Critical Acclaim for *Effective Prototyping for Software Makers*!

Effective Prototyping for Software Makers *is the first book in our field the breadth and depth of prototyping methods. Other books and articles focus prototyping method, but in this book you learn about wireframes, card sor prototyping, Wizard of Oz prototypes, and more! Renown HCI experts Arr and Berger have written a comprehensive book that is filled with practical passion for prototyping, savvy insights, and clear examples.* Effective Prototyping for Software Makers *is the sine qua non resource for prototyping and should be required reading for students, HCI practitioners, software developers, and product managers. This book is, quite simply, the best resource on prototyping that you can buy.*

Chauncey Wilson, Usability Manager, The MathWorks

Artists sketch before they paint; writers produce outlines and drafts; architects make drawings and models; aircraft designers take models to their windtunnels-all these activities are forms of prototyping. Designing and building effective software requires deep understanding, and this requires effective prototyping, but most software designers and developers don't seem to know the full range of available tools, techniques, and processes. Effective Prototyping *is written by steadfast and reliable guides who cover prototyping techniques in remarkable depth. This book is a thorough guide to prototyping for both newcomers and the experienced. It will take you step by step as well as explain the purpose of each step.*

This is the essential handbook of prototyping.

Richard P. Gabriel, author of *Innovation Happens Elsewhere*

There are many steps in the development of successful software projects, but one major key is prototyping: rapid, effective methods for testing and refining designs. Effective prototyping can be remarkably simple, yet provide powerful results without delaying the project. Indeed, effective prototyping is often the key to faster development. Up to now, there has been no single source for how it is done. But here, in this comprehensive book, Jonathan Arnowitz, Michael Arent, and Nevin Berger explain all in this essential guide to software prototyping.

Everything you ever wanted to know, but had no idea who to ask.

Don Norman, Nielsen Norman Group & Northwestern University, author of *Emotional Design*

Anyone involved in design and development of software products, whether for desktop computers, the web, handheld devices, or any other platform, will want to read Effective Prototyping for Software Makers. *This book provides a persuasive business case for prototyping as a way to reduce risk and increase the likelihood of customer adoption and loyalty. It shows how prototypes not only improve product quality, but also support collaborative work, help build product strategy, and create a shared sense of purpose among development team members.*

The book presents a comprehensive survey of tools and techniques and provides practical, detailed explanations, with illustrations, of how to plan and build prototypes.

The authors draw on their deep professional experience to recommend appropriate prototyping techniques for various stages of product development. This important advice will undoubtedly save many readers from choosing the wrong method at the wrong time.

Whether you are the manager of a development team or a developer or designer working on a user interface product, this book will expand your appreciation of prototyping and give you countless ways of doing your work better. Whether you read it cover-to-cover or just dip in for some just-in-time assistance, this book gives you a practical and theoretical foundation for making your own effective prototypes.

This is an ideal text for professional software engineers and designers who are new to prototyping as well as students in engineering, design, and human factors. The concepts and techniques presented in this volume should be considered part of the foundational knowledge for anyone in the software development field. I recommend this book to any software company that wants to improve their capability to build great products.

Jim Faris, The Management Innovation Group LLC

EFFECTIVE PROTOTYPING FOR SOFTWARE MAKERS

The Morgan Kaufmann Series in Interactive Technologies

Series Editors:

- Stuart Card, PARC
- Jonathan Grudin, Microsoft
- Jakob Nielsen, Nielsen Norman Group

EFFECTIVE PROTOTYPING FOR SOFTWARE MAKERS

Jonathan Arnowitz

Michael Arent

Nevin Berger

ELSEVIER

AMSTERDAM • BOSTON • HEIDELBERG • LONDON
NEW YORK • OXFORD • PARIS • SAN DIEGO
SAN FRANCISCO • SINGAPORE • SYDNEY • TOKYO

Morgan Kaufmann Publishers is an imprint of Elsevier

MORGAN KAUFMANN PUBLISHERS

Publisher	Diane Cerra
Publishing Services Manager	George Morrison
Production Editor	Dawnmarie Simpson
Assistant Editor	Asma Palmeiro
Cover Design	Eric DeCicco
Text Design	Yvo Riezebos
Composition	Integra Software Services, Pvt., Ltd., Pondicherry, India, www.integra-india.com
Copyeditor	Graphic World Publishing Services
Proofreader	Graphic World Publishing Services
Indexer	Graphic World Publishing Services
Interior printer	Transcontinental Printing Interglobe
Cover printer	Transcontinental Printing Interglobe

Morgan Kaufmann Publishers is an imprint of Elsevier.
500 Sansome Street, Suite 400, San Francisco, CA 94111

This book is printed on acid-free paper.

Library of Congress Cataloging-in-Publication Data
Arnowitz, Jonathan.
  Effective prototyping for software makers/Jonathan Arnowitz, Michael Arent, Nevin Berger. – 1st ed.
     p. cm.
  Includes bibliographical references and index.
  ISBN 0-12-088568-9 (alk. paper)
1. Computer software–Development. I. Arent, Michael. II. Berger, Nevin. III. Title.
  QA76.76.D47A762 2006
  005.1–dc22

                                                    2006019373

ISBN 13: 978-0-12-088568-8
ISBN 10: 0-12-088568-9

For information on all Morgan Kaufmann publications,
visit our Web site at *www.mkp.com* or *www.books.elsevier.com*

Printed in Canada.
06 07 08 09 10 5 4 3 2 1

DEDICATIONS

To Morris Arnowitz and in memory of Harriet Welton Arnowitz.
—Jonathan Arnowitz

In memory of Jack and Dodie Arent.
—Michael Arent

In memory of Gene Berger and Sam Norman.
—Nevin Berger

CONTENTS

PHASE II | SPECIFICATION OF PROTOTYPING   106

CHAPTER 6   DETERMINE CHARACTERISTICS   109

ACKNOWLEDGMENTS

Where to begin?

The easiest place to begin is with our devoted families. We couldn't have accomplished the Herculean effort of this book without the unwavering, loyal and loving support of: Jacqueline Arent, Nick Arent, Vanessa Arent, Minne Fekkes, Sarah Arnowitz, Lisa Norman, Eli Berger, Ezra Berger, and Emma Berger.

This book could not have been adequately written and produced without the vote of confidence, guidance and support of our publisher and patron saint, Diane Cerra.

We extend our sincere gratitude to the contributors, who helped in ways beyond their individual chapters: Ji Kim and Dave Rogers. We want to graciously acknowledge those special people who devoted their time to diligently and substantively reviewing the manuscript: Jim Faris, Dirk-Jan Hoets, and Deborah Mayhew. We are indebted to our tireless editor, Casey Jones.

We also want to thank those who gave us their support along the way: Laurie Vertelney, Jeff Herman, Meg Dastrup, Wendy Mackay, Don Norman, Chauncey Wilson and Mary Czerwinski. With so much guidance, any inaccuracies that remain are truly the fault of the authors.

And last but not least we want to thank the Effective Prototyping photo shoot team: Mark Detweiler, Sabine Kabel-Eckes, Sally Lawler Kennedy, and Mohini Wettasinghe. We have chosen not to use real life test subjects or users in this book. We feel to do so would be an abuse of the test participant's cooperation. So thank you team for making these illustrative photos possible by giving up your already diminished free time for the photo sessions.

Lastly, we would like to thank a few people who have personally helped us, or otherwise inspired us to get to the point in each of our lives where we could write this book.

Nevin: My first thanks goes out to my co-writers who have shouldered the heavy lifting in this endeavor. Jonathan, who held the vision, inspired us and always had wonderful wine available to keep our fortitude up. Michael who could always could be counted on for his strength, thoroughgoing and a plate of baklava for treats. In my user experience career I have always found creativity as my greatest tool. I have been inspired by creative artists and thinkers such as Alberto Giacometti, Albert Einstein, William De Kooning, Wolfgang Amadeus Mozart to name but a few.

Michael: My career in technology user experience design and management has been an adventurous and exotic Marco Polo-like journey with many inspiring influencers: Leonardo da Vinci, Wolfgang Amadeus Mozart, Wassily Kandinsky, Le Corbusier, Jimi Hendrix, Wolfgang Weingart, Laurie Anderson, Nicholas Negroponte, Philip Glass, Aaron Marcus, Philippe Starck, Ron Baecker, Joy Mountford, Don Norman, Frank O. Gehry, and Arundathi Roy.

Jonathan: It has been a bumpy road to this place where I can write a book like this with such excellent colleagues. I got where I am because of these visionary people: my thankfulness is both profound and humble (if in some cases a little late): Dr. Harold G. Marcus, Howard Thomas, Jo Ann Avalos, Alan Balch, Piet Vonk, Martin Simpson, Tasoula Georgiou-Hadjitofi, Lieven Baeten, Gijs der Waal, Esther Dunning, David Zeidman, Bill McCarthy, John Thackara, Wendy Mackay, Marilyn Tremaine, Joseph Konstan, Jose Arcellana, Motasim Najeeb, Diana Gray and most recently Michael Arent and Dan Rosenberg. For inspiration, I have turned to many times: Gustav Mahler, Friedrich Nietzsche, and the towering figure who keeps us all honest Don Norman.

Michael Arent, Jonathan Arnowitz, Nevin Berger
The San Francisco Bay Area, California, 2006

EFFECTIVE PROTOTYPING, WHY THIS BOOK?

Effective Prototyping may seem like an odd title: Who ineffectively prototypes? Actually, we all do. We'd all like to think our prototypes are effective and that we have a sophisticated understanding of prototyping. In reality this isn't true due to the simple fact no book we know of addresses these concepts. In fact, most prototypes are often either overachieving or underachieving, neither of which serves software-making purposes well. It's the effective prototype that assures your prototype will hit the mark.

OVERACHIEVING PROTOTYPE

An overachieving prototype artificially wows an audience by showing inappropriate high fidelity too early in the software creation process. An artificial high fidelity, while it may impress, will often cause many design decisions to be made prematurely — a leading cause for finding yourself designed into a corner. This usually happens due to thoughtful striving to be as thorough as possible without understanding early in the process how thorough to be. When design decisions are made early, little (or no) room remains for successfully evolving a software concept to an optimal outcome.

UNDERACHIEVING PROTOTYPE

An underachieving prototype under whelms the audience through its ambiguity, and gives the presenter maximum, even dangerous, flexibility to fill in the blanks with persuasive verbal descriptions. The lack knowing what should be thorough leads to the dangerous situation of an unshared understanding of what a prototype represents. Again, this is generally caused by a lack of guidance as to what should be thorough and what not. An undeveloped prototype leaves vague, aspects that should be concrete. The result is a prototype that leaves it to the reader to fill in the blanks.

EFFECTIVE PROTOTYPE

Overachieving prototypes close discussions early in the process by allowing decisions to be made too early. These seeming decisions can become confusing to different stakeholders. By contrast, underachieving prototypes give little to inspire the next steps of design. Effective prototypes combine the right mix of conceptual and experiential prototyping to accurately express the current state of understanding of the software product or service.

Effective prototyping is a learnable, repeatable process where the prototyping approach depends on effective analysis of the current state of requirements as well as the current needs of your organization. Effective prototyping uses the right prototyping tool, method, and process given the appropriate need. In order to succeed at prototyping, the effective prototyper must understand all of the variables involved in prototyping, including their advantages and disadvantages. The effective prototype allows the audience to understand ideas without being overwhelmed by superfluous details.

Anyone can be an effective prototyper; and anyone can prototype with software tools they already know how to use. No doubt for some people this statement raises a few questions.

THE YES QUESTIONS

Can I prototype? Yes. Anyone can prototype if they understand their goals and current stage in the software development process.

Can I prototype with the tools I already know (or have readily available)? Yes. You can adapt almost any tool to create a successful prototype.

> The back of a dinner napkin? Yes.
> Paper? Yes.
> Presentation tools? Yes.
> Office productivity software, such as a word processor or spreadsheet application? Yes.
> Video software? Yes
> Programming software? Yes

Will it be easy for me to prototype even though I haven't already incorporated it into the software creation process? Yes. Prototyping can be incorporated in any stage of the software design process, even at multiple stages for varying purposes. It's never too late to start prototyping. Almost anywhere in the software creation process, you can slip in some form of prototyping. A little and late is better than none, and your product will be better for it.

THE NO ANSWERS

Do you need graphic software experience to prototype effectively? No. Graphic software tools are just one of many tools that can be used.

Do you need special prototyping tools in order to prototype effectively? No. Depending on the method, you can use almost any tool you have available, even a word processor.

Do you need to be a designer (or an artist) to prototype effectively? No. Not all prototypes will have logos and pictures in them, and many that do require no more skill than capturing and pasting what you find on your corporate website or a clip art library.

Do you need to be a developer to prototype effectively? No.

Is implementing a prototyping process into my software development timeline going to cost a lot and take a lot of time? No. Prototyping can be included at various stages in the software development process, using a variety of styles, many of which are inexpensive and rapid.

We don't want you to just accept the above answers at face value, this book aims to prove it.

Effective prototyping means understanding prototyping characteristics, content, methods and tools.

SHIFTING PRIORITIES IN FAVOR OF EFFECTIVE PROTOTYPING

The current focus on rapid software development often uses prototyping too late in the development process. This late implementation of design work seems to occur due to a focus on the wrong priorities rather than bad practice – a focus on functionality rather than usable functionality. The industry fixation with and emphasis on software production comes at the cost of diminished emphasis and priority on the conceptual and design aspects of software product or services development. What else can explain the fact that compared to the few published works on software design and usability there is a plethora of books concentrated on software engineering and production. Until this book, not a single work was dedicated solely to one of the most important activities in software creation: prototyping. With this book explaining the characteristics, methods, and tools of prototyping, in addition to where and how prototypes fit in the software creation process, we hope to shift the priorities of software making toward software conception, design and usability.

CHARACTERISTICS

Prototyping characteristics are the many aspects that define a prototype. Until recently, the industry has only discerned between high and low fidelity, and even those terms are often misunderstood. This book defines seven overarching/primary prototyping characteristics that you will use to select the appropriate prototyping method.

CONTENT

The content of a prototype is what is contained in your prototype and what you design. A prototype can contain many different kinds of content, including information, visuals, a navigation structure, etc.

METHODS

The various methods are what can be used to create a prototype; for example, storyboards, wireframes, paper prototypes, etc.

TOOLS

Prototyping tools are the software and/or physical tools used to create a prototype. These tools include applications such as office productivity software, Visio, Acrobat, Visual Basic, etc. But really, almost any software productivity application can be a prototyping tool.

SOFTWARE IS NOT JUST DEVELOPED IT IS CREATED

The term, *software development*, stresses being driven by engineering rather than its multidisciplinary collaborative nature. The activity, *developing software*, gives us the impression that the software already exists in some ideal form to be realized by engaging in a methodical scientific process inexorably resulting in the finished software.

The prevailing practice we have observed in many companies suggest that, due to its technical nature, software will have a predictable outcome as long as the right engineering methods are followed. The reality is much different, with an overwhelming majority of written code (just like the majority of specified design) never seeing the light of day. It is not necessarily bad development that leads to wasted code or bad software, but rather poorly planned or ill-conceived development processes. Bill Buxton (one of the pioneers in human-computer interaction) made the observation that successful software making is a process more akin to filmmaking than pure engineering. Films are made, not by a waterfall process but rather by doing most of the work upfront and then iterating. A script and cast of characters are known almost in its entirety before filming even begins. When filming begins, there is a constant iteration centered on the core of the script and the cast of characters and reviewing what had been shot each day [Buxton 2003]. It is our view that prototyping should play the same role that a script and cast of characters does in films: it should be the overall plan the core is iterated on.

As a part of the software making process, we look more to prototyping as something to be done early and often. In the view of Michael Schrage, co director of MIT's media lab, prototypes are "shared spaces" that stimulate discussions, debates and decisions that foster innovation and problem resolution. You appreciate how they elicit indispensable feedback from customers and end users in usability testing. [Schrage] Prototypes also elicit feedback from the myriad of key internal stakeholders required to build software. Indeed just as Schrage envisions prototyping as a collaborative tool shared by clients and consultants, it is even more effective among the members of internal software creation teams. Regardless of who you are, this book is dedicated to making you and your team into more effective prototypers.

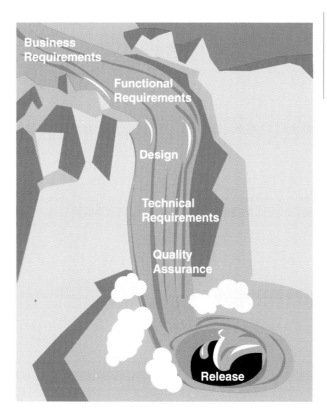

FIGURE 1 *A waterfall in action. Water falls down to the bottom never to be seen at the top again.*

In software engineering, the waterfall method is one of the prevalent processes used to manage software development projects. Waterfall, projects are broken into phases.

The waterfall diagram shown in Figure 2 shows that as the software is passed down from one phase to the next. Each team involved with the previous stage hands over the software to the next team with no additional input or responsibility required. This method is considered to be one of the easiest to manage due to the predictable and closed nature of the outcomes. The major fallacy with this process is the assumption that when a phase is done, the work of that phase has been completed forever. However, in reality, analysis rarely stops with design. Design almost never stops during the Build phase, and so on. The result is an artificial separation and compartmentalization of people who need to work together in collaboration. As shown by Ensor [Ensor 1997] in Figure 3, even attempts to bring iteration into the waterfall process illustrates that this is doomed to failure as time cannot travel backwards. For example, a new business requirement during the build phase, would have a ripple effect causing all previous steps to be revisited: this is not efficient nor realistic. Moreover, we find informal processes, undercutting the waterfall as teams need to work collaboratively to be efficient.

The Classic Waterfall Method

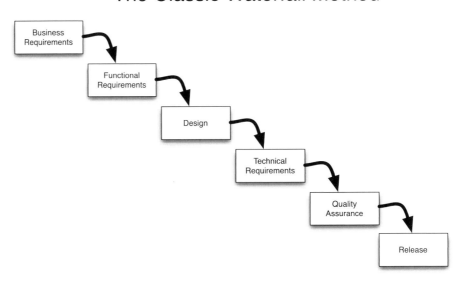

FIGURE 2 *The phases of a waterfall method as many software makers have experienced it.*

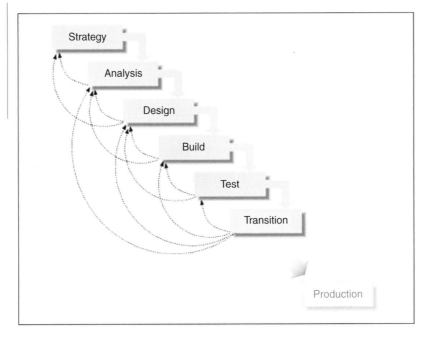

FIGURE 3 *The Waterfall method as portrayed in [Ensor 1997]: an attempt to make it iterative (time does not travel backwards unfortunately).*

SOFTWARE MAKING AND SOFTWARE MAKERS – A MODEL FOR SOFTWARE CREATION

Too often, software creation is viewed in engineering terms rather than as the cross-disciplinary process it should be perceived as. This claim should not be interpreted as anti-engineering; engineers and developers are essential allies and partners in software creation. But they are not the only partners in the complex process of software making. Many people and disciplines share equal footing: product managers, visionaries, marketers, functional analysts, sales people, graphic designers, user researchers, interaction designers, etc. *Effective Prototyping* is not intended to diminish development but to elevate the creation aspect of software making. Moreover, development resources, like all software development resources, are precious and need to be used effectively. It makes sense to perform many of the more open-ended and exploratory activities upfront where the use and costs of iterative design and prototyping are much more effective than later when laborious and costly iteration on software code is required.

We would like to introduce a new term, *software makers*, inspired by Bill Buxton's filmmaking analogy. This book is for software makers, the individuals who conceptualize, create and produce software. The term software maker encompasses the different disciplines that collaborate in the software creation process. Software makers include:

• Business analysts	• Information designers	• Usability engineers
• Cognitive and social scientists	• Interaction designers	• User experience designers
• Developers	• Product and customer support	• User interface designers
• Domain specialists	• Product managers	• User interface developers
• Functional analysts	• Product marketers	• Visual designers
• HCI professionals	• Quality assurance personnel	• And other related professionals who help create software.
• Human factors professionals	• Software architects	
• Industrial designers	• Software engineers	
• Information architects	• Technical writers	

The list is indeed long, but all of these stakeholders can improve software design by contributing to the prototyping process. While this book is primarily written for the software maker, it may also appeal to educators and students of user interface and software design. As practitioners, this book makes no claims to academic rigor, but is based on best prototyping and design practices as well as the input from many top designers interviewed for the preparation of this book as well as our own experience in software creation.

We would also like to add that our focus is intended to be platform independent. The techniques and tools mentioned in this book are equally appropriate for creating software for web, desktop, kiosk, or handhelds.

THE STRUCTURE OF THIS BOOK

Because this book is aimed at a broad audience, no assumptions are made about our reader's prior knowledge. Therefore we're covering prototyping broadly and not assuming the user has experience in more than one major discipline of software making. Likewise, we have strived to write a stand-alone book. To do this we have included guidelines and tips that only some readers will need. Also, given the broad range of software making disciplines, some sections will inevitably be too basic for some readers. Hopefully, we have clearly marked these sections, such as the HCI guideline of Chapter 10, which will strike some engineers and graphic designers as very handy, but our HCI colleagues may find them very basic.

Chapter 1: Why Prototyping – presents a case for using prototyping methods. If you are already an experienced prototyper, you may want to skip this chapter but keep it available as a handy reference when trying to convince others of the importance of prototyping. Chapter 1 includes a brief historical perspective, focusing on the influential practitioners of prototyping.

Chapters 2–13: The process of effective prototyping

The first part of this book focuses on the process of prototyping as presented in Figure 4. This part begins with chapter 2 giving an overview of the entire process. Chapters 3–5 outline the planning phase of the process. Chapters 6–8 cover the specification steps. While chapters 9 and 10 cover design and chapters 11–13 the results. For those who have never prototyped, these chapters will be a handy guide to start. For those who are already familiar with prototyping, these chapters may prove useful to round out or expand your current view of your prototyping practice. For the expert, some chapters may be more helpful than others depending on your experience and knowledge.

Chapters 14–22: The most popular methods of prototyping

The chapters in the second part cover the most common prototyping methods: how to do them and when to do them. Step by step instructions are given whenever plausible, as well as templates and sample documents. These chapters cover card sorting, wireframe prototyping, storyboard prototyping, paper prototyping, digital interactive prototyping, blank model prototyping, video prototyping, Wizard of Oz prototyping, and coded prototyping.

Chapters 23–26: Prototyping tools

The third part of this book is meant to match possible prototyping tools with your existing skills. If you're already familiar with Visio, you may want to go directly to that chapter. If you know Acrobat, then you may want to start with that chapter. The tools covered in this book are office suite applications (word processor, presentation software, spreadsheet), Visio, and Acrobat.

About the Effective Prototyping web site

In addition to this book, purchasers of this book can also get access to the Effective Prototyping web site, which will contain the templates and sample files discussed in this book. The templates and sample files will be in the native format so you can

FIGURE 4 *The phases and steps of effective prototyping.*

PHASE 1 Plan	**STEP 1** ch 3 Verify Requirements
	STEP 2 ch 4 Develop Task Flows
	STEP 3 ch 5 Define Content and Fidelity
PHASE 2 Specification	**STEP 4** ch 6 Determine Characteristics
	STEP 5 ch 7 Choose a Method
	STEP 6 ch 8 Choose a Tool
PHASE 3 Design	**STEP 7** ch 9 Select Design Criteria
	STEP 8 ch 10 Create the Design
PHASE 4 Results	**STEP 9** ch 11 Review the Design
	STEP 10 ch 12 Validate the Design
	STEP 11 ch 13 Deploy the Design

edit them/change them to suit your needs. The web site will also be a place to share your experiences with the book, offer suggestions or changes. We hope the discussion will be lively and will contribute to our continued iterations of Effective Prototyping. It is also our hope to add bonus material to the web site that we could not include in the book. The URL for the web site is http://www.effectiveprototyping.com/book

To gain access to this web site you need a password. You can get the password by sending an email to booksite@effectiveprototyping.com. In the subject line enter the first five words that appears on page 176. Your password will be sent back to you by email within 48 hours.

So let's start our discussion of effective prototyping by discussing the why of prototyping: why you should prototype and what is the business case for prototyping.

REFERENCES

Bill Buxton, Software Design from Proceedings of the Second International Conference on Usage-Centered Design, Portsmouth, NH, 26–29 October 2003, pp. 1–15.

David Ensor, Ian Stevenson, Oracle Design: The Definitive Guide, O'Reilly Books, New York, NY 1997

Jenny Preece, Y. Rogers, H. Sharp, D. Benyon, S. Holland, T. Carey. Human-Computer Interaction. Menlo Park, CA: Addison-Wesley, 1994

Michael Schrage. Serious Play: How the World's Best Companies Simulate to Innovate. Boston, MA. Harvard Business School Press, 1999

EFFECTIVE PROTOTYPING FOR SOFTWARE MAKERS

CHAPTER

1

WHY PROTOTYPING?

For many of us, prototyping is essential to creating successful software and successful user experiences. Prototyping ensures success because of its clear depiction of software requirements: instead of describing requirements it visualizes them. If done correctly, prototyping allows us to experiment in the safety of a form which can be easily changed without much loss of time or wasted effort when compared to re-programming software. Done effectively, prototyping enables us to go beyond just meeting requirements, by enabling experimentation and exploration for the optimal solutions. Done carelessly, prototyping can just as easily create a murky stew of ideas lost in redundant versions, unarticulated assumptions, and competing visions. This book aims to explain what prototyping is, good reasons for prototyping, and how to effectively prototype.

WHAT IS A PROTOTYPE?

pro·to·type *n. 1. An original or model after which anything is copied; the pattern of anything to be engraved, or otherwise copied, cast, or the like; a primary form; exemplar; archetype* [Webster's 1913 Dictionary].

pro·to·type *n. 1. An original type, form, or instance serving as a basis or standard for later stages. 2. An original, full-scale, and usually working model of a new product or new version of an existing product. 3. An early, typical example* [http://www.dictionary.com; accessed January 13, 2004].

The definition of prototype has changed little in more than 90 years. Webster's 1913 Dictionary and today's dictionary.com both classify a prototype in roughly the same way: as a model of a final product. Yet the new definition does make a subtle important difference. Unlike Webster's, the definition from dictionary.com does make a slight change using the word stages-plural-illustrating the iterative nature of prototyping.

This book specifically covers prototyping software as described by Bill Verplank, who suggests that: " 'Prototyping' is externalizing and making concrete a design idea for the purpose of evaluation" [Munoz 1992]. We like Verplank's definition because prototypes are tangible software representations, which permit the software team to experience a design without needing to program the software.

A prototype is any attempt to realize any aspect of software content. For example, the prototype can be a realization of interaction and navigation from one point in a product to another. A prototype can also be a hierarchical schema of an information design, divorced from both the look and feel of the final software. Other aspects of a prototype include:

> Current state of the art
> Requirements
> Content

The current state of the art is a checkpoint of what the software would be like if it was built with just the currently existing knowledge of the software-making team.

Requirements can refer to business requirements, technical requirements, functional requirements, end-user requirements, or any combination thereof.

Content can be any of the different content types that make the prototype: information design, interaction design, visual design, editorial content, product branding, and system performance.

For the sake of brevity we refer to any human-computer interaction as software throughout this book, regardless of whether it is a product or service, whether desktop software, mobile software, website, web application/service, or other interactive digital product.

AN HISTORICAL PERSPECTIVE OF PROTOTYPING

Software makers are not the first to wrestle with the challenges of inventing and prototyping technology. Historical perspectives help us understand the nature, challenges, and advantages of prototyping. Here we want to briefly explore three prototypers from the past: Leonardo da Vinci, Thomas Edison, and Henry Dreyfuss. Each has made remarkable contributions to design and the process of invention, and each has explored the possibilities of their inventions with prototypes.

Da Vinci left behind prototypes of concepts and ideas (in the form of drawings) that would take centuries to come to fruition. Thomas Edison used exhaustive prototyping as the engine that drove his inventive ideas. And Henry Dreyfuss used prototypes to make industrial products more user-centered and ergonomically sound. These three people illustrate how a prototype serves one primary purpose: the means of moving an idea from the human imagination to a form that other humans can readily see, understand, evaluate, use, and further develop.

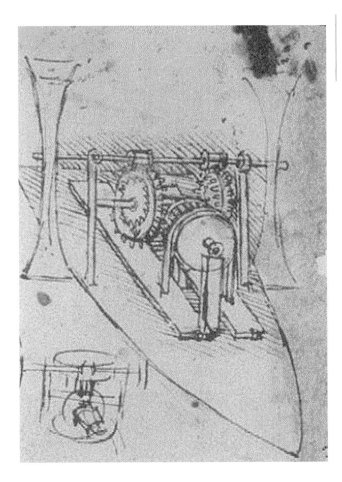

FIGURE 1.1 *A drawing of an inventive idea by Leonardo da Vinci.*

"I have often thought that one of the industrial designer's most valuable contributions to his client's product is his ability to visualize. He can sit at a table and listen to executives, engineers, production and advertising men throw off suggestions and quickly incorporate them into a sketch that crystallizes their ideas–or shows their impracticability. His sketch is not, of course, a finished design, but the beginning is likely to be there." Henry Dreyfuss, 1967

Leonardo da Vinci: The Thinking Man's Inventor

The drawings of Leonardo da Vinci (1452–1519) are some of the most fascinating examples of prototype usage for exploring innovation. During the late 15th century, da Vinci created detailed sketches of engineering ideas at the request of his patron, the Duke of Milan. These paper prototypes freed da Vinci from the contemporary constraints of what was possible to build. At liberty to push the limits as far as his imagination, da Vinci became one of history's most profound and prolific inventors.

FIGURE 1.2 *Leonardo da Vinci.*

Da Vinci's inventions would not be built for hundreds of years: flying machines, municipal construction, canals, buildings, and designs for advanced weapons.

Da Vinci's paper prototypes, and the models that others built from them, serve as proofs of concept well in advance of the technology that would eventually enable their development. Its in the same way use of prototypes will serve as the proof of concept that starts software development in the right direction.

Thomas Alva Edison: Inventor Prototyper

Thomas Alva Edison (1847–1931) was one of the most prolific and eminent American inventors. He explored ideas through extensive prototyping both in paper and in physical models. Of 1,368 separate and distinct patents he earned during his lifetime, the most recognized are the phonograph and perfections to the electric light bulb. The bulk of Edison's work was focused on creating mass-market products. He labored during a time of great industrial transition, with exciting developments in materials and production processes. Creating a prototype became not just as da Vinci used them as a source of innovation, but also as the means to communicate the manufacturing requirements: what parts were needed, what molds needed to be made, what the production costs would be, etc. These prototypes sought to improve life on a mass market level. Other American inventors in Edison's time, such as Alexander Graham Bell (1847–1922, inventor of the telephone), George Washington Carver (1864–1943, inventor of peanut agricultural sciences and food products), and John Wesley Hyatt (1837–1920, inventor of celluloid, an early thermoplastic), sought to improve daily life by reducing manual labor and introducing luxury items and entertainment to the masses.

FIGURE 1.3 *Thomas Alva Edison.*

Edison was a focused perfectionist. His models had to work consistently well because they were destined for mass production. "He would sit at one of the lab tables, chew on a wad of tobacco, and make a little drawing of a new component. He'd ponder it, pass it around among his staff, and wander off to read a couple of technical manuals. He would frown. He would spit a sluice of tobacco onto the floor, and commence to cogitate. He played with his stuff with the grace and zest of an artist, or a child. He would build a prototype and experiment with it for hours, days, weeks, months—whatever it took" [ipFrontline.com].

Edison was a tinker who believed in hard work. More scientist than philosopher, Edison's perseverance and dedication to success earn him the distinction as a model of the prototyping approach, especially rapid prototyping for the creation of the successful design. "To assist him in his invention work, Edison employed a large and diverse staff of more than 200 machinists, scientists, craftsmen, and laborers at peak production. This staff was divided by Edison into as many as 10 to 20 small teams, each working simultaneously for as long as necessary to turn an idea into a perfected finished prototype or model. Edison himself would move from team to team advising and cajoling efforts as necessary. When a particular invention was perfected, Edison quickly patented the device. With such extensive facilities and his large staff, Edison was able to turn out new products on an unprecedented scale and with unprecedented speed" [National Park Service]. Edison's iterative approach and use of multiple prototyping methods are still critical approaches to prototyping today, as witnessed by the successful use of rapid prototyping in successful software design.

Henry Dreyfuss: Designer Prototyper

Industrial designers of the last century have used prototyping and iterative design to articulate both the product's and the end-user's needs. Indeed, the struggles of industrial designer to gain acceptance into the engineering and manufacturing world resemble very closely the Human-Computer Interaction (HCI) professional's struggles for acceptance in the world of software engineering. Henry Dreyfuss (1904–1972) was the archetype of industrial designers, not least because he left behind a body of literature detailing his efforts in prototyping. Dreyfuss used prototyping to couple the perspectives of user-centered design principles, business interests, and engineering. He saw prototyping as one of the most important contributions an industrial designer makes to the product creation process because it was both essential in communicating designs to stakeholders and allowed him to evaluate designs for suitability to the target users.

Dreyfuss was a firm believer in collaborative and to a certain extend user-centered design. His techniques of design incorporated ergonomic human studies into every design he made [Dreyfuss 1967, pp. 26–28]. Emphasizing the importance of the diverse stakeholders, Dreyfuss talks of his design process in a way that is very close to what we today call *user experience design* in his inclusion of multiple disciplines. Dreyfuss claimed that a successful industrial designer is a man of many hats: design is only one of those hats. To Dreyfuss,

 FIGURE 1.4 *Henry Dreyfuss.*

an industrial designer is also a keen observer of public taste as well as someone who understands the full context of design, from concept to manufacturing, packaging, distribution, and display. Dreyfuss' concept of a designer is a user, designer, and businessperson all rolled together. The designer links management, engineering, and the consumer and cooperates with all three (Dreyfuss 1967, pp. 14–15).

"We enter into close cooperation with engineers . . . . We go over countless rough sketches. Components are arranged and rearranged. Working drawings and blueprints are made, some by the client's engineers, some by us, and frequently exchanged. Our blueprints, by the way, have letters and numerals in the margins, like road maps, so that any point on them can be easily located and discussed by phone or referred to by wire or letter. Three-dimensional clay, plaster, wood, or plastic models are developed, for we believe that three-dimensional objects should be designed in three dimensions. Perspective drawings are fine up to a point, but they can be misleading. So, as soon as possible, we get a form into clay and actually do our designing in this pliable material. It is from such models that production costs are estimated" [Dreyfuss 1967, pp. 46–47].

Dreyfuss took the concept of design and prototyping to the next level: the prototype as an illustration of a product in use that is situated in a context. In many ways his understanding of the function of the prototype is the beginning of our modern conception of the prototype. Reading his work of prototyping process, first published in 1955, reads like a work on modern user-centered design (UCD) process because it advocates the same UCD processes we apply to our prototypes to make software better: cross-disciplinary stakeholder involvement in design and user involvement in evaluation.

THE PURPOSE OF PROTOTYPING SOFTWARE

The historical needs and motivations for prototyping—innovation (da Vinci), idea refinement and requirements (Edison), and communication with stakeholders and evaluation (Dreyfuss)—are still relevant for modern software, but the drivers are more sophisticated and complex. Software prototyping is driven by a confluence of different requirements not necessarily complementary to each other if not downright contradictory. Let's mention just four examples among many others. First, revenue motivation brings successful products to the marketplace in a timely manner. Second, pressure exists to stay ahead of the competition. Third, there are risks associated with modern software design and development, such as not knowing whether the software will be desirable for users until it reaches the market. Fourth, the end user may not want what is profitable or viable for the company to produce. As such, prototypes have to be more than just tangible representations of ideas; they must reflect the requirements and the trade-offs needed to achieve the best balance among them.

Our prototyping predecessors were primarily focused on bringing manufactured products to the mass market. Although many lessons, such as user reviews and iterative design, have been learned from these historical efforts, prototyping for software is a unique activity. In the software-making process, prototypes are used for many different purposes, from developing an internal overall vision to developing products for consumption by target users. A prototype can be used to test big or small ideas. The prototype can range from lower fidelity, meaning it is conceptual, unpolished, and spare of detail, to higher fidelity, precisely representing part or all of a final user interface. The prototype can represent the simple beginnings of a vastly complex system, or it can reproduce a complex and tricky part of interaction on which user feedback is essential. Whether you have a grand plan or simply wish to see whether users understand a specific screen layout, a prototype that can be put in users' hands will help you validate, extend, and evolve your ideas, and often help you discover new ones.

Prototyping can help answer the following questions:

➤ Will the design work properly?

➤ Can the design be produced economically?

➤ How will users respond to the design?

➤ Which approach can be taken to get from concept to product?

➤ How can prototyping support product design specification?

➤ How can prototyping contribute to better product scheduling and budget planning?

Prototyping is a useful tool for solving problems in addition to raising and answering questions. Once a design concept is identified, you can build a prototype to illustrate it. Prototyping can then help extend and refine a design. It doesn't replace thinking through your design concept. But sometimes, the purpose is to come up with new concepts and simply explore.

Will the Design Work Properly?

A prototype can help visualize if your product is functionally on target. A software prototype is built around questions that you must answer before finalizing the design: Is the interaction complete? Are there any dead ends? Have we adequately covered the tasks the user wants to perform? Does the functionality represented in the prototype do its job? Prototyping exercises can help you answer the question will my design idea work?

Another purpose of "will it work?" prototyping is to test if a specific design or interaction flow works rather than an entire flow. I may want to know whether my users will be able to discover where to click to create a new object, how to select an item from one list and put it into another list, or how to manipulate the screen real estate. This type of fragmentary prototyping can be hugely influential in the late refinement phase. If testing a prototyped interactive element gives you positive results, you can proceed in that direction; otherwise, you now know you need to pursue a new direction. Any lesson you learn from prototyping is good, whether test results are positive or negative—as long as you use the results.

By incorporating feedback from customers, end users, designers, and domain specialists, prototyping can continuously furnish usability insights to successive rounds of development.

Questions you can address in a "will it work properly?" prototype are as follows:

Ease of use and learning:

➤ Is using the prototype intuitive?
➤ Can the typical user successfully accomplish tasks?
➤ Are the consequences for complex tasks evident?
➤ Is the interface easy to learn?

Customer perception of value:

➤ Is the product a worthwhile investment?
➤ Does it require costly training?
➤ Will it require frequent and/or expensive updating?
➤ Do potential customers value the functionality offering?

Look and feel:

➤ If this is a branded experience, does it bond the user to the product?
➤ Is the presentation of content legible and communicative?
➤ Do your users enjoy interacting with it?

"When I have fully decided that a result is worth getting, I go ahead of it and make trial after trial until it comes." Thomas Alva Edison

Ultimately, prototyping helps achieve successful user experiences while lowering software production risks.

Can the Design Be Produced Economically?

In the case of hardware prototyping, the cost of each component is clear: it's a physical element that has a price and an availability factor. Early hardware prototypes help a team gauge the success of a design and can also be used to calculate rough costs. In the software environment, "economical" is a matter of definition that depends on the values of the organization. Economical may mean sending programming off-shore, or it may mean low support and maintenance efforts. It can also mean that it would be expensive to sell or market. "Cost" can mean the effort expended for the complete development, maintenance, and support of a product, or it can be the rate paid for specific feature adds without adding to the maintenance budget. A prototype allows the stakeholders in your organization to evaluate how expensive this software would be. Whether or not a product or service can be produced economically depends on its context and a prototype gives this context.

If you have an exciting idea for a new interaction technique, it certainly pays off to develop a prototype to see whether the technique works for the user and to determine whether engineering can build it. One of the authors worked with a company that required innovative input devices as a market differentiator. Standard controls were considered boring–effective, but uninteresting. The search to develop something new with each product led down many roads, some of which were interesting, useful, and applicable, but most ideas were thrown out early. Prototyping allowed the entire team to see how the ideas worked in context, saving time and money by rejecting less promising directions. In this case, "economy" meant "time to market"–a brand new interaction technique, once deployed, isn't new any more, so there is some urgency to work out the issues and get the technique into the marketplace, often with the protection of a patent application.

Determining whether a design can be implemented economically must also take into consideration the values of the company producing the product. If your corporate identity rests on elegance, expect to spend considerable time working on alternatives and refining concepts as more time is spent up front exploring ideas before committing the development team to a specific path. If your product line is utilitarian and your corporate values are in product stability, you may not be prototyping as much and may have fewer questions that prototyping can answer.

The bottom line is that prototyping for determining the economy of production is really about lowering risk and financial exposure. By providing a proof of concept that can be validated internally and externally before going into production, risk is lowered. Financial exposure is lessened by allowing software engineers, marketers, and product managers to estimate the costs of actually building a specific design.

How Will Users and Other Stakeholders Respond to the Design?

The third use of prototyping is to evaluate users' and/or other stakeholders' responses to a product concept with a concrete artifact. Both big and small concepts can be tested. Testing a big concept gets user reactions to the general design direction and permit advancement to detailed design. Testing a refinement of a concept with users, especially when done with comparable alternatives in the context of use, provides some data on how to proceed with the detailed design.

To return to the distinctions between hardware and software prototyping, a hardware prototype has a "feel in the hand." A user can tell the designer whether the device is comfortable to hold: Is it the right size? Can all the controls be reached with a minimum of effort? Is the screen bright enough to read and the sound loud enough to hear? When handheld devices were first being developed, the initial models were quite large. The Apple Newton was just about the size of a tall, narrow, paperback novel; it was bulky, heavy, and the handwriting recognition technology missed the mark. Considered a technical success but a market failure, Apple abandoned the Newton line and the handheld market for almost a decade until the iPod music player. The Palm Pilot, in contrast to the Newton, was a huge success, because it fit conveniently in a shirt pocket and did not overwhelm the user with seldom used or gratuitous applications. Prototyping with users would have helped Apple discover whether users would or would not carry around a Newton in addition to which applications users would frequently use.

Software has a "look and feel." Look and feel refers to the combination of interaction techniques and visual design in addition to the emotional responses elicited from users. Designers recognize that everyone isn't going to have the same emotional response because users bring their own experiences and biases to their feelings about software. But, in general, the look and feel is developed with a target in mind, and user tests can help determine whether the target is being reached. The look and feel is what the product "says" to the user. Contrast the following affective statements that different products can make:

> "I am a sleek professional personal information device; if you use me, you'll feel hip and modern."
> "I am a trustworthy shopping website. You will always feel confident that you know what I'm doing when you use me."
> "I am clean and simple in appearance. You'll never be confused by me, and you can depend on me to do the job."

In other words, a prototype can help determine whether a product's branding attributes resonate with the user. Does your design concept elicit the feedback you were hoping to get? If so, your design is a success, if not then you know that you have a problem.

A prototype can also test market acceptance. In the case of start-up companies, prototypes are useful for securing venture capital funding, because they prove that the team has worked an idea into what looks like a product. High-fidelity prototypes are usually enough for business analysts to judge its potential for market acceptance. Likewise, interactive prototypes can gauge the reaction of users and their implementation can often discover technical constraints. We have tried to qualify this type of prototype above, because to be successful, the prototype and its use need to be carefully matched. If you intend to use your prototype as the basis of usability tests, you need to consider the learning objectives of your test. Observing the user's reaction to your prototype and eliciting comments and suggestions is different from collecting data to determine the efficacy of different task methods. The former is qualitative, whereas the latter is quantitative. These will require different types of prototypes.

Product ideas have little value if not properly communicated, distributed, and socialized. Prototypes are artifacts that can attract the attention of the marketplace or internally in the company and arouse interest. Accompanied by well-crafted messages about value and positive impact on targeted stakeholders and/or end users, a prototype can help ensure acceptance and minimize resistance. Often, prototypes are planned for completion to coincide with trade fairs, user conferences, and similar exposure opportunities. These events share designs with large populations of prospective users, collecting direct feedback in volumes difficult to achieve by other means.

A prototype can showcase an idea as a proposed reality. If well done, this speaks clearly to stakeholders and potential stakeholders. Prototypes can make the difference between making educated guesses and making informed choices to product decision makers, investors, prospective customers, and current customers.

Which Approach Can Be Taken to Get From Concept to Product?

Generative research seeks to understand what to make rather than just how to improve something that already exists. You can use prototyping to explore an idea, not really knowing where it might go, testing the possibilities along the way. Prototyping ideas generate new avenues to explore and new understandings of how people interact with software.

Participatory design is often used in generative research to involve more perspectives, especially the perspective of the user, in developing ideas. An example of a prototyping experience for generative research is blank model prototyping. Blank model prototypes are created through interactive exploration of various sizes and shapes of a handheld device and the placement of buttons on its exterior. A designer and users work with foam blocks, buttons backed with double-stick tape and other crafts materials to explore hardware form and button positioning. In the foam block exercise, participants discuss what they are doing and why. Each participant works with their own materials, and several different ideas may emerge. The foam blocks and buttons were simple shapes, proportioned realistically, but not at all refined or likely to be confused with a real product. The purpose of this exercise is to focus on physical design and manipulation, and the knowledge that can be obtained from the exercise to address the research questions and nothing more. For more information about this method of prototyping, see Chapter 19.

How Can Prototyping Support Product Design Specification?

A development organization depends on various artifacts to engineer a user experience. In more formal environments, designers produce thorough design specifications that have been qualified by usability testing, prototyping, walk-throughs, and a variety of other means. In some less formal environments, the prototypes that help develop design detail can be used as the design specification. A prototype is a much more concrete and auditable design specification than use cases or functional descriptions alone. When the prototype is used as the specification, comprehensive high-fidelity prototypes can guide the implementation. Nevertheless, prototypes do not replace documentation. The lessons learned from a prototype are important to document to supplement subsequently frozen requirements or definition documents for knowledge transfer and design rationale.

How Can Prototyping Contribute to Better Product Scheduling and Budget Planning?

Defining the scope and required resource are among the most difficult in planning a software project. Without a tangible representation of a product or product features, planning is done mostly in the abstract, based on previous experience, the skills of the team, and familiarity with the market, existing products, and targeted technology. Typically, software product and feature plans are based on a complex variety of incongruous information including marketplace trends, industry demands, feature requests from customers, competitor innovations and successes, prior project plans, team members' prior experience, and the money in the bank. We have worked in companies where the engineering effort is gauged before the interface is even roughly sketched; it is no wonder that the design options of these projects are limited to what can be force fit into the engineering schedule.

"Simplicity is the ultimate sophistication." Leonardo da Vinci

An early rapid prototype can make planned innovations, features, and product concepts much easier to comprehend. This, in turn, provides more accurate definition of the scope of work, which in turn permits better estimating, scheduling, and budgeting. This little upfront work can improve a project planning. An early prototype that includes screen layouts, interaction flows, state transitions, and performance requirements can provide the information necessary to estimate with a higher level of confidence.

"Results? Why, man, I have gotten lots of results! If I find 10,000 ways something won't work, I haven't failed. I am not discouraged, because every wrong attempt discarded is often a step forward." Thomas Alva Edison

SUMMARY

The reasons provided in this chapter have set the stage for effective prototyping by positing the essential nature of prototyping activities to ensure successful software product results. The activity of prototyping has historical significance rooted in the process of invention and in proof and protection of intellectual property. Although the definition of prototyping has changed little in more than 90 years, prototyping has evolved to become a sophisticated activity that is not only for the purpose of product conceptualization and design but for product strategy, definition, specification, and planning as well.

In going forward with the topic of prototyping, the next important question is this: How do you prototype? This book is an attempt to make the prototyping process not just understandable and manageable but also doable—by anyone with the desire to improve a product's design and learn more about user needs. This can be done with specialized prototyping tools in addition to everyday software tools with which you are already familiar. The next chapter covers the prototyping process.

WELCOME TO ARNOSOFT

Welcome to ArnoSoft, the software company that is going to help you navigate the journey to effective prototyping. ArnoSoft is a simplified archetype of a software company intended to help illustrate how the various methods and techniques of prototyping fit together.

ArnoSoft is a software start-up company that's been around for 4 years. Their core business is selling gardening equipment on the web, and they now want to branch out into household goods as well. Ceramics is their first venture into this as yet unknown field for the company. A project team has been put together of business analysts, domain specialists, designers, and developers. In addition, they have external stakeholders in the form of their venture capital investors and Acme Ceramics, their main ceramics supplier and business partner for this venture.

For now we just want to introduce a couple of key players in our story:

Alfredo Tempo *is our super sharp software architect. He's a technical guru of immense proportions. His colleagues call him il Capo. He works long hours. He is a very intense individual and resistant to change. One can usually tell how things are going at ArnoSoft by the volume of music emitting from his ear buds connected to his mpeg music player.*

Art Pince *is a graphic designer with a background in design and a degree from a major design school somewhere in New England. Despite this design background, he has changed focus and has been in the HCI business for 5 years where he has learned most of the tricks of the trade through on-the-job training. He knows what people should like and is sick and tired of putting gray beveled curves in front of users. He wants ArnoSoft to break out of the mold and do something meaningful that will transform society (as well as sell ceramics).*

Ina Owta *is a user interface designer. She is a recent graduate of an HCI university and is ready to conquer the world and make software safe for people to use. She is very idealistic and believes the only real design is user-centered design. Her main work mantra is that making the user experience really work is the only real way to make a successful product.*

Dirk Spine *is the lead developer. A solid worker but spread thin. Due to really short deadlines, his small team of coders is upset and he is trying to keep a damper on new scope so as not to cause a revolt. He also believes he should just be left alone to develop computer software without interference from people who don't know anything about computer science.*

Valmar Vista *is the company visionary. He is the man who glues the company together by his boyish enthusiasm, his drive for excellence, and his insistence to involve the entire company (much to the receptionist's horror) in every company decision. He is young, extremely wealthy, and very idealistic. So idealistic that he doesn't notice the money* *that's leaking out of the company right and left. He wants to make cool stuff for cool people. He insists that everyone call him Visty.*

The company is facing the beginning of this new ceramics project. The kick-off is looming. Although Valmar is excited, many of the folks at ArnoSoft are not so excited about this new partner, Acme Ceramics. Much to their chagrin, the CEO, Reed Dish, *insists on directly participating in the project himself as subject matter expert. The problem is that Reed believes his subject matter expertise spans over and above ceramics and extends to development, design, and architecture. He, and he alone, sees himself as the modern high-tech Renaissance man. Our cast of characters is preparing for a project kick-off meeting. Dirk wants to recommend they build something quickly just to get something in front of users and see what happens. Ina wants to suggest something different. This meeting is discussed in the next chapter.*

REFERENCES

Larry Constantine. Beyond Chaos: The Expert Edge in Managing Software Development. San Francisco: Addison-Wesley, 2001, p. 182.

Larry Constantine, Lucy Lockwood. Software for Use: A Practical Guide to the Models and Methods of Usage-Centered Design. Menlo Park, CA: Addison-Wesley, 1999, p. 497.

Alan Dix, Janet Finlay, Gregory Abowd, Russell Beal. Human-Computer Interaction. London: Prentice Hall Europe, 1998, p. 211.

Henry Dreyfuss. Designing for People. New York: Allworth Press, 1972, pp. 14–15, 26–28, 46–47.

Oscar Gutierrez. Prototyping techniques for different problem contexts. Proceedings of CHI '89. New York: ACM Press, 1989, pp. 259–265.

ipFrontline.com, Magazine of Intellectual Property and Technology. http://www.cafezine.com/index_article.asp?deptId=2&id=203&page=2. Accessed January 9, 2005.

Richard Munoz. In search of the ideal prototype. Proceedings of CHI '92, New York: ACM Press, 1992, pp. 577–579

National Park Service. The invention factory? Thomas Edison's laboratories: the creation of the Research and Development Laboratory. http://www.cr.nps.gov/nr/twhp/wwwlps/lessons/25edison/25facts1.htm. Accessed December 12, 2005.

Jenny Preece, Yvonne Rogers, Helen Sharp, David Benyon, Simon Holland, Tom Carey. Human-Computer Interaction. Menlo Park, CA: Addison-Wesley, 1994, p. 549.

Michael Schrage. Serious Play: How the World's Best Companies Simulate to Innovate. Boston: Harvard Business School Press, 1999.

CHAPTER

The Effective Prototyping Process

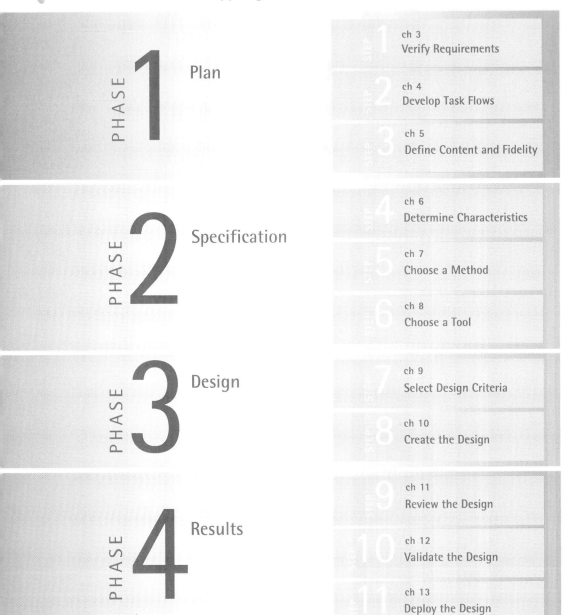

PHASE **1** Plan

PHASE **2** Specification

PHASE **3** Design

PHASE **4** Results

STEP **1** ch 3
Verify Requirements

STEP **2** ch 4
Develop Task Flows

STEP **3** ch 5
Define Content and Fidelity

STEP **4** ch 6
Determine Characteristics

STEP **5** ch 7
Choose a Method

STEP **6** ch 8
Choose a Tool

STEP **7** ch 9
Select Design Criteria

STEP **8** ch 10
Create the Design

STEP **9** ch 11
Review the Design

STEP **10** ch 12
Validate the Design

STEP **11** ch 13
Deploy the Design

2

THE EFFECTIVE PROTOTYPING PROCESS

Prototyping is a process anyone can learn and master. Although few master every aspect, there is enough latitude in prototyping that we can all find our own niche in using prototyping for communicating software requirements, designs, and ideas. That those ideas may get passed on and iterated, changed, and refined is all part of the process of software creation.

If one chooses wisely and sets expectations accordingly, effective prototyping is a repeatable predictable process of which the results are anything but guesswork. This process is not specialized, complicated, nor lengthy. Effective prototyping is a four-phase process of 11 steps that anyone with an interest can accomplish, whether to create prototypes yourself, manage prototyping in your software creation process, or any other reasonable purpose.

SCALABLE PROTOTYPING STEPS

This book presents a prototyping method in steps that are meant to be scaled to fit the prototyping activity. There will be some steps you will want to follow very closely and use the guided procedures to make sure you get every last detail correct. For quick prototyping, with less of a demand on diligence, you should know the steps and take them into consideration. For example, if you will spend 2 weeks prototyping, then spending half a day planning is not unreasonable. However, if you will just create a quick prototype in an hour, then knowing what the planning issues are and making a more cursory planning would be a reasonable approach.

PHASE I: PLAN (Chapters 3–5)

Phase I helps you to determine prototyping needs and to plan the prototyping process accordingly. You will decide what aspects of the software should or should not be prototyped to provide maximum benefit to your prototyping effort.

Step 1: Verify the Requirements (Chapter 3)

The process starts with determining prototyping requirements. These requirements are not identical to the software requirements but rather are a subset of those based on the audience of the prototype and on your current stage in the software-making process. In determining prototype requirements, you choose a focus for the prototype that influences both the task flow and prototyping content.

Step 2: Create a Task/Screen Flow (Chapter 4)

To effectively prototype, you must have some idea of how the user navigates from one screen/page to the next. Likewise, it is necessary to know what happens when a user clicks on a certain widget (or why s/he would want to). Sketching a task flow is a scalable activity: it can encompass a small or large part of the system or it can involve just one person or the whole team. A task flow can evolve as design and prototypes progress through iterations. Often, it is not simply enough to know the task flow; you must also understand the context in which the task flow takes place. Often, it is necessary to complement the task flow with a scenario or an archetypal story of your task flow.

Step 3: Specifying Content and Fidelity (Chapter 5)

Most prototyping is characterized as either high or low fidelity, with a laundry list of methods or tools thrown into one or the other category. A more comprehensive way to characterize a prototype is by first identifying the prototyping content and then setting that information against a sliding scale of possible fidelity levels. Far from having just one characteristic of fidelity, a prototype can have different fidelity levels for each of the following content types: information design, interaction design and navigation model, visual design, editorial content, branding, and system performance/behavior.

These fidelity levels more accurately characterize the prototype than just high or low fidelity. Several other prototyping characteristics (in addition to fidelity) are covered in the next step.

PHASE II: SPECIFICATION (Chapters 6–8)

The second phase of the prototyping process covers the results of decisions made in the first three steps, in which those decisions allow you to act on the planning phases. Steps 4–6 begin with defining prototype characteristics and end with choosing a prototyping tool.

Step 4: Determine the Right Prototyping Characteristics (Chapter 6)

Failing to use the appropriate prototype characteristics is a major cause of ineffective prototyping. For example, providing your target audience with too many or too few details leads to an ineffective use of your time—either in extra time spent prototyping or time spent on a prototype test that is unable to receive needed feedback. It is important to distinguish between the end users of your software and the stakeholders who will help you make the software. Step 4 details the different characteristics of prototypes: audience, stage, speed, longevity, expression, fidelity, style, and medium.

Next, you map your prototyping characteristics and content to a method that most closely matches your needs.

Step 5: Choose a Prototyping Method (Chapter 7)

Step 5 discusses how to decide which method is right for your current situation. A helpful table and worksheet are included at the end of the chapter to assist you in choosing the right method.

A WORD ABOUT OUR WORKSHEETS

The worksheets in this book are works in progress and will be subject to revision and specialization as people outside of the domains we are familiar with begin to use them. You should view the worksheets in this book as a current snapshot of possible future iterations that we plan to make available on our web site: www.effectiveprototyping.com For free updates to these worksheets as well as ability to participate in any discussions about them we invite you to our website.

Step 6: Choose a Prototyping Tool (Chapter 8)

Step 6 matches your prototyping tool to the method you selected in Step 5. We encourage you to prototype with anything you desire because we believe it is more empowering to use a skill set you already possess and a tool you're already familiar with. You can maximize the creative time spent prototyping rather than succumbing to the steep learning curve of a less familiar prototyping tool. Chapters 22 through 26 cover some prototyping tools you may already have on your computer but perhaps never realized their uses for prototyping: Office productivity applications (Microsoft Word, Excel, and PowerPoint), Visio, and Acrobat.

PHASE III: DESIGN (Chapters 9 and 10)

After specifying a prototyping strategy, Phase III focuses on executing the prototype through good design. For the accomplished prototyper, good design is already part of the professional practice, and these steps may seem naive or too simplified. For the first-time prototyper, Phase III provides a handy guide to learning how to prototype, including basic steps, good practice, and a guide through making design choices and how to execute them.

Step 7: Formulate Design Criteria (Chapter 9)

A key factor in effective prototyping is the ability to defend your prototype's design. Savvy designers have a unique sensibility for combining design guidelines with technical, end-user, and business requirements to form an elegant solution. A design rationale, based partly on design guidelines, is one of the more successful methods for outlining design decisions. However, not everyone is a designer, and it is not necessary to become one. Step 7 lists some best practices in design guidelines from the fields of cognitive psychology, graphic design, and information design. These design guidelines ensure that your page/screen compositions are not arbitrarily conceived. Even if your prototype cannot be considered the best design, it should be understandable to a general audience, and you should be able to explain the rationale for your decisions.

Step 8: Create the Prototype (Chapter 10)

Step 8 discusses methods for tying together guidelines and requirements to achieve best practice design. In the end, the quality of your prototype is based on the quality of user research, accurate definition of requirements, and your own design exploration/iteration and analysis. Your analysis can only be as thorough as your own well-rounded understanding of the guidelines and requirements as well as an appreciation for the needs of your audience.

PHASE IV: RESULTS (Chapters 11–13)

Of all the activities of prototyping, the results phase is the one that is perhaps most thoroughly covered by other texts. Therefore it is also where we spend the least amount of our attention. This section is more for the novice who:

> ➤ Is not familiar with the proper way to conduct prototype reviews
> ➤ Has never been involved with the activities and issues of usability testing
> ➤ Has little experience creating a prototype and converting it into a product

These chapters are mostly high-level discussions with pointers to where you can find more information on these well-covered topics.

Step 9: Review the Prototype (Chapter 11)

Step 9 outlines reviews with internal stakeholders and ways to ensure that an effective prototype goes on for validation. Likewise, this chapter discusses the issues around reviews: what to look for and what strategies to use.

Step 10: Validate the Design (Chapter 12)

Step 10 discusses prototype validation through usability testing and other validation techniques with external stakeholders.

Step 11: Implement the Design (Chapter 13)

The last step in prototyping is taking an iterated prototype and shaping it into a product or service concept as part of a new technology incubation process or translating it into an actual product or service to deploy to the marketplace. Implementation involves the actions required to realize a prototype appropriate to the goals and objectives of the creators.

SUMMARY

The prototyping process we described follows four phases: plan, specification, design, and results. Each one of these phases has multiple steps which are shortly described here and will be covered by the following chapters in this book.

ARNOSOFT CONTEMPLATES A PROTOTYPE

The project kick-off day has arrived. The company is reviewing its development methodology, a variation on the waterfall process, which involves some very specific engineering-driven steps. First, market requirements are drawn up. The engineers create a functional design document. The engineers develop a design. The design team makes it look good, and then the system is coded. Over the course of the past year, some elements of user-centered design have been introduced, such as some limited user research after the market requirements are done and usability testing during the quality assurance system test (which Ina likened to closing the barn door after the horse has escaped).

The first step in their process is a discussion of the marketing requirements. The ArnoSoft team is busy brainstorming requirements when Reed Dish from Acme Ceramics shows up.

Reed looks at the project schedule they are drawing on the board. He is upset that it will take so long to see an actual product. He wants the process to go much faster.

"I want to see what the thing will look like now. I don't want to sink a ton a dough into something I don't like. Make something, make something now you can . . . you know click through, do the click-click thing. Then I can decide whether it's worth my time or not."

Ina knows it's too early for design. "We can't come up with a design now; it's too soon to make the product. Or do you mean a prototype, a throw-away prototype?"

"Yeah, that's it, a prototype, but make the thing, you know, click so I can see how it works."

"A working prototype?" asked Dirk Spine, "That's extra work from my team. Our deadlines will slip. We can't possibly do that. Full stop."

"Oh come on, we need a 'can do' attitude around here!" said Reed. "I like this idea of a working prototype."

"I said a throw-away prototype," replied Ina.

"Whatever, just make it click. Oh I have to go, I got another sales call to make."

"But we're just getting started here," said Dirk.

"Well just see to it we get a click thing prototype, I gotta go pay for your salaries, later dudes." And with that Reed was gone.

"The click thing?" asked Art.

"So what do we do now?" asked Ina.

"No prototype, full stop," said Dirk.

"Maybe I can put something together," said Ina.

"How?" asked Dirk.

"I can just sketch some wireframes real quick," said Art.

"They won't click," brooded Dirk, "Whatever that means."

"Well, let's think this thing out, what would be the most effective way to prototype?" asked Ina. Let's see what Alfredo thinks.

"*My perspective is that the bulk of our industry is organized around the demonstrable myth that we know what we want at the start, and how to get it, and therefore build our process assuming that we will take an optimal, direct path to get there. Nonsense. The process must reflect that we don't know and acknowledge that the sooner we make errors and detect and fix them, the less (not more) the cost.*"
Bill Buxton

Phase I describes the planning aspects of prototyping.

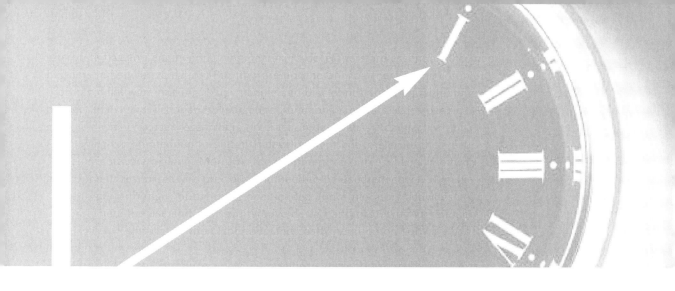

PLAN YOUR PROTOTYPE

By recognizing, adopting, and adhering to a prototyping plan you can understand and identify the requirements and assumptions of prototypes, develop task flows and scenarios to set the context, and then decide on the mix of content and fidelity relative to that context.

Because prototyping is a key design activity for transforming assumptions and requirements into a software design solution, Phase I begins with validation of those assumptions and requirements. This verification is an essential step in the prototyping process and is used to inform the overall prototyping objective through focusing on specific requirements.

Assumptions and requirements, however, are still not enough to create an effective prototype. You need more context; that is, knowledge of how the requirements and assumptions are handled and interpreted in the real world. The two proven methods for obtaining this context are to first create a **task flow** and then write a **scenario** that fulfills the task flow. If the task flow and accompanying scenario establish how the prototype will work, content and fidelity of that content determine what will be prototyped and the appropriate level of detail. A prototype can contain many different kinds of content, including information, visuals, and navigation structure. Any mix of content can be shown in a continuum from low fidelity to high fidelity. The higher the fidelity, the more representational of the intended finished product it will be.

Although we discuss products from Adobe, Apple, and Microsoft we also have had success in using various open source equivalents, such as OpenOffice products. The placement of commands often changes, but surprisingly similar results can be achieved. Although we discuss the commercial products because of their ubiquity, we do not advocate them as the only prototyping tools.

CHAPTER

The Effective Prototyping Process

PHASE **1** Plan

PHASE **2** Specification

PHASE **3** Design

PHASE **4** Results

STEP **1** ch 3
Verify Requirements

STEP **2** ch 4
Develop Task Flows

STEP **3** ch 5
Define Content and Fidelity

STEP **4** ch 6
Determine Characteristics

STEP **5** ch 7
Choose a Method

STEP **6** ch 8
Choose a Tool

STEP **7** ch 9
Select Design Criteria

STEP **8** ch 10
Create the Design

STEP **9** ch 11
Review the Design

STEP **10** ch 12
Validate the Design

STEP **11** ch 13
Deploy the Design

3

VERIFY PROTOTYPE ASSUMPTIONS AND REQUIREMENTS

This chapter focuses on transforming prototyping assumptions and requirements into a basis for a prototype design. Before you can effectively prototype, the first important activity is reviewing the balance of assumptions and requirements, including business/marketing, functional, technical, and usability ones. This review will help you determine whether you need more requirements before proceeding to build a prototype. It is also the point where you and your team can be clear about the assumptions (if any) being used as a basis for a software concept. Prototypes allow these assumptions and requirements to be validated, invalidated, modified, or substituted early in the software process thus helping you avoid the risk and costs of making major modifications to your design after discovering that the design concept and usability are faulty during the software development stage.

Prototyping can track the software's assumptions and requirements because of the continuous interplay of testing assumptions against documented requirements until all the assumptions are satisfied and requirements are validated. The nature of prototype iteration makes this interplay necessary. In one prototype iteration some requirements are validated while new questions arise to be addressed in the next iteration. As often as we have seen only one prototype produced in an entire software project, we have never seen that prototype provide all the answers. Indeed, the first prototype, as the first visualization of the software, invariably raises more questions about the requirements than it resolves. Likewise we have also seen a prototype received poorly, and see whole scale direction changes when only one or two of the key concepts needed changing. By charting both requirements and assumptions you give your next iteration a basis for keeping what is good (what was validated) and discarding what was bad (what was invalidated).

The remainder of this chapter assumes you have the basic knowledge of software requirements. It is outside the scope of a book on prototyping to go into the details of requirements gathering; there are plenty of books on this subject already. Refer to the sidebar on requirements gathering if you would like a brief review. The sidebar below is only a brief introduction to requirements; if you are interested in more in-depth coverage of the topic, we suggest Courage and Baxter [2004], Kuniavsky [2003], Holtzblatt [2005]. If you are also interested in using personas to help drive requirements or to help drive prototyping definition, we would recommend the most complete reference for practical use of personas, Pruitt and Adlin [2006].

PROTOTYPING REQUIREMENTS ARE NOT SOFTWARE REQUIREMENTS

The basic prototyping strategy advocated in effective prototyping is the practice of basing your prototype design on a mixture of requirements and assumptions. You start with some requirement (even if it is only a vision) and prototype for this requirement based on assumptions. Some assumptions will be validated, others modified, and some others not evaluated. The results are documented, leading to firmer requirements for the next round of prototyping. (See sidebar for an example.) This iterative approach eventually leads to many firm requirements and few, if any, assumptions. The rest of this chapter assumes that your requirements come from some legitimate source in the software-making process, and in our example we also ask you to believe that when a requirement is referred to as established, it has been validated through user research, marketing research, technical investigation, or other legitimate means for establishing software requirements.

In software creation, requirements arise from a number of different sources, such as businesses, market places, end users, customers, and technical opportunities. From the perspective of design and prototyping, requirements can be broken into four main categories: business/marketing, functional, technical, and usability.

Business/marketing requirements–define the needs of business or the marketplace. They are generally derived from any combination of the following: market field research, market analysis, competitive analysis, domain expertise, sales force intelligence, and focus groups. The initial product vision is often embodied in these requirements. A typical source for business and marketing requirements is a standard document, usually called a marketing requirements document (MRD), business requirements document (BRD), or a product requirements document (PRD).

Functional requirements–define the functionality necessary to support the business or marketing requirements. Similar to business/marketing requirements, functional requirements are generally derived from any combination of the following: field research (best in conjunction with user research), market analysis, competitive analysis, domain expertise, sales force intelligence, and focus groups. Usually, functional requirements are investigated and defined in parallel with business/marketing requirements. Functional requirements are also often identified as a result of user research and usability testing. Because product sales influence these requirements, they often include more functions (a.k.a. features) than those needed to satisfy the business requirements. For example, a business requirement may require form fill functionality. However, if the software is deployed internationally, it may require multiple language support in which form filling in the Roman alphabet can be functionally different from form filling in other languages, such as Asian languages based on ideograms. Functional requirements are usually found in a formal document, often called a functional requirements document or other functional specification document. Functional specifications are typically reflected in a prototype.

Technical requirements–define the technology needed to implement the required functionality. Functionality can often be compromised by the immaturity, prohibitive costs, or unavailability of a required technology. Technical requirements are generally derived from any combination of the following: technology research, technical analysis, competitive analysis, technology expertise, sales force intelligence, and other similar means. Technical requirements are sometimes articulated in a formal specification, such as a technical definition document, but they can also be found in company-specific technology architecture documents or platform-specific guidelines, such as the Windows User Experience Guidelines or the Macintosh OSX Human Interface Guidelines.

Usability requirements–define the user experience and usability requirements needed for user adoption of the software. They are generally derived from any combination of the following: user research, task analysis, competitive analysis, domain expertise, sales force intelligence, customer support intelligence, design and prototyping, usability testing, and other related means. Usability requirements, in conjunction with the other requirements described above, are transformed into user interface specifications, which are often embodied in high-fidelity interactive prototypes.

When prototyping, not all (or any) of the above requirements may be available or in a form that is helpful for prototyping. Therefore, it is important to share the prototype with key requirements stakeholders to ensure complete coverage. For business requirements, it would be best to seek out product management and marketing as these stakeholders. For functional requirements, a domain specialist or anyone who has conducted user or market research can provide input. For technical requirements, either a lead architect or software engineer can provide critical input. Usability requirements can come from user research, task analysis, prior similar experience, and usability validation of your design. However, despite coming from individual experts, all these requirements still need to be validated holistically because software is never merely a sum of its requirements. Requirements may have unwanted side effects that, before creation of the final product, only a prototype can expose.

TRANSFORMATION OF ASSUMPTIONS TO REQUIREMENTS

To illustrate a typical course for converting assumptions into requirements through prototyping, we have outlined how requirements are first elicited in the form of assumptions. These assumptions are then iteratively tested in a prototype. A prototype is completed in rounds of iterations until all the high priority assumptions are validated into requirements. Per available time and resources, this is the process of validating prototype directions to the extent allowed by a given prototyping method that enables an iteration to proceed to the next step. The entire process is a repeatable series of three steps.

To begin these three steps for transforming assumptions into requirements, you need to have the requirements necessary for proceeding with development of the prototyping schema.

STEP 1: Gather Requirements

(see sidebar on prior pages for some potential sources)

The prototype should not undertake an entire requirements-gathering process, which needs to be quite thorough; instead, it is assumed here that the software requirements-gathering process is occurring in parallel and is incomplete. So the gathering done here is just the current state of the requirements, as they are known at this moment. Depending on your stage in the requirements-gathering process, the list can be short and vague in the beginning to quite long and detailed at the end. After these requirements are gathered, enter them into Worksheet 3.1, which will look something like this.

WORKSHEET 3.1: Requirements

Project Name:
Project Date:
Product Name:
Current Phase: Design
Prototype Name:

Requirement Name (Examples)	Type	Priority	Validated? Y/N	Results	Requested Changes

This worksheet lists requirements for time management software. The requirements are currently coming from two sources: a MRD and a presentation of a wireframe sketch to a group of stakeholders.

INFORMAL PROCESS TIP

There are formal processes for software product development in almost every software company. These processes guide you through the development process and help you determine at what stage (usually extremely early) you can change requirements and when they should be frozen (usually very early). By taking the inventory of requirements suggested in Step 1, you immediately discover how far you have progressed in the software development process. Are all the requirements known and worked out? Have they been validated? If so, you should be in the later stages of the process.

If the list remains short and vague, regardless of where the company believes they are in their own development roadmap, they are still in the early stages of the software creation process. The more vague and general the requirements, the more they are open to interpretation and completion with non-validated assumptions. Too often in the software process, design and creation are crammed into the later stages when there is little time available for prototyping and validation, thus leading to high-risk software development. As a general rule, the more you base software on assumptions, the higher the risk. Conversely, the greater degree that software is based on validated assumptions, the lower the exposure to risk.

STEP 2: Inventorize the Requirements

WORKSHEET 3.1: Requirements [Example]

Project Name: Time Out
Project Date: Dec 2007
Product Name: Time Out Time Management For All
Current Phase: Design
Prototype Name: T55

Requirement Name (Examples)	Type	Priority	Validated? Y/N	Results	Requested Changes
User must be able to enter time worked by week. MRD- Use Case 1.2	Functional		Y 31 DEC 2005	1207minutes.doc	Add ability to change project code for previous entries
User wants to optionally enter project information	Usability		N		
User wants excel interface	Usability		N		
Time summary reports for managers	Business		N		
Project reports for project managers	Business		N		
Time entry reports for employees own data	Business		N		

List the state of each requirement. Make note of each requirement's origin (preferably linked to the related document). You can usually judge by its source whether a requirement is validated or just an assertion. If the requirement is validated, note when it was validated. As contradictory or complementary requirements arise later, it may become necessary to challenge old requirements that have fallen back into assumptions. You may, at any point, reclassify a requirement as an assumption if you believe that it has not been adequately validated or has been invalidated in light of newly introduced developments.

The sample worksheet lists a requirement already validated via an MRD for a time-management application and includes a link to the wireframe and the meeting minutes of the wireframe presentation. The validation also uncovered a new assumption: that users may also need to enter project information. It is listed as a direction because the assumption came from a wireframe presentation, so it is a little firmer than just a mere assumption: We know there is a need to enter project information but have no idea yet as to how. If the analysis reveals that other assumptions are hidden in a requirement, they can be fleshed out in this worksheet. For example, the requirement states time entered by week. This requirement may have additional dimensions: Maybe time needs to be entered by a configurable time period? Or maybe just by week or month? The worksheet helps to list explicit new assumptions as well as the firm requirements. Finally, the worksheet shows an assumption that users want to use an Excel-like interface because the program they are currently using has a similar interface.

STEP 3: Prioritize Requirements and Assumptions

The resulting worksheet from Step 2 is shown below. The last step in transforming assumptions into requirements is their prioritization. The priority refers to the priority for inclusion in the prototype, not priority for implementation in the software. Given that the first prototype is a storyboard, some requirements that are very important for the software are not the main concern of the prototype.

WORKSHEET 3.1: **Requirements [Example]**

Project Name: Time Out
Project Date: Dec 2007
Product Name: Time Out Time Management For All
Current Phase: Design
Prototype Name: T55

Requirement Name (Examples)	Type	Priority	Validated? Y/N	Results	Requested Changes
User must be able to enter time worked by week. MRD- Use Case 1.2	Functional	High	Y 31 DEC 2005	1207minutes.doc	Add ability to change project code for previous entries
User wants to optionally enter project information	Usability	High	Planned		
User wants excel interface	Usability	Medium	N		
Time summary reports for managers	Business	High	Planned		
Project reports for project managers	Business	Medium	N		
Time entry reports for employees own data	Business	Medium	Planned		

REQUIREMENTS AND THE BIG PICTURE

Figure 3.1 shows how prototyping requirements all fit together holistically in the software creation process. We demonstrate how assumptions are essential to the prototyping process by tracing the diagram. Only when all major assumptions are satisfied should prototyping end.

ITERATION 1: FROM IDEA TO FIRST VISUALIZATION

In the first prototype iteration, the product (or the function or new addition to the existing product) is just an idea in a product manager's or business analyst's mind. Working interactively with a designer or by sketching the idea out themselves, some of the assumptions can be visualized. This visualization provides a vague idea of the business value (i.e., is the idea worth pursuing?).

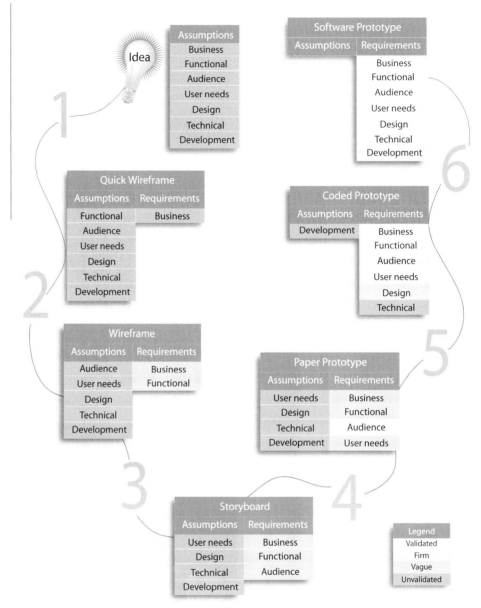

FIGURE 3.1 *Step-by-step conversion of assumptions to validated requirements. Note: The levels of gray show how refinement continues throughout the process; the darker the background, the less (if any) validation used.*

So even a quickly developed prototype can validate assumptions by providing visualizations to realize an idea. The visualization itself can communicate the value of proceeding to the next step in the process: working out the idea even further and validating its companion requirements. Also, through visualization some competing assumptions can make an idea less desirable, thereby invalidating the business requirement.

The travel and expenses reports example shown in Figure 3.3 seems like a plausible idea to the stakeholders. Starting as just an idea for travel reporting, the

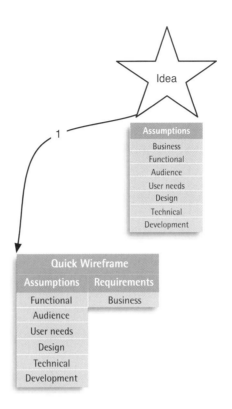

visualization provided the product manager with the idea of a new assumption: adding normal expenses in addition to travel expenses. The visualization of this new assumption has not uncovered any undesirable effects, so the project proceeds to the next step: working out the wireframe depicted in Figure 3.3 to make other assumptions clearer.

FIGURE 3.4 *Second round of iterations verifies more requirements and makes other assumptions clearer.*

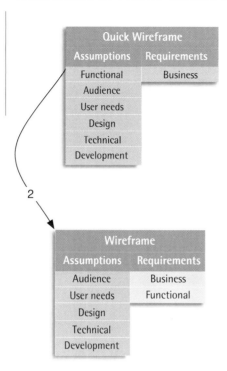

The second round of iterations is performed similar to the first prototype iteration. Assumptions and requirements are prototyped to either validate or invalidate them. Through this second round, the requirements worksheet becomes more complete and the direction of the product becomes clearer.

With the creation of the more refined wireframe shown in Figure 3.5, not only is the business case a little clearer, but the functions needed to support this business case also become clearer and better reflected in the buttons and navigation visible in the wireframe.

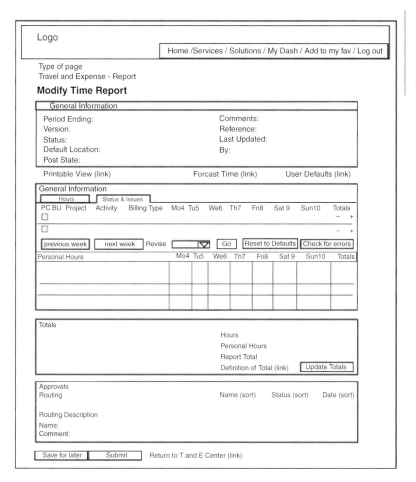

ITERATION 3: FROM WIREFRAME TO STORYBOARD

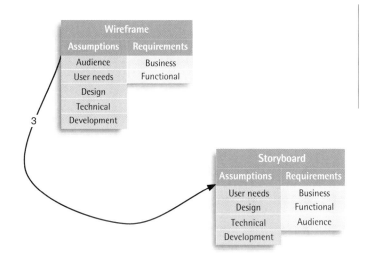

By using the recommended Worksheet 3.1, we see a definite increase in end-user–focused requirements when we get to the storyboard phase, which attempts to tell the story of the software in context. During this phase, new requirements will surface and other user requirements can be validated. For example in the storyboard picture shown in Figure 3.7, the end user does indeed need to track his project budget, validating not just optionally entering project data in the time report but also the need to have a project time report for the end user.

FIGURE 3.7 *Storyboard showing validation of the need to enter project data for an archetypal end user.*

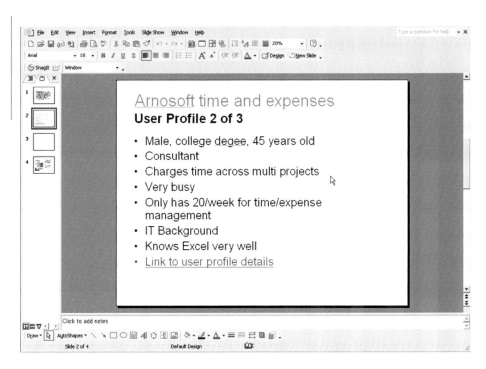

ITERATION 4: FROM STORYBOARD TO PAPER PROTOTYPE

FIGURE 3.8 *Given the more visually explicit and interactive nature of a paper prototype, requirements start being validated in rapid tempo.*

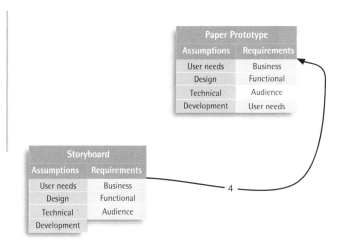

As the prototypes progress and the audience shifts from internal to external stakeholders, requirements start to be validated quickly, especially with direct user contact. Designer "requirements" about the audience suddenly become much clearer, and user needs becomes much more tangible. In the paper prototype shown in Figure 3.9, the assumption is that an Excel-like interface failed miserably in usability testing. It invalidated an assumption of the end-user needs and replaced it with a new model that fits better but will still need verification (not pictured).

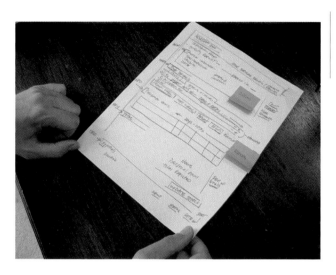

FIGURE 3.9 *An interactive paper prototype.*

ITERATION 5: FROM PAPER PROTOTYPE TO CODED PROTOTYPE

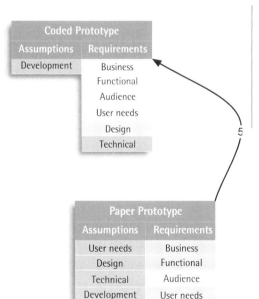

FIGURE 3.10 *Late high-fidelity prototypes come closer to resembling a software product as well as the requirements.*

In the last stages of prototyping, many open design and technical questions can be answered. The required functionality, the audience, and the business case are already firm and no longer the source of focus. Now, a high-fidelity prototype is used to firm up the remaining requirements and design details.

FIGURE 3.11 *Late prototypes resemble the real software as the requirements become firmer, and more advanced prototype development can take place with greater confidence.*

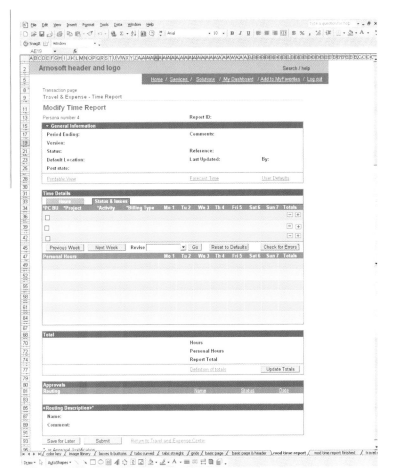

ITERATION 6: FROM CODED PROTOTYPE TO SOFTWARE REQUIREMENTS

In the last step, specifying the requirements from a late high-fidelity user-facing prototype (here in the form of a coded prototype) enables us to finally say we have validated all the software requirements. The worksheet that was the basis for evaluating the prototype requirements could now almost double for a table of contents or central reference point for the software requirements. So the journey from the interplay of assumptions and requirements is now complete; prototyping has been the primary aid in validating assumptions and transforming them into requirements. Although, it is important to note that prototyping has been an aid, not the sole source of requirements validation, such as focus groups, usability testing, market research, competitive analysis, etc.

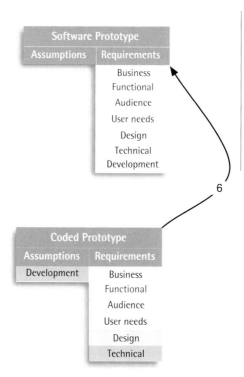

FIGURE 3.12 *Only at the end of the prototyping process do the assumptions finally give way to concrete data to base the software creation and development.*

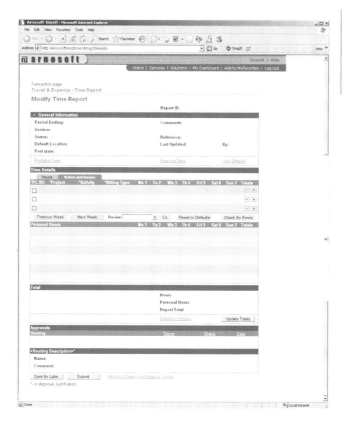

FIGURE 3.13 *The final end product for time entry at the end of the project.*

SUMMARY

We reviewed requirements setting for prototyping as the first step toward collecting prototype content. We have seen that prototyping requirements try to come as close as necessary to the actual business, functional, technical and usability requirements. However, a prototype also has the flexibility to be based on assumptions. In fact, prototyping can be used to play with assumptions while being gradually turned into concrete validated requirements. For this validation, a worksheet template supports the three-step process:

Following this validation process and using the worksheet template, you can be assured that your prototype will address exactly the right assumptions and requirements your team judges to be important. The worksheet, with the prioritization of requirements and assumptions, also helps others understand what they should and should not be looking for when reviewing your prototype.

ARNOSOFT GOES THROUGH THE REQUIREMENTS

"We should do a wireframe!" insisted Art.

"No, we should do a paper prototype, so we can conduct usability testing with it," argued Ina.

"No, we should do a proof of concept that will help us code the product; this will help my team and that is what we need in this time crunch situation, full stop," demanded Dirk Spine.

"I think all Reed wants is some proof of concept. Maybe Ina can do something in Flash for it?" asked Alfredo.

"Why should we just give Reed what he wants? If we can find some way the prototype can help the team, we should do that instead," countered Dirk.

Maybe we can find a win–win situation here. Let's start with the first step in the effective prototyping process and try to establish the requirements of the prototype as well as any assumptions.

The team starts with trying to decide the prototype requirements. They notice immediately a huge gulf between the requirements they need and the ones they have in hand. All they really have are the brainstormed business requirements. Because Reed participated in the brainstorming, the business and functional requirements are considered validated. Nevertheless, the team decided to use the step-by-step method described above by first gathering requirements as well as listing any assumptions.

Many of the requirements for the ceramic ware site are being extrapolated from the existing gardening equipment site. In the words of the CEO, Valmar Vista, "think of it as indoor gardening."

The team also decided to prioritize the business, functional, and technical requirements because a planned user research project is meant to address many of the usability requirements. After a brainstorming meeting the following worksheet was developed. After following the steps of the requirements process, a storyboard prototype was chosen because it could be quickly created and "clicked through." The results of the storyboard exercise are also reflected in the spreadsheet.

REFERENCES

Apple Computer. Inside Macintosh: Macintosh Human Interface Guidelines. Boston: Addison-Wesley, 1996.

Bill Buxton. Software design. Proceedings of the Second International Conference on Usage-Centered Design, Portsmouth, NH, October 26–29, 2003, pp. 1–15.

Bill Buxton, R. Sniderman. Iteration in the design of the Human-Computer Interface. Proceedings of the 13th Annual Meeting, Human Factors Association of Canada, 1980, pp. 72–81.

Catherine Courage, Kathy Baxter. Understanding Your Users: A Practical Guide to User Requirements Methods, Tools, and Techniques. The Morgan Kaufmann Series in Interactive Technologies. Amsterdam: Elsevier/Morgan Kaufmann, 2004.

William Cushman, Daniel Rosenberg. Human Factors in Product Design. Amsterdam: Elsevier, 1991.

Karen Holtzblatt. Rapid Contextual Design. San Francisco: Morgan-Kaufman, 2005.

Mike Kuniavsky. Observing the User Experience. San Francisco: Morgan-Kaufman, 2003.

Scott MacKenzie, R. William Soukoreff. Card, English, and Burr (1978)–25 years later. Extended Abstracts of the ACM Conference on Human Factors in Computing Systems–CHI 2003. New York: ACM Press, 2003, pp. 760–761.

John Pruitt, Tamara Adlin. The Persona Lifecycle. San Francisco: Morgan-Kaufman, 2006.

Bruce Tognazzini. First principles of interaction design. http://www.asktog.com/basics/firstPrinciples.html. Accessed June 17, 2005.

CHAPTER

The Effective Prototyping Process

PHASE **1** Plan

STEP **1**   ch 3
Verify Requirements

STEP **2**   ch 4
Develop Task Flows

STEP **3**   ch 5
Define Content and Fidelity

PHASE **2** Specification

STEP **4**   ch 6
Determine Characteristics

STEP **5**   ch 7
Choose a Method

STEP **6**   ch 8
Choose a Tool

PHASE **3** Design

STEP **7**   ch 9
Select Design Criteria

STEP **8**   ch 10
Create the Design

PHASE **4** Results

STEP **9**   ch 11
Review the Design

STEP **10**   ch 12
Validate the Design

STEP **11**   ch 13
Deploy the Design

4

DEVELOP TASK FLOWS AND SCENARIOS

In the previous chapter, we discussed how inventorizing your assumptions and requirements is but one essential step for effective prototype. Next, you'll need more information about the context and how the requirements and assumptions are combined into tasks. Two proven techniques for understanding context are creating a **task flow** and writing related **scenarios**. A task flow depicts the steps users perform to complete a task or tasks. A task flow also shows the dependencies and order of steps in a process, such as a business process or work flow. A scenario is the narration of that task flow in a specific context such as a critical incident or a day-in-the-life story using the product. With these two techniques, you should have a more vivid understanding of the software's purpose and how users would interact with it. For example, what happens when a user clicks on a button or, why would the user want to?

TASK FLOW

For effective prototyping, a **task flow** charts the user actions and thought processes to complete a task. Task flow mapping makes it possible to design and allocate tasks in a sequence of screens. They also identify new functions appropriate for inclusion in the user interface, which can then be accurately defined and specified in the context of use.

Sketching a task flow for prototyping is a highly scalable activity ranging from brainstorming potential user actions to observing and recording user performance and task accomplishment as part of a formal task analysis. Use the process described in Chapter 3 for mapping requirements and assumptions as a guideline for determining the method that best suits your situation. For further information on task analysis, refer to Diaper and Stanton [2004], or the more applied works such as Hackos and Redish [1998], or related methods such as Courage and Baxter's [2005] group task analysis, see the references at the end of this chapter.

Regardless of how user needs have been derived, they need to be represented in a task flow diagram to be usable in the prototyping process. We suggest you use either of the following two common and useful methods for sketching the task or screen flow: **a dependency diagram**, the visual depiction of a series of tasks or the steps in a task, or a **swim lane diagram**, a visual decomposition of activity flow into tasks and subtasks organized by user roles. A swim lane diagram is used for rapidly sketching alternate task schemes and can be used for initial internal design discussion. A task layer map is used to chart the interdependencies among tasks and to determine their hierarchical structure.

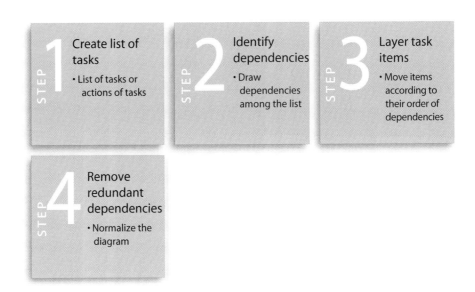

Task Layer Maps

Task layer maps are a straightforward approach to task flows that involve creating a simplified dependency diagram [Arnowitz 2004]. The basics for creating a task flow with a task layer map are to:

Step 1: Create List of Tasks

Create list of tasks
- **List of tasks or actions of tasks**

Identify dependencies
- Draw dependencies among the list

Layer task items
- Move items according to their order of dependencies

Remove redundant dependencies
- Normalize the diagram

To create a task layer map, you must first brainstorm the software steps required in a typical task, goal, use case, or the passing of data objects. This is anything that can separate the software into discrete sections of usage. For example, the image below shows how someone used sticky notes to create a list of steps for ordering ceramic ware from an online shopping store.

FIGURE 4.1 *Task layer map Step 1: actions for ordering ceramics online.*

Step 2: Identify Dependencies

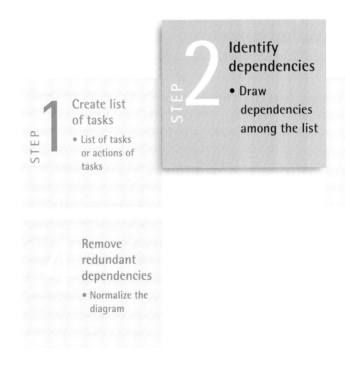

After you've created a list of all the steps, draw lines from each step to all dependent steps. The line should start without any mark but end with a dot or an arrow or other indicator of choice to determine the direction of the dependence. Draw the dependencies for every step. Figure 4.2 shows the task list after adding the dependency lines for one step.

Given the complexity of some dependencies, you may end up with a diagram that is a spaghetti arrangement of lines. Figure 4.4 shows how a diagram can look when finished. Note: To make the layering of task items (Step 3) easier, it is best to perform Step 2 by using a diagramming program, such as Visio, or using a software product with a graphing tool, such as Excel or OpenOffice.

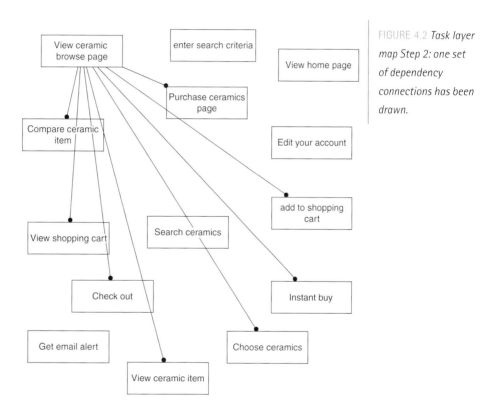

FIGURE 4.2 *Task layer map Step 2: one set of dependency connections has been drawn.*

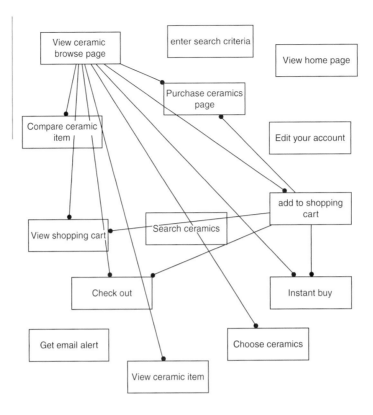

FIGURE 4.3 *Task layer map Step 2: a second set of dependency connections have been drawn.*

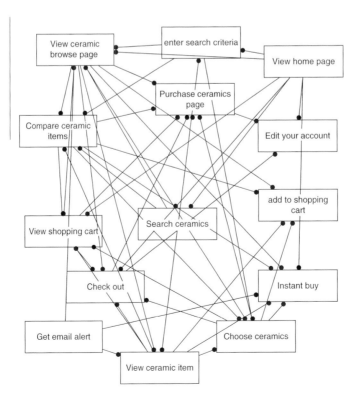

FIGURE 4.4 *Task layer map Step 2: all dependency connections have been drawn, resembling a plate of spaghetti.*

Step 3: Layer Task Items

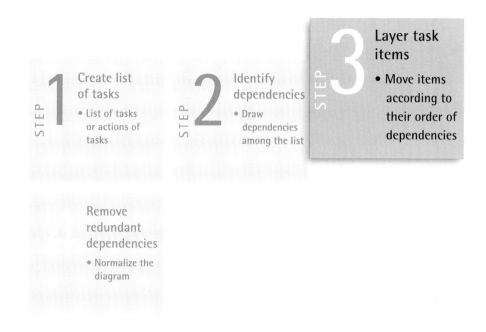

In Step 3, you layer complex dependency connections into an easier to read overview. First, divide a new empty drawing document into several horizontal rows. Each row represents a layer. Start out with six- to eight-row layers. You can always add more as you need them.

Now you start layering the drawing. Begin by placing items that have no dependencies or no arrows pointing to them in layer 1 of the diagram. Items in layer 1 are the starting points of the software. Layer 2 contains steps that only have dependencies on layer 1 steps, meaning they have only one line from a top layer step to them. Layer 3 is formed by steps that have either only a dependency on layer 2 or on both layer 1 and layer 2 steps. This process continues until each step is placed below all its dependent steps. The last steps have no steps dependent on them; they are the end points of the tasks in the software. Once the task layer map is organized into layers, the resulting drawing will look like the diagram in Figure 4.5. At the end of this step you have a dependency diagram and can proceed to the Dependency Diagram instructions of this chapter. For some people the diagram is still complex and to reduce the complexity and aide readability they often continue with the next step to remove redundant dependencies.

Step 4: Remove Redundant Dependencies

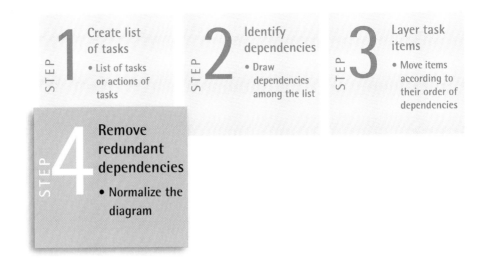

Removing the redundant dependencies simply means removing the lines that are already inferred by the chain of dependencies. For example, look at the top layer item in Figure 4.5, *Get email alert*. This item has a link to an item on layer 2, *View ceramic browse page*, and on layer 4, *View ceramic item*. The link to layer 4 is implied by *View ceramic browse page* (layer 2) link with *View ceramic item* (layer 4). Therefore the line has been removed. The resulting diagram should look something like Figure 4.5.

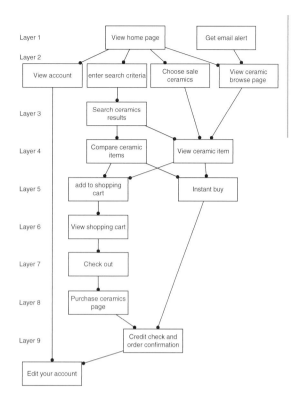

FIGURE 4.5 *Task layer map Steps 3 and 4: redundant dependencies have been removed. All dependency connections organized into layers.*

DEPENDENCY DIAGRAM

If you have an application or task flow diagram in the form of a dependency diagram, you can map this diagram to your prototype. A dependency diagram is a flow diagram in which the flow is determined by what tasks or actions are dependent. Figure 4.5 is an example of a dependency diagram. Other diagram forms and styles are possible. The sequential flow is the important aspect of the diagram not how it looks or whether it is oriented vertically or horizontally.

This diagram can be an essential aid in defining what you need or filtering out what you don't need to prototype. Often it is enough to prototype just a simple flow to illustrate a concept. This saves significant time over having to prototype an entire application just to illustrate a point or demonstrate a function. Likewise, you want to know how many tasks you need to prototype to make sure that all dependent tasks or actions are included in the prototype. Mapping the diagram to a prototype is a short process:

Step 1: Prioritize Requirements

The first step is to make a list of your high priority requirements/validations that you want to use in your prototype.

Step 2: Highlight Key Tasks

Step 2, use the list from Step 1 to highlight the key tasks in the software which will help you identify the most important screens to prototype. The dependency diagram can indicate some missing essential steps. For example, the most noticeable aspect of a dependency diagram is the clustering that occurs. The clusters show what key tasks are the most significant. For example in Figure 4.6, layers 1, 4, 5, and 9. Clusters are key application functions. If they are done wrong they will have a ripple effect through the rest of the task flow. These key tasks are prime candidates for inclusion in the prototype.

In our example (Figure 4.5), we highlighted key tasks on the basis of the clustering shown in Figure 4.6. The highlighted tasks are the home page, view item, compare item, and purchase screens. These seem to be the important screens to design. Likewise, to ensure that the prototype conforms to the task flow, you can let

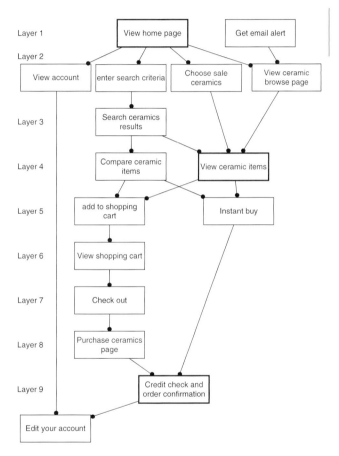

FIGURE 4.6 *Key tasks have been marked.*

the diagram direct your screen creation: creating screens represented by the next navigation steps as represented in the task flow diagram. Thus, the task flow diagram helps to guarantee that you prototype the most important application screens while being able to check the completeness of the prototype's navigation flow. Likewise, you then need to decide where the user should be taken after they reach an end point in a task. Do you go to a home page or starting window or to a confirmation page? Look at the dependency diagram and see what the next steps in the diagram can be.

Finally, items that are important for business or other requirements should be highlighted, even if they are not important for a particular task for which you're prototyping. For example, the instant buy screen could be an important selling point for the company but not important for a task.

Step 3: Identify Needs

By highlighting the lead tasks on your dependency diagram, you now have a starting point for the main windows you need to prototype. In Step 3 you list the screen elements needed for the highlighted tasks. The level of detail needed depends on both the level of fidelity and the level of available information. Worksheet 4.1 is designed to help you identify the items you need on the screen. The worksheet should first be filled in with the name of the screen followed by all the requirements from Worksheet 3.1 that will be fulfilled by the screen. Then, assign the tasks content types. For example, for the task, *View ceramic item*, a content type could be a picture of a ceramic item and a description. Next, map each content item to a corresponding requirement. On the basis of that linkage some user interface elements may come to mind. For example, with *View ceramic item* the requirement would add the price, a button to add the item to the user's cart, and a link to any related special offers. List the name of a user interface element that addresses the requirement (if known), and provide the rationale for using the chosen element. If you don't know what element to use, you can leave it blank and leave it for discussion with other team members to help fill in.

Next we'll fill out the worksheet using the example from this chapter. For each screen you prototype, map the task flow to the requirements using Worksheet 4.1. This allows you to see the relationship between requirements and task flow relevance. Likewise, the worksheet will help you discover missing or nonsensical requirements in the task flow. This means that either the task is not defined properly or the requirement is extraneous.

WORKSHEET 4.1: **Task Flow step to requirements mapping**

Project Name:
Project Date:
Product Name:
Current Phase: Scenario
Prototype Name:

Task name	Description	Requirements/ Assumptions (worksheet 3.1)	Rationale	Previous steps	Next steps

The key steps of the ceramic task layer map are shown in the following example.

WORKSHEET 4.1: **Task Flow step to requirements mapping**

Project Name: ArnoSoft Ceramics Proof of Concept
Project Date: 12 December 2006
Product Name: Cerama-Sell
Current Phase: Task Flow
Prototype Name: 1.0 release

Task name	Description	Rationale	Previous steps	Next steps
View Home page	Home page for Cerama_Sell	This screen addresses all main selling point requirements as well as main navigation	None	Account, Search, Sale specials, Browse Ceramics
Enter Search criteria	Search screen for ceramics	This screen assumes the need for a separate search screen	Home	Search results page, View item?
Search ceramics results	Results of a search result	This screen displays search results, open issue: iuf just one result go directly to view item?	Search page	View item
View Ceramic item	Ceramics detail screen	All product details and selling requirements	Search, Sale, View item Browse	Shopping cart Instant buy
Instant Buy	One click purchase screen for returning customers	Instant buy as in other ArnoSoft sites	View Item, Compare item	Credit card check and order
Check credit and order	Billing and shipping entry	Same as in other ArnoSoft sites	Purchase Page, Instant Buy	Edit Account, Confirmation page

SWIM LANE DIAGRAMS

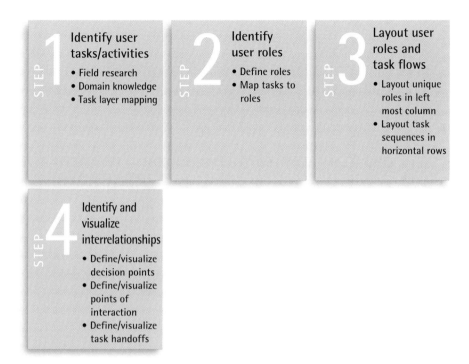

STEP 1 Identify user tasks/activities
- Field research
- Domain knowledge
- Task layer mapping

STEP 2 Identify user roles
- Define roles
- Map tasks to roles

STEP 3 Layout user roles and task flows
- Layout unique roles in left most column
- Layout task sequences in horizontal rows

STEP 4 Identify and visualize interrelationships
- Define/visualize decision points
- Define/visualize points of interaction
- Define/visualize task handoffs

A swim lane diagram (also known as a Rummler-Brache diagram or cross-functional flow diagram) is a user task/activity modeling technique that allows you to visualize the steps, interrelationships, and flow of complex processes. Process mapping is used in manufacturing-related fields to illustrate and analyze complex manufacturing processes. These diagrams have been adapted by software makers to map the who, when, and what of complex work-related processes:

> Types of people (roles) involved

> Points of workflow interaction

> Means of collaboration

> Flow of information

By mapping and visualizing processes, any gaps and improvements can be identified. In the swim lane diagram technique, you visualize the process by placing different tasks in rows (similar to swim lanes) in which the activity sequences and interaction and decision points flow through time from left to right. Each task in a row represents the organizational function or department responsible for accomplishing it. The swim lane technique is particularly useful for identifying stakeholders who are not included in a process, as well as processes where there are too many stakeholders to be able to operate efficiently [Rummler 1995].

Other types of diagrams include Unified Modeling Language (UML) sequence and activity diagrams in addition to process flow charts, which represent the business and operational work flows of a system. Generally, the start point, end points, inputs, outputs, possible paths, and the decisions that lead to these possible paths are included.

The steps involved in creating a swim lane diagram are as follows:

> Identify user tasks
> Identify user roles
> Layout user roles and task flows
> Identify and visualize the interrelationships between tasks and the different roles that carry them out

Step 1: Identify User Tasks

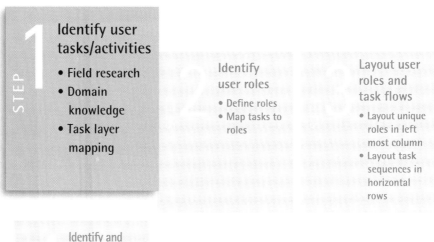

Defining the tasks to map is the initial step in creating a swim lane diagram. This information is acquired through any combination of the following:

> Field research, such as site visits and contextual observations
> Domain knowledge
> Task layer mapping (as described in the previous section)

A typical activity that is a candidate for mapping to a swim lane diagram is expense reporting. This activity involves a sequence of interrelated tasks that can be laid out in list form using note cards and sticky notes, including the following:

> Organize receipts and any other documentation of business expenses.
> Create a new expense report.
> Enter data into the expense report form.
> Review the entered data for completeness, accuracy, and adherence to policy.
> Submit the report for approval.
> Based on a work flow system and approval hierarchy, the submitted report is transferred to the next person, who is authorized to review and process it.
> Review a submitted report for approval/disapproval (based on accuracy, completeness, and adherence to policy).
> If approved, then submit to accounts payable for reimbursement processing.
> If disapproved, submit back to original submitter to make corrections.
> Original submitter makes corrections then resubmits report.
> Review submitted report again for accuracy, completeness, and adherence to policy.
> If approved, then initiate reimbursement payment processing.
> If disapproved, submit back to original submitter to make corrections.
> Original submitter makes corrections then resubmits report.
> Release reimbursement payment to original submitter.
> Reimbursement payment processed to transfer funds to employee's bank account.

Because the expense-reporting process requires accuracy, completeness, and adherence to policy, some of the tasks and subtasks are repeated for control and auditing purposes. Repeated tasks can be performed by different roles in some cases and by the same role in other cases, as the next section illustrates.

Step 2: Identify User Roles

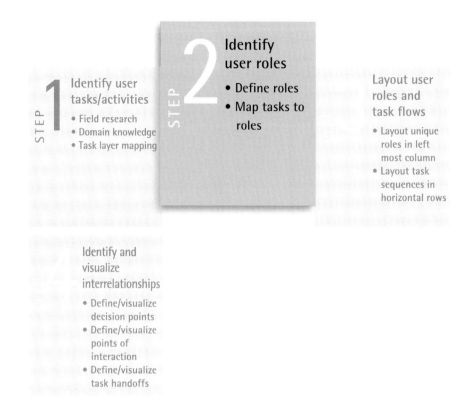

Once the tasks and subtasks are defined, a role can be assigned to each, that is, the actor performing the task (such as employee, manager/supervisor, computer system, etc.). Using the task/activity list from Step 1, a role type can be assigned to each task:

> **Employee**: Organizes receipts and any other documentation of business expenses.

> **Employee**: Creates a new expense report.

> **Travel and expense system**: Generates an expense report form and automatically assigns an unique expense report identification number. Some fields, such as employee name and ID, are automatically completed by the system.

> **Employee**: Enters data into expense report form.

> **Employee**: Reviews the entered data for completeness, accuracy, and adherence to policy.

> **Employee**: Submits the report for approval.

> **Travel and expense system**: If no data (or erroneous data) have been entered into a required field, an error message is generated.

> **Employee**: Makes corrections and then resubmits report.

- **Work flow system**: Transfers expense report to authorized person for review and approval.
- **Manager**: Reviews submitted report for approval/disapproval (based on accuracy, completeness, and adherence to policy).
- **Manager**: Approves expense report, then submits to accounts payable for reimbursement processing.
- **Manager**: Disapproves expense report, then submits back to original submitter to make corrections.
- **Work flow system**: Transfers expense report back to employee to make corrections.
- **Employee**: Makes corrections, then resubmits report.
- **Work flow system**: Transfers expense report back to manager for review and approval.
- **Work flow system**: Transfers expense report to travel and expense accountant for review and approval.
- **Travel and expense accountant**: Reviews an approved report again for accuracy, completeness, and adherence to policy.
- **Travel and expense accountant**: Approves expense report and initiates reimbursement payment processing.
- **Travel and expense accountant**: Disapproves expense report, then submits back to original submitter to make corrections.
- **Work flow system**: Transfers expense report back to employee to make corrections.
- **Employee**: Makes corrections, then resubmits report.
- **Work flow system**: Transfers expense report back to travel and expense accountant for review and approval.
- **Travel and expense accountant**: Submits reimbursement authorization to accounting system.
- **Accounting system**: Processes reimbursement payment for funds transfer to employee's bank account.

As you probably discovered during the above assignment of roles to tasks, the original list of tasks was refined and some missed tasks were added. Such refinement is common and should be done at any stage in this process if you discover missing information.

Step 3: Layout User Roles and Task Flows

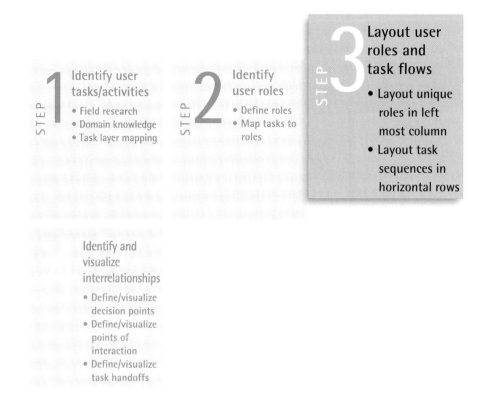

At this point, each unique role can be listed in a top-to-bottom order according to when it first appears. The tasks can then be laid out sequentially in rows that begin just to the right of a role designation (Figure 4.7). For each role, the tasks should be laid out in a horizontal temporal sequence starting from the task that is performed first to the one performed last. Now you can see why the visual representation is called a swim lane diagram. The layout of roles and associated sequence of tasks can continue to be done with note cards, sticky notes, and so forth or can be done using a software program, such as Visio.

Step 4: Identify and Visualize Interrelationships

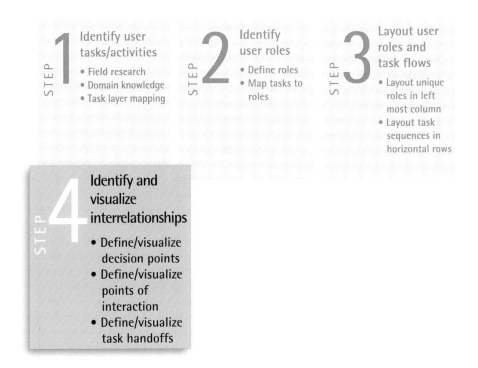

STEP 1 — Identify user tasks/activities
- Field research
- Domain knowledge
- Task layer mapping

STEP 2 — Identify user roles
- Define roles
- Map tasks to roles

STEP 3 — Layout user roles and task flows
- Layout unique roles in left most column
- Layout task sequences in horizontal rows

STEP 4 — Identify and visualize interrelationships
- Define/visualize decision points
- Define/visualize points of interaction
- Define/visualize task handoffs

The final step in swim lane diagramming is the identification and visualization of the relationships among the different tasks, including:

› Decision points

› Points of interaction with a system

› Handoff from one role to another

In our expense-reporting example, an illustration of a decision point is when a manager needs to approve or disapprove a submitted report or when a yes/no decision must be made. A decision point is often represented as a diamond shape with two vectors (a line with an arrowhead at the destination end), each leading to one of the two subsequent tasks after a decision, that is, the task after the yes option or the task after the no option.

Interaction points are generally represented by a line leading from the origin of interaction to the destination (or result) of interaction. In the expense reporting example, this occurs when an employee creates a new expense report and the travel and expense system generates the report form for data entry.

Like an interaction point, a handoff is also represented by a line leading from the handoff origin to the destination. A handoff from one role to another is demonstrated by the employee submitting a completed expense report to a manager or a manager submitting an approved expense report to accounting.

FIGURE 4.7 *Swim lane diagram for expense report tasks.*

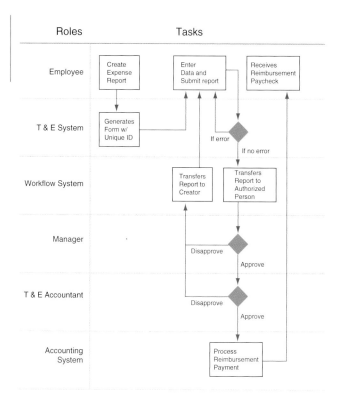

USAGE SCENARIOS

Scenarios describe how users carry out some defined task in the context of use, such as a user's work, their home or while they're shopping. Scenarios are not only an important component in the general activity of user interface design but are a necessary component in the specific activity of defining and building a prototype. Scenarios, when based on real knowledge of the user and their workplace, can help to clearly define the context of use for a requirement. They describe specific attributes about intended users, their actions, environment, daily tasks, and activities. Because they are a real-world story, scenarios are a useful tool for usability validations. The scenario will effect what you want to include in your prototype, because it portrays what the user needs to do. In the example of an expense reporting scenario, you can provide the detail that a user would like to keep track of their total budget while filling out an expense report. This amount may help them to decide whether to include an expense item or not. As a result, you may decide to include the display of a budget amount in the user interface. Additionally, scenarios support:

> ➤ Exploration of usability directions early in the design process
> ➤ Buy-in of user-centered design approach from key project stakeholders
> ➤ Identification of probable task completion times

You need little or no human factors expertise to write a scenario. Even if you've never written a scenario, you can do it by thinking of this step in its most basic form: telling a story about *someone* doing *something* (the use of your software) *somewhere*. A simplified form of scenario-based design can be used by everyone to move from task flow definition to creation of the scenario narrative. More complex and intricate methods for creating scenarios are outlined in numerous books, most notably in Rossen and Carroll [2001]. However, because most people are familiar with films, we frame scenario creation in terms of a film screenplay:

> › **Who** is your protagonist [user]? Describe the protagonist's [user's] main characteristics and main character flaw [pain points].
> › **What** is your protagonist's [user's] goal in the story? What is he or she trying to do to attain their goal [tasks/activities]? Describe the antagonist (villain) [constraints/limitations] who tries to prevent the protagonist from achieving his goal [through task/activity completion]. How does the antagonist [constraints/limitations] create conflict [less than optimal usability] for the protagonist [user]?
> › **When** does the story [scenario] take place? Now or in the future?
> › **Where** does the story [scenario] take place? Describe the geographic [physical] location [home, office, car, etc.].
> › **Why** do the actions of the protagonist [user] determine how the main conflict of the story is resolved [a task is completed]? **What** are the user actions to complete a task?
> › **How** does the protagonist [user] resolve the conflict [complete a task]? Sketch out a plot.

In addition to the familiarity with film making, starting the scenario in this way, by making the constraints into a villain, will help you consider the software in different terms—how frustrating for the user it might be to be blocked at every turn. Anthropomorphizing software, or thinking of it as a human who does or refuses to do desired action, is one approach that can apply scenarios to the idea of film making and theater, an idea first put forth by Brenda Laurel [1993].

The following are the steps for creating a scenario:

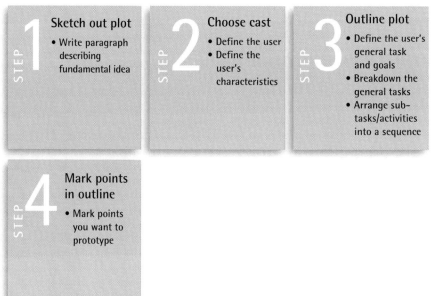

Step 1: Sketch Out Plot

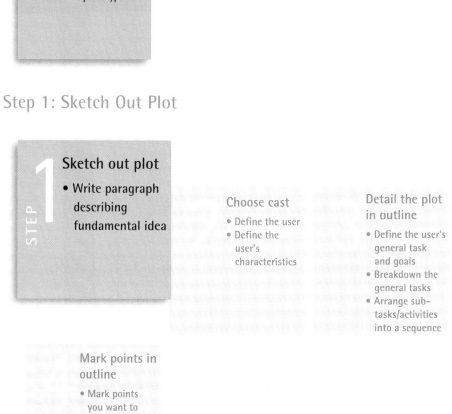

Taking the idea for a software service as a basis, write a short paragraph of how a user would apply the functionality to their benefit. For example, in the absence of online ordering software, the idea could be to send customers e-mail alerts. How will e-mail alerts help them? A story sketch could go like this:

1. The user goes to the website and looks for the latest line of Asma Ceramics. She sees the new collection is not available yet.
2. She signs up to receive an e-mail alert when in the collection arrives. A week later, she receives the e-mail alert.
3. She clicks a link in the e-mail that takes her to a view of the new Asma collection.
4. Seeing that supply is limited, she immediately orders the complete collection.

Step 2: Choose Cast

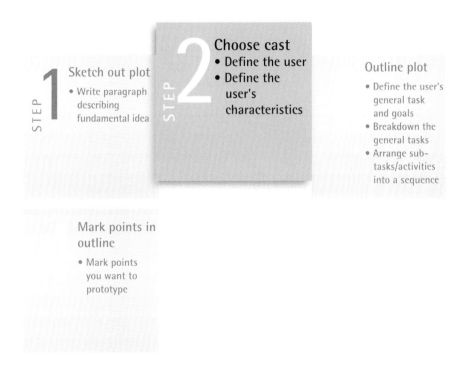

To provide a user focus for the plot, define a character you believe would most likely be the protagonist in this plot, an archetype of the main user. Let's say for our purposes it is a design-conscious working mother who has no time to shop for kitchenware because of her busy life both at work and raising her children. To more easily reference the protagonist and to make her more real for our design purposes, we'll give her a name, Rebecca.

Step 3: Outline Plot

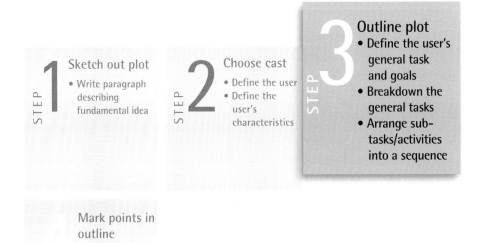

STEP 1 — Sketch out plot
- Write paragraph describing fundamental idea

STEP 2 — Choose cast
- Define the user
- Define the user's characteristics

STEP 3 — Outline plot
- Define the user's general task and goals
- Breakdown the general tasks
- Arrange sub-tasks/activities into a sequence

Mark points in outline
- Mark points you want to prototype

Outlining a plot consists of defining the task/activities in terms of user goals and then creating a step-by-step outline, inserting Rebecca (as well as any other characters) into the plot. The deconstruction of a task flow, or the breakdown of a task into finer grain subtasks and activities, can serve as the basis for the plot outline. The result is an easily scanned plot overview divided into different scenes. The ceramics example from above could take the following form:

Task: Rebecca is interested in purchasing online the Asma 2005 ceramic ware collection. Task breakdown:

1. Rebecca talks with friends about the beauty of the Asma 2005 ceramic ware collection.
2. Rebecca notes that she needs a new dinner set and would like to shop for it but has no time.
3. Rebecca becomes motivated to go to the website by seeing an ad on the Amazon website.
4. She goes to the website and looks for the Asma 2005 ceramics ware collection.
   a. Because she is in a hurry, she doesn't want to browse, so she searches for it.

b. In the search results Rebecca finds the collection but notices that it is not available yet because it's new.

c. She sees a link to register to receive an alert when the item becomes available. She clicks on the link.

d. She signs up to receive an e-mail alert when the new Asma collection arrives.

5. A week later, she receives the Asma collection e-mail alert in her inbox.

a. She clicks the link in the e-mail.

b. Her browser opens and she visits the Asma collection website.

c. She views the new collection.

d. She sees that the supply is limited and wonders whether her friends will sell out the item.

e. She orders it immediately.

f. She selects express shipping and enters her credit card information.

Step 4: Mark Points in Outline

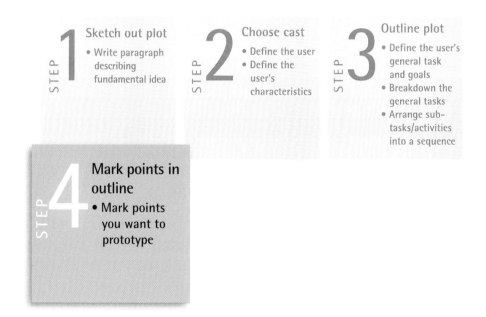

STEP 1 — Sketch out plot
- Write paragraph describing fundamental idea

STEP 2 — Choose cast
- Define the user
- Define the user's characteristics

STEP 3 — Outline plot
- Define the user's general task and goals
- Breakdown the general tasks
- Arrange sub-tasks/activities into a sequence

STEP 4 — Mark points in outline
- Mark points you want to prototype

The completed outline includes richer details as well as some forgotten steps from when the outline was done outside of the context of use. Using the plot outline from Step 3, mark the points you want to prototype. This will give you an idea for the contents that should appear in the prototype. You can also confidently talk through the steps you've chosen not to prototype.

The following list is the same as the list above but with the items the software maker will prototype listed in bold type:

1. Rebecca talks with friends of hers and they all discuss how beautiful the Asma 2005 ceramic ware collection is.

2. This reminds Rebecca that she needs a new dinner set and would like to go shopping for it. But she has no time.

3. Rebecca goes to the website and looks for the Asma 2005 ceramic ware collection.

   a. Because she is in a hurry to browse, she enters a search criterion.

   b. **In the search results she finds the new collection but sees that it's not available yet.**

   c. She sees a link to receive an alert when the item is available. She clicks on the link.

   d. She signs up to receive an e-mail alert when the collection arrives.

4. A week later, she receives the e-mail alert in her inbox.

   a. She clicks the link embedded in the e-mail message.

   b. **Her browser opens and she visits the Asma collection website.**

   c. **She views the new Asma collection.**

   d. **She sees that the supply is limited (she wonders whether her friends will sell out the item).**

   e. **Seeing that the price is right, Rebecca orders it immediately.**

   f. She selects express shipping and enters her credit card information.

Figure 4.8 is an example of a wireframe prototype created from a scenario.

An abbreviated version of using scenarios is outlined above. Scenarios have been used throughout the software-making process beyond just their use in prototyping. Entire methodologies are based on scenario-based design [Rosson and Carroll 2001] as well as the use of scenarios for requirements gathering [Beyer and Holtzblatt 1997, Baxter and Courage 2005] and usability testing [Rubin 1994].

FIGURE 4.8 *The resulting wireframe.*

ARNOSHOP LOGO/Header

My account/Help/Cart   [Search]

Shop   Registry   Ideas   What's New   Stores

Coming Ceramics for fall
Asma 2005 Collection

Lorem ipsum dolor sit amet, ut tortor, malesuada feugiat. Vel fringilla elit massa, sem quidem aenean, nulla arcu suscipit vitae mauris integer imperdiet, duis vivamus orci sed. Scelerisque ut sit, vulputate non lacus ac mauris mauris, ligula dui vel dolor, varius eu et, turpis venenatis pellentesque. Adipiscing quis erat duis donec convallis, consequat rhoncus cursus

Coming soon: (Alert me when it is in)

<View all coordinating items>

<email this>
<Print this>

Color X   Color X   Color X

Shop   Registry   Ideas   What's New   Stores   Contact Us

SUMMARY

In this chapter we discussed getting the components for your prototype by creating task flows and scenarios. Through the task flow and consequent scenario, you should now have clearly defined the users and the details of usage along with a list of the elements you need for your prototype. Regardless of the level of detail you have, you are now ready to inventory the content and decide the appropriate level of fidelity.

THE ARNOSOFT TEAM TRIES A TASK FLOW AND GETS STUCK WITH SCENARIOS

For their storyboard exercise, the ArnoSoft team needs to develop a task flow. So Ina tries to come up with a task flow that supports their "tried and true" gardening site.

Then Ina, working together with Reed, attempts to create a gardening scenario that fits this work flow. They quickly realize they're really trying to force the truth as they run into many different problems. For example, the gardening site does not allow enough keyword searches or the complex browsing practice of the ceramics buyer. Gardeners were concerned more with equipment features, but ceramics buyers cared much more for aesthetics.

The gardening scenario leads to a great number of corrections and enhancements to the gardening task flow, resulting in the undermining of key technical assumptions and business

flow. By addressing these issues, Ina discovers that new requirements are necessary. To capture these new requirements, Ina enhances the task flow diagram with the new requirements, making them stand out by using a different presentation (e.g., rounded corners and thicker lines). These new requirements are made clear to everyone on the development team that a re-scoping effort was necessary as well as a revision of the business case. This work goes beyond the responsibility of the software makers; the business stakeholders would need to meet to dis-cuss the new business case for the site. For example, Dirk realized the ArnoPlatform, the inter-nal development environment, needs a major overhaul (Reed supported this and suggested renaming it the DishPlatform). Ina also realizes the task flow may undergo an even greater overhaul when user research is conducted. The scenario written by Ina and Reed results in the following new task flow diagram:

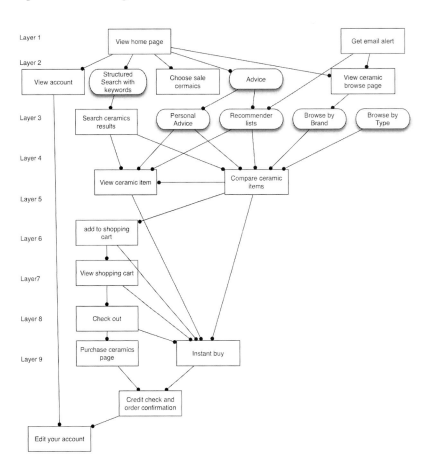

The new scenario and task flow initiate an immediate revisit of the business case, in hopes of addressing any business issues before major mistakes were made. The ArnoSoft team decides to proceed with the storyboard creation because they believe it could be done concurrently with the revisit of the business case. Also, the quick results from the storyboard would facilitate a better discussion for the business stakeholders.

REFERENCES

Apple Computer. Inside Macintosh: Macintosh Human Interface Guidelines. Boston: Addison-Wesley, 1996.

Jonathan Arnowitz. Communicating a task analysis through task layer maps. In: Dan Diaper, Neville Stanton, editors. The Handbook of Task Analysis for Human Computer Interaction. Mahwah, NJ: Lawrence Erlbaum Associates, 2004, pp. 38–45.

Hugh Beyer, K. Holtzblatt. Contextual Inquiry. San Francisco: Morgan-Kaufman, 1997.

Bill Buxton, R. Sniderman. Iteration in the design of the human-computer interface. Proceedings of the 13th Annual Meeting, Human Factors Association of Canada, 1980, pp. 72–81.

Computer Associates. AllFusion™ process modeler features, descriptions and benefits. http://www3.ca.com/Files/FactSheet/af_process_modeler_fdb.pdf#search='swim%20lane%20diagrams. Accessed February 5, 2006.

Dan Diaper, Neville Stanton, eds. The Handbook of Task Analysis for Human Computer Interaction. Mahwah, NJ: Lawrence Erlbaum Associates, 2004.

JoAnn Hackos, Janice Redish. User and Task Analysis for Interface Design. New York: Wiley, 1998.

Barry Kirwan, Les Ainsworth, eds. A Guide to Task Analysis. Bristol, PA: Taylor & Francis, 1992.

Brenda Laurel. Computers and Theater. San Francisco: Addison-Wesley, 1993.

Scott MacKenzie, R. William Soukoreff. Card, English, Burr (1978)–25 Years Later. Proceedings of CHI '03. New York: ACM Press, 2003, pp. 760–761.

Jenny Preece, Yvonne Rogers, Helen Sharp, David Benyon, Sam Holland, Tom Carey. Human-Computer Interaction. San Francisco: Addison-Wesley, 1994.

Mary Beth Rosson, John Carroll. Usability Engineering: Scenario-Based Development of Human Computer Interaction. San Francisco: Morgan Kaufmann, 2001.

Jeffrey Rubin. Handbook of Usability Testing: How to Plan, Design, and Conduct Effective Tests. Hoboken, NJ: Wiley, 1994.

Scriptologist. Writing a screenplay about a person wrongly imprisoned. http://www.scriptologist.com/Magazine/Tips/Imprisoned/imprisoned.html. Accessed January 14, 2006.

A. Shepherd. Hierarchical task analysis and training decisions. Programmed Learning and Educational Technology, 1985, vol. 22, pp. 162–176.

A. Shepherd. Analysis and training in information technology tasks. In: Dan Diaper, editor. Task Analysis for Human-Computer Interaction. Chichester, UK: Ellis Horwood, 1989, pp. 15–55.

University of Toledo, Project Enterprise. http://projectenterprise.utoledo.edu/BusinessProcessAnalysis.asp. Accessed February 5, 2006.

Usability Net. Tools and methods. http://www.usabilitynet.org/tools/taskanalysis.htm. Accessed February 5, 2006.

CHAPTER

The Effective Prototyping Process

PHASE **1** Plan

PHASE **2** Specification

PHASE **3** Design

PHASE **4** Results

STEP **1** ch 3
Verify Requirements

STEP **2** ch 4
Develop Task Flows

STEP **3** ch 5
Define Content and Fidelity

STEP **4** ch 6
Determine Characteristics

STEP **5** ch 7
Choose a Method

STEP **6** ch 8
Choose a Tool

STEP **7** ch 9
Select Design Criteria

STEP **8** ch 10
Create the Design

STEP **9** ch 11
Review the Design

STEP **10** ch 12
Validate the Design

STEP **11** ch 13
Deploy the Design

5

DEFINE PROTOTYPE CONTENT AND FIDELITY

DEFINE PROTOTYPE CONTENT AND FIDELITY

Defining prototype content and fidelity determines how much time and resources need to be spent on the prototype. A prototype with too high a fidelity wastes resources by spending time creating a level of detail that will need to be done all over again in later iterations. A prototype with too low a fidelity results in not getting enough information to validate requirements and assumptions. You select the fidelity by choosing the content and setting its fidelity. In choosing the right prototyping content and setting its fidelity correctly, it is important for a manager to consider the following points.

Beware of Too Much Content With Too High Fidelity

Well-meaning employees want to impress everyone. Unfortunately, this usually results in creating a prototype with too much high-fidelity content; because high-fidelity content is more impressive looking than low-fidelity content. When reviewing an early high-fidelity prototype, ask yourself how much are real design decisions and how much are just unnecessary details.

It Is Better to Underestimate the Content and Fidelity Than to Overestimate It

It is best to start off conservative with content fidelity levels. This requires less work and enables you to iterate the prototype to the right level of fidelity. Iteration allows you to progressively build on previous work, which prevents throwing a prototype away. For example, if you prototype with too low fidelity, it still sets a general direction to iterate on. Once the direction is decided, you can iterate and build on a direction to a higher fidelity. Once a big direction change is made in the requirements or as assumptions are invalidated, all related design work needs to be revisited if not redone completely. This commonly happens when the fidelity is too high, and usability testing or some other validation proves an assumption wrong. The work must be repeated and valuable time is lost. Therefore, it is important to get the low-fidelity stuff right first and then work out the higher fidelity details.

Fidelity Too High or Too Late

There are two fundamental rules regarding high-fidelity prototypes:

1. Prototyping best practice dictates that you should move from low to progressively higher fidelity prototypes through the design process. Early high fidelity prototypes are throw-away proof of concepts.

2. High fidelity requires a conceptual model. The more detailed the design, the more it will rely on a conceptual design to make it fit together. A conceptual model is an overall design framework that is the design rationale for things such as metaphors, language usage, and terminology. It is how the designer believes the user will conceptualize the software (e.g., desktop software as a desk metaphor). The user in turn then interprets the clues from the conceptual model into their own mental model.

The task flow in Chapter 4 established how the prototype should *work*, whereas this chapter establishes how the prototype should *look*. A prototype can contain many different kinds of content, including editorial, visuals, and navigation structure. In general, you should not prototype everything at once, especially in the beginning of a project. Even with a mature product, it may be wise, to isolate prototype content destined for revision. This chapter will help you discern between important and trivial content and decide what to include in your prototype.

THE TWO MEANINGS OF HIGH FIDELITY

high fidelity 1. A kind of sound-reproducing system whose realism of reproduction is judged to be better than average. Stereo reproduction can be high fidelity or otherwise. 2. The pursuit of perfection in sound reproduction, as a hobby or a religion (from Stereophile.com, accessed January 18, 2006).

We bring this definition to your attention to make sure you avoid falling into the high-fidelity religion. High fidelity always sounds more impressive than low fidelity. However, in prototyping, unlike sound reproduction, you want to build up to high fidelity and not just plunge in the high-fidelity religion that "a sexy looking prototype is always the best."

PROTOTYPE FIDELITY

Fidelity is the level of detail that content is rendered in the interface. Prototype content can be rendered in a continuum from lowest to highest fidelity. Specifically, the fidelity of visual look, the interaction behaviors, navigation flow, and other aspects of the user experience as reflected by prototyping content.

A high-fidelity prototyped content is more like the actual released software. For example, with the highest-fidelity visual design the software *looks* like it will when it is actually built. With high-fidelity interaction design the prototype *behaves* like the released software would. Therefore, it is possible for a prototype to have variable levels of fidelity for the different prototype contents.

Why do you want differing level of fidelity?

You might choose to do this to focus just on a new visual design or a new interaction concept, etc. By deliberately making some elements high fidelity, the audience is better able to focus on the higher fidelity items, giving them an unequal weight and thereby the lead focus. The most common prototyping mistake is reflected in the second Stereophile.com definition: when high fidelity becomes a religion. When usability testing is relegated with an almost religious fervor to extremely high-fidelity prototyping, you'll almost surely be testing too much to receive valuable undistracted feedback. In our experience, waiting to prototype only in high fidelity once all research and design is completed is to prototype too late in the game. Prototyping can uncover major problems. So it is best to start early before it is too late. Start with prototyping in lower fidelity and iterate toward higher fidelity.

Contrarily, when you want to just try out a concept, you may decide to keep the concept in lower fidelity, because the lower fidelity keeps unnecessary details from distracting the software-making team. In the early stages of design, low-fidelity prototypes are most appropriate for allowing designers to evaluate and try multiple designs, because they appropriately constrain the focus of evaluation and trial to the larger more conceptual aspects of software design—the user experience in terms of sequencing and flow.

As a design moves incrementally closer to development and its details start to fall into place, different prototyping methods are used to portray the increasing detailed solution of the software. The fidelity representations can range from low (rough hand-drawn sketches on paper) to medium (digital wireframe representations) to high (detailed renderings of visual user interfaces in Photoshop) to highest (a beta version of the actual software).

Figure 5.1 shows a low-fidelity prototype, a rough sketch in which the interaction can be approximated. There is no attention paid to a high-fidelity graphic design or even the information displayed. Figure 5.2 shows a high-fidelity visual design prototype that looks similar to the intended actual released software. It looks like what you'd expect to see on a computer screen, and as a high-fidelity prototype, it also behaves like finished software (though this complete behavior is not required for a prototype to be considered high fidelity). Some high-fidelity prototypes may only be high fidelity in one or two content aspects. More on this below.

Low Fidelity

Low-fidelity prototyping content is akin to sketches that artists and designers create early in the ideation stages of a design concept: vague and minimally formed in attributes. Low-fidelity prototypes create an early representation of its content. Low fidelity allows designers early conceptualization of page layouts, such as the rough positioning of menu areas, banners, toolbars, and content areas. One of the primary benefits of low-fidelity prototypes are usually rapid to produce. So you generally want to make your biggest mistakes with low-fidelity prototypes because of the lower cost of iterating them.

FIGURE 5.1 *Low-fidelity prototype.*

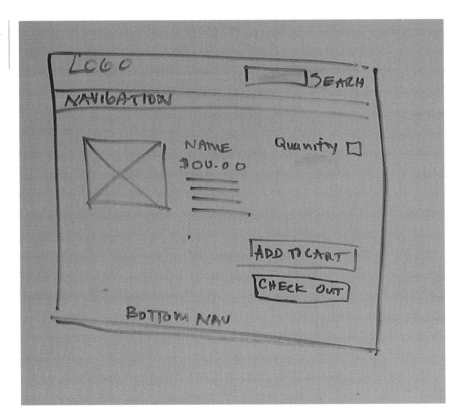

FIGURE 5.2 *High-fidelity prototype.*

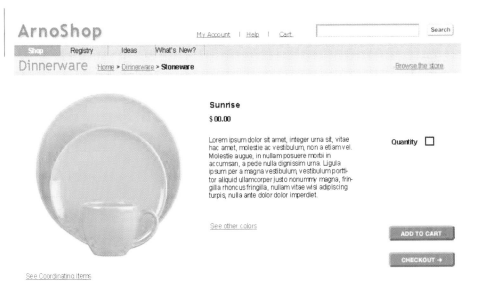

High Fidelity

People often mistake high-fidelity prototypes for the finished products. This dilemma of *demo ware* can best be surmised by the classic example of Apple Computer's "Knowledge Navigator" video prototype. Knowledge Navigator, a futuristic vision statement, was so realistically portrayed in a video scenario that the consuming public thought it was an immediately available product and made inquiries about purchasing it.

High-fidelity prototyping content has a more accurate look and/or feel to the final product. A high-fidelity prototype, like an artist or designer's comp, is rich in detail with all its attributes. High-fidelity prototypes (prototypes of mostly high-fidelity content) are intended for designers to create and try out the contents of a user interface, content such as information design, visual design, or interaction design. Ideally, the purpose of a high-fidelity prototype is to test the content with end users or at least to get their direct feedback using some other mechanism. High-fidelity prototypes also allow the designer to efficiently document the design without lengthy documents that are open to misinterpretation. Because high-fidelity prototypes are usually longer to produce, you generally want to have completed the bulk of usability testing before you create a high-fidelity prototype. Because of the high cost of iterating these, you want to refine the prototype at this stage, not make wholesale changes.

PROTOTYPE CONTENT

As the case study later in this chapter illustrates, you can avoid miscommunication and misunderstanding over what a prototype is trying to show by judiciously choosing the correct content and fidelity level for the prototype. The prototype context needs to be established by including all the different forms of content, but content can be emphasized or deemphasized through the interplay of high and low fidelity to prevent items from unwanted focus when the prototype concept is presented. Figure 5.3 shows a typical experiential prototype in which all the contents are clearly visible. Figure 5.4 shows the opposite, a prototype in which almost all the content is masked or deemphasized (low fidelity), forcing the viewer to concentrate only on the overall structure. Certain prototypes are chosen to emphasize certain content fidelities over others to evaluate them. For example, a wireframe prototype is typically much lower in fidelity than a prototype programmed in code; however, it is enough to evaluate a visual design direction, whereas a coded prototype would mean involving not just the visual design but also the interaction design, system performance, and so on, thereby detracting from the visual design. Moreover, if given the stage in software creation you're only prepared for visual design, by using a coded prototype only the visual design will be ready for prime time; the rest–interaction design information and so on–will all be placeholders. During evaluation, the stakeholders may get side-tracked by the information or interaction design and either ignore the visual design or, worse, judge the visual design poorly as not having been well thought out. Therefore, using the right level of fidelity at the right time is essential for effective prototyping.

FIGURE 5.3 *All content is visible in this prototype.*

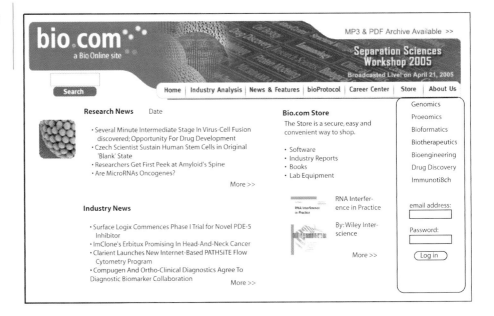

FIGURE 5.4 *In this prototype screen, all content is masked except for branding elements.*

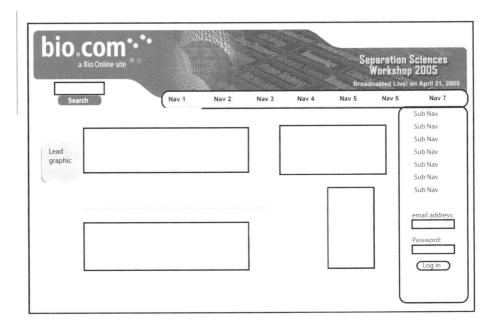

Fidelity is just one characteristic of prototyping; the others are discussed in Chapter 6. For now, we concentrate on the fidelity of different kinds of content including, but not limited to:

> Information design
> Interaction design and navigation model
> Visual design
> Editorial content
> Brand expression
> System performance and behavior

Each content category plays a different role in prototyping. Different techniques can be used for emphasizing (heightening the fidelity) or deemphasizing (lowering the fidelity) the visual and interactive components of prototypes. Given the connection of content to fidelity, think of a prototype in terms of the content/fidelity matrix shown in Table 5.1.

TABLE 5.1 **Content Fidelity Matrix**

Content	Very Low Fidelity	Low Fidelity	Medium Fidelity	High Fidelity	Highest Fidelity
Information design					
Interaction design					
Visual design					
Editorial content					
Branding expression					
System performance					

Information Design

Information design is the design and structure of information used in an interactive piece of software, including information in the form of data entry and display fields, menus, tables, graphics, messages, and other expressions of information. Information design by this understanding can also mean information architecture. Information architecture has a slightly narrower meaning [Rosenfeld and Morville 2002]:

> The combination of organization, labeling, and navigation schemes within an information system.
> The structural design of an information space to facilitate task completion and intuitive access to content.
> The art and science of structuring and classifying websites and intranets to help people find and manage information.

For our purposes, information architecture is the systematic organization, flow, and communicativeness of text-based editorial content in the user interface (see

Editorial Content, later in this chapter). Information design, on the other hand, separates textual information content (what we call editorial content) from content structure; this structure should be seen in combination with the syntactic, semantic, and pragmatic expressions of icons and other visual elements.

Because it embodies the organization, flow, and expression of screen content, information design can be the most powerful element in the user experience. The visual rendering in combination with the editorial expression of information often sets a tone—a feeling of friendliness or aloofness. Information design, by using text, can also be instructional and functionally explicit. All too often users get confused and can't find key functionality available on their screens, simply because the wrong terminology is used or the information is located outside the user's direct field of vision. Especially for information-intensive software systems, such as websites and services, providing the right information organization, placement, and editorial communicativeness is of utmost importance. Via carefully considered and well-crafted information design, designers can literally identify and speak the visual and editorial language of targeted users.

Techniques to Adjust the Fidelity of Information Design

In prototyping, information design is emphasized (higher fidelity) through more detailed visual representation of the high-level textual structure and the navigation flow (see Figure 5.5). The three most common prototyping methods used to focus on information design in software are card sorting, wireframe prototyping, and high-fidelity experiential prototyping. The easiest way to focus on the information design is to simply exclude other prototype content so only the structure or more detailed representation of information is shown. As shown in Figure 5.6, you can also focus on information design by deemphasizing the graphic elements and even the body text in a wireframe prototype, only displaying the menus, headings, buttons, and other navigational items. The most thorough and complete method to emphasize information design is by using an experiential interactive prototype (paper or digital) where all finalized information is displayed. This method is the most explicit in terms of the syntactic connection between the information and the information design that supports it. However, building an interactive experiential prototype is time consuming and makes more sense for final design refinements rather than for early prototyping.

In general, when developing the information design, you can lower the fidelity whenever a prototype is a narrative and the audience is not directly engaged with the prototype. The most common way to deemphasize information design is by using color blocks in the prototype as a placeholder for text (lowest fidelity). Selectively blocking out text allows the designer to include some incomplete elements of the information architecture. It also allows the user to block out controversial items to avoid them overtaking a design discussion, as in the example at the beginning of this chapter. One step up from blocking is the use of greeked text (low fidelity). Greeked text is purposefully unintelligible but allows the audience to see the visual design of the typography.

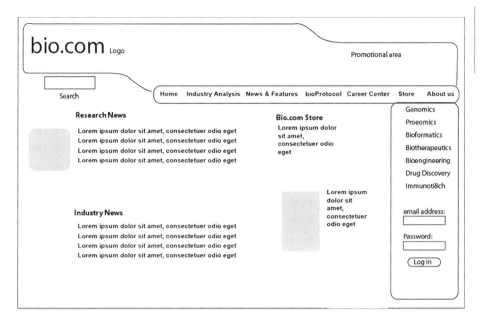

FIGURE 5.5 *Information design in high fidelity in a prototype.*

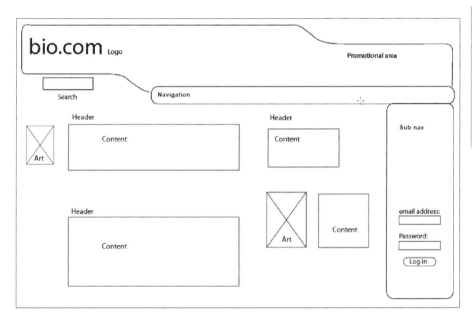

FIGURE 5.6 *Information design in low fidelity in a prototype. The only thing clear about the information design from this prototype is its raw structure.*

INTERACTION DESIGN AND NAVIGATION MODEL

Interaction design is how the user interacts with software both in the structure and the flow within a screen and among screens. The design determines how the system responds to user actions. If the user navigates to another window, is it a window where a primary or secondary task occurs? How does the system respond? Does it allow a task to be completed, provide information about errors, send warning messages, or provide processing status? Can the software anticipate a user's next action or must users always initiate their next step? These are all factors in the interaction design.

The interaction designer owns the interaction design. As with any aspect of software usability, interaction design content comes from understanding user tasks, human behavior, and testing designs with target users. The art of interaction design comes from taking a complex and often contradictory array of user interaction needs and developing a single usable design. Information designers, interaction designers structure their interfaces so that a single consistent interaction model with redundant command structures which can support a variety of users and their different styles of usage.

For an interaction designer, nothing beats the comfort and satisfaction experienced by a user who can effortlessly engage in and complete an activity. Likewise, nothing is a bigger waste then creating functionality a user cannot use or even find.

Techniques to Adjust the Fidelity of Interaction Design and Navigation Model

Interaction design and navigation are higher fidelity whenever the points of interaction and navigation flow can be portrayed in their most polished and detailed form: every link, command, and function as embodied by a user interface element is represented and their resulting action/navigation is specified. This high fidelity can be achieved in many ways, but two are the most common. One is through the level of complete narration and the other is through the level of complete interaction. Complete narration is when a storyboard includes not just a sunny day interaction but also all possible exceptions and alternate interactions and navigations. Complete interaction is when an interactive prototype has every working command, user interface controls, links, and so on, either working or at least specifying what will happen when one uses them as well as how one uses them.

One last technique for deemphasizing the interaction design is to make the prototype interactive in a way that is irrelevant for the ultimate interaction of the software. A good example of this type of prototype is a card sort, where the user interacts intimately with the prototype but in a way that has nothing to do with the ultimate user interaction of the software. In fact, card sorting is a method used to not only understand how users perceive an information structure but also how they understand an interaction scheme in the context of the information structure.

VISUAL DESIGN

Visual design is the visual language and composition of visual elements used to express the software structure and messages to users. Finding the right balance between visual structures and messaging is a complex iterative design activity. The interaction designer will tell you that the structure and message should express the use of the software. The information designer believes that the structure and messaging are meant to lead the user to desired information. The branding specialist will inform you that the structure and messaging should express the values, attributes, and qualities of a company, product, or service. As you can tell from these various purposes, visual design is key in establishing users' mental models through metaphors, analogies, concepts, and other mental associations.

The primary considerations of visual design include [Dondis 1973]:

> Layout (visual composition)
> Typographic design
> Graphic elements, including geometric/non-geometric shapes, icons, buttons, photographic images, illustrations, and animations
> Fonts selection
> Color scheme
> Visual branding expression

Because it is the most tangible piece that people can immediately grasp and relate to, most users think of the user experience purely in terms of the visual expression. Furthermore, visual elements can draw the most powerful emotions and reactions from users. The attributes of visual design make it a powerful element of the user interface and of a prototype.

The owner of the visual design is the visual designer. Visual design is only partially informed by user research. Visual design is also informed by competitive analysis, market trends, organization needs, executives' spouses, and that cool thing the designer saw when driving to work.

Techniques to Adjust the Fidelity of Visual Design

In general, the fidelity of the visual design is heightened by a color representation of the software with all graphic elements (widgets, logos, typography, color usage, etc.) (see Figure 5.7). Visual design prototypes are usually digital (or color prints of a digital interface) and are typically used late in the design process, once the interaction or information needs are firmly established (or when the prototype is meant to serve as a presentation demo).

As shown in Figure 5.8 fidelity of the visual design is low when a prototype either does not show the graphic user interface, such as in a narrative scenario prototype, or when an abstracted prototype displays just one or two design aspects, such as rough sketch wireframes and card sort prototypes. Prototypes that deemphasize the visual design by representing the user interface as grayscale sketches devoid of detailed graphic elements. The sketches often block out logos and use just text buttons instead of icons, making the designs purely textual interfaces. Sometimes designers try to suggest a visual design in a wireframe by including a company logo or using typography in a certain way. However, these are meant to be placeholders and information for designers and usability test participants to consider rather than an actual representation of the final visual design. By deemphasizing the visual design allows the audience to concentrate on just the information or interaction design.

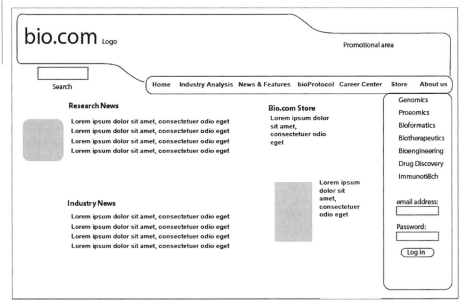

EDITORIAL CONTENT

Editorial content is the text that appears in the interface, e.g., labels, headers, titles, messages, and notifications. Editorial content also includes the usage of text, including style, flow, and expression.

Style is the type of content and the format it's presented in, such as an order form, a news story, an advertisement, etc. Style also indicates how information is syntactically presented to the user. Does it address the user as a professional or as a friend or as a salesman?

Flow consists of the method used to carry a reader through a body of content. If the content is a form with data entry fields, then flow is how the terminology guiding the user to complete the task of data entry or editing. Flow depends on the arrangement of fields and how well they are organized, grouped, labeled, and laid out. If the editorial content is in narrative or story format, flow depends on organization, presentation, and continuity in addition to any navigation required for a user to move to other screens that are part of the narrative.

Editorial expression is the voice of the content, e.g., technical, entertaining, legal, instructive, and so on.

Questions you want to ask when considering style are who is the audience and their background? What is the most important thing you need to communicate with style? Is it trust, friendliness, nostalgia, or other emotional attributes? What are the expectations for the tone of voice users would expect under a real-life situation? For example, what would the tone of a banker be and compare with the tone expressed via the bank website? What would a ceramics sales person say compared with the style expressed by a ceramics website?

Techniques to Adjust the Fidelity of the Editorial Content

Similar to other content components of a user interface, editorial content can be emphasized or deemphasized depending on the objectives of the prototype. The emphasis can range along spectrums of visual fidelity, editorial finish, and accuracy of message flow and layout. A prototype created later in the software design process typically has final or near-final edited text fully rendered in the selected font styles, weights, sizes, and colors (see Figure 5.3) to enable the usability test participant to fully experience the style, flow, and expression of text and language intended for the final product.

A prototype created early in the software process typically has the editorial content represented as shaded boxes or greeked text as shown in Figure 5.5. This more abstract representation of text is used to deemphasize the editorial content so that viewers focus on the emphasized aspects of content. This abstraction prevents viewers from reading unfinished editorial content, usually only partially conceived and written during the early conceptual phase of the software effort. In prototypes built to focus on interaction and navigation, for example, some parts of the editorial content, such as titles, subtitles, and labels, may be rendered in a higher fidelity, whereas blocks of running narrative text are represented abstractly. This allows a user to focus on navigation elements and cues on a screen and across screens while inhibiting the reading of text.

BRAND EXPRESSION

Branding is "an aggregation of all the physical and emotional characteristics of a company, a product, or a service encountered by the consumer at all points of contact. Branding is important because it communicates a brand's business proposition and, hopefully, a reason why a consumer should desire the product represented by the brand" [Roellig 2001]. The branding of products and services is often misunderstood as merely slapping on a company's logo and color scheme. Branding is actually much more. To better understand branding, we share some definitions from the American Institute of Graphic Arts' (AIGA) book, *The Dictionary of Brand* [Neumeier 2004]:

> › *Branding*: a person's perception of a product, service, experience, or organization; the art and science of brand building
> › *Brand alignment*: the practice of linking brand strategy to customer touch points
> › *Brand asset*: a distinctive feature of a product, service, company, or brand
> › *Brand attribute*: a distinctive characteristic of a product, service, company, or brand
> › *Brand experience*: all the interactions people have with a product, service, or organization; the reaction to a brand by the marketplace

Given the definitions above, we believe it is impossible to divorce branding from the other prototyping content presented in this chapter. By both the definition of brand and branding, software certainly qualifies as a major source of user exposure to an organization and its strategy, including the positive or negative associations with companies, products, and services. Interaction with software is sometimes the most intimate experience users have with a company. Therefore, how an organization expresses itself through its products and services are valuable and memorable experiences in terms of brand exposure. From this perspective, we can see why ensuring the highest quality in the user interface and user experience of software is as much a brand issue as it is a usability issue. This emphasizes the importance of including and evaluating branding as part of any planned iterative prototyping activities.

Increasing Brand Fidelity

Brand fidelity can be increased by taking an inventory of the branding elements of all the content areas and ensuring that they align and evoke desired reactions (see Figure 5.7). Examples of branding elements are:

> › Logos
> › Corporate colors
> › Company slogans
> › Company terminology
> › Company standards and guidelines
> › Corporate style guides

Decreasing Brand Fidelity

To decrease brand fidelity, ensure that branding elements are either excluded from or blocked out of prototypes (see Figure 5.8). Or you can imagine that a certain place would be a spot where company branding would be used, so use a text callout in the prototype but do not actually portray it. You can use the content-specific fidelity techniques such as using a placeholder instead of the actual logo.

A highly respected design consultant arrived at work on a project that involved rebranding a business-to-business website designed for petroleum engineers, Petroleng. The branding design consultant planned to mock up a visual concept for Petroleng. She teamed with an interaction designer who was already working on the project's interaction design.

The branding consultant used the interaction designer's new designs as the basis for her rebranding presentation because the interaction designer was working on the future of the product. Unfortunately, the interaction designer's work was quite controversial due to its use of experimental design concepts. Instead of greeking the interface content, the branding designer opted to include the complete content of the prototype so that the branding would be seen in context. The branding review meeting was prefaced by valiant attempts to set expectations.

"Just pay attention to the visual direction here and the visual branding elements."

These attempts were all in vain; the natural urge to read the text and evaluate the suggested interaction proved too powerful. The meeting degenerated from a high-level branding discussion of Petroleng to discussing the contentious interaction design and its details. This misguided focus on interaction design was more emphatic than usual due to the addition of the branding elements and the fear of finalized design decisions already existing. Instead of the prototype contents providing context to the branding discussion, the opposite happened. The branding gave context to the contentious interaction design, sparking a discussion on that instead of the branding. After the meeting the primary topic of branding was hardly discussed, although everyone congratulated the consultant on a great presentation of the interaction design. Clearly, a discussion and presentation on interaction design needed to take place, but it had occurred at the expense of the branding concept when it did not need to.

The branding design consultant was quite expensive, and there was little budget remaining for another round of work and an additional presentation. Furthermore, the company simply could not afford any more time in the schedule to revisit branding. Consequently, sign off on the whole design was forced to occur in less than ideal conditions. The consultant acknowledged that the client was happy, but she was unhappy due to the client's association of her with the great meeting on interaction design, not the rebranding effort she was hired for. Petroleng could have gotten much more for their branding money if the branding consultant had left the detailed information content out of her prototype.

SYSTEM PERFORMANCE/BEHAVIOR

System performance and behavior are characteristics of the users' experiences with the technical expression of software. How long does it take to complete a save interaction? Does a user error force the user to call tech support, or is a resolution suggested for the user?

System performance can be affected by a number of variables, including the quality of the programming code, throughput of the system, network bandwidth and traffic, and the data management and handling. System performance plays an important role in user perception of the software.

Slow performance and system response lead to dissatisfaction or, at least, vulnerability of your product to an aggressive competitor. Therefore, it makes no sense to skimp on investing in improving the system performance. Designers should take into consideration the technical requirements: web pages that behave like window–object interfaces usually have performance issues. A graphically rich website that is mostly accessed by dial-up connections will also have performance issues. Because system performance and behavior are such vitally important issues, they should be accounted for as part of the system requirements during the design.

Who owns these system issues? The interaction designer should own the system behavior issues. The wording of error messages or other system dialogs is usually the technical writer's domain. The systems performance issues belong to engineering because that group is in the best position to judge which system performance issues are affected by the design.

Techniques to Adjust the Fidelity of the System Performance/Behavior

In general, the only real method to test system performance is via an actual coded application. To provide a real sense of the system performance, this prototype (or beta release) should have all the system connections and actual data of the working application. Many people believe it is too late in the game to make huge system changes at this point because the code freeze or system test phases are near. Thus, the design team is obliged to ensure that engineering, the owners of the system performance, is involved in the early stages of design so they can raise any performance considerations and hopefully have time to resolve them without adversely affecting the design.

In the early stages of software design, a design team should not be unnecessarily encumbered by system performance and behavior emulation. Low-fidelity prototyping of just about any sort deemphasizes system performance and behavior. This lack of system emphasis enables the early most innovative stages of design to avoid being hampered by technical limitations, which may or may not be resolved in the course of developing the software. To free the design team from the confines of an actually working coded system, lower fidelity prototyping like storyboards, wireframes, and paper prototypes can be used.

HOW TO SELECT THE RIGHT PROTOTYPE CONTENT EXPRESSION

As you've just read, the content expression of a prototype can be tuned and modulated to emphasize or deemphasize various aspects and combinations of the content to receive feedback on a specific design goal. This tuning compels the viewer to concentrate on the emphasized aspects of a prototype while other aspects recede into the background.

Step 1: Define objective and focus

Define the objective and focus of your prototype. For example, if you are designing a website, the objective could be tactical, such as focusing on navigation and task flow and page layout and organization. Or, the objective could be strategic with a focus on the branding scheme, the overall software conceptual model, and so on.

Step 2: Determine emphasis/deemphasis

Based on your objective and focus, determine what aspects of the prototype content you want to emphasize and deemphasize. For example, you could choose to explore mapping interaction and navigation to a task flow and focus on interaction design and navigation within a web page as well as among pages. To have your prototype reflect your objectives, you want to emphasize the following content components:

> Interaction design and navigation model
> Information design

In turn, to avoid undue distraction in this example scenario of exploring interaction and navigation, you want to deemphasize:

> Editorial content
> Visual design
> Branding
> System performance and behavior

Step 3: Select appropriate fidelity

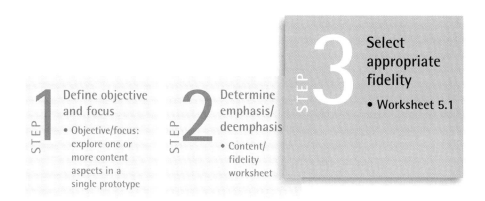

Now that you've determined what to emphasize and deemphasize in the prototype, you need to select an appropriate prototyping fidelity that allows you to achieve these objectives. You want to choose a fidelity that allows you to tune the content components to achieve your desired focus.

Worksheet 5.1 will help you select the best fidelity. Enter the information in this worksheet following steps 1–6 in the left hand column. In filling out the Content/Fidelity matrix at the top, entitled *Planned*, indicate what your audience will need in terms of fidelity for each content item. In the *Actual, current state* matrix, you will try to capture the needs given the audience needs and what you will be able to accomplish. You may wish to keep this matrix blank until the next Chapter, when going over the rest of the prototyping characteristics may alter the fidelity you can produce.

WORKSHEET 5.1: Determining Content fidelity

Step		
1	Project Name:	Author:
1	Project Date:	Internal Ref.:
1	Product Name:	Target Release:
1	Current Phase:	

2	Target Audience	Internal	External
		☐ Design team members ☐ Upper Management ☐ Lead designers ☐ Product Managers ☐ Marketing & Sales ☐ Developers ☐ Technical writers ☐ Domain specialists/Analysts ☐ QA engineers ☐ Business/financial stakeholders	☐ End-user (consumers) ☐ Customers (purchasers) ☐ Domain specialists/Analysts ☐ Financial stakeholders ☐ Business analysts ☐ Press

1	Overall prototype objective:	The purpose of this prototype is to show XXX to YYY in order to ZZZ.
2	Audience needs	This audience best relates to prototypes that XXX
2	Audience aversions	This audience is least likely to need a prototype that XXX

			Audience importance							
Content			**Not needed**	**Very low**	**Low**	**Medium**	**High**	**Very High (essential)**		
Planned										
3	Information									
4	Interaction									
5	Visual Design									
3	Editorial									
5	Branding									
4	System									
			Not needed	**Very low**	**Low**	**Medium**	**High**	**Very High**		
6 Actual, current state	Information									
6	Interaction									
6	Visual Design									
6	Editorial									
6	Branding									
6	System									

SUMMARY

In Step 3 of the effective prototyping process, we discussed the prototyping content considerations you need to address to best achieve your prototyping needs. This discussion included mixing fidelities and other variables to emphasize and deemphasize different aspects of a prototype for usability and presentation purposes. The different types of content covered in the chapter were:

- › Information design
- › Interaction design and navigation model
- › Visual design
- › Editorial content
- › Branding
- › System performance/behavior

ARNOSOFT TEAM TACKLES CONTENT

Reed, Ina, and Dirk are discussing the next prototype iteration. The storyboard was a success, but Reed still wants something more "clickable." To understand exactly what Reed wants, Dirk and Ina review the prototyping content and the fidelity level that Reed requires to get the prototype he wants and that the team needs.

First, Ina and Dirk discuss the target prototype audience with Reed. Reed at first just says, "Myself."

Dirk in disbelief says, "You want us to do this just for you?"

Ina adds, "I think other people might be interested in seeing this as well."

So together they look at the list of potential stakeholders for this prototype. They cross out the ones they believe are not going to be relevant for this prototype:

Internal	*External*
☐ ~~Design team members~~	☐ End-user (consumers)
☐ Upper Management	☐ Customers (purchasers)
☐ ~~Lead designers~~	☐ ~~Domain specialists/Analysts~~
☐ ~~Product Managers~~	☐ ~~Financial stakeholders~~
☐ ~~Marketing & Sales~~	☐ ~~Business analysts~~
☐ Developers	☐ ~~Press~~
☐ ~~Technical writers~~	
☐ Domain specialists/Analysts	
☐ ~~QA engineers~~	
☐ Business/financial stakeholders	

Reed explains he wants to make sure this site can "fly" so he is actually quite eager to also see how end users will use this prototype. In the review of information content, Reed points out that the information needed is very important. Dirk is also very concerned about the real needs of the user regarding their keyword usage. So the top priority for audience is the defined user and the internal domain specialist (a.k.a. Reed). Therefore the information fidelity that the team considered was as follows:

> *Information: High*
> *Editorial: Medium*

The team next looked at the interaction content from their desire to have the interaction design be high, but because they ultimately did not want to sweat implementation details (or use precious development resources), they decided that system performance could be low fidelity. After that, they considered the visual content and agreed that the visual design and branding could be left until later, especially while Reed and Vista argued whether it should be called Dish's Dishes or CeramaSite. Finally, they did a gap analysis of the required content fidelity with what they currently possessed (see completed Worksheet 5.1 below).

After this exercise, Dirk was sure they needed an HTML prototype. Reed wanted them to just go ahead and build it. Finally, Ina was convinced a series of wireframes shown to a focus group would probably suffice. Here is what the finished content fidelity worksheet for ArnoSoft looks like:

REFERENCES

Donis A. Dondis. A Primer of Visual Literacy. Cambridge, MA: MIT Press, 1973.

Armin Hofmann. Graphic Design Manual: Principles and Practice. New York: Van Nostrand Reinhold, 1965.

Marty Neumeier. The Dictionary of Brand. New York: AIGA Center for Brand Experience, 2004, pp. 15–17.

Larry Roellig. Designing global brands: critical lessons. Design Management Journal, 2001, Fall.

Louis Rosenfeld, Peter Morville. Information Architecture for the World Wide Web: Designing Large-Scale Web Sites (2nd ed.). Sebastopol, CA: O'Reilly, 2002.

William Strunk, Jr., E.B. White. The Elements of Style (4th ed.). New York: Longman, 2000.

The question of what to prototype relates to classic problem reduction. The designer must reduce the problem space into an ordered set of manageable subproblems.

–Bill Buxton

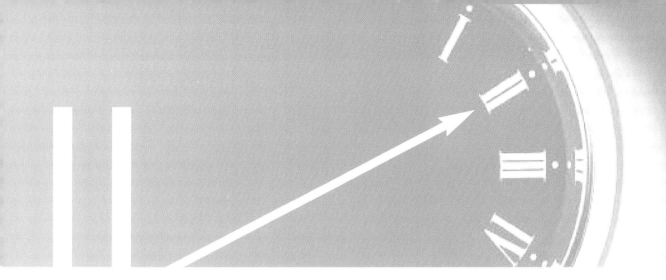

SPECIFICATION OF PROTOTYPING

Phase II involves specifying the prototyping elements that round out the prototyping strategy. In the planning phase you determined what to prototype. This phase decides how to prototype. This occurs by following the spirit of the Buxton quote here– breaking down seemingly large issues of prototype definition into small manageable chunks that can be easily understood, analyzed, and specified, including specifying the prototype itself in terms of characteristics. These characteristics give a much more sophisticated understanding than just high or low fidelity by defining exactly what you need from your prototype. Then, the specification phase continues by helping you determine the prototyping method and choosing an appropriate tool for that method. After this you are ready for the next phase: designing the prototype.

CHAPTER

The Effective Prototyping Process

PHASE **1** Plan

PHASE **2** Specification

PHASE **3** Design

PHASE **4** Results

STEP **1** ch 3
Verify Requirements

STEP **2** ch 4
Develop Task Flows

STEP **3** ch 5
Define Content and Fidelity

STEP **4** ch 6
Determine Characteristics

STEP **5** ch 7
Choose a Method

STEP **6** ch 8
Choose a Tool

STEP **7** ch 9
Select Design Criteria

STEP **8** ch 10
Create the Design

STEP **9** ch 11
Review the Design

STEP **10** ch 12
Validate the Design

STEP **11** ch 13
Deploy the Design

6

DETERMINE CHARACTERISTICS

INTRODUCTION

The fourth step in the effective prototyping process is defining the right prototyping characteristics. Characteristics should be established before selecting a prototyping method because they help define the kind of prototype needed and the prototype traits, such as fidelity and style. Defining characteristics is important because they inform the prototyper how to prototype, and they also inform a manager what should be prototyped. The methods that fit the different combination of characteristics (Step 5) are discussed in Chapter 7.

PROTOTYPE CHARACTERISTICS

As mentioned above, prototype characteristics are crucial to prototyping. The most important prototype characteristics discussed in this book are:

1. *Audience*: internal/external
2. *Stage*: early/midterm/late
3. *Speed*: rapid/diligent
4. *Longevity*: short/medium/long
5. *Expression*: conceptual/experiential
6. *Style*: narrative/interactive
7. *Medium*: physical/digital
8. *Fidelity*: low/medium/high

Fidelity is covered in Chapter 5.

In the following sections we discuss each characteristic and how they are defined and tuned for appropriate use. For now, we provide a brief overview of each:

1. **Audience**: Internal/external–the audience who will view or use the prototype; not necessarily the same as the end user of the software
2. **Stage**: Early/midterm/late–the stage in the software creation and development process in which prototyping would ideally take place
3. **Speed**: Rapid/diligent–the speed and thoroughness that a prototype needs to achieve its goals
4. **Longevity**: Short/medium/long–how long a prototype will be used; is it a quick throwaway or something that will be used throughout the software creation process?
5. **Expression**: Conceptual/experiential–how abstract or tangible the visual design and interaction behavior are expressed in a prototype
6. **Style**: Narrative/interactive–the style of participation a user is expected to take, either passive (narrative) or active (interactive)
7. **Medium**: Physical/digital–the medium in which the prototype is rendered
8. **Fidelity**: Low/medium/high–a matrix of the level of fidelity for each kind of content in the prototype (see Chapter 5)

With these characteristics, you are not simply choosing one characteristic over another. Rather, you are choosing the mix of characteristics most suitable for your prototype. Another factor to keep in mind is that these characteristics are not all mutually exclusive; some are, but others are part of a continuum. For example, prototypes are either physical or digital; there is not much room in between. On the other hand, prototypes can be strictly narrative or strictly interactive, but most prototypes combine the two. The dominating characteristic determines, for our purposes, whether the prototype is narrative or interactive.

AUDIENCE: INTERNAL/EXTERNAL

It is important to understand the audience of a prototype and also to differentiate the main stakeholders from secondary ones. A primary audience in one phase of the prototyping process, such as a product manager during the concept stage, may be secondary later when the focus of the project changes toward end users. You want to identify the primary stakeholders of this immediate iteration and identify any future audiences and the changes that are required to accommodate the different audiences.

In general, there are two different audience types: internal and external. Internal audiences include the following:

> Design team members
> Upper management

- Lead designers
- Product managers
- Marketing and sales managers
- Developers
- Technical writers
- Domain specialists/analysts
- Quality assurance engineers
- Business/financial stakeholders

External audiences include:

- End users (consumers)
- Customers (purchasers)
- Financial stakeholders
- Domain specialists/analysts

Internal Audiences

Internal audiences can be more forgiving than external users because they are more familiar with seeing rough cuts and exploratory ideas. To be more successful at getting their buy-in, include internal audiences in brainstorming and make efforts to directly collaborate with them in the prototyping process. In general, you want to make your worst mistakes with the internal audiences to avoid embarrassment with the outside world (and potential customers). Rapid prototyping methods are preferred for internal audiences because they can be easily changed, which you will need to do often, and they have more flexible interpretations. Internal audiences don't need refined information design and editorial content. An internal vocabulary can be developed that helps the prototype communicate more directly to its internal audience. The general questions you need to ask about internal audiences are:

To what degree can I assume a common understanding? This will determine how much you can get away with a rough sketch. The less shared the understanding, the more explicit and the higher fidelity the prototype needs to be.

How important is this version/iteration of the prototype? If this prototype is going to be a major internal statement on a bold new product, this requires a level of sophistication and detail as opposed to early ideation wireframes.

What is the collaborative environment like? If colleagues expect to be participants in the design, avoid an initial detailed design. Instead start with a sketch indicating a design direction and fill it in collaboratively. On the other hand, if colleagues are looking to you to be the lead, then you need to develop a clear vision of your design direction.

Design Team Members

In the beginning, design team members want to see rough prototypes that result from brainstorming and participatory design sessions. The prototype should speak the language of everyone in the audience, so don't make a prototype storyboard using Unified Modeling Language (UML) if only you and the lead engineer understand UML. Use common company lingo or the current best attempt at terminology; early user research and subsequent usability testing will correct any problems. Use a visualization method that works well for everyone.

Upper Management

Upper management usually wants to see their visions reflected in the company's products. These visions tend to be high-level strategic ideas embodied in a corporate mission statement and branding guidelines. In general, upper management responds best to high-level narrative presentations of a prototype. Only in an advanced stage of design will a motivated upper manager want to test-drive the design before it goes into production. Even then, choose carefully what is tested because management rarely fits the user profile of the software. For example, have the manager test-drive part of the application that he may know from prior experience or is the easiest part of the software to use.

Lead Designers

Lead designers should be the people you bounce ideas off of before sharing them with the rest of the design team. Lead designers also tend to have a higher appreciation for conceptual models.

Product Managers

Product managers are usually the most visually inclined audience and thus generally prefer a narrative prototype, such as a storyboard. A product manager often knows the needs of the marketplace but not necessarily how a product should be implemented or where a certain function fits into the task flow.

Marketing and Sales Managers

Marketing and sales managers are usually concerned with the product's salability, its "look and feel," (including branding expression) and the attractiveness and competitiveness of functions and features. These stakeholders want to be assured that the offering will have a good fit in the marketplace and garner maximum salability. They also want to be assured that the product demos well and that it is presented in a way that is complimentary to the company's vision and brand identity.

Developers

Developers need to understand the underlying user interface design concept, the envisioned interaction, and related task flow. For this reason it is important to have some key developers represented in almost every prototype. The developer's presence in the prototyping process assures that they understand the prototype design and that the prototype reflects the technical constraints.

Technical Writers

Technical writers need a high-fidelity and interactive prototype to help them with documentation creation, enabling them to create documentation that speaks in the same voice as the application. Understanding the prototype also helps technical writers with naming and terminology for the user interface widgets, error messages, dialog messages, and other editorial content for which they are responsible.

Domain Specialists/Analysts

Internal domain specialists and business analysts provide specialized expertise and knowledge related to the domains and marketplaces in which a software offering is targeted. They not only provide valuable customer, user, and usage information but they can also review your design work-in-progress to check for completeness of design, acceptability in the marketplace, and competitive positioning.

Quality Assurance Engineers

Quality Assurance engineers are held accountable for the quality of the implemented design. This can only occur if they understand the design intentions. Providing QA engineers access to prototypes as well as the scenarios you used to create them empowers QA staff to create the appropriate test cases needed to evaluate the software.

External Audiences

External audiences have infrequent exposure to prototypes; they more expect a finished product. Exposing a prototype to them is much more risky in that their expectations are high, and despite non-disclosure agreements or other legal protection it makes your ideas public. To get their buy-in, external audiences prefer to explore more finished software representations. Although you want to make your worst mistakes with internal audiences, external users can bring a new perspective that internal users do not necessarily provide. External audiences often catch mistakes you never knew existed. Be prepared for the unexpected and prepare an answer for when you're asked, "Why didn't you think of that!?"

External user participation in the design process calls for techniques that engage them in the design without them realizing it. Blank model prototyping and card sorting are examples of such methods that enable direct external user participation in design activities. Be mindful that, in general, external audiences want a higher level of fidelity and an interactive, not a narrative, experience. The more narrative the prototype is, the more an external user is likely to feel that you are showing a product without credibility. Higher fidelity and more interactive prototyping methods get better quality feedback as external audiences become active participants in the software design process rather than mere commentators. The main questions to consider for external audiences are:

> **How friendly is your audience?** This question helps you determine how forgiving and how high the fault tolerance of your audience is. The higher the fault tolerance, the easier it is to present lower fidelity and rougher ideas; although external audiences do need convincing for the rougher ideas.
>
> **Is the external audience a potential user?** In general, a potential user needs some background or context to understand the product, but it should not be necessary to explain how the software works. As a rule, the greater the degree to which external audiences fit the user profile, the more they expect a polished, interactive, and high-fidelity experience; users should be able to leverage their experiences and your conceptual model to guide their usage of the product. Since they were not the target user profile, product reviewers, analysts, and other non-users may not be able to take advantage of a conceptual model; consequently, they would require more of a narrative prototype.

End Users (Consumers)

End users are the consumers of software either purchased by themselves or others. Whether for business, utility, or pleasure, they need a user experience that requires little or no training to understand the basic functionality. End users are also the ultimate arbiters of how your software achieves this aforementioned goal. Testing prototypes with users is an objective way to settle a disagreement among competing design directions, tastes, and opinions and move successfully toward design resolution and decision. Users can provide feedback both on what does and does not work in terms of the user experience as well as the impressions and pains they are experiencing.

End users can be categorized in many ways for user research. For our purposes we'll focus on two: existing users, who have used your software, and prospective users, who haven't. Existing users are going to focus on the functions and features they are familiar with as well as those that are pain points for them. They look forward to enhancements that improve their use of the software and resistant to changes in functions they have already learned—especially the hard to use ones.

A new or prospective user is a stranger to your software and, as a result, can provide objective feedback and insights that those familiar with your offering cannot. These users are the best to respond about ease of use and learnability of the software because it will be the first time they are exposed to the product.

Customers (Purchasers, Not End Users)

There are some cases, such as with business software, where the software purchaser is not the end user but the customer. The customer may be less interested in an interactive prototype because she often does not fit the end-user profile. Rather, customers prefer to see demonstrations of the value of the resulting product, such as its features and functions, including product aspects that may be of little interest to the end user, such as cost savings, usage logs, etc. For customers, it is important to have a more narrative prototype based on the business case for the product.

Financial Stakeholders

Companies that rely on business partners, venture capital, and other external sources of funding often use early prototypes as a proof of concept. Typically these prototypes are visually refined but narrative in nature, usually in the form of click-through storyboards, animations, or videos. These prototypes need to convey a storyline about the goal of the product or service.

Domain Specialists and Analysts

External domain specialists and business analysts are often hired to review a work-in-progress to check for completeness of design, acceptability in the marketplace, and competitive positioning. Similar to internal domain specialists and analysts, this audience not only provides valuable customer, user, and usage information; they can also comment on how competitive the product is compared to other similar products in the marketplace.

STAGE: EARLY/MIDTERM/LATE

It's not enough that you prototype to save the costs of creating temporary coded systems, the act of prototyping itself should be done in a time and cost-efficient manner. It's not just about efficient use of resources but it's also about the effectiveness of the prototype in the overall software making process. We hope this is apparent to you by now. Although prototyping can be done anywhere and anytime, there are significant advantages for positioning the type of prototyping where it can do the most good in the software creation process. Early (Figure 6.1), midterm (Figure 6.2), and late (Figure 6.3) are characteristics capturing the best time to engage in different prototyping activities.

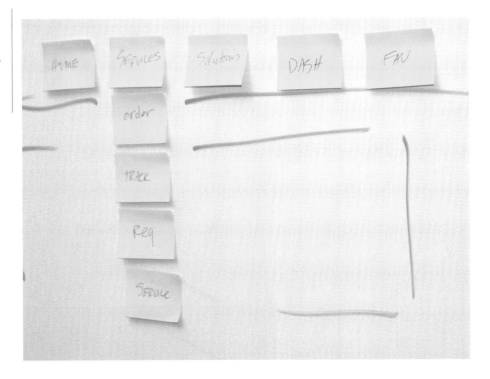

Early Stage

The purpose of early prototyping methods is to test basic assumptions and explore the conceptual design, both of which can be corrected if problems or errors are discovered using prototypes in the very early stages. Examples of early prototypes are:

> Wireframes
> Card sorting
> Storyboards
> Blank models
> High-fidelity video prototypes (to sell a concept)

Midterm Stage

Midterm prototyping methods validate a conceptual design. Midterm prototypes allow fleshing out a concept as an interactive prototype. Midterm prototypes can't be done early in the product design process because they require some expert knowledge of end users. Without this input the designs will need to be completely redone later. Examples of midterm prototypes are:

> Conceptual video prototyping
> Paper prototypes
> Digital interactive prototypes

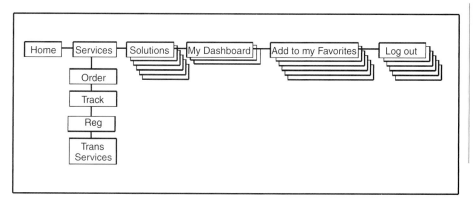

FIGURE 6.2 *Midterm prototype–the information architecture is more refined and can be used to start forming the conceptual model for the product.*

Late Stage

Late prototyping methods are used after previous design iterations lead the team to commit to a design and to refine the design so that it is ready for coding. Obviously, if done too early, these prototypes need to be completely redone as more usability validation and better design knowledge force changes. Nevertheless, it is dismayingly common for companies to forge ahead and immediately start their high fidelity prototyping early in the design process, which locks the company into suboptimal design. Late prototyping should only be conducted when the design concepts, product scope, and product vision are firmly established and when investment in the details of the user interface is a low risk. There is room for flexibility in the aforementioned areas for refinements but not for wholesale changes or wholesale challenges. Examples of late prototypes are:

> Animated prototypes (such as those created in Flash)
> High-fidelity interactive prototypes
> Coded prototypes

FIGURE 6.3 *Late prototype–prior stages of iterative design lead to a more finished representation of the design.*

SPEED: RAPID/DILIGENT

Rapid and diligent indicate how quickly a prototype can be produced and the level of detail represented in a prototype. Rapid is done in a manner often called "quick and dirty." For diligent prototypes, thorough attention is paid to detail. There is a temptation to think that rapid is associated with prototypes developed early in the design cycle, whereas diligent prototypes are created further along in the software-making process, but this is a misconception. You may need to use a rapid prototype any time in the design process when you want to quickly try out an idea or design. Likewise, if a product is mature, a diligent prototype is usually available early in the design process and can be quicker to modify than creating a rapid one. Speed determines which tools and method are preferable to use. For example, you will use a quick sketch tool for rapid or a sophisticated animation tool for diligent. Another factor in the rapid versus diligent decision is the degree to which the prototype should be reusable. If you want to portray only the general design thrust, rapid prototypes are most suitable. If you want to test the effectiveness of certain terminology on buttons or links, a more diligent prototype may be needed.

Typically, the fidelity of rapid prototypes ranges from low to medium, making them most effective in the early and middle stages of the design process. Paper prototyping and mockups in Excel or PowerPoint are typical examples of rapid prototyping methods.

On the other hand because of their high fidelity and attention to details of visual design and interaction, diligent prototypes require a longer time to conceive and produce. Diligent prototypes are most effective when used in later iterations and stages of the design process. Because of their accurate representations of design concepts, diligent prototypes can be ultimately used as a component of the specifications supplied to developers to help guide the accuracy of implementation.

The paper prototype in Figure 6.4 is rapid. Many typographic elements are greeked, and only the main navigation and rough page layout are actually prototyped along with a few visual design concepts. In Figure 6.5, the paper prototype is diligent with its precise page layout and display of actual page content. The example in Figure 6.5 took much more time to produce than the one in Figure 6.4. Even though both are digital, one clearly reflects the actual content layout, whereas the other is still conceptual and includes only sketchy content.

Rapid Speed

When used appropriately, rapid prototyping methods allow a small user experience design team to move with agility from scenarios and storyboards to multiple iterations of design. This is particularly beneficial for design teams facing constrained timelines. In fact, rapid prototyping is a successful strategy for fitting design iterations and usability testing into agile development cycles. Rapid prototyping techniques include paper prototyping, blank modeling, and wireframe prototypes in addition to prototyping with simpler office productivity products like Excel (to be covered in more detail later in this book).

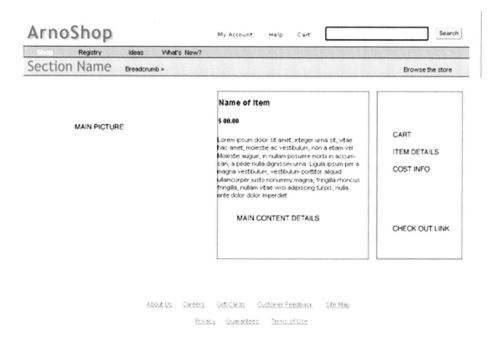

FIGURE 6.4 *Rapid prototype with medium fidelity.*

Diligent Speed

Diligent prototyping, as implied, allows a product design team to express the precise details of a user interface. Because diligent prototypes require more time to create and produce, they are typically reserved for the later stages of the design process. The diligent prototype, coupled with a user interface specifications document the most effective guide for accurate implementation of a design. The high level of detail and fidelity of diligent prototypes also makes them effective as a tool for sales and marketing demonstrations in advance of the software's completion.

FIGURE 6.5 *Diligent prototype.*

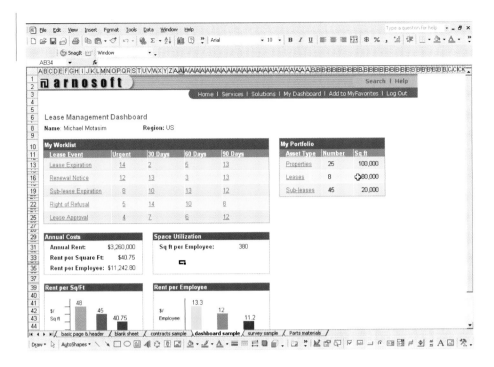

LONGEVITY: SHORT/MEDIUM/LONG

Prototype longevity refers to two aspects:

1. How long the prototype will live. Will it be a one-time throwaway proof of concept, or will it be something that is iterated and evolves into the final design of intended software?
2. How long the prototype's product influence will last. Will it be a quick short-lived sketch to try out an idea, or will it be a reference point for the duration of the software creation process?

The longer the prototype lives, the more effort and diligence you may want to put into the prototype. This also affects what prototyping tool you would pick. For example, a short-lived prototype would most likely be created and used by one person so you can use any prototyping tool. But a longer living prototype may need to be shared, and therefore a more commonly available tool should be chosen.

Short

Short-lived prototypes are perhaps the easiest to understand: the legendary (and largely unintentional) throwaway prototype. We say legendary because all too often a throwaway prototype is kept anyway for lack of a better plan; or a prototype not intended to be a throwaway ends up tossed into the prototype garbage-pail as non-implementable. Before embarking on a throwaway prototype, make sure all managing stakeholders understand a throwaway nature of what you are doing. All too often, people get caught up in the shortage of resources and the software making team end up putting lipstick on a throwaway pig.

Medium

Prototypes with a medium longevity are influential in the iteration process and stick around as a documentation of a design decision until they are eventually replaced by a successor prototype or document. Examples of prototypes with a medium longevity are a paper prototype, a storyboard, or a digital interactive prototype.

Long

Long prototypes, that is, prototypes with longevity, are those that are either influential through development or a prototype that will be directly iterated/reused in the same or compatible tool. They can also be visionary prototypes meant to set a long-term goal for a software company.

EXPRESSION: CONCEPTUAL/EXPERIENTIAL

Conceptual and experiential are the expressions of the level of implicitness or explicitness the product design should include. Conceptual prototypes do not directly resemble the look and feel of the product. Instead, these prototypes tend to focus on either the overall concept or one particular facet of the design with the goal of gaining a deeper understanding of the variables involved. Card sorting is an example of a prototyping technique that does not look like the end product but concentrates just on the information design. Experiential prototypes strive to be closer to the experience of the software. That is not to say that experiential is by definition high fidelity, because mockups and other quick system visualizations can still be experiential, such as a paper prototype.

The division of conceptual and experiential is not always so clear-cut. Often, a conceptual prototype includes some experiential aspects to provide context to the evaluator. Likewise, an experiential prototype may include elements from a conceptual prototype as a means of creating a first design iteration before everything from the concept is fleshed out in detail. For example, the rapid prototype in Figure 6.4 is experiential in that it attempts to mimic how the page layout would actually look, but there are conceptual touches such as the lower fidelity editorial content meant to show you just the information structure and not the information itself. Figure 6.7 shows a more experiential prototype that depicts how the prototyped content is actually experienced by a user.

Conceptual Expression

Conceptual prototypes isolate a subset of prototype content. In conceptualizing one or more contents, the prototyper is not hoping to develop the ultimate solution but rather to gain a deep appreciation of the issues surrounding the conceptual aspects of the content, as illustrated in Figure 6.6.

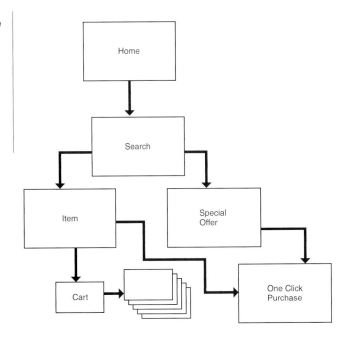

Conceptual prototypes are ideal for innovation prototyping. Innovation prototypes are helpful for brainstorming because the design is looked at in the abstract, freed from explicit details. Examples of innovation prototypes include "what if" or "blue sky" storyboards for which interaction and system performance scenarios are created and elaborated without the context of an existing product. As a story about a barely conceived product, these prototypes allow software makers free range to innovate and explore new ideas. A video prototype or Wizard-of-Oz prototype as conceptual prototype can suggest user interaction without a real system behind it—allowing for innovations that exceed current technical constraints. These types of prototypes do this by mimicking actual functionality instead of actually coding it. A video can be edited and produced to tell a story of product use, without ever directly showing the product details.

Another example of conceptual prototype is card sorting, which is a visualization of the information architecture for a web site isolated as part of a participatory design process.

Conceptual prototypes are typically used in the early and middle phases of software creation to stimulate requirements or validate design concepts. They can also stimulate and inspire the design team, freeing them from more experiential ideas to look at possible new alternatives. By providing a richer understanding of specific content rather than a vision of the whole, a conceptual prototype also prepares a design team for making more intelligent design compromises and trade-offs.

Conceptual prototypes can take various forms, either physical or digital. For a card sort exercise, cards can literally be index cards or software-based sorting. The players in a video prototype could be interacting with a physical object or another medium-paper prototype, blank model, or acetate overlay to name just three examples.

One downside to conceptual prototypes is their inherent abstract nature. Many people cannot or have trouble relating abstractions to the real world. Therefore, most conceptual prototypes require the prototyper to sell both the implementation and the subsequent interpretation.

In conclusion, it is important to point out that what separates a mediocre design from a usable design reflecting a compelling user experience lies in a basis from effective prototyping from both conceptual and experiential prototypes.

Experiential Expression

What experiential prototypes lack in subtlety they gain in richness of details and context. Experiential prototypes play only three main objectives in software making, communication, ideation, and validation, which are all of paramount importance to the software-making process.

In conceptual prototypes, designers try to isolate a subset of components into a prototyping activity, but experiential prototypes are used to try to bring it all together. The mishmash of conflicting use cases, limited budgets, organizational needs, and user requirements is reduced to a single artifact when someone creates an experiential prototype. If requirements are missing from an experiential prototype, those omissions suddenly become clearer than at any other time.

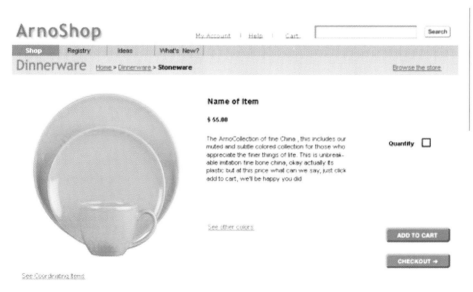

FIGURE 6.7 *Experiential prototype–a prototype that represents how the user is meant to experience what is being prototyped.*

Experiential prototypes attempt to create the actual user experience of the product, in one form or another. The prototype strives to communicate to all its stakeholders what the system precisely seeks to do and how it is designed to do it.

With ideation, experiential prototyping is the activity used to arrive at an innovative solution or to give explicit detail to all requirements, limitations, and aspirations for a software product or service. The ideation experiential prototype is usually more narrative and a lower fidelity. After the conceptual vision is agreed to, then the validation prototypes become experiential and higher in content fidelity as well as more interactive in nature.

STYLE: NARRATIVE/INTERACTIVE

The narrative and interactive styles are characteristics of either passive or active prototypes. Narrative is more passive with a predetermined user path that an audience follows. Interactive style is more active. The user has an undetermined path, which could lead to many directions.

The narrative prototype in Figure 6.8 portrays context by presenting a story. The audience usually passively listens to the explanation or story for this type of prototype (Figure 6.9). The interactive prototype in Figure 6.10 is more of a working prototype that the user can actively interact with as if using the finished software product.

FIGURE 6.8 *Narrative prototype.*

Narrative Style

Narrative prototypes are most commonly created in the early stages of software making, specifically the ideation or conceptual design phase. The quick turnaround time in creation brings agility to the system design that is only possible early in the software-making process. The narrative prototype is typically a storyboard or wireframe, often created using graphic or office productivity software such as Photoshop, Excel, and PowerPoint. These tools are ideal for a narrative prototype because of their easy linear flow from one screen to the next. With PowerPoint, you have the added advantage of being able to easily add narrative text to the screen images, allowing you to narrate the story as you present the designs.

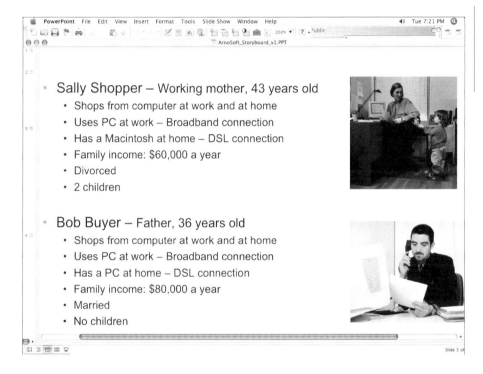

FIGURE 6.9 *Narrative prototype being reviewed by a design team.*

Interactive Style

An interactive prototype is typically a paper prototype or a digital mockup of the application created with Excel or Photoshop to create paper prototypes via printing digital images or a coded prototype like Dreamweaver and other HTML editors for testing web interfaces digitally. Higher fidelity coded prototypes can use rapid software development tools. But we have also already discussed more rudimentary interactive prototypes such as card sorting, which can take place very early in the software-making process.

The complexity of an interactive prototype lies in the fact that you cannot predict the path a user will take while using the prototype. Indeed, the prototype must be designed to allow users to make mistakes and even get lost while using the prototype.

FIGURE 6.10 *Interactive prototype in the form of paper.*

MEDIUM: PHYSICAL/DIGITAL

Physical and digital are the medium of a prototype. A medium is either physical or digital. Physical are tangible prototypes that exist usually in paper prototypes or blank models. Digital are prototypes that exist solely in a computer medium. If you are good at drawing, it may be much easier to develop a physical prototype with pen and paper. On the other hand, if you are designing a complex business form, a drawing may not be easier than a software tool with predefined widgets for quick form generation. Moreover, regarding the issue of reusing a design, it is much easier to reuse something already in digital form than to translate a physical prototype into digital format. Scanning or digital cameras make this possible, but in the end it is still often faster to just start over again in the digital media when migrating a physical prototype.

The physical prototype in Figure 6.11 is a paper prototype. The physical interaction has greater flexibility and a lower level of fidelity than the actual system performance. The digital prototype of Figure 6.7 has high visual fidelity and looks more like the actual system. A true system representation is unattainable with the physical artifact, and changes on the fly during testing are generally easier with a physical prototype than with a digital one.

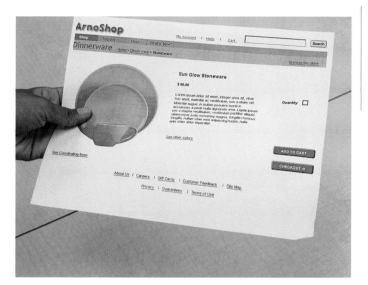

FIGURE 6.11 *Physical prototype originally created as a digital representation with a graphics tool.*

Physical Medium

Physical prototypes are versatile and can be used at almost anytime because they can be quickly sketched or drawn by hand. Sketches can provide a rough conceptual direction without heavy investment in the digital creation of the concept, allowing early physical sketches to be easily tossed aside to examine other approaches. A drawn interface's lower fidelity has the added advantage that it looks rough and unfinished, which encourages users to give broader and more open feedback.

Even though sketching is considered quick and easy, for some it is still quicker to use a software tool to create screens and print them out for a physical prototype. Some designers may choose to do all paper prototyping with software because it aids the eventual transition to a digital prototype. If starting with a paper or blank model prototype, transitioning to a digital prototype is more difficult. Often, a designer re-creates the physical prototype if he chooses to move to a digital tool.

Physical prototypes are a good match for interactive prototypes because of the flexibility of designing on the fly during usability tests or design reviews. For example, when conducting a usability test with a paper prototype, you can quickly draw up a missing screen or dialog if the user does something you did not anticipate. Likewise, if it is clear that a certain interface element or metaphor is incomprehensible, you can change it during the test.

Physical prototyping is often referred to as low-fidelity prototyping, but this is a misconception because paper prototyping can have varying degrees of fidelity. The visual design is usually in low fidelity (but again not always). The interaction design, on the other hand, is usually very high fidelity. In general, however, paper prototyping is usually very low fidelity in system performance.

Physical prototypes are one of the most commonly used in usability testing. We have even seen paper prototyping used to document the design for engineering, especially when engineering was involved in the paper prototyping exercise.

Physical prototypes are not without their risks. Paper prototypes are particularly susceptible to the fragilities of life, such as the jittery coffee drinker who can spill coffee all over your paper prototype. Or a drafty office that blows pieces of the prototype out the window.

Digital Medium

A digital prototype is flexible enough for use in either a narrative or interactive prototype. Digital prototypes can easily be incorporated into a storyboard or scenario wireframe as a proof of concept or ideation session. If the tool is easy enough to use, the digital prototype can even be directly iterated in a participatory design session. Digital prototypes are also useful because they can easily be projected on a screen for group reviews. Focus groups, multiple user cognitive walkthroughs, stakeholder roundtables, and design presentations all benefit from digital prototypes.

Digital prototyping are usually more diligent than their paper counterparts.

A management consulting company needed to redesign the way their travel and expense application handled management approvals. To test the new design accurately, management participants needed to understand the structure of the expense report. In the usability test, they were taken through a scenario where one of their direct reports entered an expense report. The user was then asked to approve the expense report in a new expense management interface. This test scenario allowed the management user to understand how expense reports were entered along with the management criteria without giving long domain-specific descriptions, thereby focusing the user's time on the interface being tested. Additionally, the tests were able to elicit some passive feedback on expense creation for the management user.

Digital prototypes are more rigid and users are less apt to suggest changes as they explore the system. This rigidity is beneficial in late stages of the design cycle and unhelpful earlier in the software creation process.

STEP-BY-STEP GUIDE TO SELECTING THE RIGHT CHARACTERISTICS

STEP 1 — Specify basic requirements
- Audience
- Time

STEP 2 — Analyze expression
- Expression

STEP 3 — Determine style and medium
- Style
- Medium

This step-by-step guide and Worksheet 6.1 will lead you through the process establishing the prototyping characteristics. The process works under the premise that you can stage the characteristic decision-making process in three steps:

Step 1: Specify the basic requirements of audience and time for your prototype based on the project constraints.

Step 2: Informed by the basic requirements, analyze expression and fidelity to help determine which further characteristics will be appropriate for your prototype.

Step 3: Finally, select the style and medium for your prototype, leaving you to holistically evaluate the characteristics you've defined to take the next step of choosing the best prototyping method to complement the characteristics you've chosen (covered in Chapter 7).

Step 1: Specify Basic Requirements

To correctly set prototype characteristics, first specify those characteristics that are immutable and are required given the constraints of the project. Because these are rigid, they have the strongest influence on the variable characteristics.

For each planned prototype, use a copy of Worksheet 6.1 and complete parts 1 and 2 of the matrix: Audience Requirements and Time Requirements. Begin by characterizing the audience target group for your prototype, using either the terminology suggested in the Internal/External Audience section or your own terminology. If the end-user population is unknown, then tailor the prototype just to your immediate audience. If the end user is known, it is important for you to specify the gap between the immediate audience and the end user. For example, even if the end user is an accountant and a financial backer is the immediate audience you want to speak to the financial backer, who may or may not know the accountant's perspective.

Next, outline the Time Requirements information in the worksheet based on your project schedule and timelines. Time requirements should include stage, speed, and longevity. To determine whether your prototype will be rapid or diligent, first circle the stage of the software process you're in–Early, Middle, or

Late. Then, enter the amount of time you have to develop and evaluate your prototype. Based on that information, circle the speed with which you will develop the prototype–Rapid or Diligent. In general, any time requirement exceeding 2 weeks' duration can be considered diligent (depending on the method and tool), whereas anything less than 2 weeks is considered rapid. Finally, indicate the longevity of the prototype.

Step 2: Analyze Expression

In Step 2 you will determine the expression. To help determine expression, whether it should be conceptual or experiential, you should review your worksheet. If the user does not understand the domain, then a more abstract conceptual prototype will be confusing and an experiential one is preferred. Likewise, this less informed user will probably require a higher fidelity prototype to understand the product. If the user does possess shared domain knowledge, you can assume they understand something more abstract and opt for a lower fidelity and more conceptual prototype.

Time is also an important consideration. An experiential prototype and a higher fidelity prototype consume more time. Or you may consider something high fidelity but more conceptual, hoping the high fidelity bridges the abstraction gap with the audience. At this point, you really need to look at your tolerance for working nights and weekends before cramming high expectations of high fidelity and experiential prototypes into a short delivery timeline.

The last consideration for expression is longevity. Longevity can throw everything overboard. The typical early, high fidelity, experiential prototype is the presentation to a venture capitalist, CEO, or the like. Such a prototype has a short shelf-life and as such can incorporate all sorts of tricks and shortcuts whether technically feasible, usable, or practical. The goal is to communicate the idea and disregard the finer points of software design for later in the process. Such a prototype is much faster to produce than an experiential high fidelity prototype meant to record the user experience requirements for development. Weighing the interplay of these requirements should help you decide whether you need something conceptual versus experiential and whether that needs to be high or low fidelity.

Step 3: Determine Style and Medium

Next, we want to determine the prototype style, which requires us to review all decisions to date. For this step you will want to also refer to your Prototype Fidelity worksheet. In general, if using an audience unfamiliar with the domain or not operationally involved in the project, you can use a narrative prototype to compensate for resorting the low fidelity and conceptual nature. The narrative would lead the audience through the interface in an easily understandable way by presenting the prototype in context, as in a storyboard. Furthermore, if you have chosen to create a high-fidelity prototype, using the narrative style allows you to limit the amount of content that needs to be high fidelity. For example, let's say you need to prototype 10 screens. If choosing a narrative method, you may decide to only create five high-fidelity screens and narrate the other five screens. With the exception of the quick throwaway, the most important rule to remember about interactive prototypes is that they require time, albeit they may be only partially implemented for the purpose of presentation to the audience.

Finally, decide on the medium. Do you want a paper or digital format? If the prototype is to be done collaboratively in a meeting, paper is usually faster. Likewise, if the longevity of a prototype is long, it is usually better to be created in a digital format. Audience is also a significant concern: Will the audience accept a paper prototype, or will they demand a digital one? Ultimately though, you must be pragmatic about all these decisions. If paper or digital is the only way you can pull something off in a given time frame, you should go with your skill strengths and let the quality of the result bridge the gap of the audience's expectations.

At the end of this decision-making process, your worksheet may look something like this example:

Determining the prototype characteristics		
Audience	Who will use the software?	Who will see this prototype?
Target group	End-User	Upper Management
Internal/External	External	Internal
Background	Accounting	No accounting
Specialized domain knowledge?	Yes	Some
Expertise required for the system?	Yes	No
Other requirements?		
Does the audience of your prototype understand the domain of the end user?	Not dependably so	
Is the audience of your prototype operationally involved in the software project?	Yes	No
Stage in the development process	Early	Middle	Late
How much time do you have to create the prototype?		
Speed	Rapid	Diligent
For how long will the software creation team refer to this prototype?		
For how long will the prototype be used, seen, presented, etc.		
Longevity	Short	Medium	Long
Expression	Conceptual	Experiential
Style	Narrative	Interactive
Medium	Physical	Digital

SUMMARY

Prototyping characteristics are much more elaborate than any previous textbook has led you to believe. It is important not to fall into the trap of choosing the wrong kind of prototype. You want to avoid overkill, which sometimes creates an unnecessary and unwarranted positive impression by detracting from the problem at hand and delivering a far more advanced visualization than required. Similarly, you do not want to waste design resources on redundant or unnecessary activities. Choosing the appropriate prototype is the only way to ensure a balanced result and an appropriate level of effort.

Specifically, we have seen in this chapter how understanding prototyping styles leads to a more effective prototyping practice. By understanding internal and external audiences, you can be assured that the appropriate characteristics and content are addressed in the prototype. By understanding early, midterm, and late stages, you are ensuring that the prototyping method chosen has the appropriate longevity to serve your prototyping needs without needless iteration because it was developed too early or too late in the process to be really effective. By understanding rapid and diligent speeds, you can confirm that you are not spending too much or too little time on the details the prototype needs to adopt to be effective. By understanding conceptual and experiential expressions, the designer is able to communicate on the right level with the audience. By understanding low through high fidelities, you learn to pick a prototyping method whose resemblance to the actual working product is appropriate to the needs of the design team. By understanding narrative and interactive styles, you can be aware of the appropriate level of audience participation. Finally, by understanding physical and digital media, you can avoid reinventing the wheel by constantly switching media. Now that you have a more informed appreciation for the characteristics of prototyping, you can go on to understand and decide among the different methods of prototyping to match your characteristics with the most appropriate method.

ARNOSOFT DETERMINES CHARACTERISTICS

Ina, Dirk, and Reed met with Art to discuss the requirements for creating their prototype. Art said he could produce high fidelity wireframes that would fit the bill, according to Art, and that led to four cacophonous voices believing they each knew the best prototyping method. Reviewing the various characteristics, they began to complete the worksheet to outline their existing knowledge.

They all knew that they were in the middle stages of their software-making process and that the audience would be users and Reed. They also realized that, to meet their deadlines, they needed to finish this prototype in 2 weeks to be ready for usability testing at the annual ceramics ware fair, which would force the prototype to have medium longevity, meaning it would probably be the last prototype created until they started building the product.

They discussed the expression and the fidelity, but those were easy decisions given their content discussions–experiential expression and medium fidelity. The more interesting discussions surrounded style and medium. Dirk thought the storyboard idea met all their needs and would work well with end users. Ina thought it would be better to get the end users' reactions to the software rather than a narrated version, which would slant their perceptions. Dirk then argued for a proof of concept prototype that could serve as a trial product, but it would take 3 to 4 weeks to create and test, and everyone, especially Reed, pointed out that they would miss their deadline. The medium discussion eventually led Ina to consider a paper prototype. The advantages of the physical medium over the digital were convincing. The group didn't even need to proceed to the next step of choosing a method because once they settled on the physical medium, Ina knew paper prototyping well, making other physical media irrelevant for the group.

REFERENCES

Oscar Gutierrez. Prototyping techniques for different problem contexts. Proceedings of CHI '89. New York: ACM Press, 1989, pp. 259–265.

Horst Lichter, Matthias Schneiderp Hufschmidt, Heinz Zullighoven. Prototyping in industrial software projects–bridging the gap between theory and practice. Proceedings of the 15th International Conference on Software Engineering. Baltimore, MD: IEEE Computer Society/ACM Press, 1993, pp. 221–229.

Robert Virzi, Jeffrey Sokolov, Demetrois Karis. Usability problem identification using both low and high fidelity prototypes. Proceedings of CHI '96. New York: ACM Press, 1996, pp. 236–243.

CHAPTER

The Effective Prototyping Process

PHASE 1 Plan

- STEP 1 ch 3 Verify Requirements
- STEP 2 ch 4 Develop Task Flows
- STEP 3 ch 5 Define Content and Fidelity

PHASE 2 Specification

- STEP 4 ch 6 Determine Characteristics
- STEP 5 ch 7 Choose a Method
- STEP 6 ch 8 Choose a Tool

PHASE 3 Design

- STEP 7 ch 9 Select Design Criteria
- STEP 8 ch 10 Create the Design

PHASE 4 Results

- STEP 9 ch 11 Review the Design
- STEP 10 ch 12 Validate the Design
- STEP 11 ch 13 Deploy the Design

7

CHOOSE
A METHOD

INTRODUCTION

As discussed in Chapter 6, defining the characteristics determines the kind of prototype you need. Step 5 in the effective prototyping process, and the individual method chapters later in the book, cover the prototyping methods, helping you decide which method to use to meet your prototyping needs. Each prototyping method, such as paper prototyping or storyboard prototyping, has specific traits that are best suited to particular kinds of prototypes.

PROTOTYPING METHODS

In this chapter, we briefly introduce each of the prototyping methods covered in the methods section of this book:

- ➤ Card sorting
- ➤ Wireframe prototyping
- ➤ Storyboard prototyping
- ➤ Paper prototyping
- ➤ Digital prototyping
- ➤ Blank model prototyping
- ➤ Video prototyping
- ➤ Wizard-of-Oz prototyping
- ➤ Coded prototyping (including scripting and HTML)

CARD SORTING
What Is Card Sorting?

A card-sorting prototype is an abstract, interactive, participatory method conducted in the early stages of the software-making process. Software makers use card sorting to determine the best information and navigation structure or to explore and verify terminology. The audience of the final prototype are internal design team members, enabling a shared understanding of the information design issues. The actual card-sorting sessions are conducted with the intended users.

How Does Card Sorting Work?

A card sorting session usually starts with a stack of terms or ideas on index cards. The cards can have terms that are intended to be pull-down menu functions, website navigation terms, or any information group that needs to be placed into a hierarchy. Users then try to group the terms in a way that makes sense. When a common thread or pattern emerges from the user data, the analyzed and synthesized results show how most participants conceptualize the information and terminology given to them.

FIGURE 7.1 *A card-sorting prototype session.*

WIREFRAME PROTOTYPING
What Is Wireframe Prototyping?

A wireframe is a narrative prototype, usually created in the beginning of the design process. The narration is usually derived from a use case or scenario, often the same scenario used in a storyboard. This prototype shows high-level sketches, visualizing conceptual assumptions about the product structure and general interaction. The primary goal of this method is to get a design team in agreement with basic concepts and design directions that guide the conceptual design in addition to more detailed design decisions.

How Do Wireframes Work?

A wireframe starts as a raw sketch of how the software could look. This could be anything from a rudimentary sketched interface on a dinner napkin to more thoroughly sketched out software screens schematics using a graphics tool. Wireframes usually have no visual design associated with them, because they are meant to be used early in the design process to determine the interaction flow and navigation model. As consensus forms around the wireframe concept, detailed designs are usually built from it. Wireframes usually stop being a central focus when a conceptual design is finalized and detailed concrete prototyping (either paper or digital) can begin.

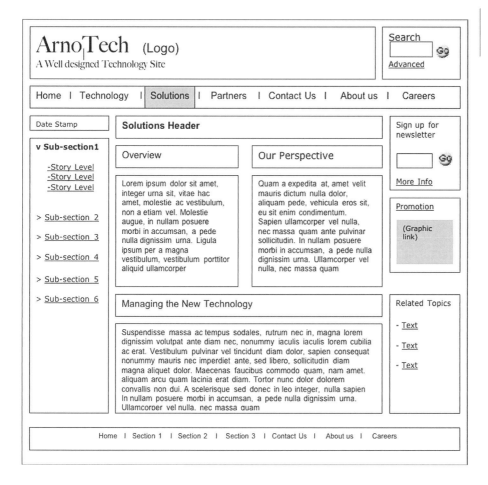

FIGURE 7.2 *A wireframe prototype.*

STORYBOARD PROTOTYPING
What Is Storyboard Prototyping?

A storyboard is a narrative prototype, usually created in the early stages of the software-making process to articulate business and marketing requirements in the form of a usage scenario or story. These stories narrate the user actions needed to perform tasks as specified by marketplace, customer, and user requirements. These requirements are gathered, analyzed, and synthesized into a scenario before the storyboarding process begins. Because requirements drive the storyboard process, they provide early insight into what users, the software, and the system are meant to do in conjunction with each other. The primary goal of a storyboard is to align the thinking of members of a software-making team as to the goals and behaviors of the product or service without detailing screen design. The intended audience is primarily internal design team members developing a shared understanding before proceeding with design. A secondary audience might be key external stakeholders who validate the direction of the team.

How Do Storyboard Prototypes Work?

A storyboard starts as a sequential scene-for-scene narrative, for example, a day in the life of a user with an envisioned product or service. As ideas mature, illustrations are inserted into the storyboard narrative, making it more and more visual as it is progressively iterated.

FIGURE 7.3 *A story-board prototype.*

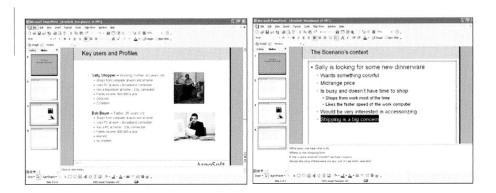

PAPER PROTOTYPING
What Is Paper Prototyping?

A paper prototype is an interactive prototype that consists of a paper mockup of the user interface. The interface is usually fully functional, even if all the functionality is mocked up on paper. Paper prototypes allow you to test a design with actual users. The intended audiences are, first, targeted users who test the design and, second, the software makers who use the prototype as a means to inform the final design iterations.

How Does Paper Prototyping Work?

Either hand drawing or printing out the user interface designs creates a paper prototype. A user can then "operate" the interface using manual or voice input. A test moderator then shows the resulting screens based on the user's input. When a test iteration is completed, the design can be corrected and refined and then retested until the major design issues are solved. It is important to use paper prototypes until all major issues are resolved to ensure that only small refinements are needed during software development.

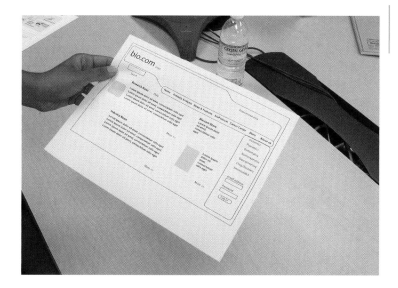

FIGURE 7.4 *A paper prototype.*

DIGITAL PROTOTYPING
What Is Digital Prototyping?

A digital prototype is almost a digital version of the paper prototype. Except, digital prototypes can range from a series of low-fidelity, narrative click-through screens for quick visualization of a design concept to a high-fidelity interactive portrayal of an evolved design which can be used as a user interface specification. In this book, low-fidelity digital prototyping is covered in Chapter 18, and high-fidelity digital prototyping is covered in Chapter 22. Digital prototyping shares the same objectives as paper prototyping, that is, they can both be used to:

> ‣ Understand task flow and context of use
> ‣ Validate assumptions in scenarios, business requirements, and user profiles
> ‣ Help shape or validate task sequencing and interaction design direction
> ‣ Help take prototypes from early rough sketches to the next level of detail
> ‣ Help inform or validate a visual design direction

A digital prototype is similar to a paper prototype in that both are appropriate during the same stage of design. A digital prototype is typically more narrative than interactive, as there are some gaps in a digital prototype that cannot be solved like they can be in a paper one. However, because it is primarily used to rapidly explore design variations, it is often a click-through or slide-show prototype unless it is being used for usability testing.

The software tools typically used to create a digital prototype are tools that can create them rapidly such as Photoshop or those typically used for office productivity, such as Excel, Word, and PowerPoint. These tools can be used to mimic minimal software interaction but generally aren't used for prototypes with complete interactivity. Just like paper prototypes, they can be used for mental model mapping in addition to visual design and other requirements validation with users. The main advantage of digital prototyping over coded prototyping is that a non-technical person can easily learn it and quickly create representations of design ideas.

FIGURE 7.5 *A digital prototype.*

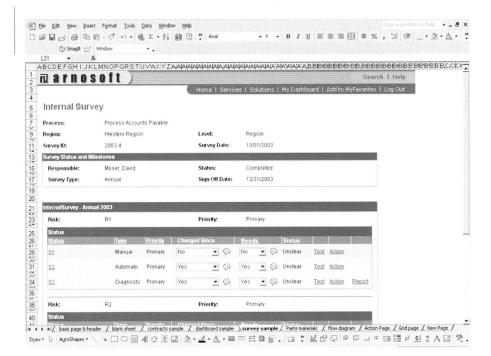

How Does a Digital Prototype Work?

Similar to paper prototyping, digital prototype is created from a collection of screen designs. A digital prototype can also comprise screen designs produced on paper and then digitally scanned. The screens can then be imported into a prototyping software application, such as PowerPoint or Acrobat, and arranged into a predefined scenario or task sequence. The content of a digital prototype can be easily arranged, rearranged, and changed to allow rapid exploration and validation of design ideas. Because of this flexibility and malleability, digital prototypes are especially useful during the early to middle stages of design, which are generally more exploratory in nature.

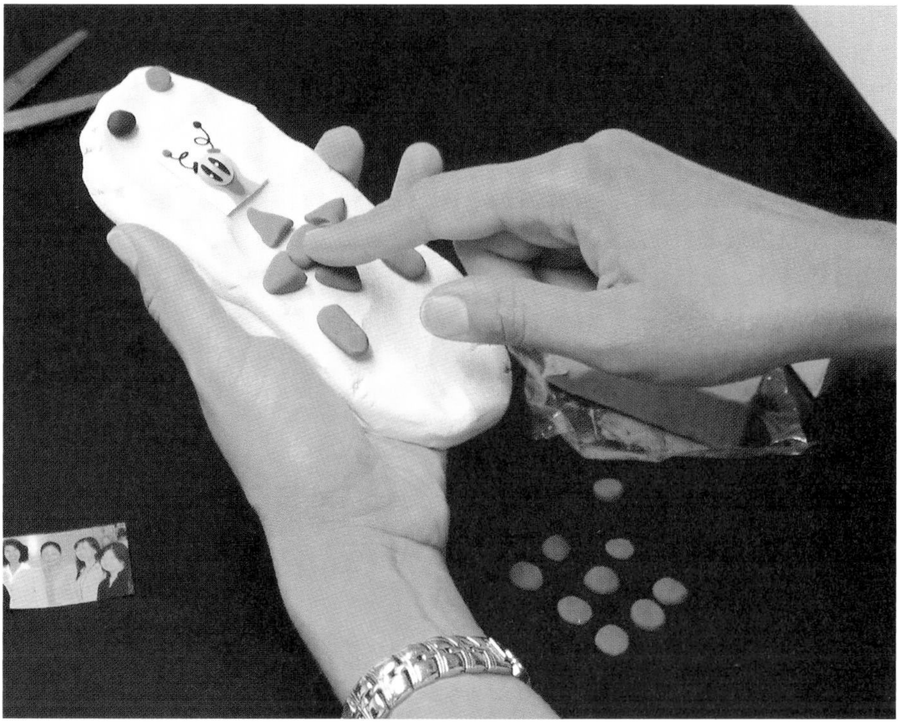

FIGURE 7.6 *A blank model prototype.*

BLANK MODEL PROTOTYPING
What Is Blank Model Prototyping?

Blank models are low-fidelity prototypes produced quickly by user study participants using readily available arts and crafts materials to represent their notions about what an intended hardware/software design could be like. This method is used in the early stages of product design to elicit user perceptions and mental models about hardware form factors and interaction controls in conjunction with a software user interface. The scene depicted in Figure 7.6 is a typical blank modeling session. A blank model user study is conducted as a one-on-one moderated session in which blank models are constructed based on a predetermined task or activity scenario and a technology product direction. This is an effective way of getting early user perceptions about the form factor and operation of a prospective design artifact, such as a remote control device used with an interactive TV service. Primarily, blank models are intended to analyze the resulting similarities and differences of the artifacts from such a study and feed the results into the ensuing design effort. The intended audience for a blank model study is primarily internal design team members so that everyone has a shared understanding of user behaviors and mental models in addition to their perceptions about how to operate devices before proceeding with a design.

How Does a Blank Model Prototype Work?

A blank model session is contingent on a clearly articulated scenario and a conceptual design direction, for example, a handheld device that can contain large amounts of information and can be accessed in a remote usage situation, such as a field sales or field automation activity. The scenario and technology concept are then used to define various user profiles to recruit user study participants. The ensuing blank model sessions are generally conducted in a room that accommodates a moderated one-on-one videotaped user study protocol. A typical blank model study begins with the moderator explaining the session objectives and the activities in which the participant will be engaged. The moderator then reviews the scenario with the participant, explaining the intended use of the arts and crafts materials relative to the scenario. When necessary, the moderator provides conversational guidance through the scenario, as participants construct a blank model from the available materials while simultaneously verbalizing their thoughts. The resulting blank models and participant verbalizations are then reviewed, compared, analyzed, and synthesized into the ongoing design activity.

FIGURE 7.7 *A video prototype. (Photo courtesy of Wendy Mackay.)*

VIDEO PROTOTYPING
What Is Video Prototyping?

A video prototype is a narrative prototype, usually done in the early stages of innovation design as part of the ideation phase of the software design process. Video prototypes allow a storyboard to be visualized by manipulating video to portray a nonexistent system as if it were fully functioning. The goal of video prototyping is to develop novel interaction ideas without developing the system. The intended audience is primarily internal design team members, creating a shared understanding of the product or service before proceeding with design.

How Does a Video Prototype Work?

A video prototype can merely be a visual representation of a software product and how it works. But for the purpose of establishing context and scale, it typically includes users portraying their appropriate roles and interactions in context. When a concept for an innovative interface is found, video prototyping usually gives way to more concrete prototyping techniques such as paper prototyping.

FIGURE 7.8 *A wizard-of-oz prototype, with the test being run on the left and the wizard controlling responses on the right.*

WIZARD-OF-OZ PROTOTYPING
What Is Wizard-of-Oz Prototyping?

A Wizard-of-Oz prototype is a method that allows a software creation team to test experimental speech (natural language) or tactile interfaces. It is also a technique that can be employed in almost any interactive usability testing session as a means to gloss over functionality contingent on emerging or nonexistent technologies.

A Wizard-of-Oz prototype is a type of interactive prototype where, during a usability validation session, the participant believes she is interacting with an actual working system using, as mentioned above, traditionally tactile interaction or natural language input methods with a computer system; however the functionality is only being mimicked.

How Does a Wizard-of-Oz Prototype Work?

A member of the design or development team or a larger scale computer system is "behind the curtain," interpreting the participant's input directives then feeding back a designed system response to the participant. This method has been adapted for use in the early stages of designing new features or products to simulate a variety of system responses, including system voice feedback and screen displayed feedback to voice input. A human "wizard" can provide both voice and screen-displayed feedback for a prototype of services such as a telephone tree user interface, an agent response system, or an in-vehicle control system.

FIGURE 7.9 *An HTML prototype script.*

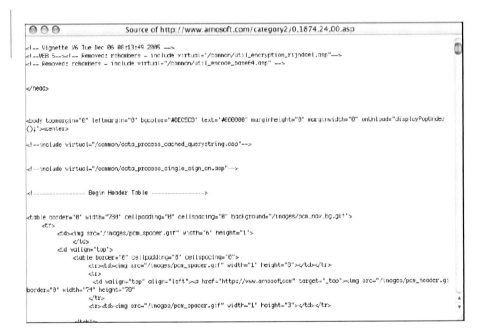

CODED PROTOTYPING
What Is Coded Prototyping?

A coded prototype is interactive and is created with a programming or scripting language, such as Java or JavaScript. Often, a coded prototype is created in the target development language and is meant to directly evolve into a final coded product.

A coded prototype generally features a high-fidelity user interface and is best created late in the design process after all large-scale changes in design have been completed. The intended audience is primarily an internal software-making team attempting to build a technical proof of concept. A coded prototype is especially good for capturing both qualitative and quantitative data via usability validation testing.

How Does a Coded Prototype Work?

A coded prototype is usually developed in a programming language or scripting code and should be considered as a later iteration of other forms of low- and medium-fidelity prototyping. A coded prototype has the advantage of allowing the software team to productively reuse code for an actual finished product.

CHOOSING THE RIGHT PROTOTYPING METHOD FOR YOU

As mentioned, the second major step in the effective prototyping process is establishing the right prototyping methods, which enable you to finally select the right tool as described in Chapter 8. Worksheet 7.1 helps you choose the right method by matching the characteristics to the method. The worksheet displays prototyping characteristics (left-most columns) and prototyping methods (top row). This overview allows you to see which methods match your needs. If the results of this worksheet ae too general, we provide a more detailed worksheet (7.2) which also attempts to show which methods are the best fit for your prototyping characteristics.

WORKSHEET 7.1: Select a prototyping method – Overview

Project Name:				Author:				
Project Date:				Internal Ref.:				
Product Name:				Target Release:				
Current Phase:								

		Methods								
Characteristics		Card sorting	Wire frame	Story board	Paper	Blank model	Video	Wizard of Oz	Digital interactive	Coded
Audience	Internal	•	•	•	•		•		•	•
	External	•		•	•	•	•	•	•	•
Stage	Early	•	•	•		•	•			
	Midterm		•	•	•		•	•	•	
	Late								•	•
Speed	Rapid	•	•	•	•	•	•	•	•	
	Diligent						•		•	•
Longevity	Short	•	•			•				
	Medium		•	•	•		•	•	•	
	Long						•		•	•
Expression	Conceptual	•	•	•	•	•	•	•	•	
	Experiential				•		•	•	•	•
Style	Narrative		•	•		•	•			
	Interactive	•			•		•	•	•	•
Medium	Physical	•	•	•	•	•				
	Digital	•	•	•			•	•	•	•
Fidelity	Low	•	•			•				
	Medium		•	•	•		•	•	•	
	High			•			•	•	•	•

• = Supported

WORKSHEET 7.2: Select a prototyping method – Details

Project Name:		Author:
Project Date:		Internal Ref.:
Product Name:		Target Release:
Current Phase:		

Characteristics		Methods								
		Card sorting	Wire frame	Story board	Paper	Blank model	Video	Wizard of Oz	Digital	Coded
Audience	Internal	+	+	+	+	+	+	+	+	+
	External	+ +	+	+	+ +	+ +	+ +	+ +	+	+
Stage	Early	+ +	+	+	−	+ +	+	−	+	−
	Midterm	−	−	+	+	NA	−	+	+	−
	Late	− −	− −	−	−	NA	− −	− −	−	+
Speed	Rapid	+ +	+	+	+	+ +	−	+	+	−
	Diligent	NA	−	+	−	NA	+	+	+	+
Longevity	Short	+	+	−	−	+	− −	+	− −	−
	Medium	+	+	+	+	−	+	+	+	+
	Long	−	−	−	−	− −	+	−	−	+
Expression	Conceptual	+ +	+	+	+	+ +	+	NA	−	NA
	Experiential	NA	−	+	+ +	+(process)	+	+ +	+	+ +
Style	Narrative	NA	+	+ +	−	+	+	−	−	NA
	Interactive	+ +	NA	NA	+ +	+	+(process)	+ +	+ +	+ +
Medium	Physical	+	+	+	+ +	+ +	NA	+	NA	NA
	Digital	− −	+	+	NA	NA	+ +	+	+ +	+ +

Content		Card sorting	Wire frame	Story board	Paper	Blank model	Video	Wizard of Oz	Digital	Coded
High Fidelity	Information	+ +	+	- -	+ +	-	+	+	+ +	+ +
	Interaction	NA	NA	+ +	+ +	+	+	+	-	+ +
	Visual Design	NA	-	- -	-	-	+	+	+ +	+ +
	Editorial Content	- -	-	- -	+ +	-	+	+	+	+ +
	Branding	- -	- -	+	+	- -	-	-	+	+ +
	System	NA	NA	NA	NA	- -	-	-	= =	+ +
Low Fidelity	Information	+	+ +	+	- -	-	- -	- -	- -	-
	Interaction	+ +	+ +	- -	NA	- -	- -	- -	- -	NA
	Visual Design	+ +	+ +	+ +	+	+	-	-	+	+
	Editorial Content	+ +	+ +	+ +	-	-	+	+	+	NA
	Branding	+ +	+ +	+ +	+	+	+	+	+	- -
	System	NA	+ +	+ +	+ +	+ +	+	+	NA	NA

Legend

+ + very appropriate

+ appropriate

- acceptable

- - not practical

NA not applicable

SUMMARY

In this chapter we presented various methods of prototyping that you can use to best achieve your prototyping goals. The chapter was devoted to brief presentations of the different methods that are covered in more depth in individual chapters, including card sorting, wireframe prototyping, storyboard prototyping, paper prototyping, digital prototyping, blank model prototyping, video prototyping, Wizard-of-Oz prototyping, and coded prototyping.

With the prototyping characteristics set and the appropriate method chosen to reach your desired goal, you're ready to choose the right tool. The tool you want may not necessarily have a one-to-one mapping to the method you want to use, and fortunately, more than one tool can be used for a particular prototyping method. As well, you can use one tool with different methods to achieve various prototype results. Ultimately it is best to create a prototype with the methods and tools you know best.[1]

ARNOSOFT PICKS A METHOD

The ArnoSoft team did not have an easy time selecting a method. Emotions ran high during the ensuing fight over the methods, which led to picking the storyboard. Art was particularly adamant. He thought using a wireframe would be the most logical step, and he couldn't understand what everyone was arguing about. In fact, it wasn't until Art spent time overnight working out sketches that he finally dropped the idea. When he worked on the wireframes, he also added the CeramaSite branding or at least a placeholder concept. Reed Dish was livid; his store is nationally well known and he thought it was only logical that the site would be named after his store, Dish's Dishes. Such a fight ensued that Visty ordered the wireframe withdrawn. With no one really advocating any alternative, they went through their selected prototype characteristics and tried to match them to a method, using Worksheet 6.1 from Chapter 6.

While completing the worksheet they discovered that wireframe and storyboard matched about equally. After their wireframe experience with Reed, they liked the storyboard advantage of masking branding and other visual design elements, while having the option to increase the visual fidelity with wireframes later.

---

[1] *Indeed, this list is not exhaustive, and you may want to add your own favorite methods to this list. We will be adding prototyping methods, as they are contributed, to our website, which we enhance with other bonus materials, such as all the worksheets and templates that we use in this book.*

REFERENCES
Card Sorting

K. Frederickson-Mele. Usability testing an intranet prototype shell–a case study.
http://www.acm.org/sigchi/web/chi97testing/mele.htm. Accessed December 15, 2005.

James Robertson. Information design using card sorting.
http://steptwo.com.au/papers/cardsorting/. Accessed December 15, 2005.

Rashmi Sinha, Jonathan Boutelle. Rapid information architecture prototyping. Proceedings of
DIS '04. New York: ACM Press, 2004.

Todd Warfel, Donna Maurer. Card sorting: a definitive guide.
http://www.boxesandarrows.com/view/card_sorting_a_definitive_guide. Accessed
December 15, 2005.

Wireframe Prototyping

Larry Constantine. Canonical Abstract Prototypes for Abstract Visual and Interaction Design;
Lecture Notes in Computer Science. Berlin/Heidelberg: Springer Verlag, 2003, pp. 1–15.

Storyboard Prototyping

M. Bekker, J. Long. User involvement in the design of human-computer interactions:
some similarities and differences between design approaches. In: S. McDonald, Y. Waern,
G. Cockton, editors. People and Computers XV. Proceedings of HCI '00. Berlin/Heidelberg:
Springer-Verlag, 2000, pp. 135–147.

Hugh Beyer, Karen Holtzblatt. Contextual design: defining customer-centered systems.
San Francisco: Morgan Kaufmann, 1998.

A. Blomquist, M. Arvola. Personas in action: ethnography in an interaction design team.
Proceedings of NordiCHI '02. New York: ACM Press, 2002, pp. 197–200.

Sari Kujala, Marjo Kauppinen. Identifying and selecting users for user-centered design.
Proceedings of NordCHI '04. New York: ACM Press, 2004, pp. 297–303.

J. Noyes, C. Baber. User-centered design of systems. London: Springer, 1999.

J. Redish, J. Wixon. Task analysis. In: Julie A. Jacko, Andrew Sears, editors. The Human-
Computer Interaction Handbook: Fundamentals, Evolving Technologies, and Emerging
Applications. Mahwah, NJ: Lawrence Erlbaum Associates, 2003, pp. 922–940.

Ben Shneiderman. Designing the User Interface. Strategies for Effective Human-Computer
Interaction. Reading, MA: Addison-Wesley, 1998.

Paper Prototyping

Anita Komlodi. The role of interaction histories in mental model building and knowledge sharing in the legal domain. Journal of Universal Computer Science, 2002, vol. 8, pp. 557–566.

Sari Kujala, Marjo Kauppinen. Identifying and selecting users for user-centered design. Proceedings of NordCHI '04. New York: ACM Press, 2004, pp. 297–303.

John Pruitt, Tamara Adlin. The Persona Lifecycle. New York: Morgan Kaufman, 2006.

Jeffrey Rubin. Handbook of Usability Testing: How to Plan, Design, and Conduct Effective Tests. New York: Wiley, 1994.

Carolyn Snyder. Paper Prototyping. New York: Morgan Kaufmann, 2003.

The Usability Company. Glossary: prototyping. http://www.theusabilitycompany.com/resources/glossary/prototyping.html. Accessed July 2006.

Robert Virzi, Jeffrey Sokolov, Demetrois Karis. Usability problem identification using both low and high-fidelity prototypes. Proceedings of CHI '96. New York: ACM Press, 1996, pp. 236–243.

Blank Model Prototyping

Richard Mander, Michael Arent. Blank models: a method for early user participation. Interact American Center for Design Journal, 1994, vol. 8, pp. 38–45.

Donald E. Rickert, Jr. A Theory-Grounded Empirical Evaluation of Special-Purpose and Generic Interaction Devices for Interactive TV. Washington, DC: George Washington University School of Business and Public Management, 1997.

Video Prototyping

Hugh Dubberly, Doris Mitch. The Knowledge Navigator [video]. Cupertino, CA: Apple Computer, Inc., 1987.

Steven D. Katz. Film Directing: Shot by Shot: Visualizing from Concept to Screen. Boston: Focal Press (Michael Wiese Productions in conjunction with Focal Press), 1991.

Steven D. Katz. Film Directing: Cinematic Motion: A Workshop for Staging Scenes. Boston: Focal Press (Michael Wiese Productions in conjunction with Focal Press), 1992.

Wendy E. Mackay, et al. Video artifacts for design: bridging the gap between abstraction and detail. Proceedings of DIS '00. Brooklyn, NY: ACM Press, 2000.

Thomas A. Ohanian. Digital Nonlinear Editing: New Approaches to Editing Film and Video. Boston: Focal Press, 1993.

Bruce Tognazzini. The "Starfire" video prototype project: a case history. Proceedings of CHI '94. New York: ACM Press, 1994.

Wizard-of-Oz Prototyping

Nils Dahlback, Arne Jonsson, Lars Ahrenberg. Wizard of Oz studies: how and why. Proceedings from Intelligent User Interfaces Conference '93. New York: ACM Press, 1993, pp. 193–201.

James Lewis. Sample sizes for usability studies: additional considerations. Human Factors, 1994, vol. 36, pp. 368–378.

David Maulsby, Saul Greenberg, Richard Mander. Prototyping an intelligent agent through Wizard of Oz. Proceedings of InterCHI '93. New York: ACM Press, 1993, pp. 277–285.

Jeffrey Rubin. Handbook of Usability Testing. New York: Wiley, 1994.

Coded Prototyping

Steve McConnell. Rapid Development. Redmond, WA: Microsoft Press, 1996.

CHAPTER

The Effective Prototyping Process

PHASE **1** Plan

STEP **1** — ch 3 — Verify Requirements

STEP **2** — ch 4 — Develop Task Flows

STEP **3** — ch 5 — Define Content and Fidelity

PHASE **2** Specification

STEP **4** — ch 6 — Determine Characteristics

STEP **5** — ch 7 — Choose a Method

STEP **6** — ch 8 — Choose a Tool

PHASE **3** Design

STEP **7** — ch 9 — Select Design Criteria

STEP **8** — ch 10 — Create the Design

PHASE **4** Results

STEP **9** — ch 11 — Review the Design

STEP **10** — ch 12 — Validate the Design

STEP **11** — ch 13 — Deploy the Design

8

CHOOSE
A PROTOTYPING
TOOL

Step 5 of the effective prototyping process covered choosing the correct proto-typing method, which determines the type of prototype to create. The tool you want will not necessarily have a one-to-one mapping to the type of prototype. More than one tool can be used for any prototyping method. A tool can also be used for multiple prototyping methods, resulting in a variety of outcomes. For example, PowerPoint and Visio can both be used to create a storyboard, and to create wire-frames. Ultimately, it is best to create a prototype with the tool you know best. For example, if Visio is better at wireframes and PowerPoint better at storyboards, it seems simple to use these two tools. However, if you have 12 years experience in Visio and know it better than any tool the combination of your talents in Visio and the learning curve of PowerPoint would argue to use Visio instead of PowerPoint.

Step 6 of the effective prototyping process guides you through the process of deciding on the prototyping tool best for you. We list the issues of some of the most popular prototyping tools and give you a worksheet to aid your decision process (shown at the end of the chapter). We do not cover all products; just those that we know are common and have credible prototyping capabilities. In the likely event that we hear from readers about other tools or tool capabilities that either aren't mentioned in this book or we don't know about, we'll update our website (www.effectiveprototyping.com) with revisions of the matrices that appear at the end of this chapter.

MANAGER'S CORNER SIDEBAR

CHOOSING THE RIGHT TOOL

In choosing the right prototyping tool it is important for a manager to heed the following points.

Using Only a Single Prototyping Tool Is Not Efficient

Prototyping requirements change throughout a project, and it is important to tailor the prototyping tool to the project needs. This ensures that you are not spending too much time with a tool inappropriate to the task or spending too much time prototyping something that should be quite simple. Keep the prototypers on track, using the best tool with the right method to ensure optimal results.

Use Complementary Prototyping Tools

Before choosing a prototyping tool, map out the prototype iterations and determine the flow of complementary tools that fulfills the requirements. That is, if one team member needs to hand over the prototype to another, ensure that the prototype is delivered in a format that is either directly usable by the successor or can be exported into something usable.

For example, an information designer may start with a wireframe using a word processor. For the graphic designer, who will do a higher level of fidelity, the word processor format is fine because elements can easily be pasted into Photoshop. The interaction designer can use the prototype by importing the Photoshop graphic elements into an HTML tool using JPEG images or via copy and paste. If the software will be a web application, the developer can sometimes use bits of the HTML from the interaction design in the final product.

Beware of Overachieving Prototypes: Prototyping With the Wrong Tool

Using the wrong tool can easily result in exposing too many details early in the design process, referred to as an overachieving prototype. The overachieving prototype, as alluded to earlier in this book, can lead to the false assumption that many design and technical decisions have been made. Although some teams welcome getting "design" out of the way, that rarely has a positive effect on the product. Rarely, if ever, will a product look like the overachieving prototype: there are too many changes ahead as design and technical requirements evolve. To avoid the overachieving prototype, use the right tool and avoid being impressed by a prototype showing high fidelity early in the design process. Instead, you should question why someone would spend so much time on a prototype when many more design and technical decisions that affect the design have yet to be made.

HOW TO CHOOSE THE PROTOTYPING TOOL

The simple way to decide which tool to use and which one will lead you to success is by following the step-by-step guidelines:

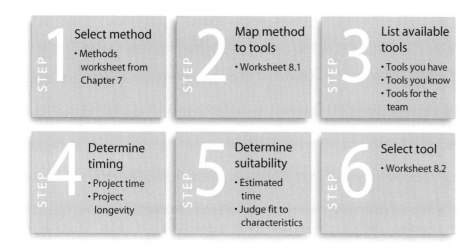

Step 1: Select Method

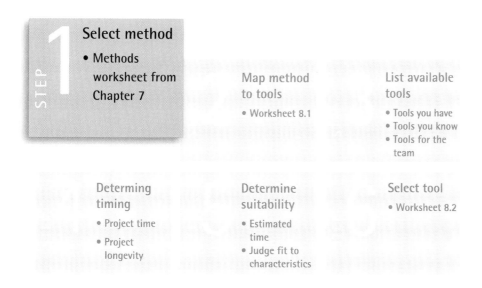

Selecting a method is the process discussed in Chapter 7. Record your selected method in Worksheet 8.1. The method you choose plays a leading role in which tool you should or shouldn't use, as illustrated in Step 2.

Step 2: Map Method to Tools

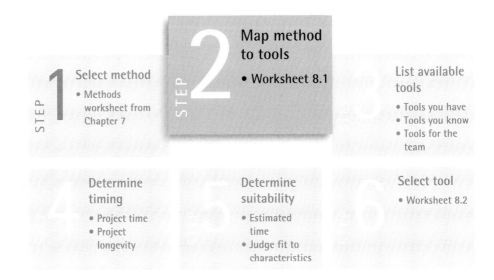

Prototyping method selection has a ripple effect on the available tools. Different methods may require different tools. Below are two versions of Worksheet 8.1. One version of the list is brand name-centric for those who have popular commercial software tools. The second list is product agnostic, featuring types of software tools:

WORKSHEET 8.1: Choose a Prototyping Tool

Project Name:	Author:
Project Date:	Internal Ref.:
Product Name:	Target Release:
Current Phase:	

	Methods								
Tools	**Card sorting**	**Wire frame**	**Story board**	**Paper**	**Blank model**	**Video**	**Wizard of Oz**	**Digital interactive**	**Coded**
Word*	NA	+	+	++	NA	NA	NA	−−	NA
PowerPoint*	NA	+	++	−	NA	NA	NA	++	NA
Excel*	NA	++	−	++	NA	NA	NA	++	NA
Visio*	NA	++	−	++	NA	NA	NA	++	NA
Paper	++	++	+	++	++	NA	NA	NA	NA
Acrobat*	NA	+	++	+	NA	NA	NA	++	NA
Photoshop	NA	+	+	+	NA	NA	NA	+	NA
VisualBasic	NA	−−	−−	−−	NA	NA	−	++	++
FrontPage	NA	+	−	−	NA	NA	−	+	+
Dreamweaver	NA	+	−	−	NA	NA	−	++	++
Flash	NA	−−	−	NA	NA	+	++	++	++
Director	NA	−−	−	NA	NA	+	++	++	++
VisualStudio	NA	−−	NA	NA	NA	NA	++	++	++

Legend

++ Very appropriate
+ appropriate
− acceptable
−− not practical
NA not applicable
* featured in this book

WORKSHEET 8.1: Choose a Prototyping Tool

Project Name:					Author:			
Project Date:					Internal Ref.:			
Product Name:					Target Release:			
Current Phase:								

	Methods							
Tools	Card sorting	Wire frame	Story board	Paper	Blank model	Video	Wizard of Oz	Digital interactive	Coded
Word processor	NA	+	+	+ +	NA	NA	NA	− −	NA
Presentation	NA	+	+ +	−	NA	NA	NA	+ +	NA
Spreadsheet	NA	+ +	−	+ +	NA	NA	NA	+ +	NA
Drawing	NA	+ +	−	+ +	NA	NA	NA	+ +	NA
Paper	+ +	+ +	+	+ +	+ +	NA	NA	NA	NA
PDF Viewer	NA	+	+ +	+	NA	NA	NA	+ +	NA
Paint program	NA	+	+	+	NA	NA	NA	+	NA
Simple programming	NA	− −	− −	− −	NA	NA	−	+ +	+ +
HTML editor	NA	+	−	−	NA	NA	−	+	+
HTML Site editor	NA	+	−	−	NA	NA	−	+ +	+ +
Animation tool	NA	− −	−	NA	NA	+	+ +	+ +	+ +
Prototyping Tool	NA	− −	−	NA	NA	+	+ +	+ +	+ +
Advance programming	NA	− −	NA	NA	NA	NA	+ +	+ +	+ +

Legend

+ + Very appropriate

+ appropriate

− acceptable

− − not practical

NA not applicable

* featured in this book

The example of Worksheet 8.1 below helps working through a process of picking the right tool for a storyboard prototype. The product names are used for clarity but are not meant to be a product recommendation. We recommend circling the top choices and crossing out those not recommended. For the sake of this exercise, Worksheet 8.1 below shows the highest recommended software in bold while the strikethrough rows are not recommended.

WORKSHEET 8.1: Choose a Prototyping Tool

Project Name:						Author:			
Project Date:						Internal Ref.:			
Product Name:						Target Release:			
Current Phase:									

	Methods								
Tools	Card sorting	Wire frame	Story board	Paper	Blank model	Video	Wizard of Oz	Digital interactive	Coded
Word	NA	+	+	+ +	NA	NA	NA	− −	NA
PowerPoint	NA	+	+ +	−	NA	NA	NA	+ +	NA
~~Excel~~	~~NA~~	+ +	−	+ +	~~NA~~	~~NA~~	~~NA~~	+ +	NA
~~Visio~~	~~NA~~	+ +	−	+ +	~~NA~~	~~NA~~	~~NA~~	+ +	NA
Paper	+ +	+ +	+	+ +	+ +	NA	NA	NA	NA
Acrobat	NA	+	+ +	+	NA	NA	NA	+ +	NA
Photoshop	NA	+	+	+	NA	NA	NA	+	NA
~~VisualBasic~~	~~NA~~	− −	− −	− −	~~NA~~	~~NA~~	−	+ +	+ +
~~FrontPage~~	~~NA~~	+	−	−	~~NA~~	~~NA~~	−	+	+
~~Dreamweaver~~	~~NA~~	+	−	−	~~NA~~	~~NA~~	−	+ +	+ +
~~Flash~~	~~NA~~	− −	−	~~NA~~	~~NA~~	+	+ +	+ +	+ +
~~Director~~	~~NA~~	− −	−	~~NA~~	~~NA~~	+	+ +	+ +	+ +
~~VisualStudio~~	~~NA~~	− −	~~NA~~	~~NA~~	~~NA~~	~~NA~~	+ +	+ +	+ +

Legend

+ + Very appropriate

+ appropriate

− acceptable

− − not practical

NA not applicable

* featured in this book

Step 3: List Available Tools

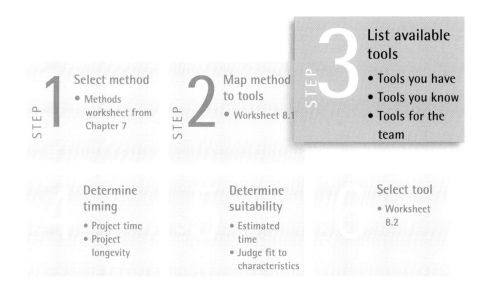

Now that you have a list of tools that will perform with the prototyping method you want, you should reduce the list to just those tools that you're familiar with and know how to use already.

If you are familiar with a tool, such as PowerPoint or Acrobat, but don't know how to use the tool for prototyping, refer to the tools chapters in the third part of this book, which explain how some of these common and generally available software tools can be used as prototyping tools.

If you're going to collaborate with other members of a team on a prototype, you may want to take stock of their software skills as well and select tools that everyone has common skills and experience with. Team members can then more readily participate in the prototyping process. Another advantage to using a common tool is the help your colleagues may provide by knowing how to use certain features and functions that you are neither aware of nor proficient in. This help alone can lead to much more effective prototyping than you could do alone.

In this next step, eliminate tools you don't know, you don't have, or you can't get. You should also eliminate tools that are prohibitive for sharing with the rest of the team. In our example below, tools like Director and Flash, which require a specialized skill set and a long development time were eliminated along with tools that were inappropriate.

The resulting list of tools for the storyboard prototype is as follows: Word, PowerPoint, Paper, Acrobat, and Photoshop. At this point you can simply choose your favorite or readily available tool. However, if you need further analysis you can move on to Worksheet 8.2 to enter the tool names for analysis of which ones will work best.

Blank Worksheet 8.2 looks like this:

Project name
Time
Longevity
Method
Next Method

Tool name	Priority	Your skills	Time/Effort	Longevity	Characteristics fit	Can your team access

After the storyboard data are added, Worksheet 8.2 looks something like this:

Project name   ArnoSoft
Time   Presentation in 5 days
Longevity   Medium
Method   Storyboard
Next Method   Wireframe

Tool name	Priority	Your skills	Time/Effort	Longevity	Characteristics fit	Can your team access
Word						
PowerPoint						
Paper						
Acrobat						
Photoshop						

POWERPOINT DRAWS: LEARNING NEW TRICKS FROM TEAM MEMBERS

As mentioned in Step 3, using common tools allows you to not only share and collaborate with team members, but also to learn new tricks with tools you already know well. One case of this occurred when a consultant designer, Lauren, was using PowerPoint to create a storyboard for a client. The client insisted on using PowerPoint because it is a presentation standard within the company. As a consultant, Lauren was familiar with the presentation capabilities of PowerPoint and agreed to use the tool. Lauren found it annoying that she needed to jump back and forth between PowerPoint and her graphics package to create the wireframes that she needed to add to her storyboard. One developer overheard her complain to a colleague. This developer was very familiar with the drawing capabilities of PowerPoint. He was able to show Lauren that PowerPoint actually included rudimentary drawing tools, not as sophisticated as those of her graphics package but enough to create much of the wireframe designs for her storyboard presentation. This increased the prototyping capabilities of PowerPoint for her and also increased her efficiency. She never would have discovered this capability on her own because she didn't think to look for drawing tools in PowerPoint. This is an excellent example of how using a common tool available to your colleagues can help increase and share everyone's knowledge of how to prototype.

Step 4: Determine Timing

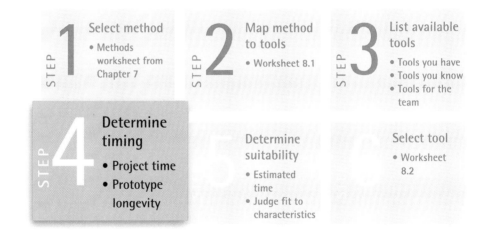

The fourth step is determining the time you need to create the prototype and how long the prototype needs to last. First, your awareness of available time determines how much of that time can be spent working with a prototyping tool and how much needs to be spent on other tasks, allowing you to scale your expectations to fit the available time. If you have only a little time available, using a tool that requires little setup and includes more efficient features is preferable over something that can create a pixel-perfect prototype that you will expend too much time on. Likewise, if the prototype will be a rapid throwaway, it is better not to invest too much time in it.

For the sake of our storyboard example, let's say the available time is short. Even if we could use a more complex tool like Director, the speed considerations would probably lead us to choose another tool. So we'll say a storyboard is needed for a presentation at the end of the week. It will inform further prototypes but will not be used for much more than that. See the filled-out Worksheet 8.2 below for how this would look.

Step 5: Determine Suitability

Step 5 maps the tools to available time and characteristics. Using Worksheet 8.2, you can estimate the time you need to create the prototype with a given tool and add those time estimates into the worksheet. Now, review the prototyping characteristics you decided on in Chapter 6. Think how well your skills with each tool map to those characteristics. In the storyboard example, which of these tools satisfy the two requirements for this prototype effort: narrative and low fidelity? In other words, do not just judge the tool's capabilities alone but also the tool's capabilities in conjunction with your skills.

Step 6: Select Tool

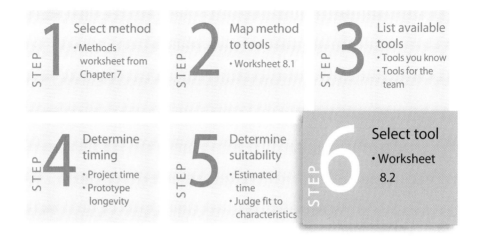

In Step 6 you select the tool. You now have all the information you need to prioritize the toolset and make a decision about which tool is the most effective, the second most effective, third, and so on. It is best to have a range of tools to choose from because companies can sometimes be very particular about the tool used to build a prototype–the alternatives will be useful. With this Worksheet 8.2 after Step 5, you can show the justification behind a decision for or against a particular tool. To determine whether a tool is a good fit, you will use the top score in each column and compare the columns:

> **First**: You can automatically assign a lower priority to those tools that do not match the project timeframe.
>
> For the example, Paper is eliminated.

> **Second**: You can assign a low priority to tools that you aren't familiar with.
>
> For the example, Photoshop is eliminated.

> **Third**: You can automatically assign a lower priority to those tools that do not match the longevity determined for the prototype.
>
> For the example, Word is eliminated.

> **Fourth**: You can automatically assign a lower priority to those tools that do not match the prototyping characteristics.
>
> For the example, the remaining choices, Acrobat and PowerPoint, both seem adequate.
>
> However, PowerPoint is already available in-house, but not Acrobat, giving PowerPoint a higher priority.

> ➤ **Fifth**: Compare if the general availability will eliminate one over the other.
>
>   For the example, Acrobat is eliminated because it is not available.

The resulting prioritization shows that PowerPoint is the first choice, followed by Acrobat.

WORKSHEET 8.2 **After Step 6**

Project name   ArnoSoft
Time   Presentation in 5 days
Longevity   Medium
Method   Storyboard
Next Method   Wireframe

Tool name	Priority	Your skills	Time/Effort	Longevity	Characteristics fit	Can your team access
Word	Low	Good	1–2 days	Short	Okay	Yes
PowerPoint	Very high	Very good	**2–3 days**	Long	Very Good	Yes
Paper	Low	Okay	2 weeks	Long	Good	Yes
Acrobat	High	Very Good	5–6 days	Long	Very Good	No
Photoshop	Low	Good	2–3 days	Short	Good	Yes, passively

WORKSHEET 8.2. Blank Template

Project name
Time
Longevity
Method
Next Method

Tool name	Priority	Your skills	Time/Effort	Longevity	Characteristics fit	Can your team access

If you have any feedback regarding this or other worksheets in this book, please send feedback to bookfeedback@effectiveprototyping.com.

NEXT STEP

Now that you have chosen the method and the tool, you have almost all the prerequisites to create your prototype. Planning is complete, and the next phase is the actual design of the prototype. In the creation phase, the prototype is built using the planning data accumulated thus far.

ARNOSOFT EVALUATES PROTOTYPING TOOLS

The new scope that was agreed to by the business stakeholders required more investment than ArnoSoft currently had, so the company resolved to meet with venture capitalists in search of a pot of gold. Visty and Reed decided a prototype would help convince the venture capitalists of their sophisticated software ideas. The effective prototyping method analysis helped Visty and Reed determine that a flash interactive prototype would be best. Because of the importance of the venture capitalist meeting for determining funding, Visty and Reed are both very concerned and put a lot of pressure on Dirk, Ina, and Art to create a functioning interactive prototype for the venture capitalist review meeting in a week and a half.

Reed comes in to see them and tells them, "Yeah, you know you got to do that clickety click thing, you know make it sing, make it click, make it work, make 'em sing."

Dirk, Ina, and Art brainstorm the prototype requirements needed to show all the major functionality and make it look as sharp as possible in their short timeline. Unsure what tool would allow them to collaborate and at the same time develop a satisfactory prototype, they decide to use the worksheet approach discussed in this chapter. They start with Step 1 in which they record the stakeholder request for a coded prototype.

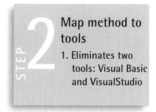

STEP 1

Select method
- Method:
  Storyboard

Coded prototype as dictated from on high. Done. That was easy.

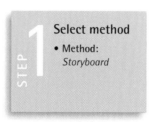

STEP 2

Map method to tools

1. Eliminates two tools: Visual Basic and VisualStudio

Then they proceed to Step 2 in which they review the list of appropriate tools for story-boards in Worksheet 8.1. That left them with the following tools: VisualBasic, FrontPage, Dreamweaver, Flash, Director, VisualStudio. In mapping a method to the tools some tools from the list can be quickly eliminated without even considering them–FrontPage was gone as not sexy enough.

STEP 3

List available tools

Remaining list:
- Word
- KeyNote
- Excel
- Visio
- Paper
- Dreamweaver
- Flash

In Step 3, after reviewing the available tools, they first removed Director because they did not have a license.

In Step 4 the team recorded the project time and longevity. They had a week and a half to make it presentable, because the third day would be presentation day. The prototype did not need to be reused at all; it was more a proof of concept than anything else for the company.

Having established the time and longevity, they began working on Step 5; Dirk, Ina, and Art realized they were left picking from Visual Basic, Visual Studio, Flash, or Director.

Reviewing the worksheet in Step 6, the team came to the following conclusions:

> *It would be quick to create a prototype with Dreamweaver.*
> *A prototype in Visual Studio would take too long.*
> *Visual Basic everyone thought was boring, but they really didn't know it.*
> *Flash seemed nice but only one person had access to it.*

It was clear that Dreamweaver would be their tool of choice; it was a shared product and the end product was a website anyway it would be perfect. They found the right prototyping tool.

Project name   ArnoSoft
Time   Presentation in 5 days
Longevity   Medium
Method   Storyboard
Next Method   Wireframe

Tool name	VisualBasic	FrontPage	Dreamweaver	Flash	Director	VisualStudio
Priority	Boring	Low	High	High	Low	~~Too long~~
Your skills	Boring	Good	Okay	Very Good	Okay	~~Okay~~
Time/Effort	1–2 days	2–3 days	2–3 days	5–6 days	Week	~~Week~~
Longevity	Short	Long	Medium	Long	Medium	~~Long~~
Characteristics fit	No	Okay	Yes	Very Good	No	~~Yes~~
Can your team access	Yes	Limited, Ina	Yes	Yes	No	~~Yes~~

They were finally about to finish when Reed enters.
"So what are you going to use to prototype for the venture capital show this Thursday?" asks Reed.
"We'll knock 'em dead. Don't worry!" said Ina.
"Okay but what are you going to use, Flash? I love Flash, click, click, click!" said Reed.
"No. We're going to use Dreamweaver," said Emerald.
"No way!" exclaimed Reed, "Use Flash. Our life is at stake here; we need clickety clickety click! Not a website."
"Okay, Reed, we will do it in Flash," said Art.
"Good, I don't care if you have to work all night, this has to look superb. I gotta go, I'm late for happy hour at the Bar."
After Reed left, Ina turns to Art, "Why did you say that? Now I have to work all night on this thing, I'm the only one who knows Flash here!"
"Because we'll do it in Dreamweaver; he'll never know the difference."

"To be as focused and as efficient as possible it is essential that the designer have the ability to isolate what constitutes a 'critical mass' of the problem under investigation."

-Bill Buxton from Iteration in the Design of the Human–Computer Interface

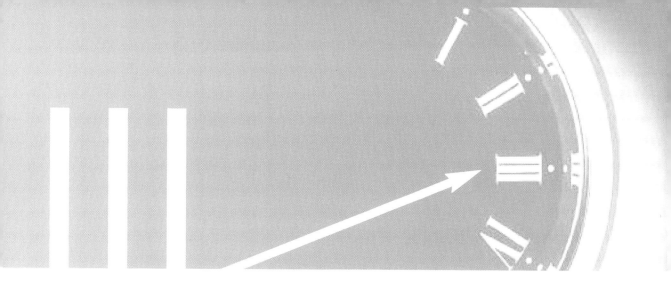

DESIGN YOUR PROTOTYPE

The previous phases covered planning and specifying your prototype, including identifying the requirements, task flows and scenarios, and content for your prototype followed by determining the prototype characteristics, choosing a method, and then choosing the tool you'll use for your prototype. This planning phase determines how you're going to use the information and tools as well as the organization of the prototype. Phase 3 covers identifying the most effective contents in addition to creating a conceptual design and navigation scheme for your prototype. This phase covers these two steps:

Step 7: Establish the design criteria
Step 8: Design and build a prototype

Determining what you need to do to complete the prototype is closely tied to the various requirements that shape the design as well as your current stage in the software creation process. In this phase we discuss the process of winnowing the prototyping task into manageable chunks for a given prototyping iteration by formulating a design criteria. As Bill Buxton mentions above, assume you have isolated a "critical mass" needed to focus and work efficiently in designing your prototype. Consequently, you'll specify the design criteria, which you'll use to formulate your prototype design (Step 7). Then, you'll synthesize the requirements and design criteria into a prototype design (Step 8).

CHAPTER

The Effective Prototyping Process

PHASE **1** Plan

STEP **1** ch 3 Verify Requirements

STEP **2** ch 4 Develop Task Flows

STEP **3** ch 5 Define Content and Fidelity

PHASE **2** Specification

STEP **4** ch 6 Determine Characteristics

STEP **5** ch 7 Choose a Method

STEP **6** ch 8 Choose a Tool

PHASE **3** Design

STEP **7** ch 9 **Select Design Criteria**

STEP **8** ch 10 Create the Design

PHASE **4** Results

STEP **9** ch 11 Review the Design

STEP **10** ch 12 Validate the Design

STEP **11** ch 13 Deploy the Design

9

ESTABLISH THE DESIGN CRITERIA

INTRODUCTION

You have already worked through the planning and specification process and already know on which requirements and assumptions you need to focus. The only thing left is to create the prototype.

Some may feel that they're ready to begin immediately. Others, especially those who have not prototyped before, may be scratching their heads and asking themselves "What do I do now?" How do you decide what goes where and why? The seasoned designer needs no help here and can skip ahead to Chapter 11 to review the prototype. For the others, it may be useful to have some design criteria to help you work through the design process, so this chapter is meant to help you choose the criteria to determine what goes where.

What are criteria? *Webster's Dictionary* defines it as follows:
cri·te·ri·on *noun, plural* cri·te·ria *also* -ri·ons
Etymology: Greek *kritErion*, from *krinein* to judge, decide

1. A standard on which a judgment or decision may be based
2. A characterizing mark or trait

The way we use criteria is to create the standard (or guidelines) by which you'll design, build, and present your prototype based. A good start is to pick the guidelines you best understand and then apply them to your situation. The more of the forthcoming guidelines you cover, the more sophisticated your resulting design will be. We do caution you not to choose more than one to three primary guidelines for your criteria. If you choose too many, the design and layout of your screens may be using a system so complex that only its creator can follow it.

This chapter is not meant to be a complete textbook on the topic of design criteria but an overview of some best practices in design from the fields of user interface design, visual design, and usability. In this chapter you'll create your design criteria by reviewing and selecting from the design guidelines outlined below. These guidelines should be based on soundly articulated requirements, verified assumptions, and best-practice design principles. At the end of this chapter we have a step-by-step procedure to help you select the criteria, if you need it. In Chapter 10, Step 8, you'll apply your design criteria to create a prototype. The ensuing design guidelines are meant, therefore, as an aid to software makers to prototype to the best of their ability but are not meant to be a substitute for a professional designer needed for the final design.

The easiest method of setting design criteria is relying on those that may be already established by your company. These can often be found in user interface or product design style guides. They may also be found in documents from a previous software project. Perhaps you can find them by inquiring with someone in your marketing, design, or usability department. Unfortunately, even with mature products, all too often there are no design criteria to be found.

QUALITY OF DESIGN AND USABILITY OF SOFTWARE

Design criteria arm you with a clear answer to the question, "Why did you design it that way?" During a presentation or design review meeting it empowers you to give a substantive answer, because design criteria are aimed at ensuring clear direction and quality in the visual and interaction design of a product in addition to its ultimate usability. Iterative prototyping based on adequately defined design criteria allows you to verify and tune the design and supporting criteria as you work toward the final design and usability on which your product will be developed.

In addition to the categories of visual design and user interface guidelines, we have also given each guideline an attribute: organizational or directional. An organizational guideline helps the prototyper organize user interface elements on a screen in a logical fashion, covering such things as groupings and associations. One example of an organizational guideline is logical groupings, in which a designer groups user interface elements into related units or chunks of information. Directional guidelines give the prototyper guidance for the flow of the page layout. A directional guideline example is for placement of information on a screen in such a way that users can visually scan it in an informative way to efficiently engage in and complete a task or activity. To maximize the usefulness and outcome of design criteria, you should choose a mix of directional and organizational guidelines.

ANALYZING CONTRADICTORY DESIGN GUIDELINES

Following design criteria does not simply mean blindly following rules that results somehow in a good user experience. You'll need to use your judgment both in the application of guidelines and in resolving contradictory rules. This is the main reason why the so-called consistent user interface is not just an elusive goal but also an invalid one. For example, you may follow a visual design guideline to conform to an information flow proceeding from upper left and leading the eye to the lower right corner of a displayed page, visually indicating that the most important information should go in the upper left corner. Then you come across a user interface guideline that all required fields should be placed near the top of the screen so they're not hidden from the user's view. If there are some technically required fields of secondary importance, what do you do with them relative to these seemingly contradictory guidelines? Analytically, we can declare the reason for this guideline is to avoid errors from users neglecting to enter data into required fields that are either not in their primary field of view or are hidden from their view. This is most likely to happen in the case of fields that require data entry and are technically essential, such as department and cost center information in an expense report that rarely change and are not perceived by the user to be important. A possible solution to this dilemma is to provide a logical default for these fields that can be automatically entered by the system, thus preventing error generation and notification. You can now place these required fields out of the user's view. With a solution like this, the spirit of both guidelines is covered. But strict consistency falls to the wayside.

VISUAL DESIGN GUIDELINES

Visual design and user interface design are often thought to be worlds apart in their approach to design. Yet their similarities are often more striking than their differences. The fact that both have their roots in psychology is but one remarkable similarity. Most of the user interface guidelines mentioned later in this chapter have roots in cognitive psychology. Most of the visual design guidelines discussed here have their roots in Gestalt psychology [Chang et al. 2001]. The other guidelines also have a best-practices characteristic of what user interface professionals call heuristics. The visual design guidelines covered here are:

- > Information flow (directional)
- > Grid-based organization (organizational)
- > Rhythm and pattern (directional)
- > Unity and variety (organizational)
- > Typographic structure (organizational)
- > Balance (directional)
- > Logical grouping (organizational)

Visual Design Guideline 1: Information Flow (Directional)

The path of the user's eye scanning across a screen and the user's resulting focus are aids in deciding where to place items in designing the layout of a screen or page. Understanding this path and points of focus, allows you to place your critical elements in places that are easy for the user to find.

A screen becomes easier to read and navigate when critical elements are easier to find and identify [White 1988].

The typical information flow and user's eye scan path begin in the upper left area of the screen and run down to the lower right. The extreme bottom of a screen display, especially the lower left corner, is where information is least likely to be noticed. Figure 9.1 shows a typical website home page in which the information would flow (represented by the arrow) and be scanned by the user from left to right, top to bottom.

FIGURE 9.1 *The information flow of a website from top to bottom/left to right.*

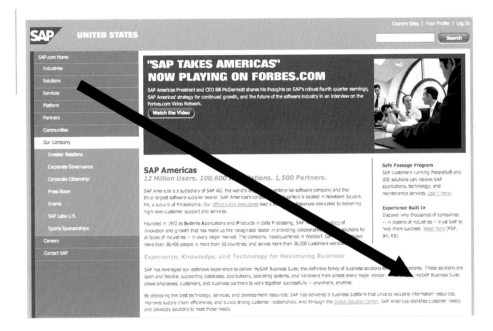

The information flow guideline can be broken into five concrete rules:

1. First priority items: Always place your most important information and user interface elements in the upper left area of an information display. Important means information that the user will want to/need to see or that the user will have to change it often.

2. Place your second most important elements below the first priority items in the center area of the screen so that they fall within the user's primary field of vision.

3. Place the third most important items in the lower right area of the information display.

4. Always place information of minor importance or elements that are infrequently interacted with in the upper right corner or below the fold of scrollable content.

5. Always place the least important information and elements that are most infrequently interacted with in the lower left area, including below the fold.

Applying this guideline provides you with a solid design rationale for the placement of content information and user interface elements on the screen.

Visual Design Guideline 2: Grid-Based Organization (Organizational)

A layout grid is a way to ensure that your design is positioned with a sense of proportion and, at the same time, provides a certain level of organization and alignment [White 2002]. A grid refers to the invisible pattern of lines and coordinates that the designer uses as both a guide and a framework for the layout of and alignment of elements on a screen as well as across related screens to achieve a final cohesive design [Hurlburt 1978].

Figure 9.2 shows an example of a layout grid. Figure 9.3 shows a web application page where no grid was used, whereas Figure 9.4 shows the same application laid out on the grid shown in Figure 9.2.

FIGURE 9.2 *An example of a layout grid for a web page.*

FIGURE 9.3 *A web page designed without a layout grid.*

FIGURE 9.4 *The same web page with the layout grid applied.*

Visual Design Guideline 3: Rhythm and Pattern (Directional)

Rhythm—movement or fluctuation marked by the regular recurrence or natural flow of related elements.

Pattern—repetition involving the exact duplication of a module uniformly spaced [Faimon and Weigand 2004, p. 48].

Rhythm and pattern, along with unity below, are our answer to the often-abused guideline of consistency. Consistency is too rigid, because things can be consistently bad and still adhere to the consistency guideline. Rhythm and pattern allow you to set up the user's expectations but still maintain a level of flexibility by keeping to a pattern.

These allow you to design different information flows and still be appropriate to your design objectives. You can design your own layout patterns and rhythms that lead the eye to follow any path controlled by your design and the arrangement of visual elements. For example, if you want the user to complete a series of fields grouped into sections, you can try a pattern layout of sections leading the user from one to the next as shown in the vertical arrangement of field groupings shown in Figure 9.5. The component from a PeopleSoft application shows a pattern of horizontal elements arranged in a way that leads the user's eye vertically down the page to more easily view and comprehend the different groups of information [Arnowitz et al. 2005].

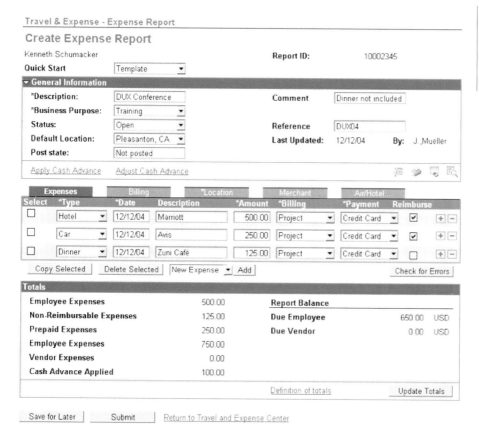

FIGURE 9.5 *PeopleSoft Travel and Expense screen showing a strong vertical pattern.*

Visual Design Guideline 4: Unity and Variety (Organizational)

Faimon and Weigund [2004] express unity this way: There should be uniformity in an overall design concept. Unity is applying the same visually consistent design concepts. Figure 9.8 shows the unity concept. In Figure 9.6 you can see how the second, third, and fifth icons really conform to the same concept even though they are different—they have a unity of concept. Variety is a variation in a design that is purposely inconsistent and is typically used for emphasizing special or very important functionality or elements. The flag icon in Figure 9.6 keeps enough of the general concept that it sticks out but does not look too foreign to the rest of the design. Variety should be used in a limited way so that it doesn't overpower the overall design and feels like it fits the design concept.

FIGURE 9.6 *A toolbar from Microsoft Word: the first icon does not follow the unity in concept, the other icons do with its predominately three-dimensional look.*

FIGURE 9.7 *Unity in concept.*

FIGURE 9.8 *Variety in the concept.*

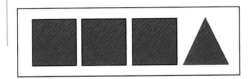

Coupled with variety, unity allows a controlled flexibility that permits variations in the spirit of the original idea, as shown in Figure 9.8. A strong underlying visual concept allows the variation to work; otherwise, changes will seem arbitrary, causing the design to look messy and uncoordinated, such as in Figure 9.9.

FIGURE 9.9 *Arbitrary changes look sloppy.*

Visual Design Guideline 5: Typographic Structure (Organizational)

Typography is more than readability of text content and labels; it also involves arrangement, flow, and communications in addition to visual and editorial expression [Felici 2003]. Typographic structure, flow, and visual expression should be carefully considered. Because it is visual and carries verbal messages, it can be a potent graphic element that is on par with images, icons, symbols, and any other visual elements that appear to a user [Tschichold 1998, pp. 82–85]. Because it has both visual and editorial communications aspects to it, typography can also evoke powerful emotional responses from the viewer.

Figures 9.10 through 9.12 are examples of the use of typography for these effects. If we look first at Figure 9.10, the *New York Times* website, a choice was made to use the traditional masthead typography at the top. The body text used is the most newspaper-like, although the overall typographic layout, arrangement of elements, and information flow were appropriately designed for the web. On the other hand, Figure 9.11, the SIGCHI Bulletin website, hopes to typographically convey a technical and design savvy as befitting an organization dedicated to good technical design. Finally, in Figure 9.12, the NeoPets site targeted to children, a typographic arrangement is used that appears fun and inviting while still using a typographic expression based on common system fonts.

FIGURE 9.10 *The New York Times website.*

FIGURE 9.11 *The SIGCHI Bulletin website.*

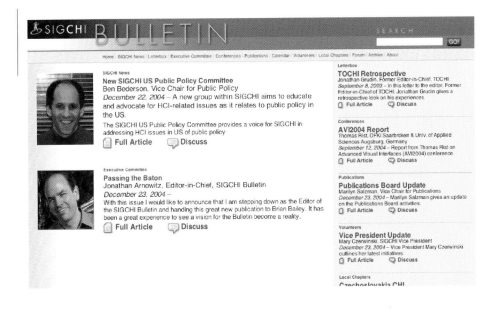

FIGURE 9.12 *The Neopets website.*

VISUAL DESIGN GUIDELINE 6: BALANCE (DIRECTIONAL)

Balance—Equipoise between contrasting, opposing, or interacting elements; an aesthetically pleasing integration of elements. When compositional elements are not balanced around a visual axis or centerline, the effect can be jarring [Faimon and Weigand 2004, pp. 102–104].

In art and visual design, balance can be expressed in two primary ways: symmetry and asymmetry. *Symmetry* is when balance is achieved in a visual design by distributing the visual weight of the design components equally on either side of a vertical and/or horizontal center axis. Symmetry in design evokes a stable static visual expression—the most familiar being classical Greek architecture. Figure 9.13 shows classical symmetric layout of a hall in the opulent Palace of Versailles. An example of a symmetrically balanced user interface design is shown in Figure 9.14. The balance in this example is expressed by the arrangement of visual elements, which are equally distributed on either side of a vertical center axis. The headline text, placed on the center axis, spans both columns.

FIGURE 9.13 *A hall in the Palace of Versailles, the embodiment of design symmetry.*

FIGURE 9.14 *A page designed in a balanced symmetric composition of visual elements and laid out on a vertical center axis.*

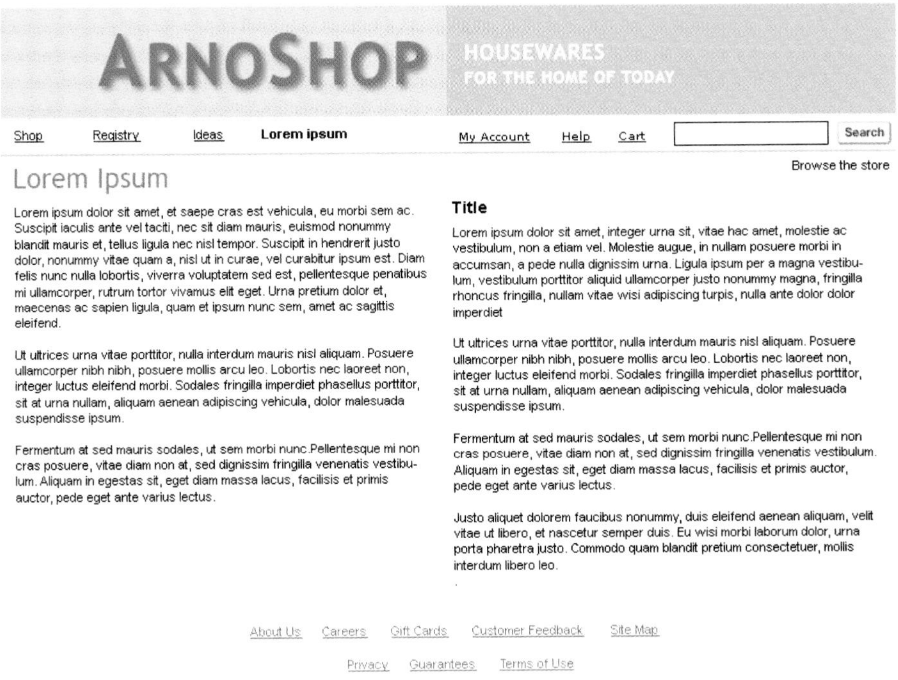

Asymmetry in a visual design is the depiction of two sides not being identical without impairing the general harmony of the design and layout. Asymmetry in design evokes an active and variable visual expression. An example of an asymmetrically balanced design is shown in Figure 9.15. This website design uses a layout in which the primary content is a large main area of focus around which the masthead (top area), the navigation menu (left column), and subordinate content area (right columns) are positioned in a balanced composition comprising different but complementary sizes and proportions.

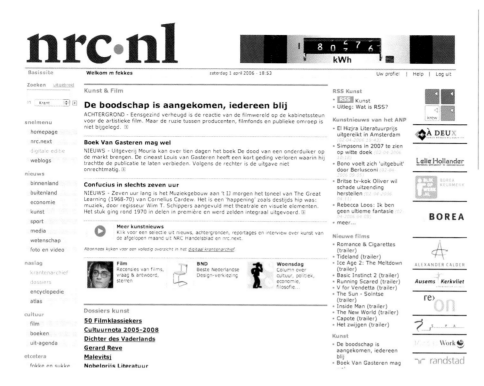

Visual Design Guideline 7: Logical Grouping (Organizational)

Our last visual design guideline involves the logical syntactic grouping of visual elements on a page. This is not just a means of organizing content and user interface elements by visual similarities in form but also by semantic expression. As shown in Figure 9.16, it is difficult to make sense of an ad-hoc arrangement of unrelated items. Logical grouping enables users to find and comprehend things more quickly and easily while also facilitating user's ability to form a mental model about the associations between and among things in a user's visual and semantic field of vision. First look at Figure 9.16 and quickly count the triangles in the picture. Now try the same thing in Figure 9.17. Because of the logical grouping and associations, you were probably able to more quickly count the triangles in Figure 9.17.

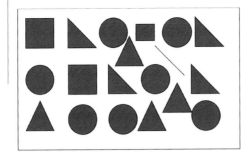

FIGURE 9.16 *A random collection of symbols. How many triangles are there?*

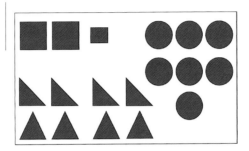

FIGURE 9.17 *A grouped collection of symbols.*

USER INTERFACE GUIDELINES

Because it is the aspect that users most initially and emotionally respond to, visual design can take you far in terms of specifically defining and evolving your prototype. However, it's not enough to just have a visual design guideline; you need to understand the user's cognitive psychological needs and motivational goals in terms of their experience in using software.

Of primary importance to the user is not only how user interface elements appear and how they're arranged and sequenced but also:

> How the interface affords users to do or learn things according to their expectations
> What and how the interface communicates and expresses itself to the user
> How the interface behaves and responds to each user interaction

A good user experience designer takes a holistic view of the software and designs it relative to users' mental models formed by their life experiences and expectations on how to do things. The goal of addressing the user interface with a set of guidelines (as shown in the bulleted list below) is to prevent usability issues from interfering with the evaluation of the prototype by internal and external stakeholders as well as others.

> Progressive disclosure (directional)
> Efficiency (directional)
> Fitt's law (directional)
> Learnability (directional)

- Speak the audience's language (organizational)
- Explicitly show required actions and fields (organizational)
- International sensitivity (organizational)
- Universal accessibility (organizational)
- Users should feel in control (organizational)
- Minimize cognitive load (organizational)
- Satisfaction (organizational)

User Interface Guideline 1: Progressive Disclosure (Directional)

A complex and overwhelming interface is usually an indication that a designer or developer has failed to understand his or her users, how they perform tasks, as well as how they comprehend, assimilate, and interact with information. Progressive disclosure is a strategy for preventing the display of an overwhelming amount of information and overly complex presentations of information to users. It is also a method for reducing cognitive overload and the need for overt memorization. Progressive disclosure involves breaking down information into task-relevant sequential chunks that are easy to comprehend, consume, and interact with. Progressive disclosure can occur within a screen or across multiple screens of information. The following are different progressive disclosure techniques to allow the user to more easily handle complex presentations of information:

> *Hide/show*–Hide and show is the most common form of progressive disclosure. The advantage of this method is that it involves hiding information from the user and then showing it when necessary and appropriate, such as the province field that appears on address forms when the user chooses to display address information for Canada. The drawback to hide/show is the failure of some users to notice when things have appeared or disappeared.

> *Below the visible scroll area*–A user interface disclosure feature most relevant for web pages in which information resides below the scroll boundary or "fold." The user reveals hidden content, such as informational content, input fields, or table rows, by scrolling them vertically into view.

> *To the right of the visible scroll area*–Another user interface disclosure method mainly for web pages similar to *below the visible scroll area* except that users scroll horizontally. Horizontal scrolling is usually more confusing for users, especially if used in combination with vertical scrolling, the user can easily get lost. If using scrolling you should pick just one direction.

Enable/disable—Perhaps the subtlest form of progressive disclosure. In this form of progressive disclosure, a user interface element is still visible but is grayed out and disabled until it is required to be enabled and active for user input. The main disadvantage of enabling/disabling is that because the element is still visible, it can be visually distracting as, for example, in a complex display of information. Enable/disable is primarily used when additional information needs to be entered by a user based on certain conditions triggered by user input, such when a user selects a range of more than one page in a printing dialogue.

Expandable regions—An expandable region is a defined area in the interface that can expand and collapse via a user interface element. For example, expanding a simple search user interface region to reveal advanced search input fields.

Tabbed display regions—File folder-like tabs (or other such metaphors) can be used to chunk complex information in the user interface by allowing it to be categorized into discrete regions revealed when users click on a particular tab. Ideally, the first or default tab is the primary information a user needs to see. The further to the right a tab is located, the progressively less important the information should be.

Menu commands—Typically, user interfaces have sets of different commands that allow users to perform a wide variety of functions. These commands are generally contained in menus and are disclosed at the time of need via drop-down or pop-up menus.

Property sheets—Property sheets are small windows (in the form of a floating palette or dialog box) that list label and value pairs that allow users to set properties. These types of windows provide a means for progressively disclosing detailed information that users need to only occasionally access.

Secondary windows—When users need to perform secondary tasks the user interface mechanism to do that is typically contained in a secondary window. An example of this is when the user is creating an invoice and realizes certain customer information does not exist in the system. The invoice task needs to be interrupted to allow the user to navigate to then enter the customer information. Once the task is completed, the user can navigate from the secondary window back to the primary window.

Hyperlinks—This form of progressive disclosure relies on navigation that redirects the user from one body of information to another related body of information that a user may seek. Hyperlinks allow users to cross-reference and disclose a semantically interconnected web of all types of information directly related to a topic or data of interest at hand. The only drawback of hyperlink-based progressive disclosure is that users may have difficulty navigating back to the point of origin because this type of navigation can involve jumping from page to page to page of information.

User Interface Guideline 2: Efficiency (Organizational)

Efficiency is a task flow and screen organization attribute. Efficiency means the user can easily and effectively navigate through the interface to accomplish a specific task or activity. Jonathan was once asked to review a budgeting application that required users to navigate five screens just to look at budget data. That was not efficient. In this budgeting application, it was more efficient for the user to have the budget data more immediately viewable by consolidating it in a single-screen view but organized in logical groups.

Another strategy for efficiency is enabling the user to complete work without having to switch between mouse and keyboard interaction. Efficiency in the interface can also be realized through the automated entry of data into fields that is contained in the system.

For interactive prototypes, efficiency can be additionally explored by trying to streamline the details and steps involved in screen level interaction—within screens and between screens. Effective methods exist for analyzing end-user efficiency, including user research and task analysis. You can find information in almost any book on user-centered design, including books from these authors: Hackos, Courage and Baxter, and Mayhew.

User Interface Guideline 3: Fitt's Law (Directional)

This guideline speaks for itself. There is almost nothing to add beyond the law itself [MacKenzie et al. 1978, p. 760]:

$$MT = 1.03 + 0.096\ ID$$

Well, maybe some explanation will help: the essence of Fitt's Law is that the smaller, more unstable, and farther away an interaction target is, the more difficult it is for users to reach and interact with that target. The first step to keeping targets usable is to ensure that your most frequently used interaction targets are large enough and preferably in a consistent location from one screen to the next. The smaller a repetitive interaction element is and the more inconsistent its placement, the more complex and difficult it is to interact with it.

User Interface Guideline 4: Learnability (Directional)

Learnability is an all-encompassing guideline that can apply to layout, content, and screen flow: make your prototype easy to learn. A user should be able to reuse current knowledge or the knowledge gained from using one aspect of the application to learn how to use the rest of the application. This is a directional guideline in the sense that once you determine a learnable direction or layout in one page, you should apply that layout/direction in subsequent pages as long as it proves to be comparably learnable.

There are three strategies for achieving learnability in a user interface:

1. Leverage professional or personal knowledge and experience of users by using metaphors and interaction models and design models that support that knowledge and experience.

2. Use computer conventions with which users are already familiar, such as familiar interaction models, menu layouts and content, icons, and interaction widgets.

3. Once you introduce an interaction method, continue to use it consistently for the same or similar types of interactions; for example, once a travel authorization user interface has been proven to be a usable design, a similar, if not identical, interface can be used for the subsequent entry of travel expenses.

User Interface Guideline 5: Speak the Audience's Language (Organizational)

This is primarily a content guideline in which the editorial and visual language of the user interface should comprise terms, images, and semantics that your audience understands. Inappropriate terminology and unfamiliar abstract icons and other graphic elements can cloud a user's ability to interact successfully with a software user interface. Figure 9.18 shows a user interface with language that might be foreign to us but includes the known terminology of its intended audience of data modelers. To provide the best design for your audience, you must frame the user interface in the editorial and visual language familiar to them. For example, because it is the actual function, the term "update" could be used in accounting software for the act of writing an invoice to a chart of accounts. However, the term "post" is the most familiar to accountants and reflects the real importance of the action. If an accountant sees the word "post," she understands that term, which more than "update" reinforces the permanence and potential difficulty to make changes to accounting data.

FIGURE 9.18 *A user interface for a contracting application. Specialized audiences may understand it but not the general user.*

User Interface Guideline 6: Explicitly Show Required Actions and Fields (Organizational)

This content-related guideline means that the user should know the required actions on a screen and the required fields for any data entry. This guideline is fairly straightforward: it should be clear and easy for the user to know what is and what is not required to take action on. Knowing required fields is especially a problem on the web, where such fields may be hidden below the fold (the invisible area in a scrolling region). There are four rules for required actions:

1. **Use a consistent convention for indicating a required action**. As part of the broader goal of avoiding user error, making required actions explicit can save users a lot of grief. You can make a required action or input field explicit by locating the action in a prominent place–in or near the screen area and user interface elements on which the actions are being taken. If only one action on the screen is required, make it the default action triggered by the return key. If multiple actions are required, ensure that the actions appear in a prominent location and are clearly identified as required.

2. **Use a consistent convention for indicating a required field**. Users are familiar with seeing the labels of required fields emphasized by a visual indicator, such as an asterisk symbol, emboldening, color coding, or some combination thereof. Figure 9.19 shows a web form where the required fields are clearly marked.

FIGURE 9.19 *A web form clearly marking the labels of required fields with an asterisk.*

2. Register

Please Note * indicates a required field

Arnoshop Login Information

Member Name:*

Password:*

Re-type password:*

E-mail Address:*

Re-type E-mail Address:*

Member Name
• Create a member name
• 3-25 alphanumeric characters long
• May not use special characters or spaces

What is a Password?
• Your secure word used to sign in
• 6-24 alphanumeric characters long
• May not use special characters or spaces

Billing Address

First Name:*

M.I.:*

Last Name:*

Company Name, if applicable:*

Address 1:*   Please include apt. or suite #

Address 2:

City:*

State or Province:*   or Province:

Zip/postal code:*

Country:*

3. **If a required action is not explicit, automate the action by having a default triggered by the return key**. Default actions, such as OK, Submit, and Save, are common to users. The required action's default status is usually reflected through some sort of visual emphasis, as shown in Figure 9.20.

User Interface Guideline 7: User Interfaces Should Reflect International Sensitivity (Organizational)

With more and more software being designed for global audiences, international and regional sensitivity is both an editorial and visual content consideration that needs design attention. To facilitate the translation from one language to another, even in prototypes it is advised to avoid jargon, national idioms, and references that have only a meaning local to the source language but may mean nothing in the target language it's meant to be ultimately translated to.

User Interface Guideline 8: Universal Accessibility (Organizational)

Universal accessibility refers to an application being useful not just for the average user but also for users with disabilities. Many people believe this guideline is the socially responsible thing to do. Often in making software that is targeted for government and nonprofit agencies, their policies require universal accessibility.

FIGURE 9.20 *A screen showing a default action (save) emphasized visually.*

Personally, we take the approach echoed by Gregg Vanderheiden during his closing plenary address to CHI 2001 when he said, "Accessibility is a usability issue because if you make it easy for people who are older or disabled then they are certainly easier for everybody."

User Interface Guideline 9: Users Should Feel in Control (Organizational)

Users need to feel like they can directly control their interaction with software in addition to getting the feedback and responses they expect or anticipate. For example, it is very distressing for users to enter data only to have it disappear or get lost after clicking the Save button. The user immediately feels a loss of control. Even if users have successfully finished a task or activity, they desire an acknowledgment or response that the task or activity was successfully completed, such as a message explicitly saying so or another result indicating so.

User Interface Guideline 10: Minimize User's Memory Load (Organizational)

Every element on the screen adds to the memory load of the user. Every navigational step does as well. How many times have you accomplished a software task and forgotten how you did it? How many times have you been unable to locate a command that is on screen in plain sight? These are two common examples of cognitive overload: there are too many elements competing for the user's attention and short-term memory. As the user tries to make sense of it all, some things get overlooked or trivialized. Reducing cognitive load involves user's perceptions and can be achieved by combining many of the guidelines we've presented above–progressive disclosure, well-organized and categorized screen information and elements, efficiency, and so on.

User Interface Guideline 11: Satisfaction (Organizational)

If it were only enough that everything the user has and needs is readily available, the design job might be quite a bit easier. However, the emotional experience of using software is so powerful it can trigger emotional responses that range from smiles of satisfaction to rage against the machine. As anyone who has ever used an application that behaved badly knows, the application may do it all functionally, but it does it *so painfully*. Complete user satisfaction can only be achieved by a complete understanding of your users. Prototyping is a way to test out your ideas on users. Among other things, it allows you to gauge and measure satisfaction as well as get information needed to prescribe and perform course corrections on your path to achieving a satisfying user experience.

STEP-BY-STEP GUIDELINES

With the above guidelines and advice, you've probably been provided with more design guidelines than you can manage. This three-step guide and accompanying Worksheet 9.1 will help you inventory and manage the guidelines that are specifically relevant to your prototyping activities.

Step 1: Review Guidelines

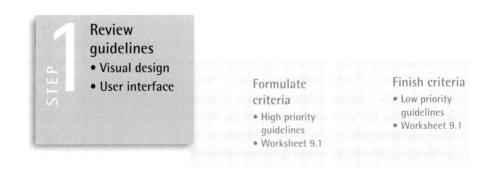

As part of your prototype planning process, the first step is to review all the guidelines (both visual design and user interface) and note the ones you believe are most relevant and important for your design.

Step 2: Formulate Criteria

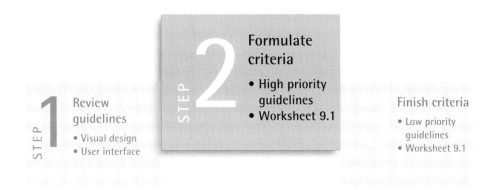

In each category (visual design and user interface) begin to formulate your design criteria by identifying the most relevant and important guidelines in a copy of the worksheet. Now from the list of checked guidelines, determine the most relevant ones from each category then circle them. These should be the ones that you believe you most want to focus on and will lead to a successful prototyping outcome.

Step 3: Finish Criteria

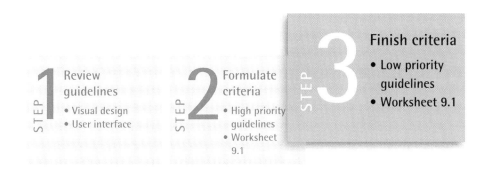

Finalize your criteria definition by prioritizing the remainder of the checked guidelines in each category from 2 to 5. This will provide you direction on which guidelines you'll base your design criteria and rationale on. It will also provide a stake in the ground in regard to socializing and negotiating your design with your stakeholders.

WORKSHEET 9.1: Prioritizing Design Guidelines

Project Name: Author:
Project Date: Internal Ref.:
Product Name: Target Release:
Current Phase:

Guideline			Priority			Justification
Visual Design Guidelines	1	2	3	4	5	
1. Information flow (directional)	1	2	3	4	5	
2. Grid-based organization (organizational)	1	2	3	4	5	
3. Rhythm and pattern (directional)	1	2	3	4	5	
4. Unity and variety (organizational)	1	2	3	4	5	
5. Typographic structure (organizational)	1	2	3	4	5	
6. Balance (directional)	1	2	3	4	5	
7. Logical grouping (organizational)	1	2	3	4	5	
User Interface Guidelines	1	2	3	4	5	
1: Progressive disclosure (directional)	1	2	3	4	5	
2. Efficiency (directional)	1	2	3	4	5	
3. Fitt's Law (directional)	1	2	3	4	5	
4. Learnability (directional)	1	2	3	4	5	
5. Speak the audience's language (organizational)	1	2	3	4	5	
6. Explicitly show required actions and fields (organizational)	1	2	3	4	5	
7. International sensitivity (organizational)	1	2	3	4	5	
8. Universal accessibility (organizational)	1	2	3	4	5	
9. Users should feel in control (organizational)	1	2	3	4	5	
10. Minimize cognitive load (organizational)	1	2	3	4	5	
11. Satisfaction (organizational)	1	2	3	4	5	

THE DESIGN TEAM SELECTS THE DESIGN GUIDELINES

When they were getting ready to create their prototype, Dirk, Ina, and Art wanted to determine the best design guidelines to follow. Because Ina was an expert in Human-Computer Interaction and Art and professional designer, they assured Dirk they could do this. However, the flu was making its rounds in the office and, unfortunately for Dirk, both Ina and Art had to call in sick during the days they were supposed to create the guidelines and get started on the design of the prototype. Left to his own devices, Dirk tried to see if he could expedite things by trying to do some of the design during Ina's and Art's absence.

Using the guided process and the guidelines worksheet, Dirk first marked six visual design guidelines he wanted to follow. This made it difficult for him to develop a screen design due to the contradictory nature of the guidelines that he chose. To simplify (a tendency he commonly has), Dirk reduced the design guidelines to a smaller set he could more easily follow and objectively validate. He chose three he understood best:

1. *Information flow*
2. *Balance*
3. *Efficiency*

Dirk interpreted these as follows:

Information flow: He put the required fields in the upper left corner, the more technically required fields second in the center of the screen, then the optional fields third in the lower right corner, and, finally, the fields that had defaults already assigned to them in the lower left-hand corner.

Balance: He interpreted that he should strive for a symmetric layout, both horizontal and vertical. Or at least come as close to it as he could.

Efficiency: He placed related information together, especially if he thought users might use it frequently. The end result would win no beauty prizes, but it got the idea across.

REFERENCES

Apple Computer. Inside Macintosh: Macintosh Human Interface Guidelines. Boston: Addison-Wesley, 1996.

Jonathan Arnowitz, Michael Arent, Diana Gray, et al. The stakeholder forest. CHI 05 Conference Companion CD-ROM. New York: ACM Press, 2005.

Bill Buxton, R. Sniderman. Iteration in the design of the human-computer interface. Proceedings of the 13th Annual Meeting, Human Factors Association of Canada, 1980, pp. 72–81.

Dempsey Chang, Laurence Dooley, Juhani E. Tuovinen. Gestalt theory in visual screen design—a new look at an old subject. Seventh World Conference on Computers in Education, Copenhagen, July 29–August 3, 2001.

William H Cushman, Daniel J. Rosenberg. Human Factors in Product Design. Amsterdam: Elsevier, 1991.

Donis A. Dondis. A Primer of Visual Literacy. Cambridge, MA: MIT Press, 1973.

Peg Faimon, John Weigand. The Nature of Design: How the Principles of Design Shape Our World—From Graphics and Architecture to Interiors and Products. Cincinnati: F + W Publications, 2004.

James Felici. The Complete Manual of Typography. Berkeley, CA: Peach Pit Press, 2003.

Allen Hurlburt. The Grid: A Modular System for the Design and Production of Newspapers, Magazines and Books. New York: Wiley, 1978.

Robert Mack, Jakob Neilsen. Usability Inspection Methods. New York: Wiley, 1994.

Scott MacKenzie, R. William Soukoreff. Card, English, and Burr (1978)—25 years later. Extended Abstracts of the ACM Conference on Human Factors in Computing Systems—CHI 2003. New York: ACM Press, 2003, pp. 760–761.

Bruce Tognazzini. First principles of interaction design. http://www.asktog.com/basics/firstPrinciples.html. Accessed June 17, 2005.

Jan Tschichold. The New Typography. Translated by Ruari MacLean. Berkeley, CA: University of California Books, 1998.

Catherine Courage, Kathy Baxter. Understanding Your Users. A Practical Guide to User Requirements Methods, Tools, and Techniques. The Morgan Kaufmann Series in Interactive Technologies. Amsterdam: Elsevier/Morgan Kaufmann, 2004.

JoAnn T. Hackos, Janice C. Redish. User and Task Analysis for Interface Design. Hoboken, NJ: Wiley, 1998.

Deborah Mayhew. Usability Engineering Lifecycle. New York: Morgan Kaufman, 1998

Alex White. The Elements of Graphic Design. New York: Allworth Press, 2002.

Jan V. White. Graphic Design for the Electronic Age. Oxford: Xerox Press Books, 1988.

CHAPTER

The Effective Prototyping Process

PHASE **1** Plan

PHASE **2** Specification

PHASE **3** Design

PHASE **4** Results

STEP **1**   ch 3   Verify Requirements

STEP **2**   ch 4   Develop Task Flows

STEP **3**   ch 5   Define Content and Fidelity

STEP **4**   ch 6   Determine Characteristics

STEP **5**   ch 7   Choose a Method

STEP **6**   ch 8   Choose a Tool

STEP **7**   ch 9   Select Design Criteria

STEP **8**   ch 10   **Create the Design**

STEP **9**   ch 11   Review the Design

STEP **10**   ch 12   Validate the Design

STEP **11**   ch 13   Deploy the Design

10

CREATE THE DESIGN

INTRODUCTION

Step 7 covered establishing design criteria to guide you in the creation of the prototype. Now, in Step 8, you take the identified and inventoried requirements, the chosen method, and the selected tool and create the prototype by using the design criteria selected in Step 7. This is the step where everything converges. To take a moment to review the design process up to this point as well as what will follow, see the sidebar on the holistic design process below. In general, Step 7 is about the process for selecting a design rationale. This step is then applying this design rationale to the prototyping content and putting it all together in a single design. After you finish this step, you'll have a prototype. After this step, you'll be able to review, validate, and iterate or implement your design.

REVIEW: THE DESIGN PROCESS

A HOLISTIC APPROACH TO DESIGNING AND BUILDING A PROTOTYPE

An effective prototype aims to achieve the right level of specificity and correctly set the audience's expectations. With the pre-work of the first seven steps, assembling an effective and relevant prototype should now be relatively easy or at least a lot easier than starting to prototype without any direction. At this point, your prototype shouldn't be shrouded in the darkness of intuition and gut feeling but exposed as a managed set of tractable requirements, content, screen layouts, and flow that will be portrayed using the most appropriate method and tool. As Bill Buxton's quote states at the beginning of this phase, we should have reduced the problem space into an ordered set of manageable subproblems. Creating a prototype can be thought of as a holistic process involving the following steps:

1. Verify requirements (Chapter 3).
2. Develop task and interaction flows (Chapter 4).

3. Determine scenario (Chapter 4).

4. Define prototype components and content (Chapter 5).

5. Gather necessary content (Chapters 4 and 5).

6. Define the design criteria (Chapter 9).

7. Design and construct your prototype (this chapter).

8. Review prototype (Chapter 11).

9. Validate prototype usability (Chapter 12).

10. Transition from prototyping to implementation (Chapter 13).

Verify Requirements

Before creating a prototype, you must first engage the team in reviewing the assumptions and requirements you intend to operate on, including business/marketing, usability, functional, and technical. The review determines whether you need more requirements or need to more explicitly define existing requirements before building the prototype. The review is also an effective tool for ensuring that the entire design team is working under the same assumptions.

Develop Task and Interaction Flows

A successful prototype not only needs to be driven by validated requirements and well-understood assumptions but also needs to be informed by task and interaction flows. Task flows result from user research, including site visits, task analysis, and domain expert knowledge. Task flows of business processes, navigation, commerce transactions, and other processes can be mapped to specific application flow. Then these flows, via scenarios, can be applied to a specific instance to understand users' environments, such as interaction with systems and other people in work, entertainment, or social activities involving software. These activities can be shown in "swim lane" diagrams.

Later, a designer can take the knowledge and task mappings acquired from task analysis and task flow diagrams and turn them into interaction flows. These interaction flows map user interactions to tasks performed in their jobs, games played, online shopping, completing and filing tax returns, and the myriad of other things people can do with software-based systems. This information becomes the basis for the design concept that appears in your prototype.

Determine Scenario

Next, you convert the task and interaction mappings into a scenario–a narrative story that describes what a user (or collaborative group of users) will do with the software. Scenarios concentrate design efforts on usability requirements and user needs. Unlike use cases, scenarios describe user interactions with software in a non-technical way, often in the form of a day-in-the-life narrative. Scenarios are often portrayed in the form of storyboards, an early form of prototyping that allows an audience, including the design team, to get an initial impression of a software design concept before committing to more elaborate representations. Scenarios also help designers develop meaningful design rationales and are important in helping designers formulate paper and digital interactive prototypes.

Define Prototype Components and Content

Not everything can be prototyped. The design team must decide which components and content achieve the prototyping goal and include them. Scenarios are an important tool in defining the content and component parts of a prototype, such as the actions users need to perform and the content needed to support those actions and interactions.

Gather Necessary Content

Once a software design concept is portrayed in a scenario or storyboard, designers can better understand the content needed to populate the software. Depending on the software concept, content can range from utilitarian forms and tables to multimedia. A software design's concept and content are often determining factors (among others presented in this book) about the kind of prototypes that will be further needed to ultimately allow designers and developers to accurately specify the software while balancing all the needs, assumptions, and requirements.

Define the Design Criteria

Design criteria include both visual design and user interface design and are used to focus a prototype's design on specific user needs. For optimal usability, design criteria should be based on users' mental models; however, it is worth noting that these criteria alone will not improve the usability of the product but rather the usability of the prototype. Visual design criteria are broken into two complementary subtypes: organizational (used for arranging screen elements logically) and directional (guiding page layout and element sequencing on a page).

Design and Construct Your Prototype

These steps for designing and building a prototype help you evolve the design concept and rationale, develop design patterns and guidelines through iterations, and then converge on a design solution and a set of design specifications:

➤ Determine the highest priority screens

➤ Block out the most important regions of your screen

➤ Layout the highest priority screen with the required elements

➤ Layout remaining high priority screens

➤ Specify each screen, overall interaction flow, and screen elements with a design rationale

Review Prototype (Internal Design Review)

After the prototype is created, a software-making team often plans an internal review to receive peer and management feedback regarding the conceptual direction portrayed by the prototype. Because of changing needs in the software making process, different prototypes need different review techniques, specific to the stage in the prototyping process.

Validate Prototype Usability (Get Valuable Feedback From Users)

Specific to prototyping during the design phase of a software product or service, design validation through usability testing or focus group sessions allows a product team to realize not only the value of the effort spent on prototyping but the value of iterative improvement and refinement as well.

This validation also allows designers to determine whether the usability and marketing or business requirements are being met. If not, a plan for iterative cycles of improvement can be developed. This iteration can be completed for both a given product release and ongoing product releases. Planning and conducting iterative cycles of prototyping and validation sessions is a strategic activity dependent on the timelines and milestones of software release cycles in conjunction with the availability of resources.

Transition From Prototyping to Implementation

Once a prototype is completed, it can be taken in a number of directions, the primary direction being validation and then iteration. At some point, however, a software-making team must move toward implementation of its design at which time the prototype can have enormous value as a component of the design specification–especially a high-fidelity prototype, which embodies the details of visual appearance in addition to interaction behavior. In fact, in some cases, a high-fidelity coded prototype can be directly transformed into a design implementation. Prototyping can also be used as a means to resolve issues that surface during implementation, such as trying to develop a work-around design solution for issues that result from technical roadblocks.

DESIGN AND CONSTRUCT YOUR PROTOTYPE

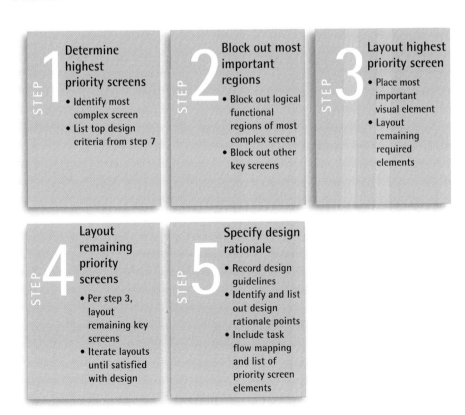

STEP 1 Determine highest priority screens
- Identify most complex screen
- List top design criteria from step 7

STEP 2 Block out most important regions
- Block out logical functional regions of most complex screen
- Block out other key screens

STEP 3 Layout highest priority screen
- Place most important visual element
- Layout remaining required elements

STEP 4 Layout remaining priority screens
- Per step 3, layout remaining key screens
- Iterate layouts until satisfied with design

STEP 5 Specify design rationale
- Record design guidelines
- Identify and list out design rationale points
- Include task flow mapping and list of priority screen elements

The prototype design and construction process is a convergence of all the work completed thus far. For example, this guide involves identifying the high-priority screens, a natural outcome of your requirements activities. Then, you will use the requirements and design criteria in addition to the content and audience definition to proceed with the rest of the design. All the while you will be using the method and tools that you chose earlier.

Step 1: Determine Highest Priority Screens

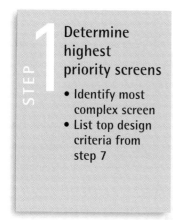

STEP 1

Determine highest priority screens

- Identify most complex screen
- List top design criteria from step 7

Block out most important regions

- Block out logical functional regions of most complex screen
- Block out other key screens

Layout highest priority screen

- Place most important visual element
- Layout remaining required elements

Layout remaining priority screens

- Per step 3, layout remaining key screens
- Iterate layouts until satisfied with design

Specify design rationale

- Record design guidelines
- Identify and list out design rationale points
- Include task flow mapping and list of priority screen elements

Based on the task flow that you mapped and the scenario that you developed, determine your high-priority screens–those that must be created for the prototype to make sense. From your high-priority screens, determine the most complex and challenging screen. Then, on a white board (or some other medium), list all the elements that will be included on this screen (Figure 10.1). Now, list the top priority visual design and user interface design criteria you've chosen. For added emphasis, it is often helpful to literally list them out on a sheet of paper. These criteria should aid you in initially blocking out your prototype screens.

FIGURE 10.1 *List of screen items on the flip chart and design criteria on the whiteboard.*

FIGURE 10.1 *List of screen items on the flip chart and design criteria on the whiteboard.*

Step 2: Blockout most Important Regions

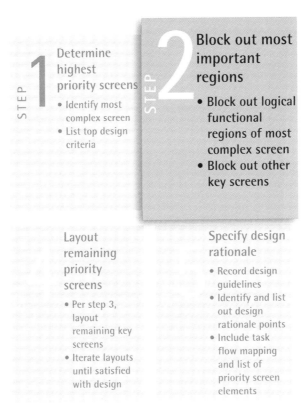

STEP 1 — Determine highest priority screens
- Identify most complex screen
- List top design criteria

STEP 2 — Block out most important regions
- Block out logical functional regions of most complex screen
- Block out other key screens

Layout highest priority screen
- Place most important visual element
- Layout remaining required elements

Layout remaining priority screens
- Per step 3, layout remaining key screens
- Iterate layouts until satisfied with design

Specify design rationale
- Record design guidelines
- Identify and list out design rationale points
- Include task flow mapping and list of priority screen elements

Create a blank area in your chosen prototyping tool for each high-priority screen you've identified. Starting with the most complex screen, try to roughly block the screen into logical functional regions, such as a branding region, header region, and navigation menu region. You can then continue to block out the remaining high-priority screens using your first screen as a guide or template. Once you've blocked out each of the screens needed for your prototype, you should be able to see a somewhat consistent design pattern emerging; it may help to display the screens in storyboard style or as a paper sequence taped to a wall. For example, in an e-commerce transaction scenario, you may decide the top part of your screens should be used for navigation and the middle region should display the most important data for the end user—the item the user wants to buy (Figure 10.2). The bottom region of the screen should show related subordinate information, such as descriptive information and secondary navigation links.

FIGURE 10.2 *Highest priority screens for an e-commerce transaction scenario roughly blocked out into functional regions.*

Step 3: Layout Highest Priority Screen

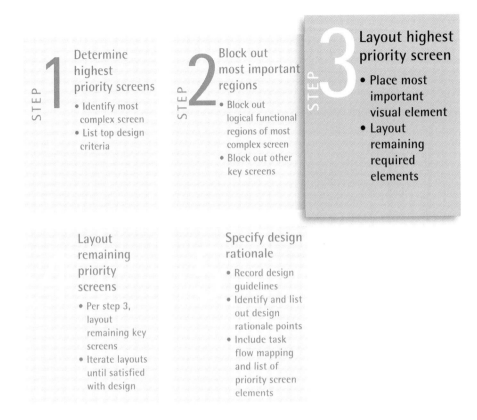

STEP 1

Determine highest priority screens

- Identify most complex screen
- List top design criteria

STEP 2

Block out most important regions

- Block out logical functional regions of most complex screen
- Block out other key screens

STEP 3

Layout highest priority screen

- **Place most important visual element**
- **Layout remaining required elements**

Layout remaining priority screens

- Per step 3, layout remaining key screens
- Iterate layouts until satisfied with design

Specify design rationale

- Record design guidelines
- Identify and list out design rationale points
- Include task flow mapping and list of priority screen elements

Now that you've roughly blocked the highest priority screens into functional regions, you can add more detailed content to the most representative screen of the prototype. First, create a visual representation of the most important, or most logical, element according to your design criteria. The functional screen regions designated in the prior step can act as a placement and alignment grid for the more detailed graphic user interface elements. Using the e-commerce transaction example, you would skip navigation for now to concentrate on the purchase item and related items that are added to the middle functional region, which resembles Figure 10.2 at the start of this step and Figure 10.3 when this step is completed.

After you add detail to the highest priority screen, you'll notice progress but are not completely satisfied with the overall design. Using the visual design criterion of unity, you realize that you can rearrange similar elements in the middle and upper right corner of the screen to get a more unified layout, as shown in Figure 10.4.

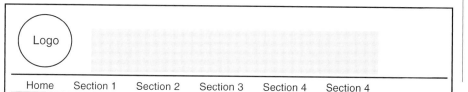

Home Section 1 Section 2 Section 3 Section 4 Section 4

STATEMENT OF QUALITY

Section Header Date 00/00/0000

Header

Lorem ipsum dolor sit amet, in ultricies felis non nibh. Ante in at, vitae ante, ante ipsum leo libero diam lorem,

Hic elementum molestie donec eget integer, donec sapien. Nunc nunc sodales. Justo pellentesque ipsum lacus quisquam, suspendisse leo nunc a mattis adipiscing, a nunc aliquam et nibh bibendum orci. Per leo. Ut ultrices metus, cras non in eu, nulla

Lead Illustration

More Info
• libero diam lorem, vel sem.
• libero diam lorem, vel sem.
• libero diam lorem, vel sem.
• libero diam lorem, vel sem.

Header

Lorem ipsum dolor sit amet, in ultricies felis non nibh. Ante in at, vitae ante, ante ipsum leo libero diam lorem, vel sem. Hic elementum molestie donec eget integer, donec sapien. Nunc nunc sodales. Justo pellentesque ipsum lacus quisquam,

Sub-Section Header

Lorem ipsum dolor sit amet, in ultricies felis non nibh. Ante in at, vitae ante, ante ipsum leo libero diam lorem, vel sem. Hic elementum molestie donec eget integer, donec sapien. Nunc nunc sodales. Justo pellentesque

Top Stories

• libero diam lorem, vel sem.
• libero diam lorem, vel sem.
• libero diam lorem, vel sem.
• libero diam lorem, vel sem.
• libero diam lorem, vel sem.
• libero diam lorem, vel sem.
• libero diam lorem, vel sem.
• libero diam lorem, vel sem.

FIGURE 10.3 *Iterative layout of more detailed content elements screen.*

Logo

Home Section 1 Section 2 Section 3 Section 4 Section 4

STATEMENT OF QUALITY   Date 00/00/0000

Section Header

Lead Illustration

Header

Lorem ipsum dolor sit amet, in ultricies felis non nibh. Ante in at, vitae ante, ante ipsum leo libero diam lorem,
. Hic elementum molestie

donec eget integer, donec sapien. Nunc nunc sodales. Justo pellentesque ipsum lacus quisquam, suspendisse leo nunc a mattis adipiscing, a nunc aliquam et nibh bibendum orci. Per leo. Ut ultrices metus, cras non in eu, nulla sem suscipit nullam

Header

Lorem ipsum dolor sit amet, in ultricies felis non nibh. Ante in at, vitae ante, ante ipsum leo libero diam lorem, vel sem. Hic elementum molestie donec eget integer, donec sapien. Nunc nunc sodales. Justo pellentesque ipsum lacus quisquam, suspendisse leo

Top Stories

• libero diam lorem, vel sem.
• libero diam lorem, vel sem.
• libero diam lorem, vel sem.
• libero diam lorem, vel sem.
• libero diam lorem, vel sem.
• libero diam lorem, vel sem.
• libero diam lorem, vel sem.
• libero diam lorem, vel sem.

Sub-Section Header

Lorem ipsum dolor sit amet, in ultricies felis non nibh. Ante in at, vitae ante, ante ipsum leo libero diam lorem, vel sem. Hic elementum molestie donec eget integer, donec sapien. Nunc nunc sodales. Justo pellentesque

More Info
• libero diam lorem, vel sem.
• libero diam lorem, vel sem.
• libero diam lorem, vel sem.
• libero diam lorem, vel sem.

FIGURE 10.4 *Iterative layout for an e-commerce transaction screen in which the detailed content elements appear more unified: headers are not aligned, and the screen is also more clearly divided into sections that align both vertically and horizontally.*

Step 4: Layout Remaining Priority Screens

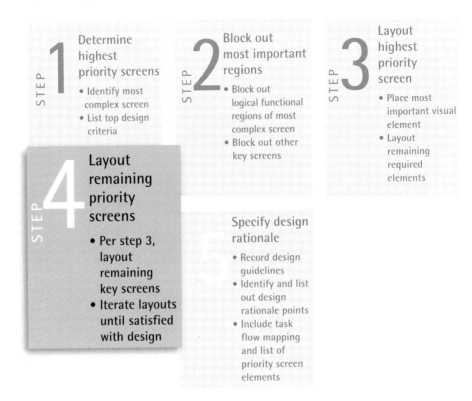

STEP 1

Determine highest priority screens
- Identify most complex screen
- List top design criteria

STEP 2

Block out most important regions
- Block out logical functional regions of most complex screen
- Block out other key screens

STEP 3

Layout highest priority screen
- Place most important visual element
- Layout remaining required elements

STEP 4

Layout remaining priority screens
- Per step 3, layout remaining key screens
- Iterate layouts until satisfied with design

Specify design rationale
- Record design guidelines
- Identify and list out design rationale points
- Include task flow mapping and list of priority screen elements

Before completing the highest priority screen in too much detail, you should begin adding detail to the other high-priority screens. As a starting point, you can continue to use the blocked out functional regions and the detailed elements of the highest priority screen.

Often, during this part of the process designers begin exploring refined layout patterns they prefer, resulting in some back and forth design among the screens to make improvements. As design refinements are created, existing designs are continually updated. As a satisfying screen layout pattern begins to emerge, iterative refinements become easier to make. Usually, by the time a designer has laid out three or four variations, it becomes easy to settle on a general design concept.

Step 5: Specify Design Rationale

STEP 1 Determine highest priority screens
- Identify most complex screen
- List top design criteria

STEP 2 Block out most important regions
- Block out logical functional regions of most complex screen
- Block out other key screens

STEP 3 Layout highest priority screen
- Place most important visual element
- Layout remaining required elements

STEP 4 Layout remaining priority screens
- Per step 3, layout remaining key screens
- Iterate layouts until satisfied with design

STEP 5 Specify design rationale
- Record design guidelines
- Identify and list out design rationale points
- Include task flow mapping and list of priority screen elements

After a prototype version is completed but before you pass it on to other stakeholders, you want to establish a clear logical (bullet-proof) design rationale based on the prototype goals; the business, functional, technical, and usability requirements applied to the prototype; and the design criteria. The rationale ensures you've met the objectives of your design and is used to set audience expectations regarding your design decisions. Setting clear expectations will help you to avoid most opinion battles that are inevitable when presenting a design–especially to strongly opinionated heavily invested stakeholders. Whenever someone suggests design changes to your prototype, such as a color, typographic treatment, interaction widgets, layout, and other factors, you can refer back to the adopted design rationale as a basis for consideration and negotiation.

To create a tangible record of the design rationale, use annotations to mark up the prototype. Refer directly to the design guidelines, requirements, criteria, and so on applied to the prototype and then explain why certain design aspects take precedence over others, such as considerations for page flow and scanning direction having priority over the visualization of brand. Include the task flow map/specification and list of priority screen elements in the documentation. These materials all play an important role in explaining the design and the outcome of the prototype.

SUMMARY

Using your preferred (or at least available) prototyping tool, you've now laid out your screens and the graphic user interface elements in a transaction or interaction sequence according to the requirements, scenario, design criteria, and guidelines. Using these design factors, the task flow, and the prioritized user interface elements, you've now established a design rationale to share with your audience, including stakeholders. Your design will not look and feel arbitrary, because you have sound reasons for your design decisions and you're ready to show the prototype to your target audience. You've created an effective prototype!

ARNOSOFT CREATES A PROTOTYPE

Dirk decided to design the highest priority screen in three passes but later realized he only needed two. With the first pass he followed the information flow guideline, placing the fields absolutely requiring user input in the upper left corner. Next, in the lower left corner, he placed the required fields for which a default could be identified so the user would not need to input them except in exceptional circumstances. This placement of field groupings resulted in this screen layout.

In the second screen design pass, Dirk tried to balance the rather lopsided groupings. Not knowing quite what to move where, he decided to use the efficiency measure, moving related fields next to each other. The screen started to balance out and look much better. When Ina returned from a sick day and Art from personal time off, they decided that even though the design was not ideal, it was good enough for the storyboard, so they moved on to other screens and decided to address this highest priority screen again in a later prototype.

Registration

Member Name:*

Password:*

Re-type password:*

What is a Password?
- Your secure word used to sign in
- 6–24 alphanumeric charcters long
- May not use special characters or spaces

E-mail Address:

Re-type E-mail Address:*

First Name:*

M.I.:*

Last Name:*

Member Name
- Create a member name that will be used for the Arnosoft Internet sites.
- 3–25 alphanumeric charcters long
- May not use special characters or spaces

Company Name, if applicable:*

Address 1:*

Address 2:

City:*

State or Province:*

Zip/postal code:*

Country:*

Registration

Member Name:*

Password:*

Re-type password:*

E-mail Address:*

Re-type E-mail Address:*

Member Name
- Create a member name that will be used for the Arnosoft Internet sites.
- 3–25 alphanumeric charcters long
- May not use special characters or spaces

What is a Password?
- Your secure alphanumeric entry used to sign in
- 6–24 alphanumeric charcters long
- May not use special characters or spaces

First Name:*

M.I.:*

Last Name:*

Company Name, if applicable:*

Address 1:*

Please include apt. or suite #

Address 2:

City:*

State or Province:*   ⌄ or Province:

Zip/postal code:*

Country:*   ⌄

PHASE

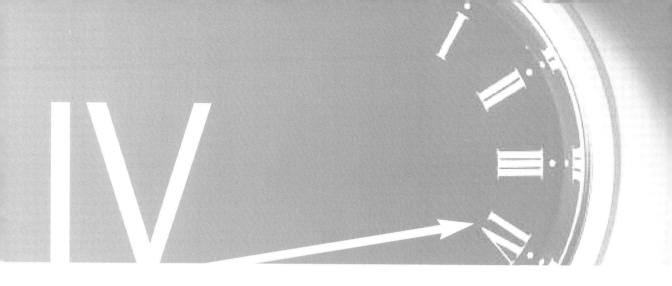

RESULTS OF PROTOTYPING

Welcome to the last phase of effective prototyping–the results of prototyping. This is what we've covered so far. In Phase I we focused on the steps needed to plan the prototyping process: the requirements (Step 1), the task flows (Step 2), and the intended content (Step 3). With the planning, you acquired a more sophisticated understanding of what will be prototyped and what is better left for later phases in the software-making process. In Phase II we determined the specifications needed for creating a prototype design (steps 4, 5, and 6). With Phase III we outlined the design of the prototype and how to create it using design principles (steps 7 and 8). In Phase IV we'll present the prototype to an internal audience (Step 9), validate the prototype with external audiences (Step 10), and proceed to next steps–implementation and iteration (Step 11).

CHAPTER

The Effective Prototyping Process

PHASE 1 — Plan

PHASE 2 — Specification

PHASE 3 — Design

PHASE 4 — Results

STEP 1 — ch 3 — Verify Requirements

STEP 2 — ch 4 — Develop Task Flows

STEP 3 — ch 5 — Define Content and Fidelity

STEP 4 — ch 6 — Determine Characteristics

STEP 5 — ch 7 — Choose a Method

STEP 6 — ch 8 — Choose a Tool

STEP 7 — ch 9 — Select Design Criteria

STEP 8 — ch 10 — Create the Design

STEP 9 — ch 11 — Review the Design

STEP 10 — ch 12 — Validate the Design

STEP 11 — ch 13 — Deploy the Design

11

REVIEW THE DESIGN: THE INTERNAL REVIEW

After you have finished an iteration of the prototype, you're ready for Step 9—the design review with your team and other internal stakeholders, including project management and development. This is the step where you internally review your work before committing to a formal validation with a broader and usually more external audience. What does the design review process look like? This can be as varied as there are practitioners. In our experience, though, the most successful review processes include the following activities:

- ➤ Define your audience
- ➤ Set goals for each version of the prototype to be reviewed
- ➤ What should reviewers expect?
- ➤ What stage in software creation process?
- ➤ What level of design finish?
- ➤ What degree of content completion?
- ➤ Decide on the presentation method (PowerPoint slides, interactive walk-through, etc.)
- ➤ Plan the next steps

MANAGER'S CORNER

Issue Management: remaining on the same page

One weakness with relying on a prototype to represent a design is the fact that it's not a static document. When changes are made, it is often difficult to track who decided on the changes, and who did what and why. The most effective solution we've encountered is to have a list of trackable and auditable issues. Fortunately, most software companies already have systems for tracking and auditing changes, such as change management processes and bug tracking. We advocate using these systems to assure quality throughout the design and implementation process. If these processes are broken at your company, we would recommend using an informal issue tracking process, such as recording the issues in a spreadsheet that is supported by an internal review and quality assurance process.

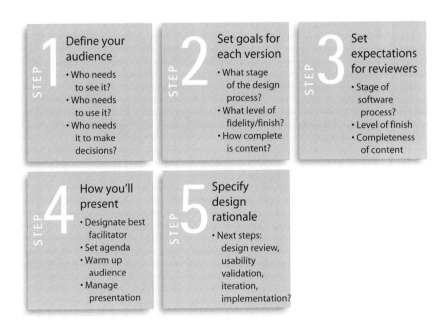

Step 1: Review your Defined Audience

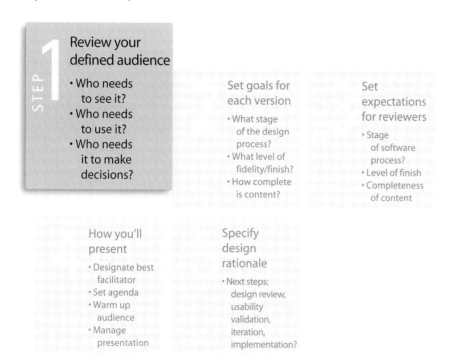

STEP 1

Review your defined audience

- Who needs to see it?
- Who needs to use it?
- Who needs it to make decisions?

Set goals for each version

- What stage of the design process?
- What level of fidelity/finish?
- How complete is content?

Set expectations for reviewers

- Stage of software process?
- Level of finish
- Completeness of content

How you'll present

- Designate best facilitator
- Set agenda
- Warm up audience
- Manage presentation

Specify design rationale

- Next steps: design review, usability validation, iteration, implementation?

The audience involved in a design review is the audience you have defined in Step 4 in Worksheet 6.1. Now that you've gone through design and prototyping activities you may need to make some adjustments to your audience definition based on any additions or changes to stakeholders or participants not originally foreseen. For example, if the CEO decides on an impromptu participation in your review, you may want to include more background in your review meeting or refine the content.

Step 2: Set Goals for Each Version

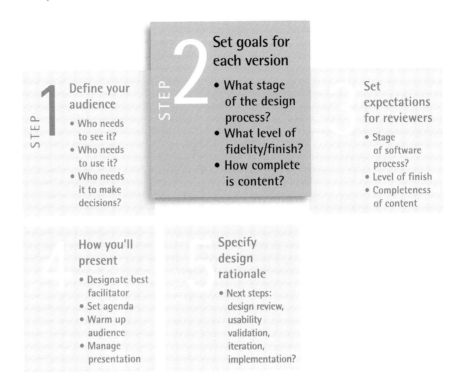

STEP 1 — Define your audience
- Who needs to see it?
- Who needs to use it?
- Who needs it to make decisions?

STEP 2 — Set goals for each version
- What stage of the design process?
- What level of fidelity/finish?
- How complete is content?

Set expectations for reviewers
- Stage of software process?
- Level of finish
- Completeness of content

How you'll present
- Designate best facilitator
- Set agenda
- Warm up audience
- Manage presentation

Specify design rationale
- Next steps: design review, usability validation, iteration, implementation?

Reiterate the goals for this version of your prototype to help communicate the purpose to the audience and stakeholders. You should be able to state the goals using the requirements and assumptions specified in Step 1 of the effective prototyping process. Remember, prototype goals differ depending on the current stage of the design process. For example, if you are trying to roughly visualize a software flow concept or the fit of information and widgets onto a screen, mention those as goals and show their relationship to the overall requirements and assumptions. If you are trying to envision how an e-commerce transaction behaves on a shopping site or how a new branding scheme looks on a brochure site, state those goals. The goal statement also helps to defer other tangential requirements coincidentally visualized in the prototype.

Step 3: Set Expectations for Reviewers

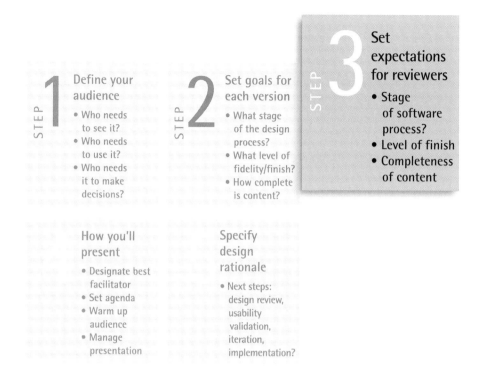

STEP 1 Define your audience
- Who needs to see it?
- Who needs to use it?
- Who needs it to make decisions?

STEP 2 Set goals for each version
- What stage of the design process?
- What level of fidelity/finish?
- How complete is content?

STEP 3 Set expectations for reviewers
- Stage of software process?
- Level of finish
- Completeness of content

How you'll present
- Designate best facilitator
- Set agenda
- Warm up audience
- Manage presentation

Specify design rationale
- Next steps: design review, usability validation, iteration, implementation?

Regardless of how the prototype is disclosed to target stakeholders, you should first articulate the effective prototyping process you've undertaken. This articulation ensures that people are informed enough to have reasonable expectations and also learn the value of effective prototyping.

After defining the audience and goals, you need to prepare the prototype reviewers. This preparation should consist of outlining information to set reviewer expectations and successfully communicate the defined goals. Furthermore, you should articulate how you reached those goals and created an appropriate prototype. Relevant information includes defining the current stage of the software creation process, the level of finish of the prototype, and the completeness of prototype content.

Communicate What You Are Doing

Communicating your goals and process, especially meeting with stakeholders in advance of prototype completion, can help set expectations. If your audience disagrees with your approach and is given no explanation for your methods, a debate will most likely ensue, leading to a negative review for all involved. Outline the prototyping strategy in advance and be clear about desired outcomes. The outline should match the scale of the review and the people in it. For example, in an informal review you can simply verbalize your ideas while sketching them on a white board, whereas a more formal presentation will introduce the expectations in depth and detail, possibly using visuals or official documentation. Depending on what type of information your audience will understand you may want to include the following points (even if you don't cover all this in your introduction, it is good information to have ready for discussion):

1. **Company's software creation process**. Setting the stage in the framework of your company's software process provides an important initial basis for review; stakeholders respond better when they believe you've considered the desires and plans of the company. First, set the prototype context within the grand plan of your company's software creation process and clearly communicate what you hope to learn from the prototype relative to the software creation process. This explanation provides context for the effective prototyping process as well as the role that the prototype plays. Include next steps as they relate to your company's product creation, iteration, and development process. If your company does not have a clearly defined software creation and release process, you can use any terms or concepts that your stakeholders will relate to.

2. **Background of the prototype**. After describing the goals, begin sketching out the prototype creation activities. What were the events that led to its creation? For example, if you are mocking up mobile software for contact handling, it's important to know that the prototype is driven by a marketplace need to handle contacts or from an engineering need to update the current product's performance.

3. **Characteristics of the prototype**. Listing the prototype characteristics (see Chapter 6) that influenced the prototype creation process makes certain aspects of the prototype and its design explicit. For example, if you assumed only an internal audience and a narrative presentation, you focused on keeping user-centered design and interaction design issues off the table. That is, a narrative prototype shows limited interactivity and an internal audience, who defines that user profiles, scenarios, and so forth are only assumptions because requirements are either unknown or not reflected in the prototype.

4. **Method you used and why**. Next, explain the prototyping method you're using along with its advantages and disadvantages. Reproducing an entire chapter from this book would be overkill; however, mentioning the salient points of the chosen method informs the audience of the rationale behind the selection. The thoroughness described above serves the immediate need of presenting the prototype.

5. **Expected outcome of the prototype**. The last step for expectation setting is describing the expected outcome of the prototype. You can list the elements you intend to include in the prototype as well as those that are out of scope. This list of elements should be presented as explicitly as possible to avoid confusion. For

example, to keep certain visual and technical design questions at bay, you may want to say up front that the visuals are low priority and low fidelity and that search is not being considered but error handling is.

Step 4: How You'll Present

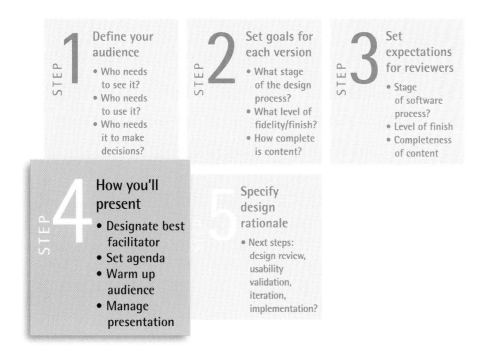

STEP 1 — Define your audience
- Who needs to see it?
- Who needs to use it?
- Who needs it to make decisions?

STEP 2 — Set goals for each version
- What stage of the design process?
- What level of fidelity/finish?
- How complete is content?

STEP 3 — Set expectations for reviewers
- Stage of software process?
- Level of finish
- Completeness of content

STEP 4 — How you'll present
- Designate best facilitator
- Set agenda
- Warm up audience
- Manage presentation

STEP 5 — Specify design rationale
- Next steps: design review, usability validation, iteration, implementation?

Now that you have expectations properly set, you are ready to disclose the prototype, which can be done in many ways, such as one-on-one discussions, conference meetings, and focus groups. But for our purposes we want to discuss the two most salient effective disclosure methods: distribution and presentation. Distribution refers to how the prototype is sent to others and accessed by them, such as via e-mail, the World Wide Web, shared server, or other means where you're not in control of user receipt to respond to any reactions. By presentation, we mean the method you use to present information to a group (either in the same room or in other geographic locations). This discussion here on disclosure does not include presentation or distribution for the purpose of validating usability (e.g., presentation to targeted users via usability testing). That topic is covered in Chapter 12.

The presentation, whether a group meeting, a brainstorming session, or a focus group, is not necessarily a slam-dunk, even considering all the care and thought that went into creating the prototype and setting expectations. A poorly planned and badly handled presentation can undo much of the good work you've accomplished to date. Expectations, once set, need to be managed, and a focus on the prototype goal needs to be maintained. However, you must also continue to foster a collaborative atmosphere; shutting participants down in the discussion and feedback process will only have a chilling effect. For a comprehensive look at effective meeting facilitation, we suggest you look at Osborn [1963] or Paulus and Nijstad [2003]. The following tips and tricks can be used to make your prototype come across more effectively.

What Makes a Good Facilitator?

In presenting, a key success factor is knowing your strengths and weaknesses. If you are not a good meeting facilitator, then find a colleague who is good, someone who conducts meetings that people like to attend. Having a colleague facilitate the meeting allows you to concentrate on the prototype presentation points without the distractions of facilitation. An impartial facilitator is also better at focusing the discussion or debate and moving the meeting beyond tangential conversations.

Setting an Agenda

Specify the agenda and send it out before the meeting, including, for example, the following points:

1. *Introductions*—If some people in the audience don't know each other, have a short round of introductions where each person states their name, role, and interest in the prototype. This might provide you with a preview of audience responses to the presentation.
2. *Background*—Briefly review the communication and expectation setting information created above.
3. *An useful prop*—Write the goals on a whiteboard or flip chart and leave them in plain sight throughout the meeting. If the meeting veers off topic, the facilitator has a readily accessible tool to restore order and focus.
4. *Requirements and assumptions*—Distribute a handout of requirements and assumptions addressed in the prototype. This list can help focus discussion around the purpose of the prototype.
5. *Scenario*—Present a scenario (one with a real name for the user) that depicts prototype usage
6. *Presentation*—Use one or a combination of the following:
   a. Present your design rationale in a handout, which usually generates a lively discussion of the requirements and assumptions used.
   b. Talk the audience through the scenario while showing the user actions depicted in the prototype. To reinforce context, include the user's name: for example, "Now Marcy clicks the look up button and selects her choice of credit card."
7. *Open forum*—Have an open question and answer period.
8. *Next steps*—To inform the next stages of the software creation process, get a list of action items from the key stakeholders.

FIGURE 11.1 *Presenting a storyboard prototype to stakeholders.*

FIGURE 11.2 *A good presentation elicits feedback that makes all issues as immediately apparent as possible.*

FIGURE 11.3 *Before presenting the actual prototype, first provide context through information such as user profiles and salient user research data.*

FIGURE 11.4 *In a good presentation, the design rationale and guidelines should be explicit so that they can be discussed at a high enough level to avoid taste wars and maintain focus on the design.*

Step 5: Planning the Next Steps

STEP 1 | **Define your audience**
• Who needs to see it?
• Who needs to use it?
• Who needs it to make decisions?

STEP 2 | **Set goals for each version**
• What stage of the design process?
• What level of fidelity/finish?
• How complete is content?

STEP 3 | **Set expectations for reviewers**
• Stage of software process?
• Level of finish
• Completeness of content

STEP 4 | **How you'll present**
• Designate best facilitator
• Set agenda
• Warm up audience
• Manage presentation

STEP 5 | **Planning Next Steps**
• Next steps: design review, usability validation, iteration, implementation?

Just as important as it is to know the background of a prototype, it is also important to share the next steps once a prototype version is completed. What actions need to be taken?

➤ Design review
➤ Usability validation
➤ Iteration
➤ Implementation

If the next steps are unknown, be explicit about the lack of direction and make it an agenda item for the meeting. Typically, unknown next steps occur in a software creation process or concept that has never been tried before, so don't worry if you don't have a plan; just be prepared to discuss future directions.

SUMMARY

Setting reviewer expectations is important for effective prototyping. Short of giving everyone a copy of this book, you will need to do some educating by informing the audience of the prototyping objectives and criteria chosen as well as the characteristics and methods. After setting expectations, choosing the right disclosure method ensures that recipients get the prototype in a useful form for evaluation. The prototype can then be disclosed without fear that it will be taken out of context by most viewers. Those who do misinterpret the prototype or misunderstand the expectations can be managed because you have prepared for them by outlining the prototype audience, goal, and design rationale. The results of the prototype disclosure are a new set of instructions to validate and iterate the prototype–the next step of the prototype process.

ARNOSOFT CONDUCTS AN INTERNAL REVIEW OF THE PROTOTYPE

Dirk, Ina, and Art completed the storyboard. In preparation for the final presentation, they decided that the storyboard needed to look flashy, which is where the advanced graphics capabilities of KeyNote came in handy. Dirk and Ina let Art take the lead in packaging the final production: adding animated slide transitions, appropriate music, and flashier slides. It was Visty's advice to do this. They showed him an early version of their work. Visty saw it and was impressed but nevertheless worried about its flash appeal for Reed as well as the venture capitalists.

Visty decided to work closely with Dirk, Ina, and Art on this to avoid anyone going overboard.

Dirk noticed that the animation settings could easily be changed and suggested to Visty that they keep the transitions fast and zippy when showing them to Reed but tune them down when showing to the venture capitalists. They all agreed.

When Art finished, Visty organized a team meeting for everyone to view the prototype and provide feedback on it before showing it to Reed and the venture capitalists. During the presentation, the team consensus was that the more subtle approach was appropriate for both Rock and the venture capitalists, so the fast approach was eliminated and the prototype was prepared as just a single presentation.

REFERENCES

A. F. Osborn. Applied Imagination: Principles and Procedures of Creative Problem-Solving (3rd rev. ed.). New York: Charles Scribner's & Sons, 1963.

P. B. Paulus, B. A. Nijstad (eds.). Group Creativity: Innovation Through Collaboration. New York: Oxford University Press, 2003.

CHAPTER

The Effective Prototyping Process

PHASE **1** Plan

PHASE **2** Specification

PHASE **3** Design

PHASE **4** Results

STEP **1** — ch 3 — Verify Requirements

STEP **2** — ch 4 — Develop Task Flows

STEP **3** — ch 5 — Define Content and Fidelity

STEP **4** — ch 6 — Determine Characteristics

STEP **5** — ch 7 — Choose a Method

STEP **6** — ch 8 — Choose a Tool

STEP **7** — ch 9 — Select Design Criteria

STEP **8** — ch 10 — Create the Design

STEP **9** — ch 11 — Review the Design

STEP **10** — ch 12 — Validate the Design

STEP **11** — ch 13 — Deploy the Design

12

VALIDATE AND ITERATE THE PROTOTYPE

In Step 9 we covered the internal review of the prototype. However, prototypes need to be reviewed and validated by external stakeholders, such as customers, end users, investors, or others, who your products are targeted to. Prototype validation, the subject of this chapter and Step 10 of the effective prototyping process, is typically achieved through usability testing, focus groups, and design evaluation sessions. It should be integral to your software-making process and project plan. Usability testing allows validation of the designed user experience, including the visual, emotive, responsive, and navigational aspects of the user experience. Focus group sessions are useful for validating the interpretation of marketing or business requirements as features and functions. The outcome of external validation may lead to prototype iterations. This, in turn, can result in effective usability and salability of your product and assure that both customer and user satisfaction are achieved.

THE STRATEGY OF VALIDATING AND ENSURING USABILITY VIA THE PROTOTYPE

Design validation through usability testing or focus group sessions enables a product team to determine the degree to which requirements are being met as well as the need for iterative improvement. Release cycles and availability of resources are critical to planning prototype iterations. For example, if a release cycle is short, such as 9 months or less, and resources are limited, then iterative design and validation is most effectively carried out over a longer term of sequential product development cycles. At the other end of the spectrum, if a release cycle is longer than 9 months and adequate resources are available, more design and validation iterations can be planned and conducted within a cycle.

To maximize the benefits of usability and functional requirements validation, prototyping and evaluation cycles should begin as early as possible in a given product release, that is, at the start of and throughout the design phase as time and resources permit. This may seem unusual for those who exclusively test finished code for usability, especially for new software product efforts. Often, validation results during the development or construction stages of the software process cannot be acted on immediately; and if action needs to be taken, it can come at the high cost of trashing and rewriting program code, introducing a further expense of errors and excessive debugging.

USABILITY TESTING: THE TACTICS OF VALIDATING AND ENSURING USABILITY VIA THE PROTOTYPE

This section sketches the steps needed to validate your prototype with usability testing, which need to be considered in their proper sequence. The steps shown below are only a sketch; we refer you to some excellent texts for their fuller treatment of these steps [Rubin 1994; Dumas and Redish 1999; Snyder 2004].

If users are in close geographic proximity, validation sessions can be conducted in a physical room or lab space with a moderator, note taker, participant, and observers. If users are scattered geographically, then these sessions can be conducted remotely using web and phone conferencing.

1. Develop a test plan.
2. Prepare a screener questionnaire (an accurate definition of the user) to pre-qualify test participants.
3. Develop a contact list of potential test participants, including a pilot test participant.
4. Designate an internal test participant recruiter or hire one externally.
5. Reserve room or lab space for the duration of the validation sessions.
6. Ensure necessary equipment for conducting each session (note-taking tools, video or audio recording equipment, etc.).
7. Prepare a schedule of validation sessions–which participants are available on what day at what time?
8. Develop a participant guide to provide users with the usage context and any objectives; include any data that may be cues to the user or need to be entered by the user.
9. Provide test stimulus–a prototype or software program to be validated.
10. Conduct a pilot session (test of the session) with a conveniently available participant.
11. Conduct validation in an appropriate predetermined number of scheduled sessions.

12. Using the notes and video recordings taken or logged during each session, review and analyze the validation data. Interpret and synthesize design successes in addition to recommendations for design improvements.
13. Prepare validation results document.
14. Prepare a presentation of the validation results and design successes and improvements.

FIGURE 12.1 *A typical usability testing situation.*

EVALUATING YOUR DESIGN

"Method developments in usability assessment include standards and guidelines, observation and monitoring techniques, attitude questionnaires, checklists, and techniques for expert evaluation. Some methods, notably performance monitoring, yield statistical data, which can show where most problems occur but do not diagnose problems or recommend solutions. Most, however, are aimed at providing designers with more incisive diagnosis, which can inform redesign. The quality of the information yield may be critical, given that selecting redesign solution may miss its target or cause secondary problems" [Doubleday et al. 1997].

Doubleday et al. [1997] suggest that evaluation leads to more successful design if a variety of evaluation methods are used. This allows the design to be considered from a variety of perspectives and increases the probability of uncovering issues that may go undetected in one method. Evaluation methods include:

External reviews–Reviews with internal and external stakeholders (except users, i.e., domain specialists, business analysts, etc.).

Usability testing–Conducted using a one-on-one protocol to validate the usability of the design with a selection of screened participants via direct review and interaction with a simulation of the design.

Focus group testing–Conducted with a targeted group to validate the conceptual premise of the design with them as well as gather task and behavior-related information from both customers and users.

Peer reviews–Carried out by a small diverse sampling of peers to validate best design and usability practices. An activity in which software or allied professionals other than the original designer or team members examine the prototype for successes, defects, and improvements. Peer review methods include critical inspections, concept walkthroughs, heuristic evaluations, and other similar activities.

Customer support feedback–Allows unstructured critical feedback by customers and end users about the software product after it's deployed and in use.

Satisfaction surveys–Allows more formal targeted evaluation feedback about the software product after it's deployed to and in use by customers and end users.

Cognitive walkthroughs–Based on predefined user's task goals, this technique involves a select group of evaluators walking through tasks or activities via a prototype and evaluating at each step how difficult it is for a user to identify and operate a given interface component most relevant to a given step in a task sequence. An aspect of this evaluation technique is how clearly the system provides feedback to each user action.

Whatever method or combination of evaluation methods that you use from the above list, the resulting data can be gathered and organized by a design team in a concentrated and longitudinal way and then systematically and continuously sifted, analyzed, and interpreted into recommendations for further action. Once evaluated, any prescriptive actions should be both tactically and strategically planned, prioritized and carried out, including:

➤ More user research
➤ More design ideation

- ➤ Design changes
- ➤ Debugging
- ➤ More prototyping and testing

How do you know what evaluation method is right for your situation? Worksheet 12.1 on choosing evaluation methods should help you make a decision about the most appropriate evaluation methods.

WORKSHEET 12.1: Choose the evaluation method

Project Name:
Project Date:
Product Name:
Current Phase:

Author:
Internal Ref.:
Target Release:

Tools	Methods								
	Card sorting	Wire frame	Story board	Paper	Blank model	Video	Wizard of Oz	Digital interactive	Coded
Internal Reviews	++	++	++	– –	++	++	++	+	++
External Reviews	NA	–	++	NA	NA	++	+	++	++
Usability Testing	NA	NA	NA	++	NA	NA	++	++	++
Focus Group Testing	+	–	+	+	NA	+	+	++	++
Peer Reviews	+	++	++	+	++	++	++	++	++
Customer Feedback	NA	– –	+	+	+	+	+	+	++
Surveys	NA	NA	NA	NA	NA	NA	NA	+	++
Cognitive walkthroughs	NA	+	NA	+	NA	NA	–	+	++

Legend

++ *very appropriate*

+ *appropriate*

– *acceptable*

– – *not practical*

NA *not applicable*

ITERATING YOUR DESIGN

The next steps, any further need for prototyping and design activity, are dependent on the degree of success achieved through testing, time and resource constraints, and the product team's level of desire and commitment to maximize design results and usability. These factors vary from project to project depending on the overall product objectives. When in doubt, consider iterating your design, especially if it is a research exploration or a new product or service effort.

Assuming that issues are identified from the design evaluation and validation activities and there is a commitment to resolve these issues, an iteration plan should be developed. This plan should contain articulate definition and prioritization of the issues with clear steps and objectives on addressing and resolving each one. As mentioned in the prior section, this plan could prescribe more prototyping, validation, and evaluation.

ARNOSOFT VALIDATES THE PROTOTYPE WITH END USERS

ArnoSoft received venture capital funding and decided to develop a conceptual design based on the storyboard. However, before creating the conceptual design, the team decided to first validate the prototype with a focus group to ensure they were on the right path. For the focus group they decided to ask some of Reed's best customers to attend.

The focus group included an overview of the software by walking through the storyboard. The group did not comment much on the interface itself–the format was too passive for that. However, the group did provide valuable feedback on end-user support they wanted: saving a wish list, creating a gift registry, and so on. Ultimately, the focus group exercise confirmed that ArnoSoft was headed in the right general direction. The team discovered a need for more online support than originally planned, but this new requirement didn't seem impossible given their new pot of gold. So the team decided to move forward and start developing a conceptual design and then a paper prototype.

REFERENCES

Catherine Courage, Kathy Baxter. Understanding Your Users. A Practical Guide to User Requirements Methods, Tools, and Techniques. The Morgan Kaufmann Series in Interactive Technologies. Amsterdam: Elsevier/Morgan Kaufmann, 2004.

Ann Doubleday, Michele Ryan, Mark Springett, Alistair Sutcliffe. A comparison of usability techniques for evaluating design. Proceedings of the Conference on Designing Interactive Systems: Processes, Practices, Methods, and Techniques. New York: ACM Press, 1997, pp. 101–110.

Joseph S. Dumas, Janice C. Redish. A Practical Guide to Usability Testing. Bristol, UK: Intellect Ltd., 1999.

JoAnn T. Hackos, Janice C. Redish. User and Task Analysis for Interface Design. Hoboken, NJ: Wiley, 1998.

Mike Kuniavsky. Observing the User Experience: A Practitioner's Guide to User Research. New York: Morgan Kaufman, 2003.

Deborah Mayhew. Usability Engineering Lifecycle. New York: Morgan Kaufman, 1998.

Jeffrey Rubin. Handbook of Usability Testing: How to Plan, Design, and Conduct Effective Tests. Hoboken, NJ: Wiley, 1994.

Carolyn Snyder. Paper Prototyping. New York: Morgan Kaufman, 2004.

CHAPTER

The Effective Prototyping Process

PHASE **1** Plan

- STEP **1** — ch 3 — Verify Requirements
- STEP **2** — ch 4 — Develop Task Flows
- STEP **3** — ch 5 — Define Content and Fidelity

PHASE **2** Specification

- STEP **4** — ch 6 — Determine Characteristics
- STEP **5** — ch 7 — Choose a Method
- STEP **6** — ch 8 — Choose a Tool

PHASE **3** Design

- STEP **7** — ch 9 — Select Design Criteria
- STEP **8** — ch 10 — Create the Design

PHASE **4** Results

- STEP **9** — ch 11 — Review the Design
- STEP **10** — ch 12 — Validate the Design
- STEP **11** — ch 13 — Deploy the Design

13

DEPLOY THE DESIGN

YOUR PROTOTYPE IS READY FOR DEPLOYMENT

The last step in prototyping is to take a prototype and either translate it into an actual software product or service, or iterate it into the next refinement. Now you must plan, set expectations, and establish some ground rules before handing it off to others for deployment or further iteration. Step 11 gives you some guidance on a successful handoff, one in which the audience or customer will be adequately prepared and properly focused on design goals, rationale, and details.

STEP 1 — **Set expectations for handoff**
- Stage of software process?
- Level of finish
- Completeness of content

STEP 2 — **Prototype distribution strategies**
- Appropriate ways for handing off
- Managing issues after handoff

STEP 3 — **Documenting prototyping results**
- Documentation
- Product design guide

Step 1: Set Expectations for Handoff

1 STEP

Set expectations for handoff

- Stage of software process?
- Level of finish
- Completeness of content

Prototype distribution strategies

- Appropriate ways for handing off
- Managing issues after handoff

Documenting prototyping results

- Documentation
- Product design guide

Regardless of how the prototype is handed off or who it is handed off to, you should invest the time to set expectations by communicating the transition process, activities, and deliverables. This ensures that those handoff stakeholders are well informed about what to expect, instead of just getting your design after it's thrown over the wall to them. (For details about setting expectations, refer to Chapter 11, Setting Expectations.)

The handoff and subsequent deployment work should be collaborative and requires continued communication with the prototype creators, regardless of whether they are in-house or consultants. We have witnessed most of the best designs go to waste when a hired consultant threw a completed prototype over the wall and then left the project. (This point is also made very cogently in Isaacs [2002, chapters 9 and 10].)

Step 2: Prototype Distribution Strategies

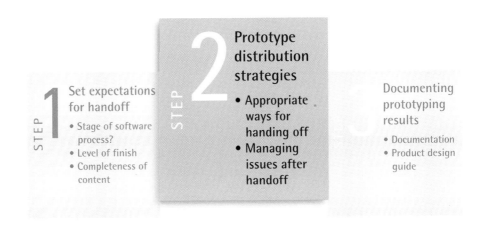

Prototype distribution strategies are the different ways to hand off the prototype so that the intended audience can effectively use it. With a deployed prototype, it's assumed that you are, for the most part, relinquishing control of it to some degree. You may even have little, if any, continued input to or discussion about it once it leaves your hands. The worst-case scenario is that the prototype must speak for itself, which is clearly not best practice but also not uncommon. You risk unsubstantiated design ideas that take on a life of their own. Best practice maintains a collaborative approach, even if it is at a reduced level. Every prototype handoff should have a well-planned transition period that actively involves the designers and their resulting prototypes.

What Are the Most Appropriate Ways to Hand Off Your Prototype?

Closed Versus Open

Regardless of the fidelity and characteristics, prototypes can be handed off in either an open or closed format. With an open format the design can be modified to reflect changes made as a result of design realization activities that occur after handoff. With a closed format the prototype can be viewed but not modified unless it is imported into a different software tool. If it is decided to hand off the prototype in an open format, then you'll need to maintain changes to it or designate someone to maintain changes resulting from such impacts as technical limitations and introduction of last-minute requirements. Likewise, an open format is useful when people are going to iterate or need to iterate your design directly in the same tool in which you created it.

Keeping the format closed is recommended when the prototype needs to be taken to the next step in either a new tool or the development environment. The closed prototype would stand as a frozen document, with iterative design performed on either a subsequent prototype or development environment. If the prototype is used for specification purposes, it is usually better to choose a closed format, such as a PDF or other read-only file type, to keep any accompanying specifications in the document closely aligned with the prototype. In addition, the closed format provides a fixed stable target from which to develop a product or service. This stable target assumes that the prototype is appropriate for providing design guidance for implementation in which all iterative changes to the design occur in a coded instantiation. Finally, if closed, the differences between the closed prototype and the new iteration must be important or they will not occur due to the difficulty of changing a closed prototype.

Going for either an open or closed format requires you to communicate the decision and collaborate with those people the design will be handed to. It is critical for your sanity and productivity to choose wisely when and with whom you collaborate. To be able and willing to collaborate with everyone you hand off to, they should:

- ➤ Have a clearly defined role to play
- ➤ Be *up to speed* with the rationale, requirements, intent, and details of the prototype

> ➤ Be able to understand how they'll effectively transition the design in terms of actual development—be it an incubator concept exploration or actual development

Narrative Versus Interactive

When the audience you're handing the prototype to does not have a shared buy-in for the resulting design or if they're having just their first exposure to the prototype, it is then best to present the prototype concepts in a narrative presentation format. You can use a storyboard that you may have created earlier, assuming that the storyboard accurately reflects the current instantiation of the design. A narrative format, such as a storyboard, is preferred for new exposure and conflicting ideas because the explicit storyline allows you to explain every step of the prototype's purpose in comprehensible terms. A storyboard frames the design goals, rationale, and details in a familiar narrative format, which allows non-experts to understand your design intentions and effectively take them over. However, it leaves detailed design implementation open and is therefore only appropriate when the design team has a continued presence.

When the handoff audience has a shared buy-in for the design or needs to directly start building from the prototype, then it is best to present the prototype concepts in an interactive presentation format. The interactive format becomes, in essence, documentation of exact system behaviors and interactions. An interactive format, such as a coded or digital prototype, is preferred when building is being continued because the interaction is functionally explicit and demonstrates exact specific system behaviors. A storyboard, on the other hand, is open to interpretation and often leaves interactive details undefined, whereas an interactive prototype waylays many of these issues. To ensure people understand the interaction properly, sometimes it is best to accompany the interactive prototype with a script. A script is especially useful because an obvious usable design for a user may be an unintuitive quagmire for an engineer or other stakeholder.

Managing Issues That Arise After Handing Off Your Prototype

The reality of modern software creation is that requirements, design details, and other factors are dynamic and can change any time. Isaacs mentions things such as unintended effects of the user interface after it has been developed, hidden user interface implications, and unintended software requirements as just three ways software requirements change and evolve over time [Isaacs 2002]. The authors' own experiences can add: scope creep, emerging technologies, and indecisive companies to that list. Changes need to be well documented and agreed to throughout the prototyping process, including after handoff. As mentioned in the previous chapter you may wish to use the same change management and bug reporting processes used for software development as the prototype design.

The following factors that may highlight needed changes can also be used to document the changes or the effects of the changes:

1. **Task flow**–Any changes made to the task or application flow will have impact on the design and the prototype representing the design, particularly the information and interaction design. Both the content and navigation model of the prototype may be affected.

2. **Business requirements and assumptions**–Changes to the business requirements can also shift priorities or emphases in the user experience, resulting in additional functions or conceptual design changes, which in turn need to be fit into the existing interaction model, information design, and screen layouts to accommodate these changes.

3. **Functional requirements and assumptions**–Functional changes affect the interaction design as well as the prototype layout. When functions or content are added, they can result in scope creep that should be avoided. However, functionality changes can often lead to time savings in other system areas. Therefore it is important to document additions, subtractions, and changes in function scope.

4. **Usability requirements and assumptions**–Competing requirements must be measured against user needs. If the user cannot achieve his goals, the product value is not only lowered but an opening is left for a competitor to leverage your work and put out a better product that addresses more user requirements.

5. **Technical requirements and assumptions**–Technical feasibility must be well documented and also challenged. If an engineer claims that any functionality is not possible, the design team should be prepared with counter examples of similar functionality that has been implemented. A challenge, when done diplomatically, often engages engineers in finding a solution that although not exactly matching your vision is close enough.

6. **Design guidelines**–Remember, design guidelines should be well defined, justified, and documented before the presentation of the prototype. If changes are made, the valid alternative considerations should be documented and decisions explained. Design guidelines are often the most expensive changes because they have a ripple effect throughout the design and may cause clashes with user requirements that are difficult to resolve.

A plan should be developed when any of the above changes are required:

➤ Who will address the changes?
➤ How will they be addressed?
➤ How will the changes be validated?

Even after a handoff, this establishes a process for addressing changes and an awareness of the costs to make those changes, which in turn determine whether the changes are truly necessary. For example, by making a minor design change, you may be required to modify the prototype completely and then further validate it for usability. This can be expensive if usability testing has been completed and the developers are required to hold the change until the next release.

Step 3: Documenting Prototyping Results

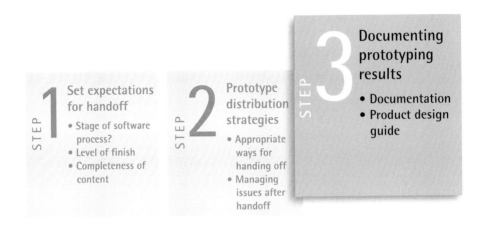

If a prototype is created and no one uses the resulting design, did it ever exist? Given the temporal nature of a prototype, documentation of the results is essential for its adoption into the software design process, especially the implementation stage. To support handoff and allow smooth distribution and implementation transitions, an official documentation and requirements repository should be established for the prototypes. It is also important to have the original prototype always accessible either on a central server, content management system, or in a document such as a product design guide, style guide, and standards and guidelines. It is important to leverage existing processes, even if prototyping is a new activity to your software creation process, because these documents already play a key role as reference documents and are viewed by internal stakeholders due to their existing role. Prototype documentation should be incorporated into a document people already use. Creating new or subsidiary documents may doom your documentation to never see the light of day.

THE PRODUCT DESIGN GUIDE

In our experience, the most ideal form of product documentation is an interactive prototype combined with documentation called a product design guide. This typically addresses a single product design. If it covers an entire company's product line, it can also be called a standards and guidelines document. If its scope is a family of applications, it can be called a user interface style guide. A good product design guide should cover the basics of the prototype and discuss all aspects of the prototype, including the prototype characteristics, content, fidelity, and design criteria.

SUMMARY

The last step in the effective prototyping process is to take an appropriately finished prototype and shape it into a product or service concept as part of a new technology incubation process or translate it into an actual product or service to implement and deploy to the marketplace. This chapter provided guidance on a successful handoff. By now you should not only be ready to plan, specify, design, and build a prototype, you should be ready to deploy the prototype and hand it off with the confidence that your audience or customer is adequately prepared and properly focused on its design goals, rationale, and details. This chapter also touched on documenting the prototyping results—an important activity throughout the prototyping process but especially important as a communication component for the prototype handoff to the stakeholders who will implement your design. This is the final chapter of the effective prototyping process. The subsequent chapters provide in-depth portrayals of the various prototyping methods that can be used to effectively prototype.

REFERENCES

Ellen Isaacs. Designing From Both Sides of the Screen. Indianapolis, IN: New Riders Place, 2002.

CHAPTER

14

CARD SORTING PROTOTYPING

DESCRIPTION

Card sorting is an early conceptual prototyping method. Card sorting prototypes derive from card sorting exercises conducted with end users and domain specialists. The card sorting sessions result in all the data you need for the synthesis of a card sorting prototype into an information structure that can serve as a model for your application's more concrete prototyping methods. For example, a card sorting exercise asking participants to arrange related commands under a common heading can be used to help create a menu bar structure for a desktop application or a navigation model for a website.

Aside from scheduling user participation, card sorting prototypes are easy to create; they require little if any technology. Stacks of index cards are the norm, though a flip chart with sticky notes works just as well. Card sorting is also fairly quick and easy to create once the list or candidate terms or concepts have been established.

The danger with isolating information in cards is that you risk skewed results if users would fail to understand the words by themselves, whereas in the context of a screen design and other contextual factors, a word would get a richer meaning with which the user would not otherwise associate. These other contextual factors may influence both the perception and the meaning of the word, which may cause usability test results to vary (sometimes greatly) from the card sorting exercises. When reviewing the results of card sorting, consider other design elements, which may alter word meanings.

Essentially, a card sorting exercise can *help* you understand:

➤ Information categorization and organization structure
➤ Titles or subtitles
➤ Sections and subsections under these headers or titles
➤ Appropriate menu groupings
➤ Inclusion, exclusion, and prioritization of information categories

- ➤ Narrowing scope of information or functional areas
- ➤ Verifying the match between the end user's mental model and the information design's conceptual model
- ➤ Correct terminology for a given interface element

In short, card sorting asks participants to organize words or concepts into groupings to extrapolate the user's mental model of the presented concepts. The exercise should validate your information design or outline a new more usable grouping of information, menus, and navigation. Card sorting can also inspire the development of a new conceptual model altogether.

Finally, a card sorting prototype serves not only as a guide to information design but also the user experience of packaging and marketing the software. In terms of overall contribution to the user experience card sorting provides stakeholders an understanding of the user's language and the way the user conceives your design.

CHARACTERISTICS

Audience–The consumer audience is the design team looking to improve naming conventions and the information design of a product. The participant audience is the end users giving their input through card sorting sessions done either one on one as a usability test or in a focus group.

Stage–Usually occurs early in the software creation process to inform the conceptual design.

Speed–Tends to be rapid. Diligent card sorting is usually a waste of time because the goal is the distillation of a larger concept, not a perfect detailed mapping.

Longevity–A short-lived exercise. Card sorting informs a more experiential prototype with more context, which replaces the card sorting with more contextually rich information.

Expression–Conceptual due to the evaluation of the information design in isolation from other design aspects.

Fidelity–Can be higher or lower fidelity depending on whether the focus is a complete information architecture (IA) or just a navigation concept (Table 14.1).

Style–Interactive, not narrative, because they lack a storyline. They require a sorting exercise that can occur in a random arbitrary order as determined by the test subjects. The result of card sorting is an information structure that is not narrative, which makes card sorting eminently interactive.

Medium–Physical or digital. Physical card sorts are easier to use for participants, whereas digital card sorting software can be more helpful with the analysis of data. However, the usability of the card sorting software can interfere in a session.

TABLE 14.1 Card Sorting Content and Fidelity Matrix

Content	Very Low Fidelity	Low Fidelity	Medium Fidelity	High Fidelity	Highest Fidelity
Information design	+	+	++	++	++
Interaction design	++	++	NA	NA	NA
Visual design	++	NA	NA	NA	NA
Editorial content	++	+	+	−−	−−
Branding expression	++	+	++	−−	−−
System performance	NA	NA	NA	NA	NA

++, Most appropriate;
+, appropriate;
−, not appropriate;
−−, completely inappropriate;
NA, not applicable.

AN OVERVIEW OF WHAT A CARD SORTING PROTOTYPE LOOKS LIKE

A card sorting session usually involves participants, a moderator, and a note taker (Figure 14.1). The moderator explains the purpose of the exercise. The participants group terms into groupings or associations they believe belong together. The terms are also prioritized. The note taker jots down not only the results of the card sorting but also the interaction of the participants during the sort, including things such as capturing important quotes while the participants think out loud.

FIGURE 14.1 *A card sorting session.*

The most common prototype resulting from the card sorting session is the affinity diagram in which aggregated results are grouped together. It is common to use statistical analysis packages, Excel spreadsheets, or to just do them by hand (Figure 14.2).

TYPES OF CARD SORTING

A card sorting prototype is the aggregation of results from conducting card sorting sessions with external participants and domain specialists. Card sorting sessions are planned by identifying what you want to test. The card sort, depending on the implementation and goal, can yield a raw site map for a website, a menu structure for a desktop application, or naming conventions for labels and messages in the user interface. In each case, as we explain below, you put the terms/words/concepts in question on a series of index cards. (There are various software applications that mimic index cards. See the reference section at the end of this chapter.)

The design of your card sorting prototype is determined by its purpose:

➤ Information architecture
➤ Navigation model for any kind of software
➤ Menu structure
➤ Terminology creation or validation
➤ Conceptual model/mental model validation

These five uses for card sorting prototypes are the most common, but feel free to use the method for any additional uses that you may discover or determine a need for.

Information Architecture

Information architecture is the organization and naming conventions of information used in software to meet user information and navigation needs. IA is a large undertaking, especially for information-based services and products, critical to the user finding desired information. Because the IA is the basis of all system information and interaction, it should be determined early in the design process, before a conceptual design has been agreed to. (This means that a card sorting for IA should also occur before paper prototyping; see Chapter 17.) An IA requires thorough domain knowledge for the creation of the card sorting exercises and also requires more lengthy and thorough user sessions. A card sorting for IA purposes should result in a hierarchical mapping of the IA or an affinity diagram, as shown in Figure 14.2.

Navigation Model for Website or Application

A navigation model usually just distills the system's site map or application structure. Card sorting prototypes for navigation models can focus more on the terminology to be used for navigating from the main screen of an application or home page of a website to its subsidiary sections. A second focus can be placed on the groupings of subsidiary sections to ensure they are both grouped appropriately and prioritized in a way that meets users' expectations. A card sorting for a navigation model should result in something similar to a site map.

Menu Structure

For a menu structure, the card labels are derived from a list of commands that need to be grouped into a menu so functionality is readily discovered by users. The cards can be handed to the participants in a randomized stack that contains some already existing best practices. For example, a menu structure has certain standard conventions (such as File, Edit, View for a desktop application) that can't be or are unlikely to be deviated from. Therefore, the designer may choose to fix column headings in the card sorting with those standard conventions.

Terminology Validation

By the time product design begins, most applications or websites already have a list of terms and a depiction of how they're grouped or related. To validate these key words, print them on cards and after thoroughly shuffling them place them into groupings by card sorting participants to determine whether the end user's organization matches the organization that the designers expected. There should be no cheating by providing prearranged groupings or column headings because this information will tip a participant to a particular direction. A think-aloud protocol and a follow-up question and answer session are essential to ensure that the designer understands the participants groupings that were created. Regardless of whether these groupings match designer expectations, understanding participant logic can help the designer determine whether her preconceived terms and groupings enable optimal ease of use. The card sorting can also be used for terminology creation by allowing participants to suggest alternate terms or by allowing them to group terms and provide labels for the groups.

Validation of Conceptual and Mental Models

A conceptual model is a design that is meant to be interpreted by an end user to make the system easy to understand. The mental model is how the end user actually interprets this conceptual model. There is often a gulf between what the designer intends and how the user interprets it. Therefore, it is important to validate the mental model against the conceptual model. To test conceptual and mental models, their key concepts can be printed on index cards with related concepts and terms then added as additional cards. If a participant's mental model matches the designer's conceptual model, the outcome of the card sorting will reflect this. For conceptual model validation, it is essential that the user is presented with the conceptual model structure (meaning key headings for the sorting) because the goal is to determine whether the conceptual model works; this is not a test of whether the tested conceptual model is the best conceptual model. Without providing an existing structure, participants create their own conceptual models, which is a test representative of the terminology validation described above.

Avoid the temptation of simply combining the card sorting prototype uncritically into a visual prototype. Note that the resulting session gives a hierarchical model of information very similar to a menu structure or the navigation model of a website. It becomes inviting to then normalize the resulting structure from the various user sessions and then directly implement them. However, remember that card sorts are abstract prototypes and therefore only concentrate on a single element of the design. Other contextual factors still need to be considered. As with all prototypes, your ability to analyze the results with a level of sophistication separates good usage from bad usage of card sorting prototypes.

STEP-BY-STEP GUIDE TO CARD SORTING PROTOTYPES

STEP 1 — Setting starting point
- Sources
- Concept terms
- Goal setting

STEP 2 — Designing the session
- Audience
- Matrix

STEP 3 — Preparing the session
- Script
- Cards
- Supplies

STEP 4 — Conducting the session
- Single session
- Group session

STEP 5 — Synthesizing results
- Analysis

STEP 6 — Preparing for reuse
- Next steps

This step-by-step guide takes you through the steps of preparing a card sorting session and synthesizing the findings into a single prototype.

Step 1: Setting the Starting Point

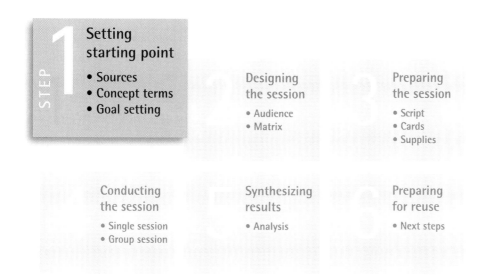

To begin preparing your cards, you must first create a starting point stack of cards. Cards are easily generated from your conceptual model, but usually the card sorting takes place before the conceptual model is created. In the absence of a conceptual model, some terminology research should help inform your choice of groupings and labels. This step can be skipped if you want to have the participants create all the terms for you.

Cards or terms are created depending on which type of card sorting you are performing (see above). Then, these cards are combined into a stack. Moderators may then choose to layout headers. Some in our industry claim this is cheating because participants should make their own headings, but it isn't cheating if you are evaluating a conceptual model. Remember that the more terms you create for the participant, the less exploratory and more evaluative your sessions will be (see sidebar, How Much Is Enough?).

WHAT IS THE SOURCE FOR THE TERMS OF A CARD SORTING STACK?

Ideally, user interviews or ethnographic research will uncover a rich source of the terms and concepts that users employ in their work. Additionally, you may wish to augment the list of terms with words from your business/marketing strategy and key marketing concepts. If your purpose is validation and the software already exists, you can simply use the existing terms. However, if your goal is to look for additional options, try to avoid using existing terms. If you don't have an existing product, look at competing products or websites of related products to see what terminology is used. Websites dedicated to the product domain (industry analysis) can provide important information on any international standards or the current terminology in vogue.

If no established terms or concepts exist yet for the product, you still need to generate some to run the sessions. Some terms can be quickly generated via a brainstorming technique such as having members of the software creation team brainstorm individually by capturing their thoughts on relevant terms and concepts that apply to the software. These items can then be clustered by like terms, which usually weeds out similar but inappropriate terms. The results from this brainstorming session are a good starter list of terms or concepts. It is best to involve the entire design team and as many other internal stakeholders as possible to create a starter list. Their involvement ensures that the card sorting terms include not just the most efficient and effective terminology but also the messages and branding that the software makers want to push to the end user.

The most important first step of preparing for and running card sorting sessions is to make the card sorting goal explicit; write it down and keep it handy. The rich information that you get can easily sidetrack you or put you on a path of looking for patterns in the card sorting that do not serve your original purpose. As interesting as these discoveries are, they actually cause regression in your prototyping progress. Explicitly stated goals help enforce the self-discipline needed to ensure that there is no scope creep during the sessions and the resulting prototype has the correct raw material for the conclusions you need.

Step 2: Designing the Session

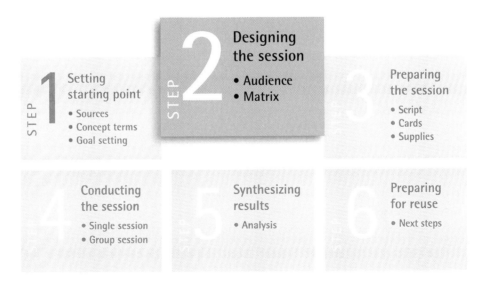

In designing your card sorting session, you want to create a card sorting matrix your software product requires. The card sorting matrix is the column headers and the number of columns and rows that the card sorting session uses. You can leave the matrix open if you want more exploratory results; for example, you can use a blank table and let participants create their own matrix. The matrix should at least include a limitation on the number of columns and a definition of the desired target output; for example, if you know there is space for only four menus in an interface, you may restrict the matrix to four columns.

While designing the card sorting sessions, always keep your target audience in mind–their backgrounds, ways of working, capabilities, and limitations. Do not use an overly complex session structure. Participants in card sorting prototype sessions have a very low threshold for complexity. When participants are asked to sort more than 10 groupings of 7 to 10 items, they can lose sight of what they are trying to structure. Ten groupings and 7 to 10 items are not magic numbers; use your best judgment to keep the list as lean as is appropriate for the domain and participants. Your research for one product may demonstrate that a user group finds a list of three groupings and 6 items too complicated, whereas your next product maintains that users of the expert system are comfortable with a much longer list (such as eight groupings and 11 items), because the users have already internalized a more complex system understanding.

Step 3: Preparing the Session

Preparing for the card sorting session consists of writing a script, printing and inventorying the cards, and obtaining the necessary supporting supplies.

Script

A script is necessary to ensure that the participants are given clear and consistent directions and that both the moderator and the participants remain mindful of what needs to be done. A written script also reminds the moderator to concentrate on the progress of the session rather than what should be said or done next. The script should include the context of the card sort, instructions, disclaimers, and so on. The instructions provide the participants with step-by-step details on the tasks to perform. Do they need to first pick their headers and then group under those? Or are the headers provided and, if so, are they fixed or can the participant change them to suit her needs? Be sure to explicitly explain that all related terms or concepts should be grouped. You may instruct participants to put the most important choices at the top of the list and the less important ones below. You should also mention the time limit, which is dependent on the type of session you are running. Sessions usually run 1 to 2 hours. You should also instruct the participants to follow a think-aloud protocol and inform them that you will periodically remind them to speak aloud during the session if anyone is quiet for a period of time.

Cards

Create an inventory of the cards needed and make sure you have them all. Then organize and sort them in a way they are easy to find. Keep each session's cards together after you print and randomize them. If you don't have time to debrief between sessions, ensure you have enough card sets for all sessions.

Supplies

Keep some pens and blank cards available. Blank cards are always useful for missing or torn cards and the ever-necessary new cards, created either by the participants or you. You may also want to have a note taker or a video camera for capturing the think-aloud protocol and other important process interactions during the session because the moderator will be too busy to do that. The video camera is also advantageous for providing contextual visual aids to accompany your results. Although this latter use of the video camera sounds very appealing and useful, in reality we've hardly ever been on a project when we were able to use anything other than the carefully taken notes of our colleagues.

Finally, bring a digital camera. It is the best method for capturing session results. You can also manually write down everything immediately after the session, but this is sometimes impractical because another session may immediately follow or other considerations may make the time after a session impractical for ruminating over the results. Assuming it hasn't been imported into a graphics editor, the camera does not lie and the images can be the results of record.

Card sorting sessions can be done one-on-one or in groups (see sidebar, One on One or in a Group?). Card sorting lends itself more easily to group sessions than usability testing because the sorting does not have errors to track that a usability test would. Group dynamics may compromise the moderator's ability to learn about an individual's mental model because that is something most people tend to guard unless alone. A group session allows for discussion and exploration of topics and ideas that a group may think of but an individual user may not necessarily think of on their own.

Step 4: Conducting the Session

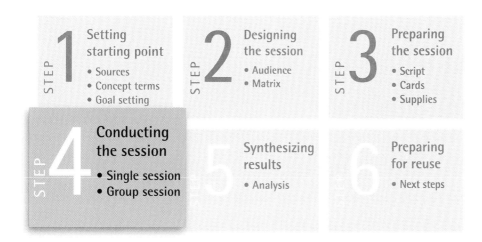

In the following example we assume a one-on-one session. Participants are usually screened for a card sorting in the same manner as a usability test. Following the script, the moderator usually uses a contextual background scenario to introduce the exercise and then instructs the participant to assemble the related information, commands, and so on into logical groups. When giving instructions, it may be preferable to not explicitly tell the participants that the exercise is for a computer program but for something they may more easily relate to, such as organizing a list of book titles on a shelf. Experienced computer users may be more readily able to work within the contextual confines of a computer program, so inform these participants they are arranging the menu options for a software application. More novice participants might yield better results with a scenario that more effectively puts them in the frame of mind of organizing, prioritizing, and grouping rather than working with computer software. Remember, your need for website (or other software) groupings is not always the best contextual factor for optimal participant results.

Through the think-aloud protocol, ask the participant to define why each card is selected. The moderator should be thoroughly familiar with each card's meaning in case any are unclear to the participant. In general, because your help will not be available to users when they are using the product, it is best to avoid most explanations unless a participant is completely lost or frustrated. In this case, even assisted data have more benefit to you than bad or no data due to a participant giving up on the task.

Step 5: Synthesizing Results

STEP 1 Setting starting point
- Sources
- Concept terms
- Goal setting

STEP 2 Designing the session
- Audience
- Matrix

STEP 3 Preparing the session
- Script
- Cards
- Supplies

STEP 4 Conducting the session
- Single session
- Group session

STEP 5 Synthesizing results
- Analysis

STEP 6 Preparing for reuse
- Next steps

After all sessions are completed, the results need to be synthesized into a card sorting prototype, either a hierarchical data structure (especially helpful for IA and site maps), an affinity diagram (helpful for more conceptual design), or some other drawing that may better suit your purposes. Some methods are disarmingly straightforward and easy, such as collating and averaging responses using Excel. If the cards have number codes, data entry can be quick and easy. Several automated tools exist for this as well (see the list at the end of this section), but before you invest too heavily, we should warn you that they do not alleviate the burden of

FIGURE 14.3 *An affinity diagram.*

Site map

FIGURE 14.4 *A site map diagram for a Dutch website.*

Homepage

Markt vandaag ▶
- fondsen ▶
  - Laatste nieuws
  - Weekcommentaar
  - Feiten & cijfers
  - Overzicht Robeco-fondsen
  - Overzicht RG ZelfSelect-fondsen
  - Indicatiekoersen
  - Resultaat fondsen
- AEX-aandelen ▶
  - Beleggingscommentaar
  - Feiten & cijfers
  - Overzicht AEX-aandelen
  - Overzicht AMX-aandelen
  - Overzicht overige aandelen
  - Technische analyse AEX-index
- Internationale markten ▶
- Beurscommentaar ▶
- Beursnieuws ▶
- Beursagenda ▶

Productinformatie ▶
- Robeco-fondsen ▶
  - Aandelenfondsen
  - Obligatiefondsen
  - Mixfondsen
  - Onroerendgoedfondsen
  - Risico-rendementsprofiel
- AEX-aandelen ▶
- Sparen ▶
  - Roparco Renterekening
  - Roparco Dividendsparen
  - Roparco Groeisparen
  - RG Groenrente Fund
  - RG RenteMAXX Fund
- Hypotheken ▶
  - Roparco Hypotheek: de feiten
  - Roparco Hypotheek: de cijfers
  - Overwaarde
- Beleggingsverzekeringen ▶
  - RoZeker KoopsomRekening
  - RoZeker LijfrentePlan
  - RoZeker OpbouwPlan
  - RoZeker PortefeuillePlan
  - RoZeker KoopsomRekening Pensioen
  - RoZeker KoopsomRekening Stamrecht
  - RoZeker PensioenPlan

Financiële planning ▶
- Beleggingsstrategie ▶
- Rekenmodules ▶
- Wonen ▶
- Pensioenen ▶
- Vermogensoverdracht ▶
- Kinderen ▶
- Beleggen en de fiscus ▶

Modelportefeuilles ▶
- fondsen ▶
- Aandelen-selector ▶

Advies ▶
- Bedrijfsprofiel ▶
- Hoe bereikt u ons? ▶
- Brochures ▶
- Evenementen ▶

Online beleggen ▶
- Opdracht plaatsen aan- of verkoop Robeco-fondsen ▶
- Opdracht plaatsen op de Amsterdam Exchanges ▶
- Uw portefeuille ▶
- Online KeyCard informatie ▶
- Tarieven Robeco Advies ▶
- Voorkeurslijst ▶

Online Tools ▶
- Open rekening ▶
- Proefabonnement ▶

conducting your own design analysis and interpretation. Remember, the quality of abstract prototypes rises or falls with the quality of the analysis and interpretation. We personally prefer manual techniques because they force you to be immersed in the data and know it thoroughly. Automatically generated data, on the other hand, can give you a quick overview and immediately usable results to iterate or tweak into a useful prototype.

The resulting prototype's style, whether generated manually, automatically, or a combination of both, is largely dependent on the data view that best allows you to get an overview of the sorting results and context.

For analysis and interpretation, the authors recommend a simplified worksheet that relies on a numeric coded system. For an example of how the authors have gathered and attempted to synthesize data from a round of card sorting sessions, see the examples of spreadsheets given in Figures 14.5 and 14.6. The method that has worked for us is to have a different spreadsheet for each individual session and also a different spreadsheet to represent the different columns of your matrix. Using numbers (a code for each card) is handy for sorting. However, for the analysis and interpretation of the actual terms, use search and replace to replace the number with the text. We use numeric words ("one, two, three" not "1, 2, 3") in the spreadsheet headers to avoid accidentally replacing them.

Step 6: Preparing for Reuse

The software development process always requires the definition of an information design or navigation structure, and fortunately a card sorting prototype provides the design team with just such an information model. The analysis is not over though. As an abstract prototype, results from card sorting sessions can be interpreted in a number of ways. Your accurate use of this information is based on the final applied analysis that you perform on the information model and implement in a concrete design. After conducting your session and synthesizing, analyzing then interpreting the results, the next step is to develop recommendations for the information structure that you have been trying to identify. Start by removing all the vague and low-priority terms and concepts. The following guidelines can help you decide what terms to remove:

➤ *Redundancies*–Better high-priority terms can replace less popular terms.
➤ *Conceptual model fit*–A compelling reason to choose a low-priority term exists if the low-priority term fits in with the conceptual model or metaphor used throughout the program. Often, a term that is perfect for an isolated circumstance is not ideal in the context of a complete application.
➤ *Cultural sensitivity*–Users understand the term, but it is inappropriate for your branding scheme/company image.

- *Appropriateness*—How appropriate is the term for a given purpose? It may be easily understood, but is it using language that may be offensive or may not fit the context or may otherwise break the conceptual model?

- *Ease of learning and retention*—If a user does not understand the term, can she easily learn it and remember its meaning?

- *Parallelism*—To what extent are terms of the same priority and the same type of term using the same form of speech or emphasis? Don't blindly follow a rule such as navigation is a noun and actions are verbs. Consistency should be internal to the information model, not arbitrarily imposed on it.

- *Internationalization/localization issues*—Do terms need to be understood by non-native speakers of the language? Will the term translate well in the interface or cause a layout nightmare? For example, using a small phrase like "Select All" barely fits on the page in English, but it becomes longer, "Alle auswählen," in the German version of the interface.

The newly trimmed down list should then be used in a subsequent more experiential iteration of your prototype. Determine the prototype's overall design. Is the design mostly task oriented or user object oriented? Understanding these patterns will give you guidance for handling the more vague or equivocal terms and concepts.

Immediately, some issue in the more experiential prototype design will jump out at you—the design looks bad with some terms because they don't fit the available screen real estate; maybe other terms have translation problems and so forth. To resolve these issues, create a prototype report outlining the names and backgrounds of the participants, the results of card sorting, and the design rationale for the recommendations that came out of the analysis. Then have a group meeting with the design team and other stakeholders to present the card sorting prototype along with your design rationale. The design rationale should encourage discussion on whether the rationale or the prototype itself needs to be refined before going further with an experiential prototype.

The resulting report should remain readily available for reference throughout the software development process and for future releases of the software. These documents can age gracefully in some domains and can become obsolete upon the product release in other domains.

HOW MUCH IS ENOUGH? DESIGNING A CARD SORTING SESSION IN COMBINATION WITH OTHER SESSIONS

As mentioned in the step-by-step guide in this chapter, the more terms you give the user, the more accurately you're able to evaluate the efficacy of existing terms by leaving it to the unbiased view of the user. A more innovative approach is using the card sorting technique without providing any group structure or specific labels. This approach helps extract users' mental models via each of their individual organization of a set of cards. The goal of this unstructured type of card sorting exercise is to assist in gathering requirements or further assessing existing requirements. Albeit, card sorting can be used to achieve different outcomes by combining different types of exercises, such as short labels plus design concept and labels plus organizational structure.

When a concept already exists, the card used can have a short label, which tests the term and nothing else. If this format comprises all included cards, you are testing the participant's conceptualization of the terms that you've grouped. However, if in addition to short labels you want to also test the concept you are designing, you should also include a phrase or brief sentence, which serves as a definition or clarification. For example, with the phrase "Shopping Cart" you could write "Shopping Cart–view and purchase selected items." During the card sorting session, ensure that users really understand the concept of each function or the meaning of each term by paying close attention to their think-aloud protocol or by asking questions when you believe they might be struggling with a card. You are neither testing labels at this point nor gathering user requirements. You're just trying to extract participants' mental models as based on a set of concepts. To gain some insight into requirements, you might ask users to propose short labels for both the groups and the individual items in the groups. This is not to say that you cannot also gather requirements when taking this route.

When designing the basic card sorting prototype session, consider what information should be prepackaged for the participant (i.e., what cards should be prepared in advance and what should be left to the participant to create). In general, only the following should be prepackaged:

1. *Those things that cannot change.* For example, if the purpose of the card sorting session is to create a Windows menu structure, the top-level terms of File, Edit, and View are already determined, as is most of the content in these menus. Do not use valuable user feedback sessions to test these known constants.

2. *Terms you do not want to change.* Some terms may be required for reasons that participants aren't aware, and you want to include them because they will bias the user's context of use (which may be what you want, but be explicit about it if it is).

3. *Terms you want to test and evaluate.* Selected terms you may want to test in later usability evaluations.

4. *Terms required for context.* For example, some participants (depending on their profiles) may require that you provide context so that the meanings of groupings and labels are not ambiguous (e.g., enter, as in enter data [type information into a field] or as in enter store [navigate into an online store]).

5. *Terms required to evaluate a conceptual design.* Requiring the participant to use a prepared card set evaluates the effectiveness of a given conceptual model.

Finally, be aware that if you are giving the participant a high level of freedom, both a good structure and a clear mission are required. Such an exercise should not be undertaken lightly. Not all participants will be successful at this type of exercise. Letting participants get lost and then struggle to finally arrive at what they believe is the best solution does not always provide you with the results you're seeking. In this type of session, you must refrain from the temptation to "correct the user" so you can get the complete picture of a user's pain points and points of struggle.

SESSIONS: ONE-ON-ONE OR IN A GROUP?

A One-on-One Card Sorting Session

A one-on-one card sorting session can seem surprisingly familiar to a usability test with the exception that it can be brief, sometimes completed in only 30 minutes. A participant is usually placed at a table with a stack of preprinted cards, a stack of blank cards, and a thick marker (a thick marker shows up best on digital pictures). Or, the user sits in front of a computer if the card sorting is done digitally. The room usually has a video camera. If no video camera is available, a note taker, in addition to a moderator, should be included in the session. It is preferable if the note taker is out of sight, similar to a usability lab test observation protocol.

The cards are usually laid out for the participant, either randomly or alphabetically. This initial display of all cards is usually helpful in providing the participants with a quick overview, allowing the participant's mental model to start forming immediately. Having stacks of cards may inhibit the participant from obtaining an overview of the cards and their meanings. As a result, piles shift often as the participant loses context or, worse, confuses the context of the rest of the items in a pile.

The participant is instructed to sort the cards and use the think-aloud protocol to elucidate the logic behind groupings. The think-aloud protocol helps designers to mediate among seemingly contradictory results, especially when one participant has grouped differently from the others. For example, the moderator could discover that a participant completely misinterpreted a term's meaning and inform the participant of the true definition.

As the participant begins to sort the cards, he should place the cards underneath one another in a column. The moderator should be aware of the time and prevent the participant from spending too much effort on any uncertainties. Creating a concept problem/issue stack may suffice to keep the session on track. The session note taker should document which cards caused problems, whether they were successfully grouped or not. Remember, the card sorting session is not intended to force the participant to sort every card with grim determination, but rather to understand the important high-priority terms and concepts without having to sweat the details they clearly care less about. As with all good design, the point of the card sorting session is to derive the general organizational thread that runs through all the sessions rather than focus on a minutely specified and detailed perfect system.

At the end of a session, a digital camera can be used to capture the results. The moderator should feel free to use any available physical or digital means to capture the information. Results can be entered into a spreadsheet. Applying number codes on the cards speeds this process.

A Group Card Sorting Session

A group card sorting session is run differently, more like a focus group. The group session attempts to maximize limited time with a large number and variety of users. The session starts in much the same way as the one-on-one session with the instructions, card display, and note taker, except that the moderator encourages discussion and debate among participants during the card sorting exercise instead of the think-aloud protocol used for one-on-one sessions. This type of exercise takes much longer, usually 2 to 4 hours. However, the results are quicker to synthesize, analyze then interpret than those from a series of one-on-one card sorting sessions. The downside of a group card sorting session is that the results are only as good as the moderator's ability to manage any data skewing that can result from group dynamics, such as domination of a session by one or two persuasive participants. An additional factor is that participants are usually more willing to be open and exploratory alone than when in a group session, regardless of the moderator's skill and effort. Be aware that a group session can result in a significant loss of context because users typically use software in their own personal space rather than as a public group activity.

RUNNING THE CARD SORTING SESSION

One recommended method is to create a columnar format that summarizes all the grouping combinations:

First order of priority (headers): Show the most popular item for each grouping made into headers.

Second order of priority (boldface and placed at the top): Then, create a table with a "header" and all the terms and concepts underneath.

This can be done either digitally or, as pictured in Figure 14.3, with sticky notes on a large whiteboard or flipchart. After this is done, embolden the ones that were near unanimous or very popular. These then tend to stick out so you can see a pattern of popular terms. Put these terms at the top. The terms underneath should be in successive order of popularity. So a term that was sorted five times in the same pile goes above one that was sorted three times, and so on. The resulting data are a pattern of popularity and priority.

Numbers or letters can be used to mark certain characteristics of each concept or term. First, use numbers to mark whether a given term was popular with a specific user group or not. Have the numbers relate to a list of user groups you've defined from your user research or other means, such as a list you've brainstormed and then recorded on a flipchart sheet. Next, match the main results with a letter as the term or concept relates to a given task in the software. This could be done by referring to a list of tasks or scenarios from a user research document (i.e., a task analysis) or from a list of tasks you've brainstormed and listed on a flipchart sheet.

Next, color code the sticky notes so that the vaguest ones get a darker color, making them recede into the background. Deciding what should recede into the background is based on several factors:

> Context derived from the think-aloud protocol or group discussion

> Terminology that product marketing needs to push for business reasons

> Vaguer terms that can easily get absorbed by more popular terms

> Terms that are copyrighted or trademarked by other companies

> Trade-offs between similar terms. A term may be preferred by half of the participants and another term by the others. With a domain specialist try to identify the most effective of the two

> Conceptual trade-offs. Try to apply the conceptual models you'd like. Demote terms that contradict, break, or don't match the conceptual model

> Collaborate with a domain specialist to create an affinity diagram (Figure 14.3) of all the terms and concepts (or, better yet, include that as a step in your card sorting exercise). Let the affinity diagram of related terms break a tie of which subsidiary term should come next after a higher priority term or concept

When this exercise is complete, it is advisable to take a digital snapshot of this diagram that represents the unadulterated results before you continue your analysis. Remember, not a single term or concept should be removed or deleted at this point. This is the basic card sorting prototype.

EXAMPLE SPREADSHEETS

Figures 14.5 and 14.6 show sample spreadsheets for analyzing card sorting results. These spreadsheets are available in the book area of the effective prototyping website. These spreadsheets are designed for more simple analysis. If you have more complex needs, try one of the software packages listed at the end of the References section.

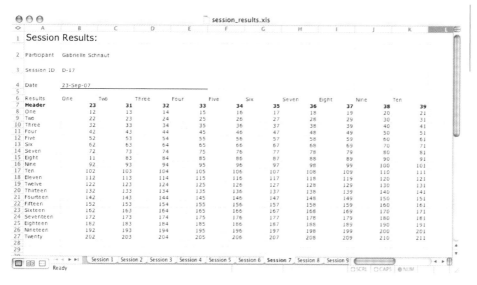

FIGURE 14.5 *A spread-sheet with multiple tabs showing all the sessions.*

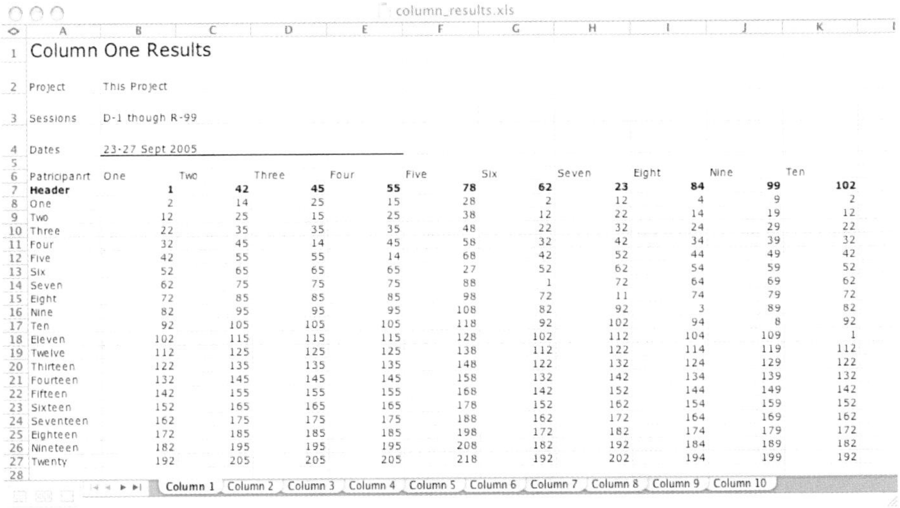

FIGURE 14.6 *A spreadsheet with multiple tabs showing session results for columns. Because these results are driven by formulas, by using the templates from our website you only need to enter the session spreadsheet results.*

Column One Results

Project	This Project									
Sessions	D-1 though R-99									
Dates	23-27 Sept 2005									
Participant	One	Two	Three	Four	Five	Six	Seven	Eight	Nine	Ten
Header	**1**	**42**	**45**	**55**	**78**	**62**	**23**	**84**	**99**	**102**
One	2	14	25	15	28	2	12	4	9	2
Two	12	25	15	25	38	12	22	14	19	12
Three	22	35	35	35	48	22	32	24	29	22
Four	32	45	14	45	58	32	42	34	39	32
Five	42	55	55	14	68	42	52	44	49	42
Six	52	65	65	65	27	52	62	54	59	52
Seven	62	75	75	75	88	1	72	64	69	62
Eight	72	85	85	85	98	72	11	74	79	72
Nine	82	95	95	95	108	82	92	3	89	82
Ten	92	105	105	105	118	92	102	94	8	92
Eleven	102	115	115	115	128	102	112	104	109	1
Twelve	112	125	125	125	138	112	122	114	119	112
Thirteen	122	135	135	135	148	122	132	124	129	122
Fourteen	132	145	145	145	158	132	142	134	139	132
Fifteen	142	155	155	155	168	142	152	144	149	142
Sixteen	152	165	165	165	178	152	162	154	159	152
Seventeen	162	175	175	175	188	162	172	164	169	162
Eighteen	172	185	185	185	198	172	182	174	179	172
Nineteen	182	195	195	195	208	182	192	184	189	182
Twenty	192	205	205	205	218	192	202	194	199	192

Column 1 | Column 2 | Column 3 | Column 4 | Column 5 | Column 6 | Column 7 | Column 8 | Column 9 | Column 10

NEXT ITERATION IF YOU WOULD LEAVE THIS PROTOTYPE

If performed early in the process, card sorting prototypes can also influence conceptual design storyboards and paper prototypes as well. Card sorting prototypes usually feed directly into more experiential prototypes, such as paper prototypes or interactive digital prototypes.

REFERENCES

Catherine Courage, Kathy Baxter. Understanding Your Users. San Francisco: Morgan Kaufman, 2004.

K. Frederickson-Mele. Usability testing an intranet prototype shell–a case study. http://www.acm.org/sigchi/web/chi97testing/mele.htm. Accessed December 15, 2005.

Mike Kuniavsky. Observing the User Experience. San Francisco: Morgan Kaufman, 2003.

James Robertson. Information design using card sorting. http://steptwo.com.au/papers/cardsorting/. Accessed December 15, 2005.

Rashmi Sinha, Jonathan Boutelle. Rapid information architecture prototyping. Proceedings of DIS '04. New York: ACM Press, 2004.

Todd Warfel, Donna Maurer. Card sorting: a definitive guide. http://www.boxesandarrows.com/ view/card_sorting_a_definitive_guide. Accessed December 15, 2005.

Available Card Sorting Software [Courage and Baxter 2004]

- USort//EZCalc<RM> (www.3.ibm.com/ibm/easy/eou_ext.nsf)
- WebCAT<RM> (zing.ncsl.nist.gov/WebTools/WebCAT/overview.html)
- WebSort (www.websort.net)
- CardZort/CardCluster (condor.depaul.edu/~jtoro/cardzort/cardzort.html)

CHAPTER

15

WIREFRAME PROTOTYPING

DESCRIPTION

Wireframes range from the classic sketch on the back of a napkin to full design comprehensives used for documenting the design to programmers. An early wireframe is intended to provide an early approximation of a software idea. Regardless of the medium in which it is created, the wireframe has a short lifespan. Its quick production allows experimentation with many different visualizations during the early stages of product design. This quickness makes the wireframe a low investment in time, cost, and effort, but it is also short-lived due to its nature of addressing immediate needs only. Though short in lifespan, wireframes usually inform a more thorough and longer living prototype, such as a storyboard or digital interactive prototype. Furthermore we say wireframes have a short lifespan, they are nevertheless among the most influential and most important prototype methods because the most innovative ideas tend to arise from them. The low resource investment means that more risky ideas can be tried, reiterated, and even thrown away without much cost to the overall project.

Different Perspectives of a Wireframe

It takes too long and is of questionable value to build a wireframe that encompasses an entire software program or website. Wireframes are more appropriate for brainstorming and exploration. Because extra energy shouldn't be spent with a diligent wireframe, it is helpful to have a plan and clear perspective on the critical elements and sequencing when preparing to build a wireframe. Use the process worksheets outlined in Chapters 3 through 13 to help you create this plan. Consider focusing on one of the following wireframe options:

- ➤ High-level structure wireframe
- ➤ Single-path wireframe
- ➤ Arrangement and sequencing

High-Level Structure Wireframe

A high-level structure wireframe focuses on the structural aspects of an application or website. As an example, the wireframe for a magazine website might start at the home page and then describe the section level pages like a table of contents. Main stories could be highlighted, but no actual article is completely visible. The section page may focus on navigating to an individual list of articles, but you only create one or two sample section pages. The article page itself may in turn only demonstrate the method of navigation within the story, to related articles, and to other interesting links. Again, you only create one or two article pages. This high-level pass is a good way to begin a wireframe because the results can be available fairly quickly and it provides an understanding of the overall structure without going into too much detail. Once you build the structure for a certain level or section, that structure becomes the template for further design. Having established the template, the wireframe can more easily be fleshed out by increasing the fidelity on specific contents or components.

Single-Path Wireframe

The single-path wireframe is used to follow a critical path through the software. Which path to highlight depends on the goals of the design. The basis for the critical path should be the most important task flows and scenarios from Worksheet 4.1: Task Flow Step to Requirements Mapping (from Chapter 4). The critical path could be an area in which the user might have difficulty when using the software, using such techniques as the critical incident. This critical path could also be defined by the business requirements: what path supports the essential business case. For example, in a commerce site, the critical path is one that the user might take from the home page through to a successful purchase. Building a wireframe to follow any of these critical paths gives the audience the context from which to understand the prototype.

Arrangement and Sequencing

An important trait of the wireframe is its ability to have the many different aspects and components of a design arranged. The ability of the prototyper to determine the placement and sequencing of elements, such as content, images, graphics, widgets, promotions headers, and the like, gives a wireframe form beyond just a simple structure. It is important that early wireframes keep the visual details of different elements in their lowest fidelity so that the focus of the wireframe remains on general arrangement and sequencing issues. Specific descriptions can be saved for later higher fidelity wireframes or other higher fidelity prototyping methods.

CHARACTERISTICS

Audience–Wireframes are primarily an internal stakeholder document. Showing wireframes to external audiences should be done very judiciously to avoid the typical outsider complaints that it doesn't look finished or that they don't understand it. The abstract nature of wireframes means that you have to trust your audience to be able to take a leap in faith to understand and appreciate the direction they are heading. Furthermore, although users are very important stakeholders for branding, visual direction, and navigational structure, their turn to evaluate the design comes later in the process than the wireframe stage. Wireframes are more for setting the design direction, which is more properly placed in the stage of design that involves vision and concept exploration.

Stage—Wireframes are traditionally considered early-stage prototypes when their vagueness is an accurate reflection of the state of the requirements and assumptions as well as the design direction. The earliest wireframes start as very low fidelity. These wireframes can increase in fidelity for certain types of content as you get closer to the project's midterm. Making completely high-fidelity wireframes doesn't make much sense, because to achieve a certain level of fidelity you ultimately need to include interaction, for which wireframes are not appropriate.

Speed—Wireframe prototypes are rapidly produced prototypes. This gives them their flexibility and benefit for the most creative and innovative work. A sketch wireframe can easily be tossed aside without fear of having lost much work. Given its inherent short life cycle, a diligent wireframe makes no sense.

Longevity—By nature a wireframe is a short-lived prototype. It is built at a low fidelity in the beginning of the design process and iterated quickly to foster quick design decisions. A wireframe acts more like a blue print for designers to use when designing something such as a website or for the storyboard team when they are building out ideas for a narrative. As a wireframe matures it becomes richer in detail; however, it is never suitable as an interactive prototype because it is generally too abstract to make the inclusion of interaction worthwhile.

Expression—Wireframe prototypes hover between conceptual and experiential. They are abstract to the extent that they concentrate on window and screen layout as well as rough sequencing structure without all content and widget details. The user needs to interpret what the content would be like. However, the user is given a visual frame of reference, a sketch of what the product can evolve to be like. This can serve as later inspiration for how the design can take shape.

Fidelity—Wireframes are lower-fidelity prototypes accenting the visual design, page layout/structure, and high-level navigational models. Although physical wireframes are definitely low fidelity (and destined to remain that way), the digital ones can easily evolve into more detailed storyboards or digital prototypes, at which point they cease to be wireframes any longer (Table 15.1).

TABLE 15.1 Wireframe Content and Fidelity Matrix

Content	Very Low Fidelity	Low Fidelity	Medium Fidelity	High Fidelity	Highest Fidelity
Information design	+ +	+ +	+	+	+
Interaction design	+ +	+	NA	NA	NA
Visual design	+ +	+	+	+	−
Editorial content	+ +	+ +	+ +	+	−
Branding expression	+ +	+ +	+	−	− −
System performance	+ +	NA	NA	NA	NA

+ +, Most appropriate;
+, appropriate;
−, not appropriate;
− −, completely inappropriate;
NA, not applicable.

Style–Wireframe prototypes are usually narrative; any interactivity they have is of a sketch-like nature, which usually requires a narrative to explain how it operates or what it should do.

Medium–Wireframe prototypes can be physical or digital. Physical wireframes, such as hand-drawn images or images printed on paper, are easier for some people to create. However, physical wireframes probably have a shorter life span than digital versions, which are easier to update and iterate. Although it may be better to inherently build in a short lifespan so that the wireframe is eventually discarded for more detailed and comprehensive prototyping, wireframes are usually digitally produced because they are not only easier to produce using digital tools, such as Excel or Photoshop or Word, but also because they are easier to share with others for example via e-mail. They are especially useful when team members are not co-located. Wireframes can also be included as part of a high-level design requirements document.

AN OVERVIEW OF WHAT A WIREFRAME PROTOTYPE LOOKS LIKE

A wireframe has a rough sketch-like appearance that looks similar among all wireframes. That is not to say that all wireframes look alike. The wireframes shown in Figures 15.1 and 15.2 represent the same application page, but their emphases and communication purposes differ in representation of a specific stage of design, the design intent itself, and, perhaps, skills of the author.

The hand-drawn wireframe example in Figure 15.1 demonstrates a simple and straightforward skeletal expression. The wireframe is devoid of visual design details, explicit content, and interaction widgets. It reflects only the structure of the screen and logical arrangement of the general page components, but none of the specific

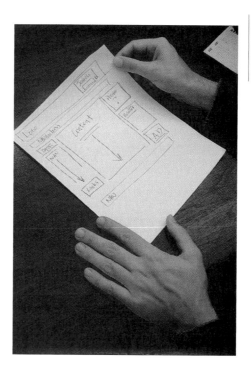

Logo Tag line	Illustration	Search

Navigation Bar

Date Stamp	Header		Promotional area
Navigation To sub sections	Sub Head	Sub head	
	Text Block	Text Block	Promotional area
			TK
	Sub head		
Possible links to partner sites	Text Block		

Bottom Navigation bar

An Overview of What a Wireframe Prototype Looks Like | 277

details of the page, which are meant to be expressed in later higher fidelity design iterations [Constantine 2003]. The arrangement of screen elements and notions of page sequencing are only meant to be a general guide–not an exact template for any final design. The final arrangement and visualization of interface elements in addition to page sequencing come from the results of further design iterations and specifications. All high-level page and window components are represented as boxes with text labels. The arrangement of these boxes highlights their relationships and the visual flow of the interface elements. At this stage, the naming conventions are generally unknown, and the text labels assigned to the page element boxes are only functional placeholders. Very minimal representations of screens and pages, the arrangement of their elements, and their sequencing are the essence and intent of wireframes.

The web page wireframe shown in Figure 15.2 uses a systematic and hierarchical labeling system for the different sections. By using a labeling system arranged in a hierarchical fashion, you can easily reference the different sections of the wireframe in a supporting document. Additionally, the hierarchical labeling enables a quick understanding of the design intent of the arrangement and flow of the page elements. When wireframes are represented in an ordered sequence, it is easy to understand the page elements and their arrangements in relationship to each other both within a page and across pages.

Let's walk through the wireframe example shown in Figures 15.2 and 15.3, which represent the same page in more detail. At the top of each page is a frame indication of the logo with accompanying marketing illustration and the search component. The actual graphic logo, which has not been finalized yet, is only represented in text format. The accompanying marketing illustration and search component are indicated simply with a box and a label. The global navigation bar in the next box down describes all the sections that have so far been approved. The currently displayed section, "Solutions," is highlighted using a gray tone and bold text. There is no indication at this point of the graphic treatment of the final design, whether it will be tabs, graphic rollovers, or a color indicator. The highlight merely reflects that this page will use a highlighted navigation element. The main content area is contained in two similar boxes to underscore the common theme of each text area. The text area content is represented in greeked text as a placeholder (see sidebar). The sub-navigation menu on the left uses generic labels at this stage, referring to where the navigation is positioned in relationship to the main navigation. Sub-navigation menu text labels will be added as the content becomes better understood and defined. In the promotion box on the right, the graphic, which has not been built yet, is only a gray placeholder, labeled with the reference of what it is and that it will be a graphic link.

The main take-away from this wireframe example is the directness of the information expressed without using graphic or visual design elements. In this way the design can begin to take form conceptually without creating a detailed visual design. Because at this point the specific design details are either not known or explicitly not included to avoid distraction from the more important goal of getting an overall understanding of the design structure.

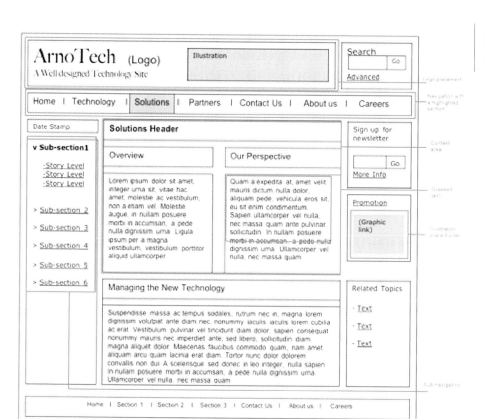

FIGURE 15.3 *A detailed web page wireframe.*

LORUM IPSUM

Greeked text is a tool used by graphic designers as a placeholder for content that is not yet written. Although called greeked text, it is actually Latin text derived from the writings of Cicero. Using greeked text enables you to fill in content areas to get a better feel for typographic design and how content will work in your design in advance of the actual content. You can find greeked text on the web that is available for your use. At the following website, you can generate as much greeked text as you need: http://www.lipsum.com/.

It's also important to note that greeked text is used in various prototypes, including interactive prototypes to ensure that some aspect of the design is being tested in the hopes that actual content doesn't interfere with the ability to legitimately test other characteristics, such as interaction, navigation mechanism, page layout, and graphic design.

DIFFERENT GOALS OF WIREFRAMES

Wireframes can serve many tactical goals in the software creation process:

1. Help you understand the meaning of a requirement
2. Serve as a quick visualization of page structure, content placement, and page sequencing

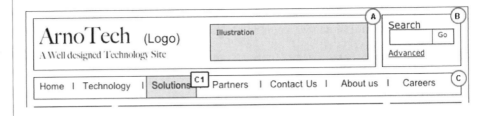

3. Provide an idea sandbox to play around with different product ideas, functions, and requirements

4. Aid in documenting early design requirements or issues (they are a great communication medium)

5. Define scope of ensuing design and production work

6. Help quickly discern the pulse of the team and its creative direction

7. Inform planning of more diligent prototyping methods

The Meaning of a Requirement

Often in software creation, use cases or scenarios or some other text explanations describe business, marketing, or functional requirements. The problem with text descriptions is that they are open to many different interpretations. Furthermore, as discussed in Chapter 3, requirements defined early in the process are actually better characterized as assumptions that need to be validated. Often, it is not until the product is built that any problems with the requirements are uncovered. One way around this dilemma is to visualize the requirements early in the design process with a wireframe to make sure that what is stated in the use case is what is understood by the design team and other relevant stakeholders.

A Quick Visualization to Understand Scope, Structure, and Layout

Often, the translation from requirements to design is held up by abstract discussions of project scoping, flow structure, screen or page layout, and other aspects of the software architecture. A visualization of these aspects can clear up that discussion and help make abstract principles concrete and tangible. Using wireframes for early visualizations of applications and web pages often leads to productive decisions and an end to fruitless conversation in ways more abstract discussions cannot.

An Idea Sandbox to Play Around With Different Product Ideas/Functions/Requirements

Because wireframes are quick and easy to create, the design team can generate many alternate designs or quick variations. Quick sketches lower the costs and reduce the effort of iteration and allow anyone with ideas or alternatives to either draw something on their own or work with a visual designer to mock up a new idea and have it reviewed by the team for future direction. Very often a sketched idea will not literally make it into the final product but can influence changes and improvements to the design that are essential.

Make Sure All Members of the Software-Making Team Are on the Same Page

A wireframe can help gauge the pulse of a team to make sure the members are in agreement about the design and the requirements that drive the design. A wireframe series of screens can be used not only as a basis of discussion but to clarify any confusion about design intent as well.

A public visualization allows all stakeholders and team members to develop a shared understanding through a focused discussion on requirements and how those requirements are being addressed. Wireframes should be thought of as a sandbox of ephemeral "throw-away" visualizations that allow swift and effective iteration of design ideas. Once ideas are agreed on, they can serve to help document the requirements.

A Medium to Begin Documenting Requirements or Issues That Have To Do With Early Designs

Wireframe prototypes can also be used as a medium to begin documenting requirements or issues related to early designs. To be effective in presenting early requirements, these sketch-like visualizations should be accompanied by text descriptions or annotations, which fill in the blanks inherent in abstract sketch visualizations.

A Quick Visualization of Task Flow Through an Idea

Wireframe prototypes can also be used to string together several ideas into a task flow. The flow can then easily be checked with domain specialists or a user focus group for proof of concept before committing to a concept or idea.

Inform More Diligent Prototyping Methods

We mentioned above that wireframes are an early rapid prototyping method. Because of the rapid production and low barrier to usage, a wireframe can also be used to quickly sketch ideas throughout the process. For example, if a given concept is not working during usability testing, you can rapidly create alternate concept solutions as wireframes and the team can evaluate them before implementing them in a more diligent interactive prototype.

WHO PARTICIPATES IN THE WIREFRAME CREATION PROCESS

Because wireframes are so quickly and relatively easy to produce, anyone can create them. Indeed, a good designer would be served well to encourage all team members to visualize their ideas by sketching screens and then arranging and rearranging them in desired sequences. If team members believe they don't have adequate drawing skills, they could be encouraged to participate in team wireframe sessions in which a visual designer facilitates a participatory design session where all team members can help brainstorm user experience ideas via wireframe. And try to remind team members that anything from paper and pen to a software program, such as PowerPoint or Photoshop, can be used for sketching, and that rectangles are the fundamental unit of design at this stage.

Although it is important that the major stakeholders all participate at one stage or another in the wireframe process, typically you create a wireframe and share it with the team. A wireframe owner is the person who must make sure that the different stakeholders get a chance to give their input as needed. As a wireframe progresses and is fleshed out, different stakeholders, such as developers and product managers, can become involved or at least sign off on aspects of the wireframe that concern them. The wireframe creator is ultimately responsible for seeing that results are documented correctly and shared with the team. If the wireframe is not documented, the design rationale can easily become forgotten, leading to the "why did we do that?" syndrome and its corollary, the "arriving late and changing already" syndrome. The documentation needed to avoid these undesirable syndromes does not need to be anything more than notes in the margin of the physical drawing or annotations on a digital document. A wireframe also needs to be shared with the team so that other team members do not reinvent the wireframe or contradict it in other documents. Sharing a wireframe and its documentation also ensures that a wireframe influences the ultimate design.

STEP-BY-STEP GUIDE

In the software development process, a wireframe provides the basis for a shared understanding of a software product's structure, visual direction, and/or branding strategy. The wireframe process starts with articulated requirements in any state of finality. These requirements are quickly created with a wireframe.

Wireframe creation can first begin with the elemental structure of the design and then move to fuller and more detailed display of the design, showing placement of different design elements. Avoid the temptation to immediately get into the details. Without the underlying structure, the placement of detailed content will not have the correct relationships among interface pieces.

Creating a good wireframe involves five steps:

Step 1: What Is the Source of the Wireframe Content?

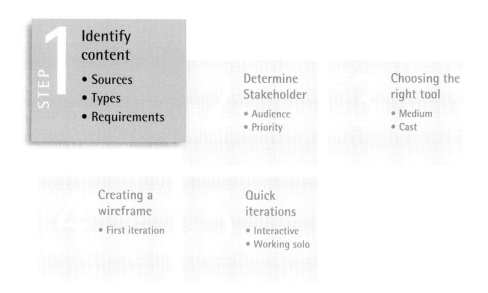

Before discussing wireframe content, it is important to note that you may start prototyping with no information. Start with some assumptions and rough ideas and then begin to draw. However, before you start wasting time creating wireframes that are already known to be useless, it would be valuable to first do some quick internal research. In this research you want to bring together as many requirements and assumptions that have already been gathered up to this point, in sources such as:

> Site maps and task flow diagrams
> Results from participatory design sessions with the team
> Results from any preliminary user research and studies, such as paper prototyping, card sorting, etc.
> Competitive analysis information
> Business requirements documents
> Functional requirements documents
> Existing designs

For explanations of these sources, see the sidebar on Wireframe contents. What is important is that you assure any knowledge already gained by the organization is reflected in your prototype.

WIREFRAME CONTENTS

Site Maps and Task Flow Diagrams

Site maps and task flow diagrams are helpful in initially defining the flow structure of the wireframe. From a site map or task flow diagram the team has a high level view and can decide which pages to prototype and how those pages fit into the overall design schema (see Chapter 4).

Participatory Design Sessions With the Team

Participatory design is always a helpful part of any design effort whether it is a wireframe or other type of prototype. Keep in mind that the people involved in your participatory design sessions affect which issues are discussed and possibly the direction of the wireframe. Once a wireframe is created, the design discussions can more effectively continue with a tangible representation for reference. A note of caution is that early design sessions can often drive a wireframe to become too detailed early in the process. It is best to focus on sketch-like high level representations and make notations about desired future directions.

Results From any Preliminary User Research and Studies

Although a wireframe is usually done early in the design process, user research or user studies may have preceded it. Any knowledge gained from these earlier studies can inform a wireframe as it is built.

Competitive Analysis

Understanding competitors' applications or websites is always helpful as a starting point for conceptualizing and visualizing the design of screens and task flows. But proceed with caution. As you can learn from other's mistakes, you can also duplicate them. Not understanding the reasoning and decisions behind a design can lead you to the same problems your competitors may be suffering from.

Business Requirements or Other Requirements

Any idea or vision for a software project can be made into a wireframe. Use of cases, scenarios, and other text descriptions all may capture what the software or website should do, but the visual representation can demonstrate, even in rough sketches, how those results can be accomplished.

Existing Product or Website Redesigns

For extending and improving existing products or services, already deployed application or website designs can easily be used as the basis for building the wireframe. The existing page structure and content placement allow you to quickly generate and iterate wireframe concepts. The danger here is using too much of the existing design and thus limiting the possibilities for new useful ideas that could derive from the wireframing exercise. Working at the conceptual level with low-fidelity wireframes makes the prototypes quicker to iterate, easier to discard, and easier to change.

Once you have gathered the content information, you should have a richer understanding of what the product should look like, how it needs to behave, and what visual elements the wireframe needs to support.

Step 2: Who Are the Stakeholders?

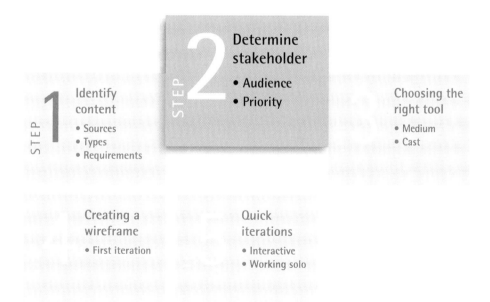

STEP 1
Identify content
- Sources
- Types
- Requirements

STEP 2
Determine stakeholder
- **Audience**
- **Priority**

Choosing the right tool
- Medium
- Cast

Creating a wireframe
- First iteration

Quick iterations
- Interactive
- Working solo

Your audience is one of the primary influences on deciding how to best represent the content. If the audience is only composed of team members, then you may waste effort-making sample text or making a visually refined wireframe. For a rougher wireframe, you trade off a higher quality that the finer touches might add to help ideas come across better. In general, internal audiences can have a higher tolerance for rough sketches.

An external audience, even external to the team but internal to the company or organization, may want to see you put a better foot forward in your wireframe. *The rougher a sketch is, the lower the perceived level of finish.* Among insiders, that perception can be less important, but to the outside world you want to give the impression you know what you're doing and that you're professional designers, so there is a need to set expectations accordingly. For example, client presentations should almost always be done with the most highly refined fidelity possible, such as using greeked text instead of blocks for masking.

Step 3: What Tool Do I Use?

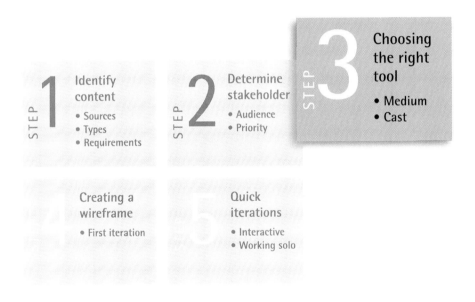

Finding the right application in which to build your wireframe is important. The application determines the speed with which you develop a wireframe and how flexible you can be with it. The wireframe in Figure 15.2 was built using Microsoft Word. There are many other applications that can be used for building wireframes, such as Visio, Photoshop, PowerPoint, Illustrator, Excel (and the equivalent programs StarOffice, OpenOffice, and Apple), and Dreamweaver. The best application to use can be a matter of which application you know best or understanding which application best serves your prototyping needs.

In choosing what application to use, consider these four principles to help guide you (see Chapter 8 for more general guidance on choosing the right prototyping tools):

1. Keep it simple.
2. Build and edit quickly.
3. Share it with others.
4. Migrate to the next step.

Keep It Simple

It is important that a wireframe remain focused only on the structure of the design. Save the detailed visual and interaction design for later stages when prototypes need a higher degree of visualization and interactivity. The success of a wireframe can hinge on the simplicity of its execution. Building a complex wireframe can affect the schedule by taking too long (see Build and Edit Quickly). A complex design that strays from the focus on structure can become sidetracked from the goal that needs to be accomplished.

Build and Edit Quickly

Because a wireframe is built near the beginning of the design process, it is important to consider finding an application that facilitates rapid production and iteration. When starting to design an application, everyone on the team can feel the impatience and pressure to make decisions and "get it going." In the minds of some production managers and developers that means "start the coding" or "begin the visual design." If the wireframe production process takes too long, there is a chance that the time for early discovery will run out and the team will need to go ahead prematurely with development or miss their delivery deadline. Choosing an application in which there is a high level of competency helps to increase the speed with which a wireframe can be built and iterated.

Sharing With Others

When making the application choice, the team's collaborative needs should be taken into consideration. Is the application available to others on the team who need to be a part of building it? Adobe Illustrator can allow you to create simple graphics, because it has great text tools for building wireframes. But the key question is who else on the team knows how to use Illustrator? Is the application available company-wide or is it only installed on a designer's computer? This is not to say you can't use Illustrator. This prototyping tool decision is best resolved when the collaborative needs of the team are examined. If multiple team members need access to a wireframe in a collaborative environment, then application knowledge and access are deciding factors.

Migrate to the Next Step

Wireframes are rarely an end to themselves. Sometimes, if a wireframe is developed beyond a more traditional mockup, you may want to consider working in a tool that allows you to migrate your design into a more advanced tool for further development into a more sophisticated prototype. You may also want to use one that allows you to use the same tool. For example, mocking something up in Excel as a wireframe can easily be adapted to a higher fidelity prototype by using the hyperlink feature to navigate among screens.

Step 4: How Do I Do It?

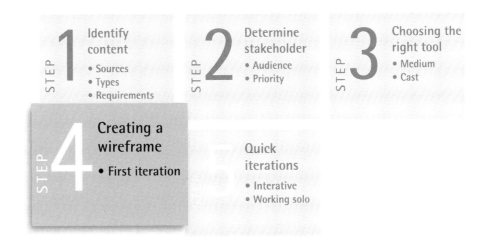

The most important step is to draw something quickly, either on paper or the computer. Don't spend time analyzing–just draw. The first idea in a wireframe will launch many more ideas, and you will correct and refine your ideas as you go along. With speed comes the ability to iterate, as none of these dynamic refinements will occur if you spend so much time getting a first draft done that looks like a finished product. There is nothing that inhibits free discussions and new ideas more than a prototype that looks already finished. When confronted with a finished-looking wireframe, people look reactively to fix the design rather than think of new ways to do the same thing. So feel free to make the first wireframe very sketchy as long as it communicates what you are trying to design. Try following these instructions to help you along.

Start at the design framework level by creating a screen layout using simple graphic or text boxes with a black outline and no fill. By beginning in this manner the structure of a screen as well as the sequencing of screens and their components can quickly be defined. When this overall framework is built, you can begin to better define each blocked area. The labels at this stage can be generic: global navigation, logo, main content, and page navigation. As the basic structure is filled in with content, all the important elements that comprise the design can be accounted for.

Global elements common to all pages, such as navigation or header icons, can be identified and become reusable screen elements used repeatedly across an entire wireframe.

As the wireframe evolves, the different sections can be labeled in greater detail and the content can become less generic. Dummy, or greeked, content can be flowed in, and widgets can be described with simple boxes. For example, an input box can be described by a slim rectangle and a pull-down menu by a rectangle with a "v" on the right side to indicate the pull-down widget. Illustrations and graphic elements can be indicated with gray or colored boxes. We recommended that illustrations and graphics not be used if possible. In the end the degree to which a wireframe is described visually is up to you, but by keeping the graphic elements to a minimum, a wireframe can quickly become a representation of the requirements rather than a design direction taken too early. If the requirements are not in alignment, a new iteration or a reexamination of the requirements, which in turn may lead to a new wireframe, is necessary anyway. When the requirements begin to stabilize and wireframe iterations begin to be minor refinements instead of re-conceptualizations, the wireframe process is finished and the team is ready to go to the next design step: something more interactive or fuller narrative like a storyboard.

Once the wireframe has its base components on which you have iterated several times to better represent your product, it now provides a good representation of the content that can effectively be used to gain agreement across the team regarding the initial design direction. Finally, a wireframe will begin to seem confining with its limited visualization, indicating that it may be time to move along in the prototyping process and abandon your wireframe for a prototype with more details and interactivity.

Wireframes can be used to test an interaction concept, conceptual design, content placement, structural elements, and sequential flow in the software or website. As such, a wireframe should minimally depict these elements, whereas other content elements should be masked or deemphasized (lowering their fidelity). The emphasized elements can be sketched, such as the logo shown in Figure 15.5 or typeset as in Figure 15.6. The main point is that these emphasized elements have a higher fidelity than the less important masked elements. The less important elements can be masked either by blocking out the space as done in Figure 15.5 or by using greeked text as done in Figure 15.6.

If a wireframe is intended to be a proof of concept for the branding strategy, then all elements of that strategy need to be included in the wireframe. All elements that are not playing a major role in the branding strategy should be masked. For example, if the interaction within an article is important but not the article itself, then the links, buttons, and other navigational elements should be displayed in high fidelity and the article text should be masked. Branding elements can include almost any element that will be branded as a specific part from the company or organization, including logos, images, advertisements, and content messages.

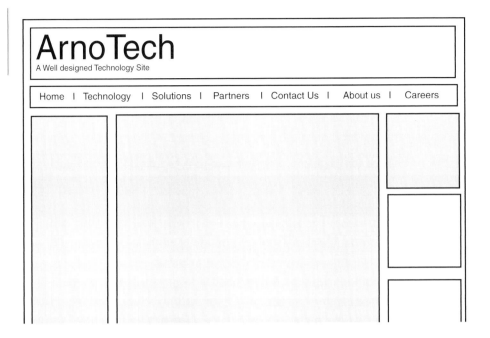

FIGURE 15.5 *Wireframe detail with low-fidelity logo and blocked text.*

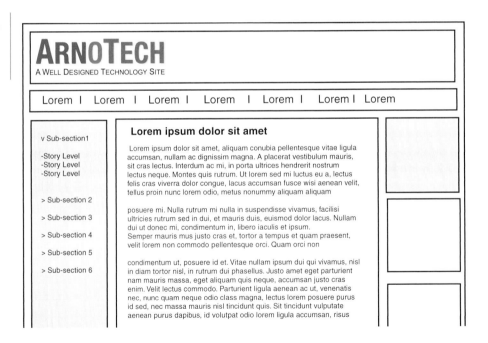

FIGURE 15.6 *Wireframe with high-fidelity logo with greeked text.*

Step 5: How Do I Evolve It?

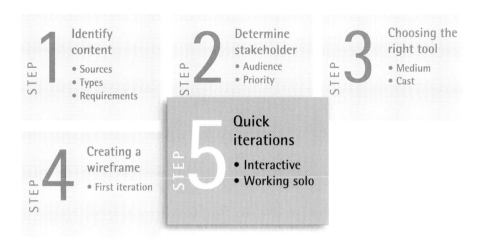

The final step consists of rapid iterations with the wireframes. By far the most dynamic and exciting parts of this step are those collaborative sessions with other stakeholders. Evolving a design in real time as experts brainstorm ideas can be one of the most rewarding design activities in the software creation process. However, in today's business world of globally distributed workforces, it's not always possible to sit around the table and create with your stakeholders face-to-face. You may need to distribute your wireframe via e-mail or provide access through a globally available server and receive responses via e-mail or telephone. You can also give a short presentation highlighting the wireframe and ask people for feedback that will be incorporated in the next design. Even when undertaking these distributed reviews and iterations, wireframes should still be done rapidly. Try to make the turnover time quick and create many versions. If you are receiving contradictory feedback, mock up that aspect in several different ways in a wireframe to see if it has potential. In Step 5, the quick iterations are designed to exhaust ideas to arrive at solid design directions that migrate into other prototyping activities.

CASE STUDY: THE HIT AND RUN WIREFRAME

Jonathan and Nevin once worked for an enterprise software products company with a very low designer-to-developer ratio. They were both involved full time on other projects but kept receiving requests from many teams but didn't have the capacity to help. After some successful rapid prototyping experiences, Nevin developed a wireframe template in Excel, a program they both knew very well and one that the other teams had access to and most certainly had used before. The wireframe templates included copy-paste building blocks as well as the company approved visual standards, including colors and icons. This template allowed the authors to quickly build wireframes on demand. After receiving a request for a wireframe, they would go into a meeting with the development team members and the tool on their laptop, ready to create the wireframe prototype in that meeting. For this software company, Excel proved to be the ideal tool due to its wide availability and utility to help the authors and other team members create prototypes rapidly.

The requesting development team performed the background work described in Step 1 of the wireframe process. At the collaborative meeting the developers would begin to state their needs while Nevin or Jonathan used Excel, starting with the wireframe template, to start creating wireframes to visualize the team's ideas.

This initial wireframe would expose errors in assumptions and missing requirements and lead to some immediate revisions. The result of the meeting was always an infinitely clearer view of the requirements for everyone involved and a rudimentary design to continue to work from.

LEAVING WIREFRAMES: THE NEXT ITERATION

The next logical prototype step after a wireframe is a higher fidelity interactive prototype such as a storyboard or paper prototype. Depending on the tool used to create your wireframe, you may be able to develop the next iteration of the prototype using the wireframe sequence as a basis. For example, an image of the wireframe structure could be directly used in a graphics tool, such as Photoshop, as a background layer on top of which you can build more detailed screen representations that are then used in a prototyping tool, such as PowerPoint or Flash.

REFERENCES

Larry Constantine. Canonical Abstract Prototypes for Abstract Visual and Interaction Design. Lecture Notes in Computer Science. Berlin/Heidelberg: Springer Verlag, 2003, pp. 1–15.

Thomas Tullis. A method for evaluating web page design concepts. Proceeding of CHI '98 Extended Abstracts. New York: ACM Press, 1998, pp. 323–324.

CHAPTER

16

STORYBOARD PROTOTYPING

DESCRIPTION

Storyboards are a narrative prototype. They narrate a scenario illustrating how the use cases and functional requirements are played out in the context of a user's actual tasks. The storyboard usually follows a specific plot or storyline to tell the story illustrated with interface mockups or illustrations of end users using/interacting with the software.

Storyboards are most often created early in the software design process. A storyboard is also used to help software teams flesh out the convergence of ideas early to assure that everyone on the team is on the same page. Storyboards create a great artifact for a shared understanding of what the goals of the software should be and what the software should do. Later in the process, the storyboard can act as a check to keep the team focused on the core solution.

Storyboards allow stakeholders who are less involved in the design process to get up to speed by providing a common understanding of the domain and the initial software design. Technical writers, quality assurance testers, and information architects are among the people who greatly benefit from the storyboard. Marketing and sales can also often take the internal storyboard and, with a little sprucing up, reuse it as marketing demonstrations or presentations to potential customers and clients.

User research, whether performed before or after the initial storyboard creation, can enrich and augment the storyboard. When new research significantly changes the storyboard, the change in the storyline or the players in the storyboard inform the team what parts of their prior work need to be revisited. Moreover, when new scope threatens to creep into the project, the storyboard provides the discipline to ensure that the feature really gives added value to the software.

Storyboards can be as simple or as complex as you want them to be. You can narrate a single user session, which comprises only a few screens, such as a quick e-commerce purchase. Or you can use a storyboard to string together related use cases to understand how they work together, such as in the fulfillment system for the e-commerce purchase that must incorporate use cases from accounting, supply chain and customer relation management.

A storyboard can evolve and grow as your understanding of the product grows. A storyboard can begin as just a text narrative and then can become enriched with dialogue, screen visualizations, or videos. A storyboard can start out as the main prototype early in the software creation process and, if used correctly, can fade into the background as other prototype methods are used later. But a storyboard will always remain as a trusted friend, guiding the software makers and keeping them focused on the software's context of use.

A storyboard can depict either a pie-in-the-sky software concept or an iteration of an existing system. To be based on the real world, we recommend not rushing ahead to create a storyboard without having good initial feedback from domain specialists and users. Informed user research is needed early in the storyboard process. Otherwise, you risk an unrealistic storyboard, which would need to be started all over again if found to be invalid. Minor improvements and iterations are a natural part of the storyboarding process, but a complete rewrite of the previous effort is a waste of time, and won't serve anyone's purpose.

A storyboard is not validated in the sense of usability testing; instead it is validated by a review by domain experts and/or user researchers. Storyboards can also be shown to users, customers or other external experts for validation, this is usually done as part of a focus group. These participants can be asked to validate the storyboard if their real-world experiences match the storyboard, and if not what is missing. This early validation can set the context and strategy for ongoing user research, which is particularly valuable in days of short user research timelines and discount user research methods.

A storyboard can be an essential design artifact to help you understand the following:

> ➤ Do you have an accurate understanding of the domain?
> ➤ Do your existing use cases or function set make sense?
> ➤ Are your use cases or function set complete?
> ➤ How will the envisioned software be used to achieve users' goals?
> ➤ What is the value proposition of the software for the end users and/or customers?
> ➤ What are the other contextual factors that affect how a user interacts with the software?

CHARACTERISTICS

Audience—In the beginning the storyboard is and to a certain extent always remains an internal stakeholder document. Even when being shown to external audiences, this occurs judiciously. In general, these external audiences only see a subset of the entire storyboard, usually the most compelling parts, or those relevant to a focus group, sales demo, or analyst presentation.

Stage–Storyboard prototypes are early to midterm prototypes.

Speed–The storyboard can be rapid or diligent. A rapid storyboard can easily be iterated into a diligent one. What starts as a brainstorming vehicle can end up being a sales demonstration once the design process is completed.

Longevity–The longevity can vary greatly. How long will a storyboard be used in the development process? Is it just to get a common understanding of what the software should be? If so, then the storyboard need progress no further than a quick sunny-day story with sketch-like visual examples. Is the storyboard going to live beyond the software creation and act as a sales and marketing tool? This calls for an iterative approach that ultimately ends in a presentation worth showing to the outside world. If a storyboard will be used only in the initial stages, then a physical storyboard works as well as a digital one. If, however, the storyboard will help drive use case definition and user requirements and act as an evolving understanding of the user, then a digital format is required because of the ease with which it can be updated and refined.

Expression–Storyboard prototypes are concrete because they are, by definition, rooted in a concrete real-world context with their narrative style.

Fidelity–Storyboards are usually lower fidelity in the beginning. Physical storyboards are definitely lower fidelity. Digital ones begin as lower fidelity (and may remain that way) but can evolve in fidelity as they are updated with screen shots from more interactive prototypes.

TABLE 16.1 Storyboard Content and Fidelity Matrix

Content	Very Low Fidelity	Low Fidelity	Medium Fidelity	High Fidelity	Highest Fidelity
Information design	+	+ +	+ +	+	− −
Interaction design	− −	+	+ +	−	−
Visual design	+ +	+ +	+	+	− −
Editorial content	+ +	+	−	− −	− −
Branding expression	+ +	+	+	+	+
System performance	+ +	+	NA	NA	NA

+ +, Most appropriate;
+, appropriate;
−, not appropriate;
− −, completely inappropriate;
NA, not applicable.

Style–Storyboard prototypes are narrative, not interactive.

Medium–Storyboard prototypes can be physical or digital. Physical storyboards are easier for some people to create and can also be more fun; however, they have a shorter life span than digital versions, which are easier to update and iterate on. A physical storyboard is also intended more for internal consumption, whereas the digital prototype can also be shown to stakeholders outside of the software creation team.

AN OVERVIEW OF WHAT A STORYBOARD PROTOTYPE LOOKS LIKE

A typical storyboard has a narrative, which it combines with visual elements to represent key scenes that reinforce the storyline. The most common storyboard approach is to begin with a purely narrative document, such as the one pictured in Figure 16.1. This outline forms the script that the storyboard will follow. Depending on where you are in the software creation process, the storyboard is then enriched with visuals that are either simple pictures of users interacting with the system (avoid showing the actual system) or include sketch wireframes of the interface or even screen captures of digital prototypes of the actual interface, as shown in Figure 16.2. The drawings can be rough, not polished. As you can see on closer examination, Figure 16.2 is not a high-fidelity prototype but just a simple wireframe. You also only need to visualize key moments and let the narrative fill in the gaps.

FIGURE 16.1 *A storyboard narrative.*

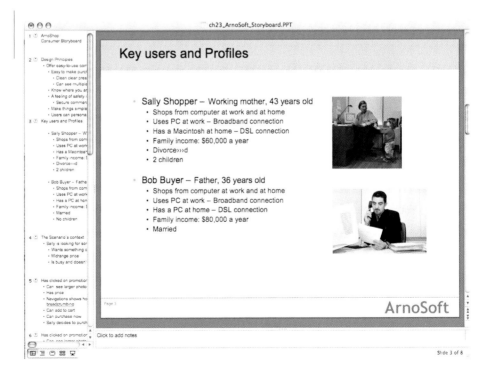

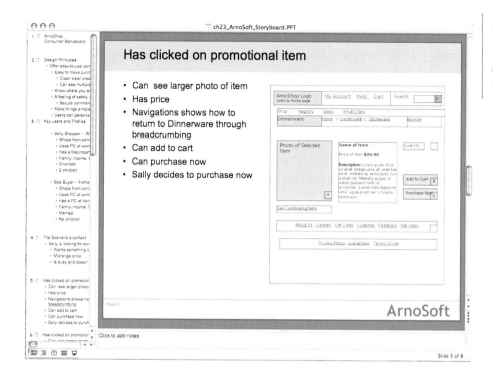

FIGURE 16.2 *A story-board with a mockup page added to the narrative.*

TYPES OF STORYBOARDS
High-Priority Task Scenarios

High-priority task scenarios are the most common focus of a storyboard. They are scenarios built around the highest priority functionality within the design, strung together in a logical way. The scenario starts at the beginning of a high-priority task and follows the task through its steps to its conclusion. This is the easiest way to map to existing use cases. This works well for simpler systems with a smaller number of user experience design resources. A focus on high-priority tasks uses the logic that in getting these critical tasks correct will be more forgiving if the less common tasks are poorly designed.

This is also the most common storyboard technique because it is the least rigorous and quickest to complete. The shorter time to achieve results speaks to software creation teams, which are always under aggressive deadlines. It can be successful as long as one does not equate high priority with merely most often performed. Making that assumption, this high-priority perspective is the most common but also the most common source of errors in software. The myth is that the most common tasks are the main tasks that a user would be engaged in with the system. In very few systems is this actually true. A major cause for mistakes that end users make do not occur during the most common tasks but in ancillary tasks with far-reaching consequences. These ancillary tasks tend to be overlooked because of their so-called low priority. Before exclusively focusing on the most common scenarios, look critically at the software you are designing.

A Day in the Life of a User

Creating a storyboard of a day in the life of a user is an ideal way to understand user routines, habits, and how a user might incorporate a system into their daily life. The scenario begins when the user starts a task, with or without a computer, which leads to the first software activity for the day. The scenario then follows the user through the course of a typical day to understand how he might use or incorporate the software into his daily life. This storyboard perspective has the advantage that the user not only touches on high-priority tasks but all the likely tasks performed in a given day. If there are special days, for example, a regular day when the user carries out some routine task, such as generating reports, then the scenario can branch off to cover that special activity. Software programs that benefit from this perspective include personal productivity tools, personal websites, information applications, and consumer websites. The negative side to this focus is the reliance on personas to follow a "typical" or archetypal user because a scenario is needed for every persona that works significantly differently from the one portrayed in the storyboard. Another downside is that by taking the perspective of a single end user you may be missing requirements for software that necessitate or encourage collaboration among work groups. To avoid this pitfall, see Pruitt and Adlin [2006] regarding the appropriate usage of personas and methods for creating them.

A Day in the Life of a Work Group

A day in the life of the work group is an ideal way to understand how a group of users intend to use common system parts together. By focusing on the group, you don't miss key points that relying on a single user perspective would result in. A storyboard of the work group day allows multiple personas to play a central role instead of just one. It also allows a plot line, much like a movie, where interrelated but separate tasks flow together. This type of storyboard often starts with a list of personas, the cast of characters. Also included are personal motivations regarding work associated with the personas. Once the personas and plot are elaborated, the information is threaded together to represent persona use of the system to achieve a group goal through performing individual tasks. This scenario approach is best for work group-related software or for software that relies on a collaborative element, such as enterprise software, complex collaborative environments, and project management software.

Critical Incidents or Critical Task Situations

Critical incidents are key defining moments for software, where extraordinary usage, as opposed to everyday usage, proves its real value. Warning detection systems, security systems, and software with peak seasonality, such as tax processing software, are all examples of systems defined by extraordinary usage. Because some software systems are meant to be used much differently in critical moments than in daily moments, it is important to ensure that the development team has not overlooked these occasions. Products like safety software or even accounting software have different types of usage depending on circumstances. For example, users may not have much interaction with budgeting software until the yearly company-wide budgetary process begins and suddenly time becomes critical and many people are involved. For an appreciation of the real usability challenges of the system, it makes much more sense to storyboard the critical incident rather than a typical day in the life of a single budget analyst. A critical incident storyboard follows a user or work group through a typical critical incident in the software usage. This scenario should start at the onset of the critical incident or juncture and continue until the incident is resolved. Critical incidents come from user research, where both good and bad user stories provide a context-rich background and cogent reference point for the storyboard. Of course, it is important to pick a common critical incident and not an edge case. When you design for the edge case, you end up with the word processor that is annoying to use when writing a letter but works perfectly for generating cross-reference tables.

Sunny Day

For exploratory storyboards, a design team often starts with a sunny-day scenario to flesh out the best-case use of the software when a user successfully uses the system. This focus allows the team to concentrate on the functionality of the software independent of quality assurance issues and exception cases (which should both be addressed later in the software-making process). The main advantage of the sunny-day approach is that it is quick and easy to write. Sunny-day storyboards can work for almost any software where the team is first coming to grips with understanding the system being built. The sunny-day approach, though universally applicable, has an equally universal short lifespan. When a thorough understanding emerges of the software's workings in the sunny-day scenario, then reality needs to set in and the team needs to learn about and address the real-world constraints of the software. For this added context, the sunny-day approach should be converted into one of the other storyboard perspectives above. This conversion process can be made easy by simply enriching the sunny-day content with more contextual information.

Who Participates in the Storyboard Creation Process

Storyboard creation is a key activity in which all major stakeholders can involve themselves in the software ideation process. In the act of creating a storyboard narration, the context is set by dealing with such issues as:

- ➤ Who will use the software?
- ➤ Under what conditions will they use the software?
- ➤ How will the software's functions and features adequately support user tasks or activities?
- ➤ How will the software's usage affect others in a collaborative or workflow environment?

This context could potentially drastically redefine, narrow, or expand a given requirement or use case by fleshing out the specific conditions in which it will be used.

If all major stakeholders are not involved, a resulting storyboard may not be an accurate portrayal of the usage situations needed to inform the design. The storyboard owner then becomes the person who validates the storyboard's details with others and gets them to sign off and commit to the narrated storyline. The easiest way to get broad stakeholder agreement is to include them all in a group meeting to flesh out the storyline together. This process is more time intensive in the beginning but is usually well worth the investment as a shared vision and understanding of the requirements emerges. The storyboard is more of a reference document when it's created in a group process rather than just a coalescence of knowledge left to an individual for validation.

STEP-BY-STEP GUIDE

A storyboard does not need to be digital. A storyboard could be a series of sketches in the form of flipchart pages adhered to the walls of a team meeting room. For the design team, this display serves as a constant reminder of the usage and task context. The disadvantage of a physical storyboard is the difficulty of updating it without rewriting or redrawing the entire storyboard. A physical version is prone to being accidentally erased, torn, or otherwise ripped up. A physical prototype is also less likely to be shown to the outside world. This makes a digital version more advantageous for editing, updating, and showing to the outside world. A digital version can be created in storyboard-like software—software that can easily move from one slide or scene of the storyboard to the next, such as Keynote, PowerPoint, or other presentation software. (Because we believe presentation software is ideally suited for this task, we include on our website a template that can be opened by PowerPoint, KeyNote, or Impress.) Animation software or even certain graphics programs also work well.

The creation of the storyboard follows these seven steps:

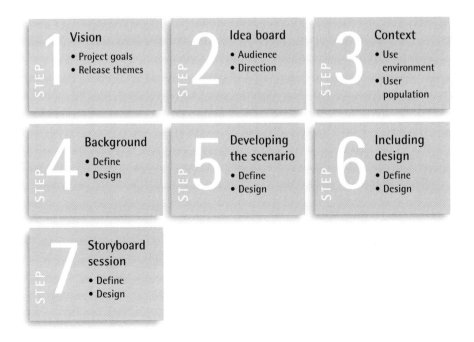

Digital presentations are better for their longevity and ease of communal use. Almost everyone has presentation software of some kind. We discuss using the presentation software; however, with some adaptation you can follow this process using any tool, including a white board.

Step 1: Vision

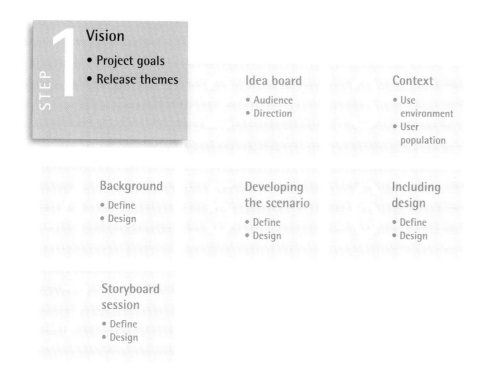

Vision Statement and Project Goals

In our experience, every good project starts with a clear vision and purpose. A clear vision keeps everyone focused on a common target. A clear purpose ensures that scope never creeps out of control. A vision always sounds like a nice-to-have, but it is a must-have statement defining what you are trying to achieve.

If one does not already exist, you can start storyboarding by trying to identify a vision for your software product or service. A vision does not simply give you free range to write platitudes; those kinds of visions are worthless. A vision tries to distill the reason for why this software will be a success in the marketplace. A vision becomes a slogan or quick phrase that helps guide our design decision-making process. Without a vision, the only guide to design decision making is best-guess and prior similar experience, which are helpful in setting up navigation models but less helpful in other user experience aspects such as branding and color usage. To help make a vision concrete, we strive to sneak in the terms of the goals of the project. An example of a bad vision is this: "The purpose of this project is to make money and keep us employed." Although undeniably true at the base level, it is not the purpose of the project; rather, the project is to make "A mail client so compelling that users will feel the need to switch from their current one to ours" or "A new way to enter time management that users do not view as an administrative annoyance but as an aid to their work." What we particularly admire about this last vision statement is that it contains two measures: one against scope creep, so that users don't view the product as an annoyance, and one to aid their work. When considering a new piece of functionality or requirement, both of these examples make the following clear: If it does not meet both of these goals, discard the idea.

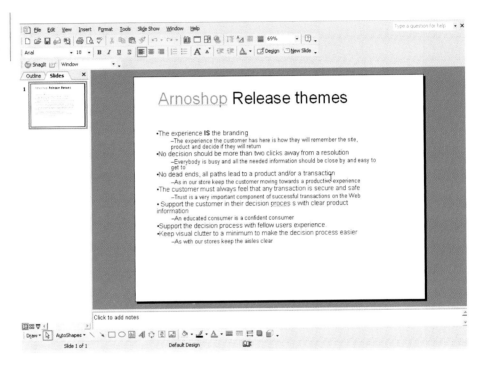

FIGURE 16.3 *Release themes in a storyboard.*

Release Themes

After a vision statement is developed for your software as a whole, try to narrow down the vision to your desires for the current software release. These release themes also become guidelines and aphorisms to help guide design, development, and scoping decisions and are especially important when the storyboard will be used for a long time.

To help brainstorm the release themes, you can hold sessions that include brainstorming activities on whiteboards or flipcharts. For example, you can ask participants what they want to achieve with this release, in light of the stated vision, and ask them to list three to five things on sticky notes. Next, you can group like goals together and synthesize the themes as a group. This is a rapid (about half an hour) and very effective method for arriving at compelling release themes.

Step 2: Idea Board

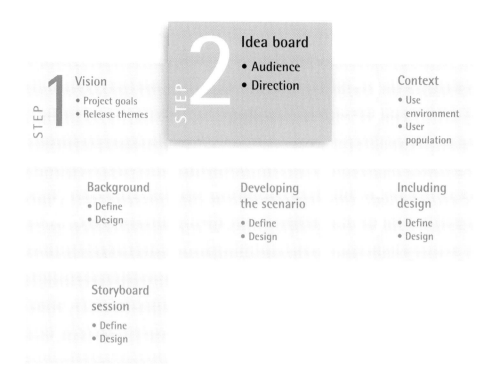

The idea board is a list of images, products, people, and writings that become sources of inspiration or guidance in the product (and thus storyboard) development. In the idea board section of the storyboard, you can develop images that fit the coming release. You can shamelessly assemble competing products or other existing products you'd like to emulate or compete with. You may also try to cut out pictures of the various personas defined for your product. You might add artistic images, quotes, or even sound bites that communicate the ideas you'd like to achieve. The idea board is sometimes a surprising source for ideas or the germs of ideas that help us design better software, but its primary purpose is to inform audience segmentation and other contextual information (company profiles and work groups). Idea boards are difficult to understand until you see one, so feel free to take ideas from the idea board shown in Figure 16.4.

Company/Organizational Profiles

If relevant, try to develop company and organizational profiles from your target audience/users. Imagine these organizational profiles are archetypal companies that are the primary market targets. The profile includes company size, products and services offered, the organization chart, their website design (by taking screen shots of similar companies on the web), location, and so on. Any information that can be considered helpful for distilling requirements or for giving you better context to the storyboard is added. In developing company profiles it is important to

FIGURE 16.4 *An idea board for use with a storyboard.*

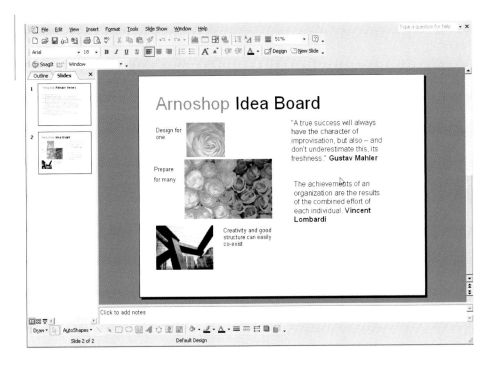

Step 3: Context

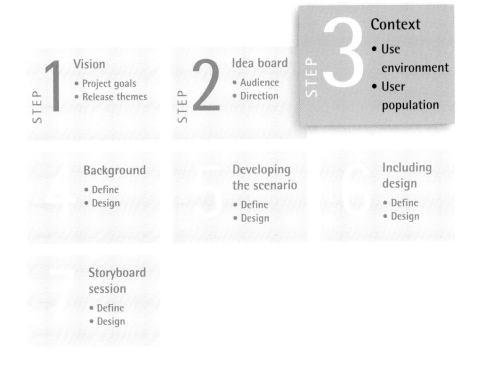

distinguish between traits needed for product requirements (e.g., this software is for companies with 10,000 or more employees) versus details needed only for context (such as this particular company is located in Detroit). You want the context traits to help drive the scenario, but they shouldn't unduly influence the requirements. You want to ask yourself is a requirement being derived from a company only because that company is located in Detroit or because it is in a large city like most of the target companies.

Cast of Characters (User Segmentation)

The cast of characters is where you specify the audience segmentation, either in the form of personas or user groups and user types. You can describe the personal backgrounds of users as reflected by user research. Try to use pictures of the real users, but you can also use archetypes found in your idea board. In your specification of end-user backgrounds, try to include all relevant background information that will influence how personas perform tasks. In some instances this can include personal information; for example, on an e-commerce site for singles, a person's relationship status plays a key role in the profile. Likewise, if the company profile suggests the employee turnover is quite high, this would attract users with certain traits. There are many methods for creating end-user profiles; refer to Kujala and Kauppinen [2004], an excellent critical summary of these approaches.

Step 4: Background

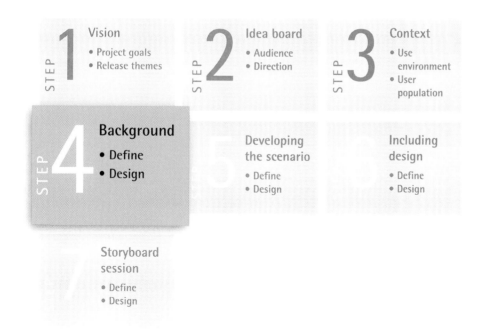

The goal of the background session is to set the scene—all the underlying and historical information needed to understand the scenario when it begins. For example, if the scenario begins with the registration of a document, the background will cover the reasons why the user needs to register the document, what the document is, and what challenges exist. Background information can be derived from any number of means, such as user research, domain experts, and personal experience.

Step 5: Developing the Scenario

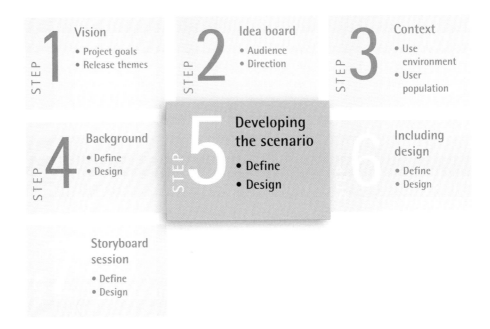

The heart of the storyboard is developing the scenario in a slide or frame format, which is broken down into three parts:

➤ Title (covered in this step)

➤ Implementation (covered in Step 6)

➤ Scenario details (covered in Step 6)

Figure 16.5 shows the typical layout of a storyboard scenario slide.

Title

The title is a headline-like description of a step in the scenario. The title doubles as the title area of the presentation slide. For example, buying a book on an e-commerce site might have the following titles:

1. User searches for book

2. User browses search results

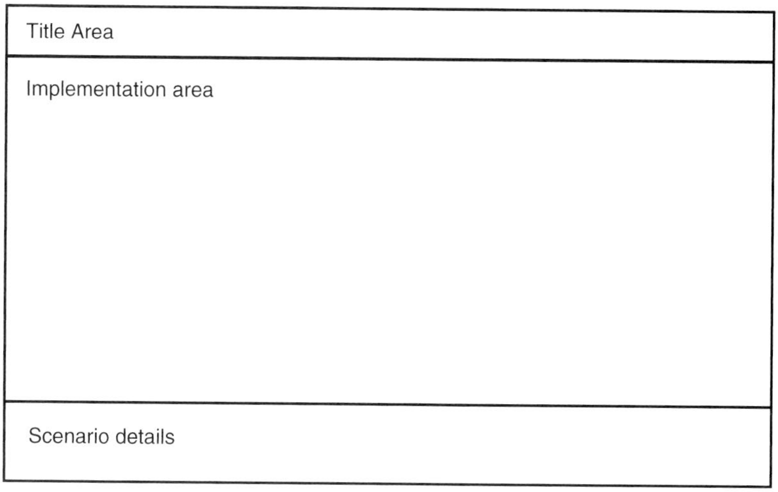

FIGURE 16.5 *The typical layout of a storyboard scenario slide.*

3. User adds book to shopping cart
4. User browses related items
5. User checks out selected items
6. User logs in to account
7. User completes purchase
8. User continues to browse website

The title is the most stable part of the prototype slide. The title establishes the scenario scope. Early in the process as you flesh out a scenario, the title may change often, redundant slides may be deleted, or scenario titles may be deemed too high level, causing a single slide to be split over several slides for more detailed specification.

WHAT IS THE SOURCE FOR THE SCENARIO?

A storyboard scenario can cover many variations in source materials. If your process is in the early stage of a product effort and you don't have access to a user study, software requirements, or use case, the storyboard can still use the domain knowledge and collective experience present among team members to flesh out assumptions. As the information sources become more grounded in user requirements (domain specialists, user research, market studies, competitive analysis, etc.), the scenarios can be enriched and acquire more credibility. In general, it is best to stick with a pure storyline until more confirmed contextual information arrives to inform the storyboard. That information can be visualized through rough sketches. Remember, the screens do not need to speak for themselves because they are part of a narrative that gives semantic context to the rough sketches. Sometimes the screens can be visualized more abstractly by using greeked text, blocked layouts, or even just pictures of end users interacting with software (without actually showing the software itself). In the latter case the focus can shift from the screen content to how the users interact with the software.

Implementation

The implementation section is where the visualization or interaction is specified. Implementation specification can be bullet points outlining the action involved or a mockup, character sketch, or screen capture. Usually, the storyboard starts with just a text description. When visuals become available, the interaction details are added to the scenario details section (described below). If maintained, the storyboard evolves from sketches to more refined screens and eventually to screen shots of the actual implementation. The original scenario details provide the narrative background required to give a demonstration or presentation to external audiences.

Step 6: Including Design

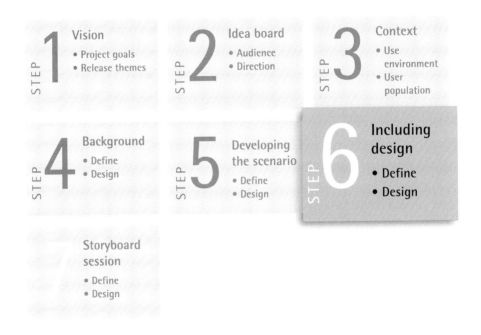

STEP **1** — Vision
- Project goals
- Release themes

STEP **2** — Idea board
- Audience
- Direction

STEP **3** — Context
- Use environment
- User population

STEP **4** — Background
- Define
- Design

STEP **5** — Developing the scenario
- Define
- Design

STEP **6** — Including design
- Define
- Design

Storyboard session
- Define
- Design

Scenario Details

The scenario details section is the "notes" section of most presentation software. The notes section includes the original text specification for the interaction and any implementation notes needed by the developers, designers, or product managers.

Step 7: Storyboard Session

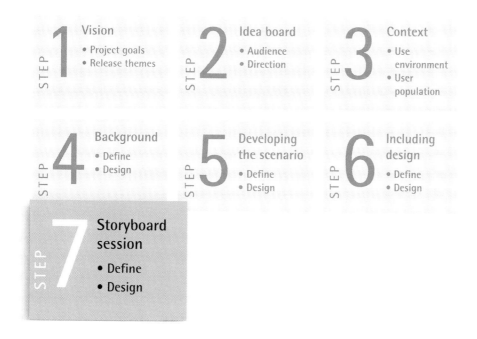

In the software development process, a storyboard helps everyone to understand both the software's domain and how the software will be used in context. Storyboards provide domain understanding by first defining the user and/or their company profiles. These profiles are then put into the context of a real-life scenario describing how the software works. For this scenario to be effective, a domain specialist and user researcher are required to share their findings with the entire group conducting the storyboard; otherwise, the scenario has no grounding in reality. This enriched domain and user knowledge is subsequently shared with anyone who reviews or sees the storyboard. The audience of the storyboard can also include other domain specialists who can validate the domain knowledge reflected in the storyboard. This approach leads to a scenario that better reflects use in real-world conditions.

FIGURE 16.6 *The story-board session with stakeholders.*

HOW THE STORYBOARD SESSION WORKS
Best-Practices Storyboard Planning

A storyboard can be started at any time in the design process. However, to be considered best practice, the storyboard needs to eventually include both domain knowledge and user research. Therefore storyboard planning needs to follow some guidelines:

1. Early storyboards, done before user research and/or domain specialists are engaged, should be ideation storyboards that are quick and easy to produce and are exploratory. The process needs to be short to ensure that participants have an open mind to changing, modifying, or throwing out their assumptions after user research data become available.

2. Information from domain specialists and user researchers should be treated with more credibility than the ideas and intuitions of the rest of the team. Design informed by the real world always yields higher results than those informed by intuition or best guesses that are not informed by direct user and domain knowledge.

3. Domain knowledge and user research should not dictate the design but establish the context in which it takes place. Informed design can be innovative; however, design dictated only by the current state of the domain cannot.

4. A suggested storyboard iteration schedule could follow this timeline:

   a. One week for blue-sky ideation storyboarding with a design/vision team.

   b. One week for more informed deep-dive storyboarding. This storyboarding exercise should include more stakeholders and should occur after or at least in parallel with user research. The more user research that occurs in the later stages of the deep-dive phase, the greater the risk that the design team will need to completely re-do early parts of the storyboard that tend to get discredited by field research.

   c. One to 2 days for iteration sessions held after evaluation and validation (see the section below). Agree on the number of iterations needed to go on to the next stage in software development (see the end of the chapter for possible next steps). This time limit ensures that the storyboard won't be an overkill effort.

5. Iterate as necessary. New products require more iterations than existing products. The authors have fought the temptation to give a magic number of iterations. The more you storyboard, the more efficient you become at it. In general, when a consensus is reached on the general domain understanding and the software requirements, the storyboard is finished.

How the Storyboard Is Iterated

The storyboard is iterated by incorporating stakeholder feedback into the storyboard that improves the real-world representation of the storyboard. The entire design team in a group meeting can then review changes. These review meetings are often informative because many team members can be inspired through their reactions to the new information. These inspired ideas often result in valuable participatory design sessions. Each new design creates a new iteration ready for a new evaluation or for the next step in a company's software creation process. Thus as the storyboard evolves, the storyboard presentation provides a natural mechanism to share the storyboard evolution with the design team.

In summary, an iterative storyboard will help you gain the following insights and advantages:

➤ Domain knowledge
➤ Software use and task context
➤ Shared vision and understanding among stakeholders
➤ Future design focus: reference and guideline
➤ High-level user/stakeholder validation

Working for a software company, Jonathan was assigned to lead the user experience effort for the introduction of a work management product that would track the work done on a company's large assets, such as factory machinery or cars and trucks. After some initial work that wasn't going anywhere, it became clear to Jonathan that the team understood neither the domain nor the requirements. He proposed a storyboard session with a domain specialist so that everyone could understand a "day in the life" of the typical users of the system. In parallel, user research would be conducted to validate assumptions from the domain specialist.

Together the team and domain specialist started with the high-end goals of the project, one of which was that the software must be very plain and easy to use, because the user is not very sophisticated. During the storyboarding exercise, it gradually became clear to the team that the product was way more complex than anyone had imagined. As the team started to work out their simple example of a worker going out on the shop floor, everyone came to realize that this user would not be carrying a laptop computer. Common terminals, personal digital assistants, or some other system would be required. The storyboard exercise, with its immediate use of contextual information and product narration, brought out conflicting product assumptions and real-world situations that helped focus user research.

Although the storyboard was useful for clarifying the direction of the work management product, it also successfully addressed other stakeholder issues. For example, when the team's management questioned the increase in product complexity and scope, the storyboard served as an ideal presentation, which the management agreed with. Using narrative and storyline instead of click-through screens put the problem clearly in lay terms.

The storyboard success was evident throughout the product development. When too many complexities were introduced, team members would quickly remind everyone on the agreed themes of simplicity and speed. Memorable quotes from user research were added to the storyboard to help drive these requirements. One of the more notable examples was a manager of employees who said, "I must have a simple system, they must be turning wrenches, not typing into a computer." The employer was emphasizing not just the need for simplicity but also the need to minimize computer usage by the target users, who were expert mechanics not computer operators.

This work management product storyboard had value for both explicitly showing functionality context and informing team members about the domain. Even though other forms of prototypes were being developed, the storyboard continued to be a reference point to keep these prototypes on track.

NEXT ITERATION GOING BEYOND THIS PROTOTYPE

Once a storyboard session is complete, storyboard scenarios initially help forge a common understanding and aid in requirements iteration and project scope assessment. The most likely next steps after early storyboarding are either an abstract prototyping method such as card sorting or another conceptual design prototype, ultimately ending in some form of interactive prototype. If the product is already mature and has an existing conceptual design, then the next logical step after the storyboard is an interactive prototype, usually something low fidelity like a paper prototype. At that point the trail reverses, the storyboard, which initially informed the first interactive prototypes, is updated with the new information derived from the interactive prototype validation with users.

REFERENCES

M. Bekker, J. Long. User involvement in the design of human-computer interactions: some similarities and differences between design approaches. In: S. McDonald, Y. Waern, G. Cockton, editors. People and Computers XV. Proceedings of HCI '00. Berlin/Heidelberg: Springer Verlag, pp. 135–147.

Hugh Beyer, Karen Holtzblatt. Contextual Design: Defining Customer-Centered Systems. San Francisco: Morgan Kaufmann, 1998.

A. Blomquist, M. Arvola. Personas in action: ethnography in an interaction design team. Proceedings of NordiCHI '02, Norway, 2002, pp. 197–200.

Sari Kujala, Marjo Kauppinen. Identifying and Selecting Users for User-Centered Design. Proceedings of NordCHI '04. New York: ACM Press, 2004, pp. 297–303.

J. Noyes, C. Baber. User-Centred Design of Systems. London: Springer, 1999.

John Pruitt, Tamara Adlin. The Persona Lifecycle. San Francisco: Morgan Kaufman, 2006.

Janice Redish, Dennis Wixon. Task analysis. In: Julie A. Jacko, Andrew Sears, editors. The Human-Computer Interaction Handbook: Fundamentals, Evolving Technologies, and Emerging Applications. Mahwah, NJ: Lawrence Erlbaum Associates, 2003, pp. 922–940.

Ben Shneiderman. Designing the User Interface. Strategies for Effective Human-Computer Interaction. Reading, MA: Addison-Wesley, 1998.

CHAPTER

17

PAPER PROTOTYPING

DESCRIPTION

Paper prototypes are best when used during the conceptual design phase preceding and informing the first detailed screen designs. These sketches of screen ideas can be drawn on paper or rendered in a digital format and printed. To mimic the working system, multiple screens and supporting interface elements are created in paper form. The system "works" by having the moderator play the role of the computer, displaying and removing paper as needed to represent system interactions. Through this interaction, users and other stakeholders can evaluate a paper prototype.

Many definitions of paper prototyping are too narrow, that is, strictly as a usability testing method. For our purposes here, we define paper prototyping as follows:

A paper prototype is any interactive visual representation of a user interface/user experience that uses the physical material of paper rather than digital computers.

Paper prototypes are essentially interactive prototypes, although they can include some storyboard-like narrative scenarios to bridge gaps in the prototype's design. Paper prototypes can be done rapidly or diligently or any combination thereof as long as the software is depicted on paper in some way. These depictions can be in low- to high-fidelity visual design. They can be used for mental model mapping via user studies, design analysis and decision making by a design team, as well as for interaction design and validation of visual design and other requirements of users. They can also be used to internally try out a design concept as well as to sell it to internal stakeholders.

Paper prototyping is most often used interactively in conjunction with a one-on-one, think-aloud usability protocol. In this protocol, a user simulates computer input either verbally or pointing to a paper screen representation. The user experience is observed as both the computer system responses are simulated using the paper representations together with verbal monologue of the test participant. Paper prototypes can also be used in narrative form with a cognitive walkthrough, where stakeholders either talk through the prototype or are talked through the prototype by the designer. In either case, the audience can comment on the paper prototype's conformance to requirements and ability to meet needs.

All too often, paper prototyping means simply 'low-fidelity prototyping.' There is some aspect of low fidelity inherent in a paper prototype, but not all aspects are necessarily low fidelity. The inherent low fidelity refers to a paper prototype's innate inability to mimic actual digital system performance or behavior. There are strategies for coping with this lack of true representation, just as there are strategies available for conducting user studies with paper prototypes. Furthermore, there are a number of different strategies to include or exclude an application's look in a paper prototype, discussed below in the "how to" section.

Paper prototyping can be used to evaluate different aspects of a system. Task flow and context of use, that is, insight into user motivations and task expectations, can be studied through creation of a prototype to represent a specific task. Since paper prototypes are usually scenario driven, using business or marketing requirements and user profile definition and storyboarding can be used to validate and refine those scenarios. Paper prototyping can also shape task flow and interaction design. This prototyping method can occur before any articulate visual definition of the user interface exists and inform the visual design direction. In fact, paper prototypes are an effective aid in validating the early direction of a visual design. On the other hand, a paper prototype could include high-level visual definitions, especially if the product is mature.

However, a paper prototype excels as an aid to interaction design. The creation of a paper prototype forces the designer to think on a level of detail of interaction that most early prototypes do not achieve.

CHARACTERISTICS

Audience—To evaluate the conceptual design, the audience needs to be users. For more specific requirements evaluation, the prototype's audience can be any stakeholder (usually internal) who wants to review the prototype's representation of specific requirements.

Stage—A paper prototype is meant for the midterm point of software design; it's best done immediately after a conceptual design is established. In the early stages, you won't have enough requirements to warrant investing in a paper prototype, nor will you have a complete conceptual design on which to base the paper prototype. At later stages, there isn't enough time to act on the findings of a paper prototype evaluation.

Speed—Paper prototypes hover precariously between rapid and diligent. Precarious because it is easy to get caught up in the details and end up spending hours on something intended to take a few minutes. Furthermore, even complex system paper prototyping is considered rapid: this can be misleading. Given the level of detail required to achieve a working paper prototype, it is very diligent work indeed in terms of interaction and information design. Nevertheless when compared with the time a coded prototype would take to achieve the same thing, paper prototyping is undeniably rapid.

Longevity—A paper prototype has medium longevity. It usually lasts until there is either a product specification based on the prototype or it's replaced by a digital prototype. Usually a paper prototype is referenced in

later stages. Paper prototypes can be kept for later reference, but this is often impractical. Impractical, first, because storing the paper prototype in an orderly manner in cubeville is precarious at best. Secondly, knowing the interaction design requires the original moderator, who may or may not be available (this is a problem shared by most physical prototypes).
Expression–Paper prototypes are concrete because they address the finest granularity of details regarding system look and feel.
Fidelity–Paper prototypes vary in fidelity. They are usually high fidelity in interaction design and information design. They can range in fidelity in branding and visual design if those elements exist. However, paper prototypes are inherently low fidelity in system response and behavior.

TABLE 17.1 **Paper Prototyping Content and Fidelity Matrix**

Content	Very Low Fidelity	Low Fidelity	Medium Fidelity	High Fidelity	Highest Fidelity
Information design	− −	−	+	+ +	+ +
Interaction design	NA	− −	+	+ +	+ +
Visual design	+	+ +	+	+	−
Editorial content	−	+	+ +	+ +	+ +
Branding expression	+	+	+	+	+
System performance	+ +	NA	NA	NA	NA

+ +, Most appropriate;
+, appropriate;
−, not appropriate;
− −, completely inappropriate;
NA, not applicable.

Style–Paper prototypes are usually interactive because they can be functionally complete and allow a user to operate the system. However, if the intended audience does not match the user profile (business or technical stakeholders, for example), then it is possible to opt for a narrative approach. With paper narratives, the designer walks the audience through a scenario, illustrating the scenario with the prototype at each step.
Medium–Paper prototypes are physical prototypes. They are by definition not digital prototypes, even if they are printed from a digital source.

WHAT DOES A PAPER PROTOTYPE GET YOU?

What are the benefits of paper prototyping? In her book about paper prototyping, Carolyn Snyder [2003, p. 13] lists them:

➤ Provides substantive feedback early in the development process–before you've invested effort in implementation.

➤ Promotes rapid iterative development. You can experiment with a diversity of ideas rather than betting the farm on one.

- ➤ Facilitates communication within and between the product management and development teams, and between them and customers.
- ➤ Does not require any technical skills, so a multidisciplinary team can work together.
- ➤ Encourages creativity and experimentation in the product development process due to its cost effectiveness.

In addition we would like to add these additional benefits of paper prototyping:

- ➤ In early stages of the software-making process, it allows the most complete interactive evaluation when compared to any other midterm prototyping method.
- ➤ Includes visual design, information design, and interaction design in any desired combination.
- ➤ Can be completed purely from either physical or digital tools or a combination thereof.
- ➤ Offers greater on-the-fly modification and flexibility than digital prototyping.
- ➤ An inviting medium for design experimentation and critical analysis.
- ➤ Allows the design team to engage early in mental-model mapping.
- ➤ Evaluates the usability of software independent of system behavior.

We would like to discuss each of these benefits in greater detail below as well as add a few caveats about when not to use paper prototyping.

Provides substantive feedback early in the development process–before you've invested effort in implementation.

Because paper prototyping requires no computer programming of any kind, it is possible to get an early evaluation on designs and/or design directions before any investment of costly development resources [Virzi et al. 1996]. This minimal investment not only saves the costs of rework but also improves quality if conducted early in the software-making process. Quality is improved through the quality of the design as well as avoiding code development for a bad design that will be thrown out later because improving it is too costly.

Promotes rapid iterative development. You can experiment with a diversity of ideas rather than betting the farm on one.

Iteration is cheap and quick with paper prototyping, providing the designer with more design cycles in which to refine the design. Often the refinements result in a design that bears little resemblance to the original design, meaning that the iterative process successfully uncovered issues. With other methods, an initial design will often be refined but never completely iterated as paper prototyping allows.

Facilitates communication within and between the product management and development teams, and between them and customers.

The early production of a paper prototype gives the entire team a tangible design artifact. Because of its lack of completeness, the first versions of a paper prototype are often not employed in usability tests but rather refined based on revised requirements. These requirements changes arise from discussion and analysis among the members of the product design team and other relevant stakeholders, such as product managers and developers. By including a diverse group of stakeholders, the prototyping sessions become a shared experience on the good and bad points of the user experience design, allowing the design and development teams to share understandings and goals.

Does not require any technical skills, so a multidisciplinary team can work together.

Akin to returning to basics, the arts and crafts techniques we learned in our earlier school years are effective in creating paper prototypes. Paper prototypes can be created quickly with varying combinations of simple tools such as pencils, pens, scissors, adhesive tape, glue sticks, and paper. Paper prototype development generally follows storyboard development in which similar arts and crafts techniques can be used.

Encourages creativity and experimentation in the product development process due to its cost effectiveness.

As alluded to above, using the paper prototyping method early in the design process affords the designer an opportunity to make mistakes. More specifically, in the spirit of experimentation, paper prototyping affords software makers the opportunity to purposely try multiple designs with very little expenditure of time and money.

Allows the most complete interactive evaluation when compared to any other early or midterm prototyping method.

Paper prototyping is usually conducted after some conceptual design has been done, enough to provide guidance on the detailed design of the system. At this stage, screen layout and content details are first defined, which in turn leads to iteration of the conceptual design so that the two can be revised and iterated in parallel. This parallel work allows validation or other evaluation of the conceptual design without waiting for the working system to be available.

Includes visual design, information design, and interaction design in any desired combination.

Although paper prototyping is primarily a user interface and user experience design rough-sketch medium, it is also an opportunity to experiment with combining the early visual design, information design, and interaction design concepts. Paper prototyping allows easy experimentation with different combinations or compositions of these design aspects before the design team moves on to rapid, interactive digital prototyping.

Can be completed purely from either physical or digital tools or a combination thereof.

A paper prototype can be easily created with any tool, allowing for easy cross-discipline collaboration. For example, a visual designer can create paper prototypes with prints from a graphics application such as Photoshop, while a developer can create them in a modeling application such as Visio, and an interaction designer can create paper prototypes by sketching or cutting or pasting items on sheets of paper. This flexibility allows paper prototyping skills to be dispersed throughout a software-making organization, thus reinforcing the positive synergies of collaborative design, such as a more concentrated and coordinated design effort, more timely analysis and decision making, and input from the entire software-making team.

Offers greater on-the-fly modification and flexibility than digital prototyping.

Paper prototyping is essentially a sketch medium that maps user perception models to more concretely evolving task and interaction flows. In the spirit of sketching, paper prototyping allows ad-hoc generation of variant ideas that can be laid out on a large wall or whiteboard space. These ideas can be discussed and compared more readily in these physical forms than through the constrained view of a computer monitor. The same physical layout techniques can be used after a one-on-one paper prototyping session to allow participants to reflect on their thoughts and feedback during an evaluation session.

Inviting the user to experiment and critique.

Paper prototyping is also a sketch medium for participants in paper prototype user study sessions. The physical medium is well suited to participatory design as it allows participants to interact with a system without the need of a computer, a running system, or any other technical limitations. Participants can add or subtract from what is in front of them or even sketch something new. Using the materials and techniques described above, a participant can be encouraged to visualize a work task or other activity with the paper medium. Participants can then be further encouraged to re-draw elements they're not satisfied with and add them as new pieces, or tear off already attached pieces and move them around, and so forth. It's important to remember that the paper artifacts are not precious; they're malleable, and participants should be comfortable experimenting with them. Participants can be further encouraged to change and rearrange components as well as change their minds and ideas while verbalizing their thoughts and critical comments aloud. The net results of this activity are that the participants' mental processes and perceptions can be recorded and mapped and the resulting paper artifacts are visual evidence of those processes and perceptions. This information has high value for a design team while they perform critical and comparative analysis of the results to better identify and understand user thought patterns, perceptions, and activity performance.

Mental-model mapping.

According to Don Norman in his book, *The Design of Everyday Things* three different aspects of mental models must be distinguished: the design model, the user's model, and the system image. To successfully design interactive software, the designer's model must match as closely as possible to users' understanding of how to perform tasks and operate a system to do that. The system image, i.e., how a system appears and functions in the mind of the user, must be faithful to both the design model and the user model; that is, it must be designed with frequent user participation and intuitively understood by the user. Paper prototyping is a simplified physical format that members of a design team can use to understand how users perceive a task or activity environment as well as perform certain tasks and activities in that environment. With this information the design team can take steps toward successfully reconciling the various aspects of mental models into a product that is easy to learn and use.

Evaluates the usability of software independent of system behavior.

One of the primary reasons for early prototyping with paper or other physical materials (such as blank models) is to optimize the relationships of design and user models as well as to sketch system images without confronting computer system constraints and behaviors. Paper prototypes provide usability design knowledge and direction that can drive designers and engineers to create systems that support and accommodate maximum usability. Designing usability, user experience, and software systems involves negotiation and bargaining to achieve the correct balance among business needs, sales, usability, and engineering.

OVERVIEW OF WHAT A PAPER PROTOTYPE LOOKS LIKE

Paper prototyping uses paper or cardboard artifacts to represent the user interface of any kind of computer-based system, ranging from server administration systems to desktop computers, from websites to handheld devices.

The paper prototyping process begins by first making hand-drawn or printed representations of screen designs or screen components such as dialog boxes. These paper

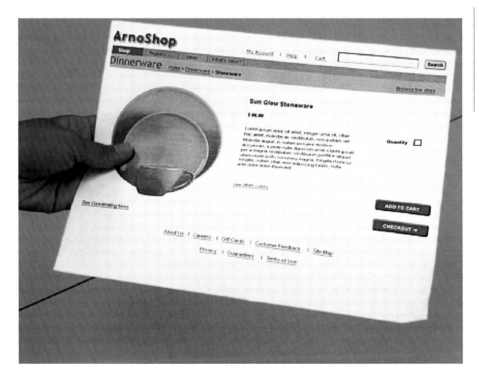

FIGURE 17.1 *The main screen of a paper prototype. In this version, the main screen is created digitally.*

FIGURE 17.2 *A paper prototype in use with the facilitator playing the role of the reactive computer system.*

visualizations are then collated into sequences of screen flows. Then, by placing one screen down in place of another, the prototype moderator can mimic a running system.

STEP-BY-STEP GUIDE TO CREATING PAPER PROTOTYPES

Paper prototypes as sketches allow a design team to explore divergent user experience concepts by having the various team members reflect on a task storyboard or scenario; members then create a series of sketch screens to represent their ideas, using arts and crafts supplies (though digital images which are printed out work as well). After sketching a series of screens, the team can review and evaluate what they've done to determine if they need to sketch more screens and concept variations. This is a rapid, iterative approach to successfully exploring, then evaluating, variations on a user experience theme.

The steps involved in creating a paper prototype:

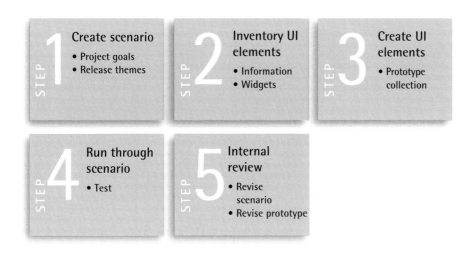

Step 1: Create Scenario

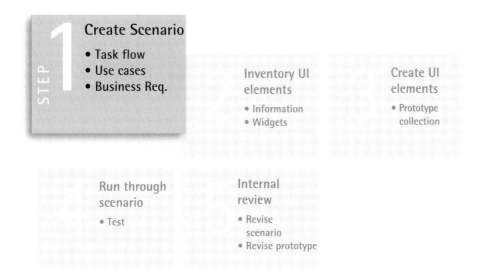

Use a scenario narration to portray the main user goals and the tasks needed to perform with the system. If you have created a storyboard, it is a good source for the scenario. (If no scenario exists, you should be able to brainstorm a few scenarios in 2 to 4 hours.)

In our experience, the completion time required to create a paper prototype for an average complex desktop application is 1 to 2 weeks. For websites and Web applications, which have much more limited interaction capabilities, the time can be trimmed to 1 to 2 days. Iterating a paper prototype can usually occur in half a day, depending on the complexity of the changes. If wholesale changes are needed, usually half the time taken to create the original prototype is required.

Creating the scenario step means creating a task or user activity scenario that covers all the main functionality that should be included in the prototype. This functionality, in the midterm of a software creation process, should already be known and documented, at least in the form of use cases, task flows, or business requirements. The scenario should follow a typical user through the routine usage of the product. Some common exceptions should be planned for, but because you don't have enough contextual information to be prepared for all contingencies, don't worry about them at this stage; you will address those later when you prepare to present or test the prototype.

Step 2: Inventory UI Elements

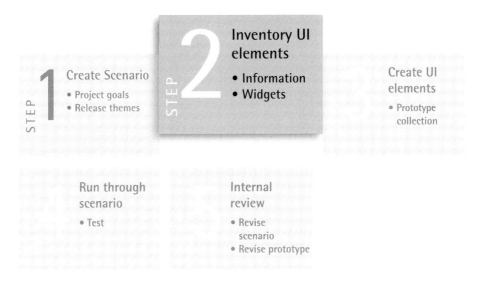

Create a checklist of all interface elements needed to support the scenario (1 to 5 hours maximum).

In the next step, the scenarios are used to inventory the main screens of the product; that is, what information is needed and what secondary or other windows and widgets are needed (modal dialogues, pull-down menus, messages, etc.). This process should result in a list of items, each with a check box next to it and a space to write the document where the item resides and a place for notes to jot down during the internal review of Step 5.

Step 3: Create UI Elements

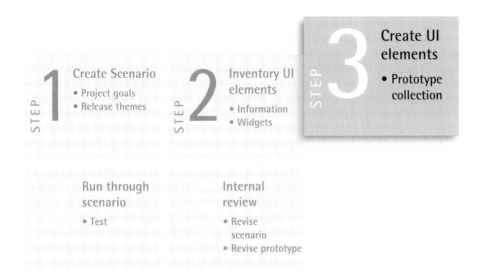

Create every item on the checklist (average, 1 to 3 days, 3.5 day maximum for most systems. Very complex systems may require more time).

In Step 3, you need to create the screens and other user interface elements.

For some tips on paper prototype creation, see the sidebar Making a Prototype From Paper.

When you finish, you should have some means of collecting and organizing the prototype into organizational units (we use the traditional colored folder system: red for main screens, blue for modal dialogs, green for menu items, etc.). The last thing to do in this step is to review the inventory list created in the previous step and check off each item that was created; it will save you a lot of trouble in the next step.

Step 4: Run through scenario

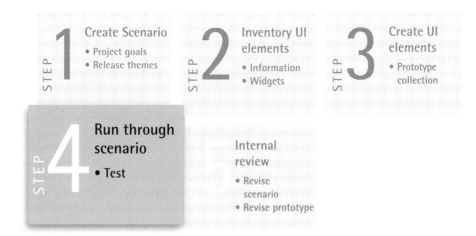

Perform your own dry-run through the scenario with the paper prototype and create any missing parts (4 to 8 hours; 1.5 day maximum).

In Step 4, you run through the scenario. Place the paper prototype screens in an orderly fashion on one table. On a second table, place the starting window for the prototype. Then, try to go through the scenario by *operating* the paper prototype. You should be able to fill in forms (use a sticky note so that you can remove your entries later and not need to reprint everything), click on buttons or links (with your finger), show the system reactions through pieces of paper representing windows or pull-down menus, etc. In this run through, you should catch the missing pieces and any requirements that were overlooked. This gives you a chance to revise your checklist and quickly create a few more screens before the internal review. For those who need a more detailed process for this step, please see the guided activity for the prototype test below.

Step 5: Internal Review

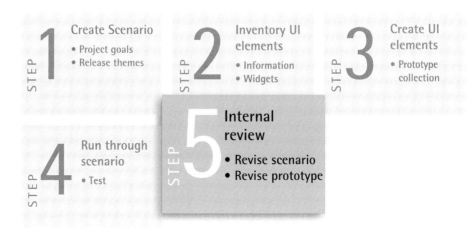

Show the prototype to relevant stakeholders (1 day; 1.5 day maximum).

For the internal review, you bring in a couple key internal stakeholders (more if you can manage it) and show them the prototype. It is critical to get someone from development to review the prototype and acknowledge the direction. Often you will get some technical feasibility feedback, which will return you to altering the scenario, changing the inventory, and creating more user interface elements. You will feel like a user interface element foundry, but in the end (and in record time compared to any alternative), you will have a completely functional and totally robust prototype of the software that will not crash, unless a strong draft blows in during the review.

MAKING A PROTOTYPE FROM PAPER

When creating a paper prototype, the drawing-challenged have the tendency to want to design the screens in a graphics package and print the results. While this is a legitimate approach, it can be an ineffective approach, if the visual fidelity is too high. Ineffective, because users tend to feel freer providing feedback on screens with a less polished look. So how do you create paper prototypes if you can't draw by hand well? We've provided some tips below.

Pull-down menus—Prepare a list of all the pull-down menus you need to define. In a word processing program, create a table with 5 to 6 columns using 12 or 14 point type (bigger type is more legible) and an easy to read print font (e.g., Verdana or Helvetica) and use double-spaced lines. Word processor columns support list creation. In the columns, type the menu name first then all the menu commands. If you're creating more than 5 to 6 menus, add another row to the table and you get another 5 to 6 menus to type. If rows are breaking across pages, there is a setting in most word processor table properties that prohibits rows from crossing pages. The menus are created by cutting each column into a strip of paper after you print the document. When a user taps a finger on the menu command, you place the resulting menu list on the prototype.

Fields and tables—To create fields, use a spreadsheet application and make the columns wide enough for the longest label and very wide for a text entry field. Tables can also be mimicked in a spreadsheet program by making the grid columns much wider and the row height much higher than normal; then, add borders to draw the table.

Dialog windows—To create a simple dialog, use a word processor document. Make the margins narrow, about half a page. First, type the window title of the dialog. Skip two lines, then type the dialog text. Add the field labels, if any. Then, on the bottom line, in boldface, type OK<tab>Cancel<tab>Help.

The time–pressed prototyper will draw by hand the borders around the buttons. The prototyper with a more generous deadline will use the software to draw rectangles around the button text, add rectangles for the field areas, and draw squares for the check boxes. Finally, select all the text and draw a border around it. Print and cut.

Main windows—Don't try to design an entire window; instead, break it down into smaller parts that can be pasted or laid out together. For example, for a paper prototype of a Web application, it is much easier to draw a form (say in a form design program) and a table (in a spreadsheet program) and print them separately. Then cut and paste together into a single composition.

Menu bars—A menu bar can be made in two easy ways. Method 1: in a word processor, set the page orientation to landscape. Set the background to light gray. Using bold text (again, 12–14 point Verdana or Helvetica) create your menu text on one line with each word separated by a<tab>. Print the page, but only cut out that one-line strip. Place the menu bar at the top of the paper prototype "window". Method 2: in a spreadsheet, set the page orientation to landscape. Increase the width of the cells to equal the distance of the menu bar in the spreadsheet window. Select the entire second row, format the cells with a light gray background. Set text to bold and 12 to 14 point Verdana or Helvetica. Type one menu item in each cell. Print and cut out.

Progress bars–On a yellow sticky note, either draw a watch or cut and paste a watch from a magazine ad. Next to the watch, write in block letters: "Please Wait!" At any prolonged pause during the paper prototyping session, place the watch over the paper interface. The facilitator should ignore any input performed by the user while the watch is displayed, unless there is a Cancel button next to the watch.

And the best part is, you can re-use all this. Even if you're creating a paper prototype for a new product, it will probably still need menu bars, dialogs, forms, and tables. You have just created templates. Ones that will surely need to be modified, but they'll give you a head start on your next prototype.

OPERATING THE PAPER PROTOTYPE

The first type of paper prototype user study session is an **interactive technique** that involves a participant and a facilitator. The two engage in a role-playing dialogue in which the participant details completion of a pre-defined task or task set while simultaneously constructing an improvisational representation of a user interface from readily available paper-based materials. This session's purpose is to understand user thought processes about task environments, specific tasks, and how to complete them using computer technologies. This information is generally gathered in the initial stages of product conceptualization and design to serve as one of several bodies of information that inform a nascent design.

Sitting face to face across a table, the facilitator begins a session by activating a video recording device, then explaining the study's purpose and the think-aloud procedure. The facilitator further describes the use of the paper materials and office supplies on the table for constructing a representation of a user interface to accomplish the described task. Useful supplies include paper, scissors, pens, pencils, clear adhesive tape, and a glue stick.

To get the participant in the right frame of mind, the facilitator has the participant read the task scenario aloud and turns the session over to the participant, who begins talking and gesturing through the task scenario, while at the same time creating a visualization of the user interface in collage fashion using the materials. From time to time, the participant may falter, requiring the facilitator to provide just enough prompting and guidance for the participant to continue through the session. Once a session is complete, the facilitator has the participant reflect on it and verbally articulate the overall experience, including both walking through the scenario and constructing the paper visualizations. This reflection period provides useful information about user thoughts and perceptions on the tasks performed, especially in terms of the user interface artifacts he or she has constructed. The participant's reflections often reveal clever means of performing tasks in addition to potential cognitive breakdowns in task performance due to certain user interface characteristics, such as too many controls and modalities.

The next type of technique, **paper prototype as interaction and task flow design**, is also meant to be used in the early stages of software conceptualization and design. Members of a product design team are engaged in interactive sessions using a large empty wall or whiteboard with visualizations of tasks and subtasks represented on paper, such as sticky notes. This ideation technique logically follows the *interactive technique*, user study, paper prototype sessions mentioned above, and, in fact, should be informed by these and any other user research conducted to date. This paper-based technique, which involves mapping task flows and interaction sequencing, is used to visualize user behaviors and software behaviors as they relate to task scenarios as identified by the design team.

Similar to the *interactive technique*, the third paper prototyping technique also involves a facilitator and an individual participant, but the paper prototypes are created by designers in advance of the session. This **paper prototype feedback session** is used to get user opinions about early design and task flow ideas represented on paper. Using a pre-defined scenario, ideally informed by user research, storyboarding, and the two previously mentioned paper prototype techniques, the facilitator guides a participant through a series of tasks while simultaneously presenting the visualizations on paper. The objective is to capture the participant's verbal and gestural feedback for review and analysis by the design team. These sessions are typically recorded on video or audiotape for later examination.

STEP-BY-STEP GUIDE TO TEST THE PROTOTYPE

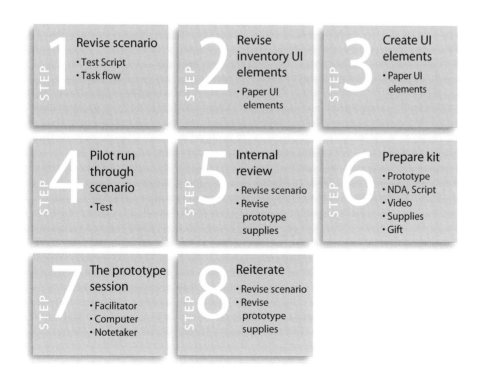

STEP 1 — Revise scenario
- Test Script
- Task flow

STEP 2 — Revise inventory UI elements
- Paper UI elements

STEP 3 — Create UI elements
- Paper UI elements

STEP 4 — Pilot run through scenario
- Test

STEP 5 — Internal review
- Revise scenario
- Revise prototype supplies

STEP 6 — Prepare kit
- Prototype
- NDA, Script
- Video
- Supplies
- Gift

STEP 7 — The prototype session
- Facilitator
- Computer
- Notetaker

STEP 8 — Reiterate
- Revise scenario
- Revise prototype supplies

Usability testing, its theory and application, is outside the scope of this book. There are excellent books about usability testing, one of our favorites is Jeffrey Rubin's *Handbook of Usability Testing.* And as mentioned, there is Carolyn Snyder's work specifically on usability testing with paper prototypes. Here, we would like to highlight the steps involved, not so much for usability testing, but for operating a paper prototype, especially if you do not get the guidance as described above in Step 4. Whether it is operated by the user, as in a usability test, or a domain specialist or members of the design team is not so important; the important part is the set up and proper facilitation of the prototyping session.

During actual paper prototyping sessions, it is usually most effective to include internal stakeholders as observers or facilitators. Allowing internal stakeholder participation is vital to reinforcing the importance of design and to make powerful advocates of the design within your organization. The steps involved in a paper prototyping session are:

Below we briefly cover each step in turn.

Step 1: Revise Scenario

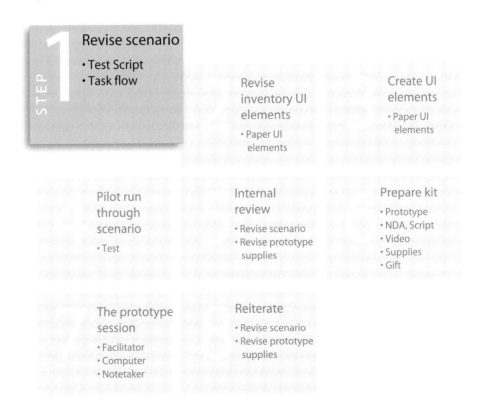

STEP 1

Revise scenario
- Test Script
- Task flow

Revise inventory UI elements
- Paper UI elements

Create UI elements
- Paper UI elements

Pilot run through scenario
- Test

Internal review
- Revise scenario
- Revise prototype supplies

Prepare kit
- Prototype
- NDA, Script
- Video
- Supplies
- Gift

The prototype session
- Facilitator
- Computer
- Notetaker

Reiterate
- Revise scenario
- Revise prototype supplies

From your previous internal reviews, you probably have tweaks you want to make to the scenario. Because many aspects of the prototype depend on the scenario, changes to the scenario cause a ripple effect in the prototype inventory of screens and user interface elements. Changes should be kept to a minimum, but if they're necessary, you'll want to make changes to the scenario before testing begins. Once you change the scenario, you should track the changes to determine if you need to revise the inventory of user interface elements.

Step 2: Revise Inventory UI Elements

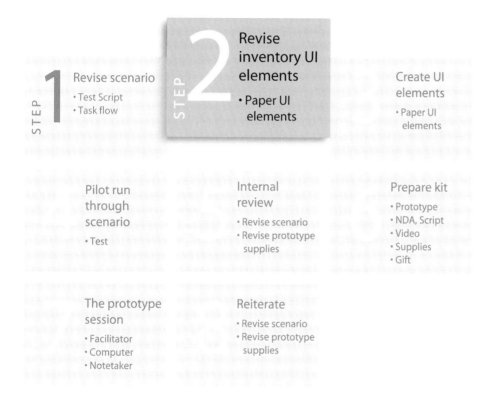

STEP 1 Revise scenario
- Test Script
- Task flow

STEP 2 Revise inventory UI elements
- Paper UI elements

Create UI elements
- Paper UI elements

Pilot run through scenario
- Test

Internal review
- Revise scenario
- Revise prototype supplies

Prepare kit
- Prototype
- NDA, Script
- Video
- Supplies
- Gift

The prototype session
- Facilitator
- Computer
- Notetaker

Reiterate
- Revise scenario
- Revise prototype supplies

At this point, you may have run through the paper prototype numerous times only to find some vital piece of the interface missing. It's a good time to review your checklist for completeness and try to anticipate the problems you'll encounter once the prototype is exposed to a session participant–users gesturing or verbalizing a click on something to see what it does and, of course, users just using it in a way you didn't anticipate. In any case, developing a set of user interface elements will be useful.

Step 3: Create UI Elements

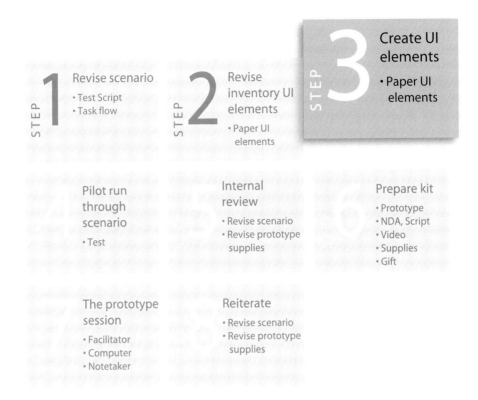

At this point, you want to create all the user interface elements. At the same time, you may want to anticipate problems by printing blank menu bars or blank menus or empty dialogs with only a border and OK and Cancel buttons. These empty materials will be waiting for you, or the participant, to create necessary interactions on the fly, just in case the truly unexpected happens, which it usually does.

Step 4: Pilot Run through Scenario

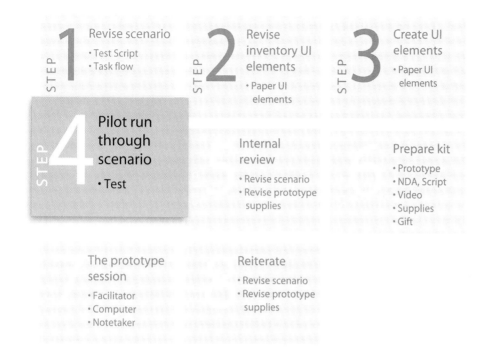

STEP 1 — Revise scenario
- Test Script
- Task flow

STEP 2 — Revise inventory UI elements
- Paper UI elements

STEP 3 — Create UI elements
- Paper UI elements

STEP 4 — Pilot run through scenario
- Test

Internal review
- Revise scenario
- Revise prototype supplies

Prepare kit
- Prototype
- NDA, Script
- Video
- Supplies
- Gift

The prototype session
- Facilitator
- Computer
- Notetaker

Reiterate
- Revise scenario
- Revise prototype supplies

You don't want to go in front of a user or stakeholder with a prototype that hasn't been tried out first. This is a good time for a pilot run. Just have anyone in the office readily available try it out. Don't worry so much if they can use it, but rather focus on whether you are prepared for everything they do. The pilot will ensure that you haven't created a half-baked prototype, the king of all prototyping faux pas.

Step 5: Internal Review

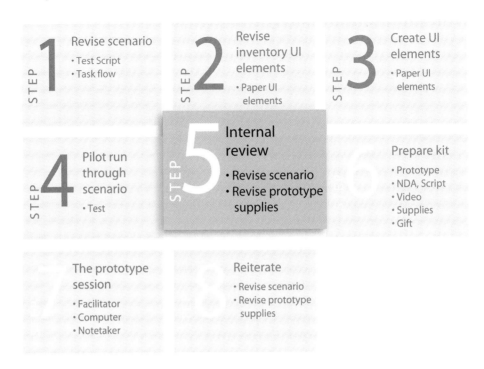

STEP 1 — Revise scenario
- Test Script
- Task flow

STEP 2 — Revise inventory UI elements
- Paper UI elements

STEP 3 — Create UI elements
- Paper UI elements

STEP 4 — Pilot run through scenario
- Test

STEP 5 — Internal review
- Revise scenario
- Revise prototype supplies

Prepare kit
- Prototype
- NDA, Script
- Video
- Supplies
- Gift

The prototype session
- Facilitator
- Computer
- Notetaker

Reiterate
- Revise scenario
- Revise prototype supplies

After the pilot run, it is prudent to run the prototype through a few key stakeholders for one last check and to discuss the results of the pilot along with possible issues and solutions. This may trigger one last visit to the scenario, which in turn will trigger a revisit to the inventory and possible modifications of existing elements and creation of new elements.

Step 6: Prepare Kit

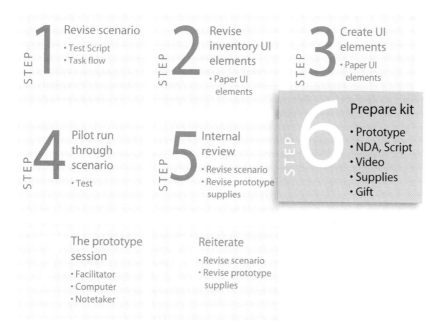

STEP **1** Revise scenario
• Test Script
• Task flow

STEP **2** Revise inventory UI elements
• Paper UI elements

STEP **3** Create UI elements
• Paper UI elements

STEP **4** Pilot run through scenario
• Test

STEP **5** Internal review
• Revise scenario
• Revise prototype supplies

STEP **6** Prepare kit
• Prototype
• NDA, Script
• Video
• Supplies
• Gift

The prototype session
• Facilitator
• Computer
• Notetaker

Reiterate
• Revise scenario
• Revise prototype supplies

Before running the prototype evaluation session, you have some administrative tasks. You want to arrange the prototype in a way that makes it easy to find the various user interface elements. If using an external participant, you may need a signature on a non-disclosure agreement. You should also write a script including the scenarios that the user should perform and how the paper prototype is operated (using the index finger to simulate a mouse, think-aloud protocol, etc.). You also want to prepare materials such as pens, sticky notes, and blank paper to make user interface elements on the fly when necessary, and it frequently is. You should have a video camera so that you can provide incontrovertible evidence to reluctant colleagues in case it turns out their designs, however elegant and beautiful, just don't work. Last, if going to an external disinterested party, you need an honorarium or gift to thank them for their participation.

Step 7: The Prototype Session

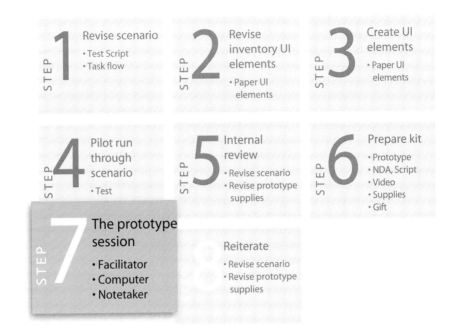

STEP 1 — Revise scenario
- Test Script
- Task flow

STEP 2 — Revise inventory UI elements
- Paper UI elements

STEP 3 — Create UI elements
- Paper UI elements

STEP 4 — Pilot run through scenario
- Test

STEP 5 — Internal review
- Revise scenario
- Revise prototype supplies

STEP 6 — Prepare kit
- Prototype
- NDA, Script
- Video
- Supplies
- Gift

STEP 7 — The prototype session
- Facilitator
- Computer
- Notetaker

Reiterate
- Revise scenario
- Revise prototype supplies

Now you're ready to run the session. It is out of the scope of this book to go into great detail of the mechanics of facilitating a paper prototyping evaluation session, but we do give you other hints in our sidebar, How to Operate the Paper Prototype. Regardless of your mission, it is always important to have at least a facilitator and a note taker support each session.

Step 8: Reiterate

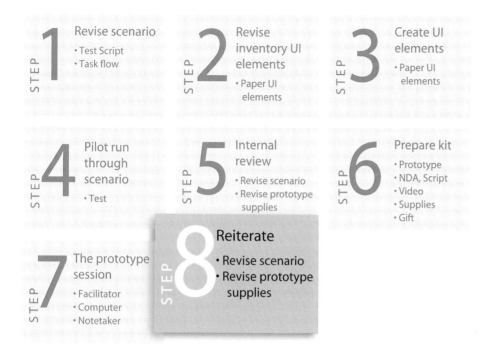

STEP 1 — Revise scenario
- Test Script
- Task flow

STEP 2 — Revise inventory UI elements
- Paper UI elements

STEP 3 — Create UI elements
- Paper UI elements

STEP 4 — Pilot run through scenario
- Test

STEP 5 — Internal review
- Revise scenario
- Revise prototype supplies

STEP 6 — Prepare kit
- Prototype
- NDA, Script
- Video
- Supplies
- Gift

STEP 7 — The prototype session
- Facilitator
- Computer
- Notetaker

STEP 8 — Reiterate
- Revise scenario
- Revise prototype supplies

After the revealing experience of seeing someone operate the paper prototype, you're probably ready to immediately perform invasive surgery on it–don't. After each session, review and evaluate what went right and wrong. Whether things went right and/or wrong, you should wait until after all your planned user sessions are completed to do an overall comparative review and evaluation before any re-design and next-step decisions are made.

CASE STUDY: THE PAPER IS MIGHTIER THAN THE COMPUTER

Sometime, somewhere, in a small European country, Jonathan was working as a user experience consultant. He was involved in a point-of-sale information kiosk project. The kiosk would be installed in various department stores throughout this small country and the consulting company Jonathan worked for was deciding whether to use touchscreen or a trackball and keyboard or just keyboard-based navigation. This project was done more than 10 years ago when the notion of an average consumer to use a computer to get commercial or public information outside their home was the big idea du jour. Since time and money were of the essence, the department store company needed to make a risky investment decision sooner than later.

Jonathan suggested creating three designs for the three navigation systems and testing the designs without any hardware investment. The project manager's fateful reply was, "You find a way to do that, and I'll fly you to Costa Rica!" With dreams of tropical beaches dancing in his head, Jonathan proposed a paper prototype process that constrained user input to just the allowed channels.

First, all the different designs were quickly created on paper, using a few graphics programs and some of the department store's catalogs. The assembled paper product represented all the intended functionality of the system. Internal tests showed that these concepts could work, so he moved on to try out the design with the targeted users.

The touchscreen-based design would use only single-click action with an index finger anywhere on the "screen." The keyboard-based design also used finger-based input but via a paper mockup of the keyboard, and users could not touch the screen. (In the end, using an unconnected keyboard served his purposes best.)

For the trackball and keyboard method, a more traditional paper prototyping protocol was used. First though, users went through some exercises of pointing and clicking with a real trackball.

A fourth system was also tested, using a standard mouse only. This input mechanism was the same as the trackball without the trackball exercise. This bright idea was serendipitously discovered when Jonathan forgot the trackball one day.

All four systems were tested without any need for a major hardware investment, except for the keyboard and the trackball, which was readily available anyway. The paper prototyping method saved the company an immense amount of money. It also saved the department store client an immense amount of money, since all four tests failed miserably. Apparently, in 1994, there was no need for a point of sale kiosk in a department store (or at least not one that the client was willing to build). As one test subject was quoted, "But I am in the department store already, I can just walk over to the men's department myself."

Meanwhile, Jonathan never made it to the exotic beaches of Costa Rica, but the dream remains.

NEXT ITERATION AFTER A PAPER PROTOTYPE

Paper prototyping is the end of the conceptual design stage and an important bridge to the more detailed interaction design stage of software making. The next logical step is to use the results from paper prototype evaluations to inform further design discussion and analysis as well as synthesis into digital interactive prototypes. Those digital prototypes can be used to validate the next iteration of design. This validation is most effectively achieved through iterations of digital interactive prototypes in conjunction with qualitative usability testing.

REFERENCES

Sari Kujala, Marjo Kauppinen. Identifying and selecting users for user-centered design. Proceedings NordCHI '04. New York: ACM Press, 2004, pp. 297–303.

Anita Komlodi. The role of interaction histories in mental model building and knowledge sharing in the legal domain. Journal of Universal Computer Science, 2002, vol. 8, pp. 557–566. (Presented at: I-KNOW '02; 2nd International Conference on Knowledge Management; Graz, Austria, July 11–13, 2002.)

Donald Norman. The Design of Everyday Things. New York: Doubleday, 1988

John Pruitt, Tamara Adlin. The Persona Lifecycle. San Francisco: Morgan Kaufman, 2006.

Jeffrey Rubin. Handbook of Usability Testing: How to Plan, Design, and Conduct Effective Tests. New York: Wiley, 1994.

Carolyn Snyder. Paper Prototyping. San Francisco: Morgan Kaufmann, 2003.

The Usability Company. http://www.theusabilitycompany.com/resources/glossary/prototyping.html

Robert Virzi, Jeffrey Sokolov, Demetrois Karis. Usability problem identification using both low and high fidelity prototypes. Proceedings of CHI '96. New York: ACM Press, 1996, pp. 236–224.

CHAPTER

18

DIGITAL INTERACTIVE PROTOTYPING

DESCRIPTION
Introduction

A **digital interactive prototype** is similar to a paper prototype in that they are both appropriate for the same stage in the software-making process; however, a digital prototype can range from a more narrative style, such as a PowerPoint-based prototype to a fully interactive high fidelity coded prototype (covered later in this book). The style of digital prototype we're covering in this chapter is essentially an interactive wireframe, hence the name, digital interactive prototype. The interactivity can vary in fidelity with sometimes limited and sometimes complex interactions built into them. A digital prototype can often mimic many interactions but rarely all of them. However, the representation of system performance in a digital prototype is generally minimal if even existing. For the sake of brevity, we will refer to Digital Interactive Prototyping as a Digital Prototyping from here on.

The software tools used for digital prototyping are mostly nontraditional prototyping tools such as office productivity products like Excel, Word, PowerPoint, etc. These tools can mimic software interaction but fall far short of the complete interactivity of a paper or coded prototype. More traditional tools include Dreamweaver and Photoshop. Just like paper prototypes, digital prototypes can be used for both mental model mapping via user studies, design analysis and decision making by a design team as well as for interaction design and visual design validation with users.

The main advantage of a digital prototype over a coded prototype is that a nontechnical person can create a digital prototype whereas a coded prototype generally requires the specific skill set of a programmer or scripter.

In general, digital prototypes, like paper prototypes, are best when used during the initial conceptual design phase preceding and informing the first detailed screen designs. These prototypes can be rendered in digital format, which is especially helpful for the ever-increasing practice of remote usability testing where test moderators are in separate locales from their test subjects, where paper or other physical prototyping is not possible and coded prototyping is not practical due to time or skill constraints.

Digital prototyping shares the same objectives as paper prototyping:

> Understand task flow and context of use
> Validate assumptions in scenarios, requirements, user profiles
> Shape or validate the task sequencing and interaction design direction
> Take early prototypes to the next level of detail
> Inform or validate a visual design direction

The above aspects are discussed in the previous chapter on paper prototyping and are not repeated here. Unlike a paper prototype, though, the digital prototype affords the possibility of greater fidelity in visual design and interaction design.

DIGITAL PROTOTYPES AND REMOTE USABILITY TESTING

Remote usability testing is becoming an increasingly essential part of the standard usability test plan as globalization increases and Human-Computer Interaction budgets are cut. This has put paper prototyping in decline. Unfortunately, it has led to an increase in coded prototyping too early in the process in the hopes of meeting the full interactive needs of usability testing. This is where digital prototyping comes to the rescue.

When we worked at PeopleSoft designing and testing financial management software, one of the primary usability challenges we faced was how to conduct low-fidelity prototype testing to allow for adequate geographic and market region coverage in addition to an adequate sample size of test participants. Since PeopleSoft had key customers and markets distributed worldwide, using paper prototypes in a physical lab was not practical and the time and skills it took to create coded prototypes was not sufficient given the project schedule's meager allowance for design iteration. The PeopleSoft Financial Applications design team created medium-fidelity prototypes and made them available to test participants over the Web.

Because PeopleSoft applications were mostly Web-based, mockups of them were created in Dreamweaver to mimic them. These HTML prototypes could be easily made available and shared over the Web.

In addition to the medium-fidelity prototypes created in Dreamweaver, under Nevin's influence (see Case Study below), the application Excel was also used to create low-fidelity wireframe prototypes for remote testing at an earlier stage of the design process (more details later in this book). The hyperlinking capabilities of Excel allowed linking of screen designs created in individual worksheets resulting in what seemed to test participants to be a functioning low-fidelity prototype. No matter what tool was used to create them, prototypes were usually shared over the Web using a Web conferencing application, such as WebEx® or NetMeeting®. A digital video recording tool was used to capture the user's interaction and verbal feedback from each session for later review and analysis.

CHARACTERISTICS

Audience–A digital prototype can be easily distributed to allow your audience (including test participants) to be exposed to and feedback on the conceptual design or specific examples of user interaction. For specific requirements evaluation, the prototype's audience can be any stakeholder, such as a product manager, who wants to review the prototype from their particular perspective. For example, developers can review the prototype purely from an implementation and technical requirements perspective.

Stage–A digital prototype is primarily meant for the midterm stage of design. In the earlier stages there are generally neither enough requirements nor a conceptual design to warrant investment in a digital prototype. Digital prototypes can be useful in later stages for testing alternative designs when implementation problems crop up during development.

Speed–Digital prototypes can be either rapid or diligent. As you will see in the section on prototyping with Office Suite software, these prototypes can create screens from sketchy abstract interfaces to high-fidelity interfaces that almost exactly reflect how the developed screen should look.

Longevity–A digital prototype has moderate to extended longevity. It usually lasts until a specification for the actual product replaces it. However, given its digital format, it can be a reference point for years after the design stages of the project finish. Portions of a digital prototype can be easily repurposed for future products.

Expression–Digital prototypes are experiential because they delve into the finest granularity of details regarding system look and feel.

Fidelity–Digital prototypes can vary in fidelity from low to very high in almost any aspect, with the exceptions of system performance and interaction. System performance and interaction are often tedious and difficult to fully implement without reverting to the diligent effort of a coded prototype. Digital prototypes are usually high fidelity in terms of information design. They can be high fidelity in branding and visual design if this is a prototype objective and those elements already exist and can be copied into the prototype.

Style–Digital prototypes are usually narrative, or partially interactive. When employed in usability testing, the digital technique is often combined with the Wizard-of-Oz technique to bridge the gap between those things that are interactive and those that are not implemented in the prototype.

Medium–Digital prototypes are, of course, digital.

TABLE 18.1 Digital Prototyping Content and Fidelity Matrix

Content	Very Low Fidelity	Low Fidelity	Medium Fidelity	High Fidelity	Highest Fidelity
Information design	− −	+	+ +	+ +	+ +
Interaction design	− −	+ +	+ +	+	− −
Visual design	+	+ +	+ +	+ +	+ +
Editorial content	+	+ +	+ +	+ +	+
Branding expression	+	+	+ +	+ +	+
System performance	NA	−	− −	− −	− −

+ +, Most appropriate;
+, appropriate;
−, not appropriate;
− −, completely inappropriate;
NA, not applicable.

WHAT DOES A DIGITAL PROTOTYPE GET YOU?

What are the benefits of digital interactive prototyping? They are very similar to paper prototyping:

➤ Provides substantive feedback early in the development process
➤ Promotes creative exploration through rapid iterative development
➤ Facilitates communication among stakeholders
➤ Does not require advanced technical skills
➤ Visual design, information design, and interaction design can all be included in the prototype
➤ Digital prototyping allows a design team to become informed about potential usability directions of the software, independent of the system behavior
➤ Digital prototyping allows the design team to engage early in mental-model mapping (see Chapter 17, mental-model mapping)

Some advantages over paper prototyping include:

➤ Digital format tends to have a longer lifespan than paper and can be referred to across projects.
➤ Digital prototypes can stand on their own, without excessive moderator facilitation, because they usually contain navigation hyperlinks that users follow from one screen to the next. Paper prototypes require an expert moderator to guide users through them.
➤ Digital prototyping is easier than paper for implementing narrative style.
➤ Prototypes are completed in a purely digital format for safer digital storage.

Some disadvantages over paper prototyping include:

➤ In early stages of the software-making process, paper affords the most complete interactive evaluation.
➤ If the visual fidelity is high, digital prototypes may discourage users from critical comment on the prototype.

Points in Common with Paper Prototyping

Provides Substantive Feedback Early in the Development Process

Because digital prototyping requires no computer programming, it is possible to get an early evaluation on designs and design directions before any investment of costly development resources. As in paper prototyping, this saves the costs of rework and improves quality, if conducted early in the software-making process.

Promotes Creativity Through Rapid Iterative Development

Iteration is both cheap and quick with digital prototyping because there is no code, and some software tools, such as PowerPoint, provide at least some interaction built into the tool. This ease of building interaction gives the designer an opportunity to investigate scenarios with a digital tool that normally has to wait until late in the design process. By having earlier digital artifacts, designers and other software makers have a chance to experience a more finished prototype earlier than ever before, allowing much greater freedom to innovate and iterate. Innovation is improved due to the lower cost of trying new designs, and they can be thrown away if they don't work. Quick iterations can result in more creative design explorations as a multiplicity of variations is achievable before coding begins.

Facilitates Communication Among Stakeholders

Digital prototypes allow for concrete software visualizations earlier than ever before in the software-making process. This visualization often speaks more clearly to non-specialized stakeholders about the product than the more abstract and traditional use cases, requirements documents, or other specialized system representations. These early or midterm visualizations allow the team more agility to change approaches, rather than wait for a late digital visualization for some stakeholder to finally realize that the misunderstandings or mismatches of assumptions among team members has created serious usability and design flaws in the product.

Does Not Require Advanced Technical Skills

You can use the software skills you already possess. As long as you have some software experience, almost any software tool you're skilled with can be used to create a digital prototype. Whether you are savvy with a word processor, presentation software, graphics packages, or spreadsheets, they can all be used to create digital prototypes ranging from low to high fidelity. This low technical threshold empowers many collaborators who have never prototyped before, to participate in prototyping activities. You'll need a good process to support this because multiple prototypers can be a curse if not managed well.

Visual Design, Information Design, and Limited Interaction Design Can Be Included in the Prototype

As with paper prototyping, digital prototyping allows much more prototyping in the way of visual and editorial content to be included. Visual design and information design can range from the lowest to the highest of fidelities, based on needs defined by your prototyping objectives. Interaction design is more medium fidelity, relying on narrative or Wizard-of-Oz techniques to fill in the gaps of missing capabilities. This is a shortcoming when compared to paper prototyping, which allows a designer to create or modify designs on the fly.

Usability of the System, Independent of the System Behavior

Digital prototyping allows you to create a prototype independent of what is technically possible and practical due to technical and performance limitations and issues of an implemented system. Unlike coded prototypes, the considerably lower effort it takes to create these prototypes means you are not constrained to what can actually be implemented due to any technical or performance reasons. In the late stages of design, these are important issues to deal with but in the earlier stages in which you're exploring design directions and possibilities, you don't want to be saddled with constraints that will prevent you from accomplishing your objectives at that stage of the process.

Digital Advantages Over Paper Prototyping

Digital Format Has a Longer Lifespan Than Paper and Can Be Referred to Across Projects

The digital format has a life that can span not only one project but can be shared among other associated projects. We have found it useful to open past digital prototypes and reuse bits and pieces in new projects. Digital's greater flexibility over paper gives it one advantage in terms of longevity. If part of the software-making team is collaborating from a distant location, another advantage is that digital prototypes can be easily e-mailed or shared from a common file server. This is also an advantage over coded prototypes, which can also be widely available but often require special and expensive software to edit or have technical restrictions that make them difficult to share; for example, if the coded prototype is created on a Macintosh computer by the design team but everyone else is using an open source Linux system.

Digital Prototypes Stand on Their Own as Users Often Follow Preset Functionality to Navigate From One Screen to the Next

In usability studies, digital prototypes (unlike paper prototypes) need no moderator to operate them. Digital prototyping software usually includes some form of rudimentary interaction such as hyperlinks, paging, etc. These features are often sufficient to allow test participants to guide themselves through the intended interactions based on their own understanding and perceptions. Since there is no affordance for direct manipulation interactivity in a paper prototype, a moderator or someone familiar with the project needs to facilitate the use of the prototype.

Digital Prototyping Is Easier Than Paper for Implementing the Narrative Style

Digital interactive prototyping differs from both paper and coded prototypes in trying to implement everything, as the latter two forms may not be a practical use of time. Given the rudimentary linking and other interactive support of most digital prototyping tools, implementation and maintenance problems can occur. For example, an Excel prototype that includes a series of links could require extensive link checking throughout the prototype if a change is made to one page of the design. Digital prototypes are best when used to represent the big picture of complex software. For simple applications or applications-based on strict templates, this may pose little problems. In our experience, applications are always more complex than they seem, thus digital prototyping can often only be used to create key screens or main tasks due to time constraints. However, in a usability test or other presentation, the designer cannot predict which screen will be requested by the audience. Therefore, it becomes necessary to resort to a narrative approach. In a digital prototype, narration is often a key partner with interaction. It is sometimes the case that a digital prototype may be developed using a combination of different tools. A login screen in HTML may lead to an Excel prototype, which will then launch a series of PowerPoint prototypes. If these files are not (or cannot) be linked, then the presentation may rely on Wizard-of-Oz techniques in which an operator launches the appropriate files from behind the scenes. Paper prototypes don't encounter any of these issues.

Prototypes Are Completed in a Purely Digital Format

A digital prototype is completed in a digital format, which means it is easy to store and share over digital media as well as for later reference. Physical prototypes can often get misplaced or damaged over time, whereas storing digital prototypes safely and archiving them well assures long-term survival. Moreover, unlike coded prototypes, which can cease to run on upgraded operating systems, the digital prototypes are more reliable. For example, a prototype done in spreadsheet will almost always open in new versions of the software.

Disadvantages Over Paper Prototyping

Paper Affords the Most Complete Interactive Evaluation Than Any Other Early or Midterm Prototyping Method

During the testing of a paper prototype, screen elements can be augmented, edited, even created spontaneously. This is practically impossible with digital prototypes. Thus, during user studies, paper prototypes are more complete in their ability to meet, or be adapted to, participant needs without anticipating them.

Less Inviting for the User to Experiment and Critique

When user study participants or stakeholders experience a prototype representation of software running in Excel or Word, it is a cue that the product is still a sketch.

As participants walk through a prototype, they usually feel comfortable talking critically about functionality, though less so than with a paper prototype. However, as we have experienced in some usability evaluations of prototypes with higher visual fidelity, there is a substantial decrease in participants' freedom to think critically about the screen. However, users were particularly adept to comment on pieces that were not visualized with high graphic fidelity, i.e., some rougher screens and omitted visualizations shown in a mostly higher fidelity digital prototype. Therefore, it may be best to visualize just enough of the prototype to provide context, using narration as a starting point for usability testing or stakeholder critique.

Overview of What a Digital Prototype Looks Like

A digital prototype can range in appearance from a series of connected wireframes to screens of extremely high fidelity. If the prototype is using both visual and interaction high fidelity, sometimes the only way to tell it from the real thing is the menu bar or other interface idiosyncrasies that give away its graphic nature. In Figure 18.1 only the Photoshop interface elements on the left betray it; the rest looks exactly like an application built with PeopleTools, a PeopleSoft development tool.

FIGURE 18.1 *The main screen of a digital prototype for a web site with a Photoshop tools palette displayed along the left side.*

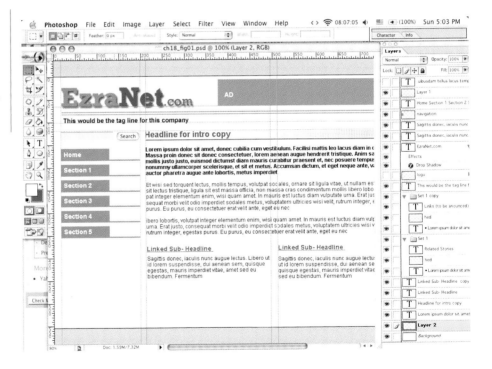

STEP-BY-STEP GUIDE TO CREATE A DIGITAL PROTOTYPE

Digital prototypes allow a design team to explore divergent user experience concepts. While reflecting on requirements, a storyboard scenario or articulating a task flow, software makers can begin creating a series of sketch screens using the low-fidelity digital tool of their choice. In a collaborative design session, the team can interactively review and evaluate the prototype to refine and improve them during meetings. If arguments about direction come up, the prototype can represent many different variations. This is a rapid, iterative, and multidisciplinary approach toward successfully exploring and evaluating user experience variations.

Here is a general outline of the steps involved in creating the digital prototype. You'll notice this guided procedure for digital prototyping is very similar to the paper prototyping procedure but with nuanced differences.

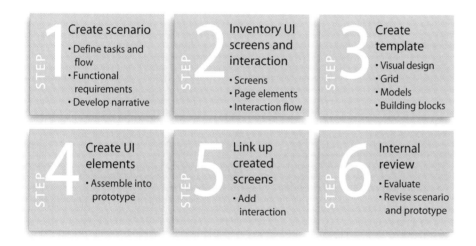

STEP 1 — Create scenario
- Define tasks and flow
- Functional requirements
- Develop narrative

STEP 2 — Inventory UI screens and interaction
- Screens
- Page elements
- Interaction flow

STEP 3 — Create template
- Visual design
- Grid
- Models
- Building blocks

STEP 4 — Create UI elements
- Assemble into prototype

STEP 5 — Link up created screens
- Add interaction

STEP 6 — Internal review
- Evaluate
- Revise scenario and prototype

In our experience, creating a digital prototype for the average complex desktop application takes 1 to 2 weeks for low visual fidelity. A high visual fidelity would take about 50% more time. If the visual design already exists and you have a template set up for it, the prototype creation can take less time than the low-fidelity version. Likewise, an individual screen can be created in a matter of hours or minutes depending on the complexity. Creating a template for mass production of the high-fidelity prototype screens of an application can take as long as 1 to 2 weeks, though this can often take place 30% to 50% in parallel with the first iteration. For websites and Web applications, which have much more limited interaction capabilities, the time can be trimmed to one to two days.

Step 1: Create Scenario

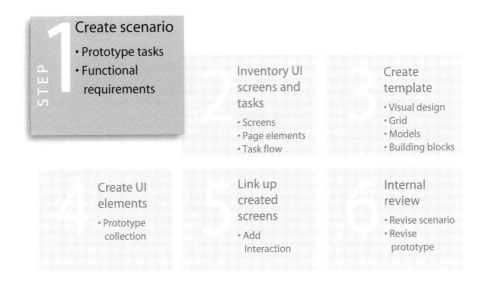

Write a scenario narrating the main user goals and tasks to be performed with the system. Storyboards provide good source material for scenarios. If no scenario exists, one can usually be brainstormed in 2 to 4 hours.

As in the paper prototyping, the task scenario should cover all the main functional requirements and user tasks you want to include in the prototype. This functionality, in the midterm of a software creation process, should be documented in the form of use cases, task flows, and business requirements. The scenario should follow a typical user through the routine usage of the product. Plan for the common exceptions you can think of, but don't worry about addressing all problems at this stage; you'll deal with those later when preparing for prototype evaluation.

Step 2: Inventory UI Screens and Tasks

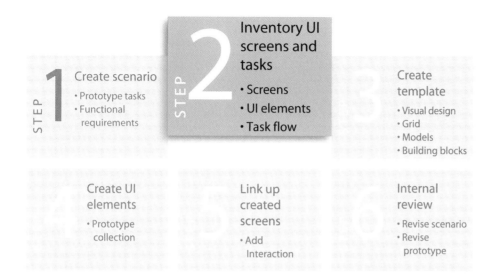

Create a checklist of all UI screens, elements, and task flows needed to support the scenario (1 hour, 5 hours maximum).

As in paper prototyping, the scenarios are used to inventory the main product screens and the information needed to create them, including what secondary windows and widgets are needed, such as modal dialogues, pull-down menus, messages, etc. The end result should be a list of items each with a check box next to it; a space in the list to enter the name of the file (if digital) in which the item resides; and a place to jot down notes during the internal review of Step 6. Also, create a task flow diagram that can also be checked off during Step 6.

Step 3: Create Template

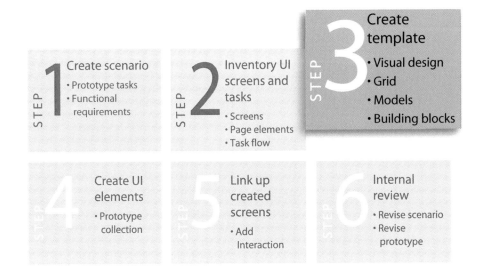

Make templates or examples for every screen type and interface widget. The templates can be used as models or building blocks to construct screens.

After an inventory is created, the real efficiency of digital prototyping is realized via the creation of a template you will use in your chosen software tool for the creation of screen designs. Check individual tool chapters to see how they support or do not support the creation of prototype templates. The template is composed of the following elements:

1. **Visual Design**–the colors, typography, layout and other required graphical element requirements.

2. **Grid**–horizontal and vertical spacing of elements. Very often, pixel-level control is not possible due to technical restrictions. Ensure that your grid accurately reflects the granularity of the development tools; this will make your digital prototypes seem real if that is a desirable objective.

3. **Models**–model layouts are window, page, or screen types that use the same layout elements. All the standard elements, those elements that are used on every screen, such as a menu bar or high-level navigation, are put on the model. Then, you only need to use the model; for example, in a model layer in Photoshop or a master slide layout in PowerPoint. The model serves as the background, or at least the starting point, for a UI design so that the prototyper doesn't have to reinvent it for every screen design.

4. **Building Blocks**—building blocks are UI components needed to build the user interface, such as panes, check boxes, data input fields, tables, etc. They are kept in a separate layer, slide, or document used as a central repository of UI components for the development environment.

To create the template you create a document in the prototyping tool to use the foreground, background, and type colors from the visual design (if specified). Also, the document should have default fonts and type sizes (if specified) and include any branding art (company logo, special images, etc.) that is required in the document (preferably placed where they are required to appear). Next, create the model layouts based on the existing product or conceptual design (if you have one). Finally, in a separate area or document, copy and paste the graphical elements that are required (look and appearance of tabs, buttons, look up list widget, icons, etc.).

To use the template, identify the screen you want to create. If a model layout has been created for it, either use it, or copy and paste it so you can use it. Then, create the screen using the standard items from your graphics library. If you need to make new items, create them and place them in the library. If there are building block compositions or combinations you will use repeatedly, add them to the template library as well so that they can be copied when needed.

Step 4: Create UI Elements

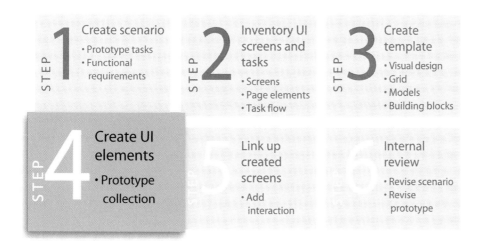

Create every item on the checklist. (Average, 1–3 days, 3.5 days maximum. Complex systems might require more time.)

Create UI elements either in your prototyping tool or cut and paste them from other applications. If you are unsure how to proceed, see the prototyping process sections or the individual tool sections. When you finish creating all screens and UI elements, you should have some means of collecting and organizing the prototype pages into task flows or another organizational system (Excel has worksheets, PowerPoint has contiguous slides, Photoshop has layers, etc.). Last, you want to review the inventory list you created in the previous step and check off each item that has been created.

Step 5: Link up Created Screens

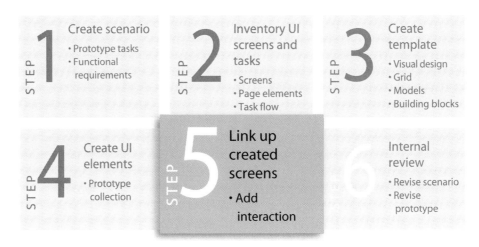

Combine components in a manner that follows the scenario or task flow.

Next, run through the scenario using the prototype and be certain you can navigate from one screen to another. If the prototype is meant to be user operated, implement the interaction in the way supported by the tool. This is referred to as low-fidelity implementation—implementing interaction through a mockup rather than actual functionality, which would be hyperlinks in Excel, slide changes in PowerPoint, macros for layer changes in Photoshop, etc. This will assure that task flow follows the intended sequence. You can use the checklist to avoid overlooking anything.

Step 6: Internal Review

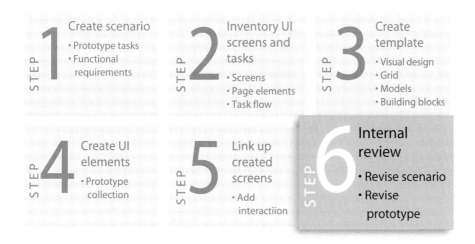

STEP 1 Create scenario
- Prototype tasks
- Functional requirements

STEP 2 Inventory UI screens and tasks
- Screens
- Page elements
- Task flow

STEP 3 Create template
- Visual design
- Grid
- Models
- Building blocks

STEP 4 Create UI elements
- Prototype collection

STEP 5 Link up created screens
- Add interactiion

STEP 6 Internal review
- Revise scenario
- Revise prototype

Show the prototype to requirements stakeholders (1 day, 1.5 days maximum)

In the next step, use your digital prototype to run through the scenario with some key internal stakeholders. Feedback from product managers and business analysts usually focuses on the prototype's ability to achieve its business goals. It is also important to have at least one person from the development team review the prototype and acknowledge the direction from a technical and implementation perspective. Often, feedback about the technical feasibility of your design will send you back to your scenario to make modifications–possibly necessitating changes to your inventory list and the creation of more UI elements. After receiving internal feedback, the prototype is ready to be revised and iterated before being shown to external audiences, such as a focus group or usability test participants.

CASE STUDY: USING EXCEL AS A PROTOTYPING TOOL AT PEOPLESOFT–NEVIN'S STORY

It is not very often that we are introduced to a new tool to use in prototyping which does not involve having to purchase or learn a new application but merely relearning one we already know. However this happened to Nevin. From that introduction he was able develop a new and useful way of creating compelling digital interactive prototypes. Here is his story:

I was first initiated to Excel as a software prototyping tool while working at PeopleSoft. I was assigned to a project late in the design phase. The project had some prototype already developed. While reviewing them I couldn't figure out what program they had been built in. I contacted the developer who created them, Mark Miller, to send me a copy. What he sent was an Excel file. This caught me off guard, I didn't know Excel very well nor thought you could do anything but spreadsheets with it. I did notice that no matter how quickly I sent him changes; new corrected prototypes were quickly turned around and delivered to me. I was impressed with the agility and speed with which these prototypes were turned around.

The early iterative design phase of the project was nearing its end where most of the pages had been sketched out. It then became my job to convert them to Dreamweaver as was our process at the time. I gathered up the latest printouts of the prototypes and spent about two weeks rebuilding them in Dreamweaver. When I had finished, I sent them to the lead developer for review, only to hear an entirely new concept was decided on, which he had produced in Excel. I groaned thinking about how much work it was going take to update them and maintain the Dreamweaver files. So I decided to abandon my Dreamweaver endeavors and proofed the Excel prototypes.

Soon after my involvement with the project ended I decided to find out more about using Excel for prototyping. Mark gave me a 15 minute explanation on how he used Excel. I can only explain that as he showed me, I saw how really simple it was. I just instantly "got it."

Developing a Template

After this initial introduction to Excel prototyping, I quickly realized that many of the features could support not just a robust prototyping tool but could be a total prototyping environment. The grid makes alignment of art and text a snap, the tabbed worksheets can hold multiple Web pages of design. The hypertext feature can mimic interaction between worksheets. I then built a template for PeopleSoft which included all the UI elements needed to create a prototype. First there were the graphics. I dedicated a worksheet page to become the image library of the most often used graphical elements. By simply copying and pasting graphics from established pages or art folders I quickly was able to gather enough images to cover the most common pages.

I also created worksheets with common buttons. Some were merely captured graphics but others were made by coloring, adding borders and text to table cells. I also created pages containing the different configurations of tabs that were used in PeopleSoft applications. I then created example pages that could house the element that I had put in the template.

The Test Case

I had taken my Excel template and was showing it to different groups within PeopleSoft trying to show how it worked. There had been interest from developers who were experts already in Excel and saw it as a way for them to visualize their design ideas without having to use HTML which they hated and Microsoft Paint which they found difficult to use.

Some members of the user experience group quickly saw the use for this new approach and adapted it to their work. But many were a bit put off by the fact that it was Excel and weren't open up to the new idea. I had been using Excel in my own work when I was drafted into a "Dream Team." It was a project that you both

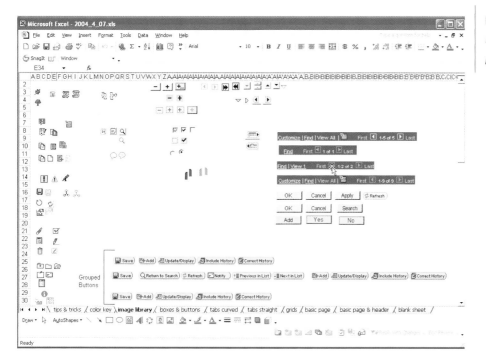

FIGURE 18.2 *The image library from the template.*

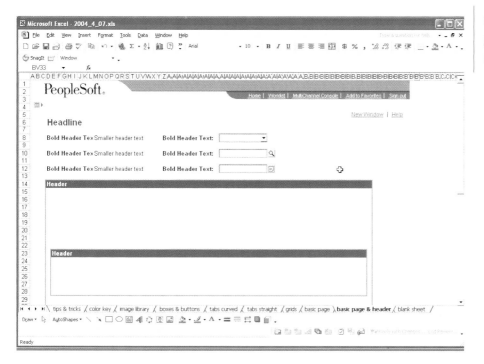

FIGURE 18.3 *The sample pages from the Excel template.*

FIGURE 18.4 *An example interface in Excel.*

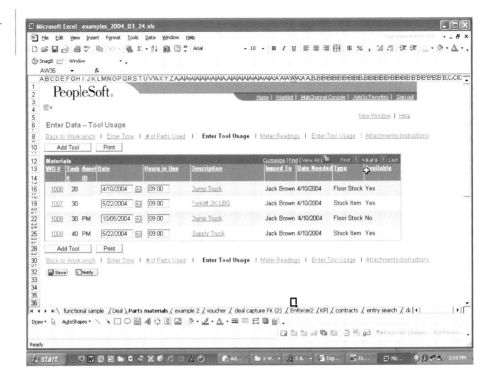

want to be on and dread at the same time. It was a major redesign of an existing project on a very very tight deadline. The directive came from on high so it would have a great degree of visibility leaving little room for error. Early in the project, one meeting that I was called into had to do with some early ideas that needed to get prototyped on a quick turn around basis. It was late Thursday afternoon, and the developers were on the hot seat. The prototypes needed to be delivered by Monday. There was a general moaning from the loss of a weekend but the real concern was that it just couldn't be done even with the loss of a weekend. It was then that I offered the use of the Excel template as a means to get the job done on time. There was interest in what I had to offer and so an hour meeting was set up for 8 o'clock the next morning. I was all ready to give my usual one hour demonstration to the developers. Many doubted that I could help them but the boss was there so they were there too. I was about half way through the demonstration when the meeting seemed to be breaking up. But before any one left they asked where they could get a hold of the template. The VP of Engineering stayed and we talked. What had happened was that they didn't need anymore explanation they had "got it" and were ready to start using it. Soon after I was assigned to another project but the VP of Engineering made sure to stop by and thank me, letting me know that with the Excel tool they were able to make that deadline.

NEXT ITERATION AFTER A DIGITAL INTERACTIVE PROTOTYPE

Once a digital prototype has been created, reviewed internally then validated via usability testing, a software making team can then move on to a coded prototype or, in some circumstances, begin developing the actual software product or service. It is common that a digital interactive prototype can be used by developers as a form of user interface specification for the final software. Consequently, a digital interactive prototype can be the last prototype iteration before the release of the product.

REFERENCES

Mackay, Wendy E., et al. Video artifacts for design: bridging the gap between abstraction and detail. Proceedings of DIS '00. Brooklyn, NY: ACM, 2000.

CHAPTER

19

BLANK MODEL PROTOTYPING

DESCRIPTION

Introduction

Blank model prototyping is closely related to paper prototyping. It's another form of physical prototyping that involves the representation of both hardware and software user interfaces. Blank model artifacts are used during a participatory design process to elicit users' perceptions and mental models about innovative design concepts involving hardware devices in combination with software operating systems and user interfaces, especially portable ones. Examples of these devices include mobile phones, personal digital assistants (PDAs), digital music players, electronic tablets, and other similar portable devices. Because handheld devices are generally produced in large numbers for the mass market, early prototyping methods such as blank models can contribute to mitigating the risk of design failure, expensive manufacturing tooling errors, and ultimately, to stave off rejection in the marketplace.

Blank model prototyping is a rapid role-playing technique using readily available arts and crafts materials, such as clay, wood, foam, paper, and plastic together with pens, scissors, and other appropriate tools. These materials allow blank model study participants to construct rough physical representations of a technology idea according to a predetermined scenario. The blank model method is used by product designers to understand users' preconceptions about technology concepts and their potential uses as well as to identify design and usage patterns that inform product design [Mander].

A Blank Model prototype is a moderated participatory design process that involves a facilitator and participant, who attempts to construct a representation of an imagined technology artifact out of provided materials and tools. In the blank model activity, the facilitator engages the participant in a dialogue in which the participant thinks aloud about using an initially undefined technology to perform a task or an activity based on a scenario. The scenario details are progressively revealed by the facilitator; this progressive method allows the user to focus on particular aspects of the prototype at a given time rather than being distracted by too much information. A blank modeling session is usually captured on videotape for later review and analysis by the design team. Ultimately, blank model sessions should include a representative sampling of individuals to engage in the study and create artifacts.

CHARACTERISTICS

Audience–The intended audience for the sessions are targeted end users. For the resulting prototype, due to the highly innovative nature of the work, the intended audience for the results of blank model prototyping are solely the internal design team. Showing the results of blank modeling to even internal stakeholders outside the design team could lead to misunderstandings or misinterpretations and misuse of the results.

Stage–Early in the process.

Speed–Blank models are rapid prototypes.

Longevity–Short. Even though short lived, the results from a blank model study can have a profound impact in terms of shaping a usable and useful new technology concept, especially if it is destined to set the direction for an innovative mass market product.

Expression–Because they are constructed from physical materials, blank models inherently have experiential aspects, while at the same time, they can also be conceptual. The conceptual aspects result from the rough and imprecise session artifacts. The high abstraction requires interpretation with the help of concrete participant feedback.

Fidelity–Because they are imprecise and sketch-like, and usually unfinished, blank models are generally very low-fidelity.

Style–Blank model prototypes are a hybrid of interactive and narrative. The process is scenario-driven. The sessions themselves mix a narrative with interactive ideation/construction on the part of the participant.

Medium–Blank models are physical prototypes.

Overview of What a Blank Model Prototype Looks Like

A blank model prototype can take many shapes and forms, depending on the user's interpretation of the given scenario, that represent a form factor with specific controls and control layout. As shown in Figure 19.1, a blank model is essentially a rough sketch of a study participant's scenario interpretation and *may not even be fully realized relative to what participants have verbalized*. That is why recording participant verbalizations is so important–to allow the design innovation team to fill in any gaps left by the participant in the prototype artifact itself. These gaps often occur because a participant may have had a difficult time articulating a certain control or representing a desired function and interaction as a physical component.

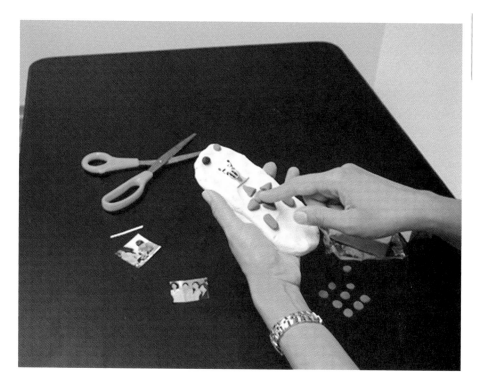

FIGURE 19.1 *An example of a Blank Model artifact.*

Who Participates in the Blank Model Creation Process

Blank modeling is a participatory design method most effectively used by design or technology innovation teams. The blank modeling goal is to collect potential user impressions and ideas about a nonexistent hardware/software technology, including required functions, controls, and interactions needed. A blank model prototyping team typically comprises advanced technologists, user experience designers, and usability specialists. A blank model study can also be planned and conducted by a single person with a combination of these skills.

What Are the Benefits of a Blank Model Prototype?

A blank model study engages users in the early stages of technology innovation and ideation to capture their thoughts about performing the relevant tasks without necessarily being constrained or limited by known technologies. This method keeps users from being prejudiced by a designer's preconceived notions. New technology ideas and approaches are common positive side effects of these sessions. The results are both the recorded verbalizations from the study participants and the physical artifacts that each participant has constructed. This detailed information is especially valuable in defining new product ideas and in shaping emerging or advanced technologies into useful products. Rarely will a resulting prototype ever be built, but the sessions often inform the design process by exploring new or uncharted areas of end-user interaction.

The advance of television and video recording technologies in conjunction with regularly updated passive and interactive TV content and service offerings from cable and satellite providers continues to spark the desire for the Holy Grail of remote control devices. Following this quest in the mid-1990s, a team of advanced TV designers working for Tele-TV (an interactive TV venture) used blank modeling and other participatory methods to explore the design of a better remote control. This team hoped to create a remote that offered not just usable and useful interaction to consumers but also included new functionality such as e-commerce services, on-screen TV guides, and movies on demand. Not only was it important to get user perceptions about remote control functions, their related controls, and their layout, but equally important was user feedback about the form factor and the fit and feel of the device while being held.

Form factor: The overall shape of a three-dimensional object, ranging from free form to geometric or combinations thereof.

As a result, clay was one of the key arts and crafts materials used in this study. Each of eight study sessions began with the participants talking about the form factor desired in an advanced remote control device, while at the same time forming the device with clay. Once each form factor was modeled in clay, a participant would proceed to use other materials, such as pen and paper or wooden and plastic shapes, to add buttons or other components to the base form according to their desire and need. In the end, the study yielded eight individual blank models that were analyzed and evaluated to identify patterns regarding:

> - Overall form factor
> - Functions
> - Controls and other hardware components, such as a display
> - Interactions and device responses
> - Any other salient factors from the sessions

This information was valuable for deciding whether to go forward with:

> - A new custom designed and manufactured device
> - A modification and re-tooling of an existing device
> - An existing device

Another point of strategic decision-making was whether to proceed with a device that could control different brands of TVs with functions specific to Tele-TV's broadband subscription services or a universal device that could control different TVs, support Tele-TV's services plus control additional devices attached to the TV, such as VCRs, etc. Feedback from the blank model study and later usability testing of a higher fidelity prototype resulted in the decision to go with a universal device [Rickert].

From the interactive TV case portrayed in the sidebar, you can see that blank models not only help design and innovation teams with tactical decision-making but strategic decision making as well.

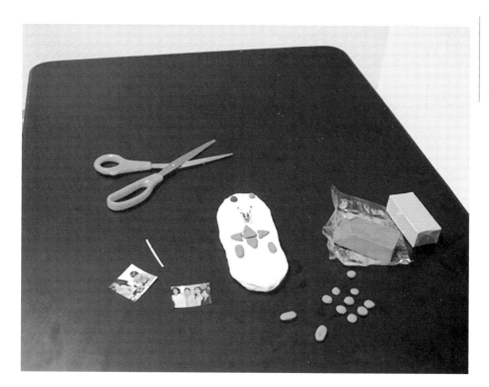

FIGURE 19.2 *A model of a device to remotely control interactive TV services.*

Essentially, a Blank Model prototyping in the early conceptual stages of hardware technology with software interactivity can help you understand:

➤ Users' desires and perceptions about scenarios that portray tasks and activities in new and inventive ways
➤ Design criteria and requirements that impact business decisions about future technologies conceived for use in new and novel ways
➤ Feasibility of transferring advanced usability concepts to commercial products

STEP-BY-STEP GUIDE TO BLANK MODEL PROTOTYPE CREATION

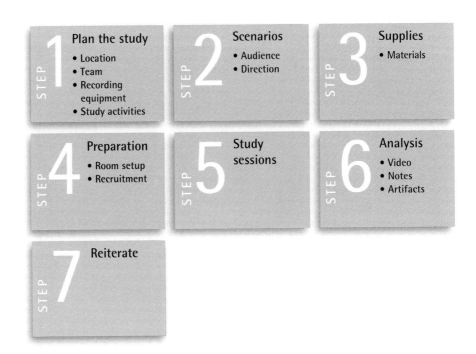

Unlike most of the prototypes described in this book, blank models are created by study participants who are identified as potential users of a yet to be defined technology or technology artifact. Because a Blank Model prototype is created in one-on-one facilitated sessions from common materials, the artifact does not function as a working prototype but instead acts as a vehicle for comparative analysis and interpretation using facilitator observations and participant verbalizations. The outlined steps include approximate time frames for this rapid prototyping method. Some of the project activities, such as participant recruiting, do not need to occur in a sequential order.

Step 1: Plan the Study

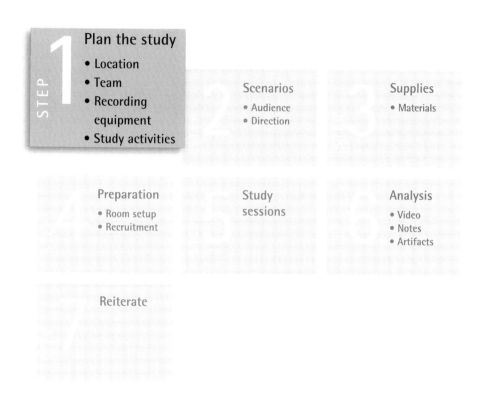

First, you must plan for the study by preparing for the location, the team, recording equipment and the study activities. The location can be a design or usability lab or onsite at the user's location or in an ad-hoc session room. It is common to have the study take place in a locale near the user but not necessarily at the user's home or office (although this is of course also possible). A team consisting of a moderator and note taker needs to be assembled. For continuity, it is important to always use the same note taker and moderator. The study relies not only on accurate note taking but also on the inclusion of a video artifact in the study analysis. Lastly, the study focus and activities should be explicitly stated in the plan: what are the project goals and desired outcomes.

Step 2: Scenarios

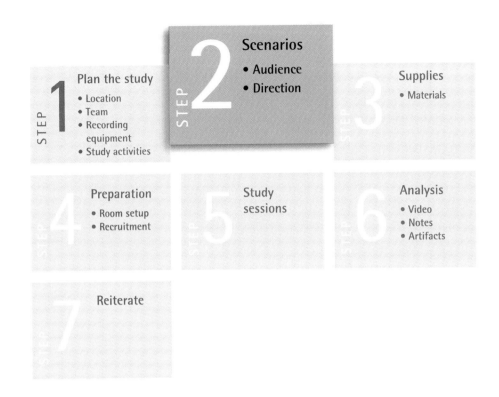

The blank model session centers on an end-user trying to complete a scenario. The team initially develops a scenario comprised of a series of tasks based on the tasks or activities that prospective users are meant to engage in. An example of a task appropriate for blank modeling is the use of a handheld device to capture images and enter notations about real estate opportunities. The task, in this example, involves capturing images of real estate properties and entering notes about necessary details for each property, such as location, measurements, physical conditions, etc.

Step 3: Supplies

STEP 1 Plan the study
- Location
- Team
- Recording equipment
- Study activities

STEP 2 Scenarios
- Audience
- Direction

STEP 3 Supplies
- Materials

Preparation
- Room setup
- Recruitment

Study sessions

Analysis
- Video
- Notes
- Artifacts

Reiterate

A checklist of required arts and crafts materials should be created, and those materials acquired. The checklist is especially useful for ensuring that you have enough materials for each of the sessions. Common materials include colored clay, magazine clippings, screen cut outs (like a paper prototype), and styrofoam or wood blocks or plastic handles, etc.

Step 4: Preparation

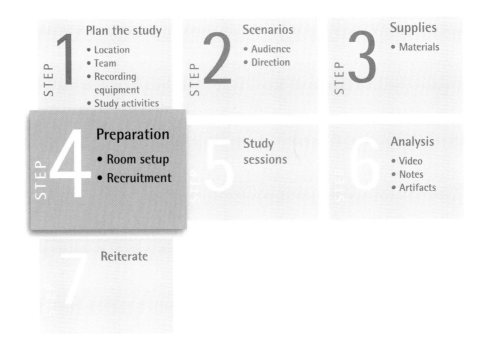

As with any study involving users, a key component to successful blank modeling is the ability to accurately recruit study participants and set up the location. Proper recruitment is contingent on an accurate screening questionnaire and a skilled recruiter or recruiting service. As for the room, a lab or other suitable space is needed to allow uninterrupted conversation in a relaxed setting. Video cameras and note takers should be placed out of view or, if that's not possible, then in the background.

Step 5: Study Sessions

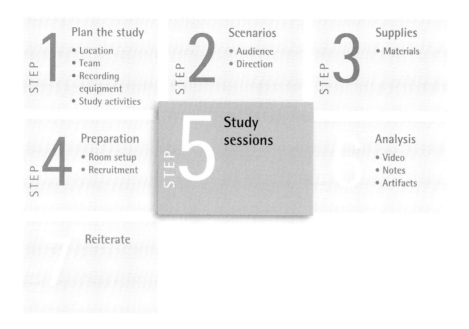

A session usually lasts for about an hour. The facilitator engages the participant in a dialogue based on the predefined scenario while the participant ultimately constructs a single artifact from available materials. This construction activity usually involves cutting, drawing, adhering, and shaping. At the same time, the user verbalizes what the pieces are and the functions they'll perform. For more details, see the step-by-step guide to running a blank model session below.

Step 6: Analysis

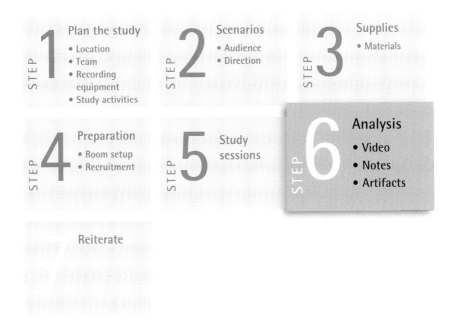

When the blank model sessions are complete, the team analyzes and evaluates the study results, which include the blank model artifacts, the session video recordings, and any handwritten notes. The team then figures out the next steps, which can be further innovative exploration of the concept or transfer of the ideas into a product effort.

The analysis of videotaped dialogues and created artifacts inform the ongoing design of a useful device, especially a newly conceived device. The blank model artifacts are particularly valuable as they help the design team find and identify emerging patterns in the user's mental model and articulations of a device and its operation relative to the task being performed.

Step 7: Reiterate

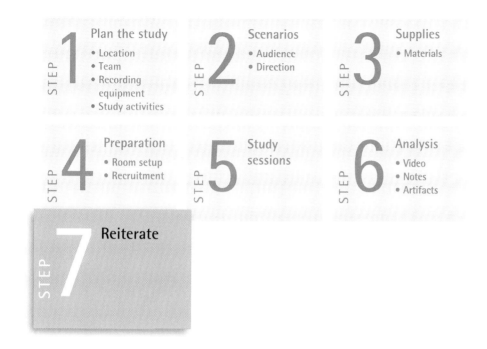

Generally, decisions on next steps follow a blank model study:

➤ *Abandon* the project effort due to feasibility issues related to lack of a market-place, risky business conditions, or lack of availability of technologies to create a working concept prototype or commercial product.

➤ *Postpone* the project effort to a later period when the marketplace appears to be ready for the novel technology, the business climate is less risky or technology is more readily available to create a working prototype or commercial product.

➤ *Continue* forward to design and build a concept prototype.

FIGURE 19.3 *A facilita-
tor conversing during
a Blank Model study
session.*

The Blank Model Prototype Creation Session

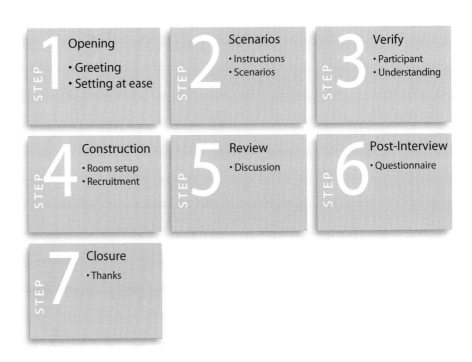

STEP 1 — Opening
- Greeting
- Setting at ease

STEP 2 — Scenarios
- Instructions
- Scenarios

STEP 3 — Verify
- Participant
- Understanding

STEP 4 — Construction
- Room setup
- Recruitment

STEP 5 — Review
- Discussion

STEP 6 — Post-Interview
- Questionnaire

STEP 7 — Closure
- Thanks

A series of scheduled blank model sessions can commence once the base scenario is adequately defined, developed, and refined; the study participants are recruited; and the location is set up with the required arts and crafts materials, recording equipment, and any other requirements. A blank model session is a one-on-one protocol involving a facilitator and a study participant. A third person may be present to take notes and manage the recording equipment. There also may be project personnel or stakeholders observing from a separate room.

Step 1: Opening

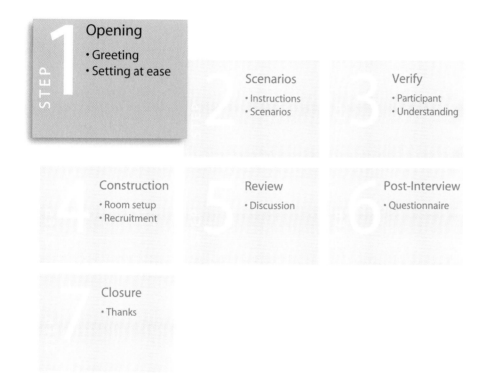

The facilitator tries to put the participant at ease by introducing the session purpose as well as the materials present on the table. The facilitator reminds the participant that the session requires about an hour. Note: The ideal duration for a blank model session is approximately 1 hour. Beyond an hour, participants generally become tired and less articulate in their verbalizations and blank model constructions.

Step 2: Scenarios

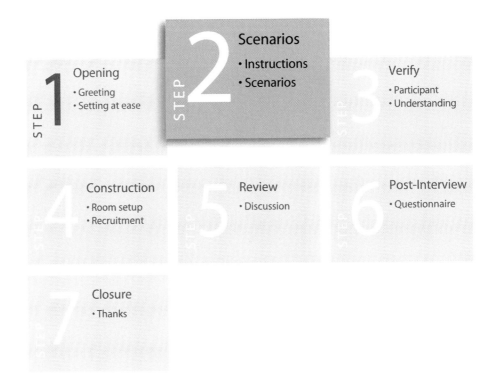

After the participant understands the purpose and general goals of the study, the participant is requested to read the scenario aloud, setting the stage for the desired think-aloud protocol during blank model assemblage.

Step 3: Verify

Once the facilitator is certain that the participant grasps the scenario, the participant is guided to begin verbalizing the task requirements, such as accessing an onscreen TV program guide while sitting in the living room at a distance from a TV.

Step 4: Construction

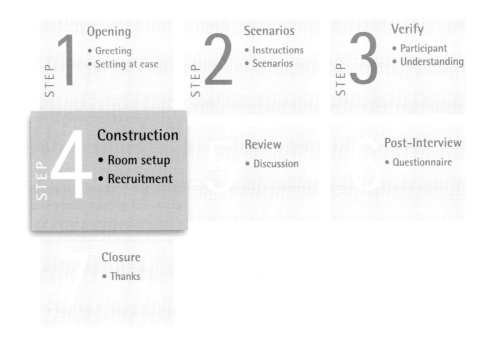

While verbalizing a task, the participant begins constructing a physical artifact from the available materials. The artifacts will allow performance and completion of the tasks. If the participant has difficulty verbalizing or articulating the physical details of the artifact at any time, the facilitator may provide guidance in the form of questions to stimulate the participant's consideration of his actions from other vantage points.

Step 5: Review

Once the participant has completed the blank model construction, the facilitator prompts the participant to verbally reflect on the activity accomplished and assess the constructed artifact. This reflection allows the participant to revisit the session and make any improvements or changes to the constructed artifact.

Step 6: Post-Interview

The facilitator then conducts a post-session interview with the participant, drawing upon predetermined questions and issues raised during the blank model session.

Step 7: Closure

The facilitator closes the session and thanks the participant.

The design innovation team can now:

➤ Analyze and interpret the information obtained

➤ Consider the themes, patterns, concerns, and dead ends observed

➤ Summarize any tactical and strategic design implications

➤ Decide on directions going forward

CASE STUDY

At Apple Computer in the early 1990s, Michael was a member of a small team of user interface designers, whose charter was to explore advanced digital camera hardware and software user interface concepts. Michael and Richard Mander, a usability expert, wanted to initiate the exploratory design work by engaging in participatory activities with users similar to prior work that was done by human factors specialists in Denmark [Ehn & Kyng]. In advance of concept design activities, Michael and Richard wanted to engage potential users by getting them to talk about capturing and subsequently organizing or viewing images while simultaneously handling physical artifacts. Richard and Michael had the idea to set up a series of moderated sessions involving a very general scenario about capturing photographic images. Participants would be asked to imagine (and verbalize) in detail what they would most want the device to do what that device would be like. While verbalizing, the participant would assemble (from at hand arts and crafts materials) a rough physical likeness of the artifact described. This technique was meant to ultimately record and map different user mental models and perceptions about the scenario; how they might roughly represent those ideas with a physical artifact; and what they would do with the images after the capture process. Participants with different backgrounds were recruited with the hope that they might use image capture devices in different ways for different reasons, such as for real estate sales, tourism, and other purposes. The materials to be used for representing participant ideas included clay, images cut out of magazines, and pieces of wood, plastic, and metal to name a few. Some of the verbalized ideas included not only the details of capturing photographic images but also capturing audio to go along with and describe the images. In addition, many participants wanted to be able to organize and filter images inside of the camera device. As a result, the assembled artifacts had rough representations of various elements:

➤ Picture taking controls
➤ Controls that allowed in-camera picture organization and management
➤ Audio capture and playback controls
➤ Viewfinder
➤ Lens
➤ Panel for view finding and viewing captured images
➤ Screen representations showing various views of what the participants expected to see while interacting with the device; for example, slide show functionality

The artifacts from all of the sessions were collected and analyzed to determine if any conceptual and design patterns could be distilled to inform the team's design direction. These patterns included the following features, to name just a few:

➤ Types of desired controls
➤ Placement of controls
➤ Use of controls
➤ Placement of lens
➤ Types of viewfinders
➤ Placement of viewfinder
➤ Desired functions and navigation
➤ Screen layouts
➤ Different form factors, which allowed desired ways of holding and operating such a device
➤ Different types of UI widgets

Each of the sessions was captured on videotape to allow detailed analysis. The results and findings of the sessions were documented in a report then shown to the design team. The outcome of the blank model study not only helped concretely shape the immediate design direction of the camera with software device but also drove the next level of prototype–a rapid assemblage of readily available hardware components with software to create a rough working prototype that could be tested in the field. This, in turn, evolved into a progressive iterative prototyping process that ultimately led to a detailed high-fidelity product concept design that was validated via user participation.

NEXT ITERATION AFTER BLANK MODEL PROTOTYPING

The usual prototype iteration following a blank model study and its resulting proto-types is a proof-of-concept hardware prototype with software interactivity. Generally, moving to a proof-of-concept prototype is a decision based on business risk and market factors in addition to availability of technology to actually build and test the prototype. In some cases, strategic decision making permitting, the next iteration of a blank model effort could be a Wizard-of-Oz prototype using larger scale technolo-gies in lieu of miniaturized components that may not be readily available, such as for a personal digital assistant (PDA) concept.

REFERENCES

Richard Mander, Michael Arent. Blank models: a method for early user participation. American Center for Design: Interact Journal, 8(1), 1994: 38–45.

Donald E. Rickert, Jr. A Theory-Grounded Empirical Evaluation of Special-Purpose and Generic Interaction Devices for Interactive TV. Washington, DC: The George Washington University School of Business and Public Management, 1997.

Carolyn Snyder. Paper Prototyping. New York: Morgan Kaufman, 2004.

P. Ehn, M. Kyng. Cardboard computers: mocking-it-up of hands-on the future. In: J. Greenbaum, M. Kyng (eds.), Design at Work: Cooperative Design of Computer Systems. Hillsdale, NJ: Lawrence Erlbaum Associates, 1991, pp. 169–195.

CHAPTER

20

VIDEO PROTOTYPING

INTRODUCTION

A video prototype is a narrative method primarily used in two ways. First, video is used to sell visionary technology concepts internally to product decision makers and externally to prospective customers and entrepreneurial funders; this method is referred to here as visionary video prototyping. The second way involves using and reusing video artifacts through the participatory design process to research, brainstorm, design, iteratively prototype, and evaluate a nonexistent software product; this method is referred to here as holistic video prototyping.

Visionary Video Prototypes

Visionary video prototypes are most effectively used to portray future technology concepts and scenarios such as those involving multiple modalities in conjunction with multisensory interaction. These prototypes are narrative and rarely include any end user interaction. The visionary method is best used for prototypes that are difficult to render and build with more mainstream prototyping tools. This method generally involves high production values and their associated high costs. The result of such design and prototyping activity is essentially a short feature film.

Holistic Video Prototypes

On the other hand, there is a more holistic form of video prototyping advocated by Wendy Mackay. Researchers at the University of Aarhus [Mackay et al. 2000] developed a video participatory design process as a means to create an interactive prototype. This process includes video prototypes created throughout the design process as the results from incremental and iterative design activities. Then in turn, these video artifacts can be used as inputs for further iterative design activities, including observing and recording user activities, exploring divergent design directions via brainstorming, converging on a workable design, and finally evaluating the design.

This holistic design methodology can include not only using video as a prototyping medium but also leveraging video for other purposes as well; for example, the video recorded during field studies can provide a contextual framework for brainstorming a video prototype. Likewise, a brainstorming video in conjunction with video from field studies informs design convergence sessions in which video is used as an iterative prototyping medium.

Video prototypes are used as design artifacts for usability testing and evaluation, which can include the use of a Wizard-of-Oz–like method where a system, having no existing functionality, can be mimicked by acting out the functionality on camera. To complete the holistic cycle, the video capture of the testing and evaluation sessions suggest directions for further field studies, help the design team identify new issues for additional brainstorming and, finally, provide the necessary validation for design decision making.

Visionary and holistic prototypes both use special effects and camera tricks to mimic the functionality of a working system. These prototypes are most effective for portraying either future technology concepts or software functionality that are difficult to render and build. This difficulty can be due to the software not yet existing or to the inclusion of functionality beyond the capabilities of mainstream prototyping tools, such as those that involve multiple modalities. Some of the best known examples of video prototypes are the visionary ones from the early 1990s-Apple Computer's "Knowledge Navigator" and SunSoft's "Starfire." These have lived beyond their expected lifespan and have reached the public domain as cult classics.

The seminal Knowledge Navigator vision video portrayed a university professor using a futuristic "smart book" electronic device to engage in a conversational interaction with an anthropomorphized personal digital agent and a remote colleague using voice recognition, synthesized voice, and real-time digital video conferencing, among other advanced technologies.

StarFire depicted a business scenario about a project leader defending her project positioning and funding from another project's threats. This pre-Web scenario involved putting together a complex business presentation in a short time frame via just-in-time access to an extensive information base.

WHAT IS A VIDEO PROTOTYPE?

Depending on the recording medium, a video prototype is digital. Since there is nothing really tangible about a video prototype, it really doesn't qualify as a physical prototype. The primary video medium today is digital, which allows much more flexibility in terms of creative expression, image manipulation, and compositing in addition to distribution opportunities. Typically, a video prototype is not interactive but can portray a highly interactive product through the narrative format. For example, the aforementioned Knowledge Navigator video has a conversational dialogue between a college professor and a digital agent. Technically, a video prototype can feature large quantities of video content, such as the interactive TV prototype described in the coded prototypes chapter. This particular prototype is, in fact, video and interactive but is classified as a coded prototype, because it was created in a visual programming language and is highly dependent on scripting for its interactivity. This particular example proffers the notion that to effectively prototype, you don't necessarily need to stick to the strict prototype classifications presented in this book. You may find ways to better achieve your prototyping objectives by combining different prototyping methods.

Who Makes Use of Visionary Video Prototyping?

The primary users of visionary video prototyping are technology innovators who need to express their ideas and concepts in a narrative storytelling medium but have found other methods inadequate to represent those ideas. This is especially true of ideas that involve high interactivity combined with emotion-based or sensory-based expression between humans or between humans and anthropomorphized technology systems that behave and respond as humans.

Narrative video is an ideal medium for innovators to sell advanced ideas to entrepreneurial funders as well as research and advanced technology decision makers. Video prototypes can also be used as a public relations tool to show innovative ideas and forward thinking concepts. The ability of video prototypes to demonstrate interactivity with video content makes them well suited for prototyping premium TV services, video editing software, or video content management software.

Video prototypes require an interdisciplinary team to conceptualize, storyboard, design, and produce them. The team could include a variety of disciplines, such as conceptualists, designers, script or scenario writers, technologists, storyboard artists, video content creators, video/special effects producers, user researchers, and others. Because of the number of disciplines required, video prototypes (especially narrative ones) portraying innovative concepts require a sizeable investment and are typically fueled by research or marketing budgets.

What is probably of more interest to the readers is the Mackay approach, which uses more modest video techniques in an accessible method. Assuming that you have a video camera (you can use the one that you record usability test sessions with), the Mackay approach can be done with little preparation.

What Are the Benefits of a Visionary Video Prototype?

For the visionary flavor, video prototyping is generally a high fidelity prototyping medium. To achieve the highest visual and audio quality, the Knowledge Navigator and StarFire video prototypes were originally shot in 35-mm film and converted to video. Because of the feature movie production quality, people often mistakenly think that video prototypes portray finished products or services. The Knowledge Navigator was so realistically portrayed in a movie-style scenario that consumers believed it was an available product and made inquiries about how to immediately order it.

HOLISTIC VIDEO PROTOTYPING

Low- to medium-fidelity interactive video prototypes can be created and produced on small budgets using the Mackay method, which is how we refer to it since we draw heavily on the article [Mackay et al. 2000] where she describes the process. Mackay's approach results in prototypes meant more for an internal audience for whom production values don't need to be high. Rough prototypes can be created from digital storyboards or scanned paper storyboard frames. Medium-fidelity video prototypes can be created from wireframe or higher fidelity images. In any of these cases, the digital images can be imported into an inexpensive desktop video editing application, such as Adobe Premiere Elements, where you can sequence and time-code them and even add titles, transitions, and special effects.

Characteristics

Audience—Due to the highly innovative nature of the content, the intended audience for video prototypes is initially the internal design team. Video prototypes can live longer and be subsequently used as presentation artifacts to show innovation prowess and advanced technology ideas to decision makers and investors. As mentioned, some video prototypes can reach the public.

Stage—Visionary video prototypes are generally created early. They are meant to help formulate product ideas for the future. Holistic video prototypes can occur in the early to medium phases of product design since they are intended to support user research and the iterative design process.

Speed—Because of the time and resources involved in conceptualization, storyboarding, and production, video prototypes fall completely in the category of diligent.

Longevity—Because high-production video prototypes are generally created in the early conceptual stages of new technology explorations, their longevity is based on the intellectual and creative cachet of their content and the persuasiveness of their creators. The Knowledge Navigator video is a good example of a video prototype still capturing the imaginations of people today as an idea that has not yet been fully realized this many years later. Because of the power of electronic storage, distribution, and instantaneous information access, video prototypes (or any kind of prototype for that matter) can be a powerful vehicle for spreading forward-thinking ideas and keeping them alive for generations. You're probably saying to yourself, "That's just like movies." Yes, video prototypes can have the same persuasive storytelling power and extensive legacy as a popular movie. Video's potential is what makes the high risk and investment so attractive to some.

Expression—Because they represent visionary or nonexistent product ideas, video prototypes are both conceptual and experiential. They generally entail moderate to high-fidelity scene renderings depicting innovative technology concepts involving software.

Fidelity—With their high production values, visionary video prototypes are high fidelity. Holistic video prototypes can range in fidelity depending on which part of the iterative design process they're being used for.

Style–Video prototypes are designed and produced as narratives, using scenarios and storyboarding. Video prototypes are passive, although they can depict many different forms of interactivity ranging from gestural to voice initiated.

Medium–The medium falls into the digital realm, not just because most videos are digital, but also because the prototype is not a tangible medium that a user would interact with, which is our definition of a physical medium.

FIGURE 20.1 *Scene from Sun Soft's Star fire vision video.*

FIGURE 20.2 *Video brainstorming session. (Photo courtesy of Wendy Mackay.)*

FIGURE 20.3 *Video storyboarding. (Photo courtesy of Wendy Mackay.)*

FIGURE 20.4 *Shooting a scene for a video prototype. (Photo courtesy of Wendy Mackay.)*

"Video artifacts may serve multiple roles in any design process. They capture not only the basic functions of the software, but also more subtle considerations of the software as it is used in real world contexts. By recycling video artifacts, we can move between activities that stress the specifics of the interaction and those that explore the general principles underlying the design, integrating the two and bridging the gap between abstraction and detail" [Mackay et al. 2000].

Regardless of fidelity, a narrative video prototype is essentially a short movie. In a single frame, Figure 20.1 shows the most definitive visual aspects of a video prototype, an audio-visual expression of an advanced technology look and feel along with notions of how people might use and interact with it. This paper-based book is not able to effectively portray the interactive, navigational, and audio output aspects of the scenes shown in video prototypes, especially those meant to simulate advanced technology expressions. Our website's Book area has a link to the Knowledge Navigator video so that you may experience the strong emotive effects of this example of video prototyping.

Who Participates in the Video Prototype Creation Process?

The primary users of low-fidelity (lo-fi) video prototyping are software makers who employ video prototyping as a means to rapidly design a prototype interactively with other design team stakeholders. In lo-fi video prototyping existing video can be combined with newly captured video and quickly leveraged to portray functionality that doesn't exist in a current system. With video, one can mock up the prototype in noncomputer technical ways by using more theatrical methods, including special effects, the use of props and sets, and other "smoke and mirror" tricks that allow a viewer of the video to suspend disbelief and imagine the prototype to be an actual functioning artifact. Software makers can then try to envision how a product should work and test those assumptions with end users, refining the video prototype to an actual specification for a software concept to be built.

STEP-BY-STEP GUIDE

The following step-by-step guide covers the holistic video prototyping method.

STEP 1 — Observation of users
- Observe/videotape experts
- Analyze clips
- Create use scenarios
- Develop storyboards

STEP 2 — Video brainstorming
1. "Say it"
2. "Show it"
3. "Act it"
4. "Videotape it"

STEP 3 — Video prototyping

Top down
- Identify functions
- Identify interactions
- Link design scenarios

Bottom up
- Create video prototypes
- Develop software prototypes

STEP 4 — System evaluation
- Collect user feedback
- Conduct field study
- Analyze data

Step 1: Observation of Users

STEP 1

Observation of users

- Observe/videotape experts
- Analyze clips
- Create use scenarios
- Develop storyboards

Video brainstorming

1. "Say it"
2. "Show it"
3. "Act it"
4. "Videotape it"

Video prototyping

Top down
- Identify functions
- Identify interactions
- Link design scenarios

Bottom up
- Create video prototypes
- Develop software prototypes

System evaluation

- Collect user feedback
- Conduct field study
- Analyze data

Video prototyping can start with video capture during the user research phase. These videos can include user task performance (with think-aloud protocol). After the user research, key issues should be distilled and all clips demonstrating the key problems or key solutions should be compiled into videos, one set of video clips per issue. For example, if capturing the use of an expense reporting application, all key problems/successes associated with approvals should be compiled on one tape, all key problems/successes around splitting hotel receipts on another, etc.

Design team members should watch the compiled user research videos and construct scenarios (like those created for a storyboard prototype) that cover all the end-user activities. For the expense reporting example, the team would develop a scenario in which users create various expense reports then submit them for approval.

Paper or digital storyboards are then developed from the scenarios. A storyboard illustrates each task step of a scenario. Visualizations in a storyboard can include a screen capture of the software, a still from the video, or a drawing or wireframe. The visualizations are then arranged to match the storyboard scenes, which are then paired with the video compilations. This composite video then shows the challenges for an entire scenario rather than just a single action. Each of the design team members should review the storyboard and watch the clips associated with them. Each should take notes on possible solutions as well as comment on how the accompanying visualization either fits or doesn't fit the feedback from the user research videos. The end result is a sequence of video comments with your end-user scenario and some ideas for a design solution. These ideas will be carried forward in the video brainstorming session in Step 2.

Step 2: Video Brainstorming

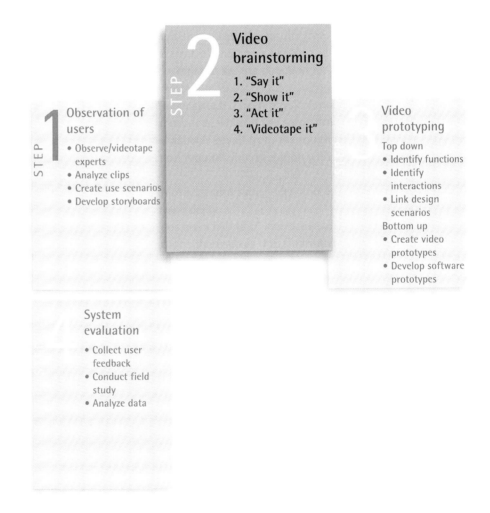

During the video brainstorming session, use the video camera and a few design team members and brainstorm ideas in four stages, which according to Mackay are:

➤ "Say it"
➤ "Show it"
➤ "Act it"
➤ "Videotape it"

Say it–State your idea, which everyone present should feel free to do.

Show it–Explain the idea on paper or draw it on a whiteboard.

Act it–This is the innovate part of brainstorming. Act out the scenario to show how it works. Any team members present can ask questions regarding the activities expressed during acting. In the expense report example, say someone has an idea that the solution should provide an Excel-like table structure in which a user can easily enter one expense item at a time. The user acts it out by going to a computer (literally or virtually) then performing the task while simultaneously speaking the solution aloud for capture on the video. Then, another design team member refers to the split receipt problem and wonders how the grid entry system would resolve that.

Videotape it–Team members brainstorm possible solutions, which are then videotaped. When the brainstorming session ends, multiple solutions to the identified problems and issues should have been raised and clearly recorded on video.

Step 3: Video Prototyping

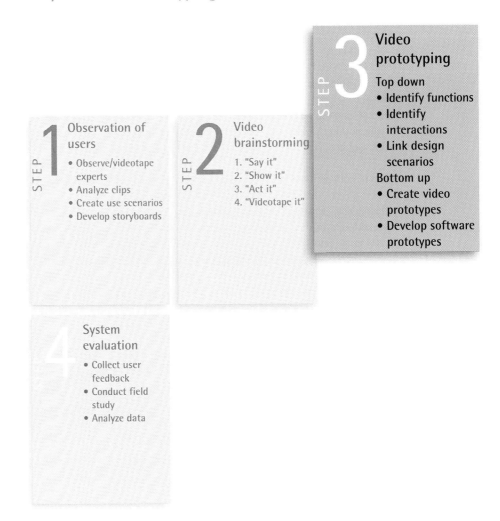

STEP 1 Observation of users
- Observe/videotape experts
- Analyze clips
- Create use scenarios
- Develop storyboards

STEP 2 Video brainstorming
1. "Say it"
2. "Show it"
3. "Act it"
4. "Videotape it"

STEP 3 Video prototyping

Top down
- Identify functions
- Identify interactions
- Link design scenarios

Bottom up
- Create video prototypes
- Develop software prototypes

4 System evaluation
- Collect user feedback
- Conduct field study
- Analyze data

In the design phase, synthesis of video brainstorming artifacts into a single design solution is the goal. First, you act out the most promising solution and build on the alternative solutions from the brainstorming tapes and the video clips from the user research. Rich context is added to the solutions from user research, collaboration with team members, and the actual acting out of the solutions. This means no real design needs to be done, though obviously it can be done and combined with wireframes, computer mockups, or white board mockups drawn and shot as part of the video. It is important that a member of the development team be included in this exercise to check for technical feasibility. The video prototypes are iterated until they represent realistic and well-defined goals. The results of the iterations can then be reviewed by users, and based on their feedback, the videos can be reworked. After a few iterations you (and your team) can review the results then select what worked best from each and edit them into a single design solution for system evaluation.

Step 4: System Evaluation

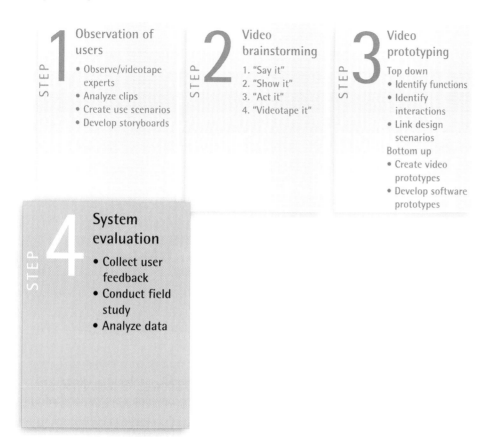

STEP 1 — Observation of users
- Observe/videotape experts
- Analyze clips
- Create use scenarios
- Develop storyboards

STEP 2 — Video brainstorming
1. "Say it"
2. "Show it"
3. "Act it"
4. "Videotape it"

STEP 3 — Video prototyping

Top down
- Identify functions
- Identify interactions
- Link design scenarios

Bottom up
- Create video prototypes
- Develop software prototypes

STEP 4 — System evaluation
- Collect user feedback
- Conduct field study
- Analyze data

The video artifacts are presented to users as part of a feedback and evaluation process. Users can look at the videos and give passive feedback, but they can also act out the solutions to determine if the solutions work for them. These "acting out" sessions should be captured on videotape for later internal review and synthesis.

HOW TO CREATE A VISIONARY VIDEO PROTOTYPE

To manage the need and cost for expensive high-end video production, narrative video prototypes are usually preceded by storyboards, possibly a low-fidelity jump frame video sketch known as an **animatic**, or other types of low- or medium-fidelity prototypes, including rough coded prototypes rapidly created in a time-based visual programming tool, such as Macromedia Director. These methods can be expedient and inexpensive ways to gain closure and acceptance of concept directions. The considerable risks of creating high-end video content and special effects can be off-set by shooting preliminary versions of scenes with a consumer video camera. You can then use the relatively inexpensive and popular video, graphics, and audio creation tools currently available to refine and iterate your ideas before committing them to high-end video shoots and content production. Using digital video as an inexpensive preliminary sketch medium for movies has been explored in the past by filmmakers, such as Francis Ford Coppola.

The most widely used form of animated prototyping is the **animatic**, which is an animated storyboard and interactive video pre-visualization tool. Animatics are generally low-fidelity jump frame videos that can be either digital narrative or digital interactive forms of prototyping. Animatics are typically used as a rapid, proof of concept vehicle to keep the initial cost and risk of video production to a minimum until a more finalized concept and user experience is achieved. As a result, animatics appear as roughly cut video with inconsistent and unpolished audio-visual scene presentations and transitions. Animatics are especially useful in prototyping interactive TV or Web-based video services concepts. The animatic technique can be useful as an early representation of a software game concept, including the thematic expression and interaction model. A third use of the animatic technique is as a sketch medium for narrative video prototypes of advanced technology ideas similar to Knowledge Navigator.

As mentioned earlier, video prototypes are essentially short films and should be driven from storyboards created by a vision team, which could include other key stakeholders, including user researchers, marketing representative, conceptualist, information architect, user experience designer, development representative, director, producer, script writer, and other movie production personnel. The storyboard contains the technology concept vision embodied in a scenario depicting intended usage. The storyboard frames need to be translated into all or some of the following component parts for production and compositing into a video sketch format or a final cut movie with high production value:

> Discrete segments or scenes of narrative content
> Any required special effects within or overlaid on the scenes
> Transitions between scenes
> Graphics, such as titles, credits, images, etc.
> Soundtrack
> Voiceover narrations

Once the narrative content, audio, and any other movie components are produced, they can be imported into a time-based digital editing program, in which an editor or producer assembles, sequences and scores the media components along a timeline. Whether it is a rough or final cut, the movie can be critically reviewed by the vision team and producers to decide whether it is ready to be shown externally or needs further editing and evaluation.

Because both film and video are flexible and wide-ranging audio-visual canvases for creative and intellectual expression, the content can be almost anything a person imagines. Video prototypes can represent software concepts related to entertainment, business, communications, desktop applications, and much more. Content for a video prototype can be derived from the lower fidelity artifacts of previous prototyping methods that is then re-created as high-fidelity content. This content typically includes professionally produced video, graphics, and special effects in addition to refined editorial content and the application of a branding scheme. In addition, video prototype content may also include an underlying soundtrack, audio special effects, and voiceovers. In terms of exploring ideas through iterations of low- and medium-fidelity prototypes, this type of content can be relatively quickly and inexpensively created using relatively low-cost, time-based media creation tools.

NEXT ITERATION AFTER VIDEO PROTOTYPING

Visionary video prototypes: Because of the large investment of time required to design and produce video, graphics, special effects, audio, and/or animation content, typically no iterations are generated for visionary video prototypes. The final produced version is usually the end of the prototyping project.

Holistic video prototypes: Holistic video prototyping involves video use throughout the participatory design process. Since holistic video prototyping doesn't necessarily require high-end video equipment and high production values like visionary video prototyping, it is more practical to use as a method throughout the complete design process from user observation through usability evaluation. During the design phase of holistic video prototyping, programmers can create coded software prototypes driven by the video prototypes that were also created in the design phase. The evaluation of these prototypes leads to convergence on a single software offering, which can then be implemented.

REFERENCES

Hugh Dubberly, Doris Mitch, The Knowledge Navigator [video]; Cupertino, CA: Apple Computer, Inc., 1987.

Steven D. Katz. Film Directing: Shot by Shot: Visualizing from Concept to Screen. Boston: Focal Press (Michael Wiese Productions in conjunction with Focal Press), 1991.

Steven D. Katz. Film Directing: Cinematic Motion: A Workshop for Staging Scenes, Boston: Focal Press (Michael Wiese Productions in conjunction with Focal Press), 1992.

Wendy E. Mackay, et al. Video artifacts for design: bridging the gap between abstraction and detail. Proceedings of DIS '00. Brooklyn, NY: ACM, 2000.

Thomas A. Ohanian. Digital Nonlinear Editing: New Approaches to Editing Film and Video. Boston: Focal Press, 1993.

Bruce Tognazzini. The "Starfire" video prototype project: a case history. Proceedings of CHI '94. New York: ACM, 1994.

CHAPTER

21

WIZARD-OF-OZ PROTOTYPING

DESCRIPTION

A Wizard-of-Oz (WoO) prototype was originally created to allow software makers to test nonexistent or experimental speech or haptic interfaces [Dahlback et al. 1993]. A secondary goal of WoO is the ability to explore innovation with technologies that may exist but are not yet prototyped; the main example being an unfinished design. This latter function allows a software maker to test the design direction for an incomplete design to get a proof of concept from users before committing to the design any further.

Like all prototyping, a WoO prototype is based on suspension of viewers' disbelief. It is a type of interactive prototype, where during a usability validation session, the participant thinks he is interacting with an actual working system using traditionally haptic interaction or natural language input methods. In fact, a member of the software-making team, or a larger scale computer system, is "behind the curtain" interpreting the participant's input directives and feeding back a designed system response. This method has been adapted for use in the early stages of new software feature or product design to simulate a variety of system responses including voice and screen feedback. A human wizard can provide both voice and screen feedback for prototypes of technology, such as a telephone tree user interface or an agent response system. WoO prototyping usually stops being a focus when system development is well underway and major changes are no longer necessary or possible.

Haptic input: The term haptic comes from a Greek word meaning touch or contact. Hence, haptic input involves physical contact between the computer and user. This contact may be via the hands using a mouse; fingers or stylus touching the screen; feet using a pedal; or even the tongue using a special joystick. But unlike a traditional mouse, the intensity and force of the touch is a key aspect of the input. Without WoO techniques, it would be impossible to test innovative haptic interfaces, because the technology per definition does not yet exist to truly test it.

Natural language interface: a natural language interface is an interaction technique that uses a person's voice as the basis for human-computer interaction as opposed to learning a computer language or computer commands. The user either speaks into the computer or types commands as if speaking in a conversational manner to another person. The computer then interprets the commands and reacts accordingly. As with haptic input, the WoO technique allows testing of innovative natural language interfaces that can't be technically modeled yet.

WHAT IS A WIZARD-OF-OZ PROTOTYPE?

As mentioned above, WoO prototypes are primarily used to explore innovation with technologies that don't yet exist or that exist but are not yet commercially available due to cost, immaturity of technology, inadequate scale of a technology, or other reasons.

The intended audience of a WoO prototype is the prospective early adopter of an advanced technology, including buyers and users. For prospective buyers, a WoO prototype is an effective demonstration of both technology innovation and a potential new business or market trend. A WoO prototype is also used to elicit feedback in usability testing or cognitive walkthroughs with targetted users. In both cases, the WoO technique allows the audience to see envisioned technology before it exists. This preview allows the audience to validate or invalidate the vision before too much work is spent realizing it.

ETHICAL CONSIDERATION

Many people have raised ethical questions concerning the WoO method. The main worry is that the WoO prototype is in essence a deception: you create the impression of an existing technology or design where no such thing exists. This is particularly egregious when approaching buyers, but nonetheless deceptive when a naïve user is led to believe a product actually exists that is in reality vaporware. Full disclosure is not simply the answer; legitimate business or legal reasons may exist for not disclosing. We believe that these ethical dilemmas can be addressed by a simple disclaimer at the beginning of a WoO session or during a debriefing session that what they are seeing is a prototype of possible developed software. In essence the problem is the same for all prototypes, but because with WoO prototypes there is a greater chance the user does not see the Wizard and may believe the system is real. A boilerplate disclaimer used as part of a nondisclosure agreement before seeing the prototype could be as follows:

> *The software you are about to see is experimental in nature, and therefore you should not expect it to look or act in a finished manner. The technology itself may or may not be in a finished state. As such, seeing and interacting with this software is no guarantee that the product or functionality will ever be released, or if it is, it may look different than its current form.*[1]

The statement is inserted in the standard nondisclosure agreements, which preclude discussion with outside parties and, also, excludes use of the prototype as a sales demonstration of any kind. It is important to sensitize all members of the software-making team to this issue to ensure that no statements or promises are made that cannot be fulfilled. More informally, if the wizard is a person, you can simply acknowledge the WoO at the end of the prototyping session by having him come out from behind the curtain.

Characteristics

Audience–WoO prototypes are meant to be shown primarily to internal design teams, even though they can also be effective as technology demonstrations to external stakeholders. For the design team, a WoO prototype enables exploration of software technology ideas regardless of availability or maturity of technologies. The suspension of disbelief (man behind the curtain) aspect of WoO prototypes is meant to bridge the gaps caused by the lack of technology. This bridging leads session participants to believe that these technologies are, in fact, available and mature. WoO prototypes are also effective as proof of concept demos for both internal stakeholders, such as management, and external stakeholders, such as technology funders. They provide a seemingly realistic crystal-ball view of a future technology experience.

Stage–The WoO prototype is a typical midterm prototype because it requires a fidelity level that is only possible with a conceptual model of some kind to support it.

Speed–Due to the need to accomplish adequate suspension of disbelief, WoO prototypes require some diligence to create. Those prototypes with a larger, more powerful system behind the curtain can be rapidly created depending on the technical skills of the team as well as the level of complexity of the system being prototyped.

Longevity–WoO prototypes have a relatively short lifespan, they are medium to short. The short lifespan is due to the prototype ceasing to exist once performance is achieved and results documented. After conceptual design and thorough interaction design, a WoO prototype can be used to test new design ideas or new technological ideas. WoO can also be used to simply skip over unfinished designs in the prototype. After the sessions, findings show that either an envisioned design

---

[1] *Please consult your company or organization's legal advisors for wording that will suffice for your situation.*

received validation and is sent on to the development team for further specification or the interaction design needs to be iterated and a new WoO prototype created.

Expression–These experiential prototypes attempt to portray a working system and its responses by using sleight of hand. The conceptual aspect of WoO prototypes is the suspension of disbelief created by this illusion.

Fidelity–Because of the required suspension of disbelief, WoO prototypes generally tend to be high-fidelity, especially if they portray a voice response user interface or are used for demonstration purposes. WoO prototypes employing a larger system behind the curtain, such as a hardware/software prototype of a mobile or portable device, can start out in the medium-fidelity range. Often a design team will iterate these prototypes several times, increasing the fidelity of every iteration.

Style–WoO prototypes can be either narrative or interactive. The interactive WoO prototype is used to determine if a sampling of users understand how to complete a representative activity. However, WoO prototypes can be considered narrative since they often serve as presentations or demonstrations or proofs of concept for selling advanced technology or research ideas to management, possible investors, etc.

Medium–WoO prototypes are digital.

Overview of What a WoO Prototype Looks Like

The most definitive aspect of a WoO prototype is not so much the look but how it is set up to effectively suspend disbelief or otherwise hide missing functionality from the user. The method for achieving this trick depends on the type of technology being prototyped. We will discuss two examples: a natural language system and a Web user interface.

For the simulation of a natural language interface, the user should think that the computer is interpreting his language input and responding appropriately. Let's say that the input mechanism is a microphone. The user testing environment has the user interacting with a computer, following a standard usability test script to perform several tasks by talking into the computer using natural language. In the WoO approach, the user's input is not interpreted by a computer, but rather by a person in another room who manually executes the commands by operating a computer. For this method to be effective, a note taker must carefully document the user's syntax. A list of expected terminology or syntaxes that the WoO operator faithfully follows must be devised; otherwise, the test degenerates into a communication test between two people.

In the Web interface, an unfinished screen design is tested as in a traditional usability test. However, certain links that require complex server action are instead sent to an unseen computer operator who manually displays the results on the participant's screen. This can be mimicked; for example, by making Web page text appear as a link but it is instead a signal to the hidden operator to enter a URL and display an image or trigger an audio response on the participant's computer. Another example is a submit button which needs to react differently based on what a user inputs. The WoO operator observes the input and prepares the resulting screen. When the user clicks the submit button, the Web browser navigates to a screen created by the operator. The resulting screen could be either chosen from a library of possible outcomes, or even created dynamically by the operator. When creating a prototype for a complete system is not feasible, WoO allows an incomplete design to be tested when most, but not all, of the interaction has been completed. Incomplete design aspects can be manipulated by the operator or even narrated by the moderator. For Web-based WoO sessions, it is effortless to simulate Web interface interactions if the participant and operator are using remote Web meeting client software wherein a user can lose control of the screen without realizing it.

FIGURE 21.1 *A WoO prototype session. The test participant (seated) thinks she is interacting with a complex system. The operator in the next room (on the right) is actually mimicking the interaction.*

Who is Involved with Wizard-of-Oz Prototypes

Neither Dorothy nor Toto not even the good witch of the North! rather a WoO prototype session is conducted by a team of at least two people. One person performs the role of the moderator, and the second person plays the role of the wizard or runs the computer system that serves as the wizard. The moderator should be someone very familiar with the interaction design concept to be able to accurately provide ad-hoc information on system interaction that occurs during the session. Even though the moderator is most likely working from a script, unexpected questions and issues will pop up. These unexpected interactions are part of every participant session, regardless of the prototype method chosen, but easily understood answers are more critical for maintaining the illusion desired from a WoO. The wizard role should be played by someone who can maintain the conceptual vision while also possessing technical knowledge of system possibilities to grant or create interactions that align with the technical capabilities.

What Are the Benefits of a WoO Prototype?

Primarily, the WoO technique allows testing of experimental interactions before they actually exist. For example, if the software team is creating speech recognition software that responds based on the tone of voice, the WoO method allows the team to set up a usability test where the user interacts with the system using both natural language and tone of voice. However, instead of trying to build a prototype to recognize a user's tone of voice, the wizard can recognize tone of voice and trigger the designed response. If the results are disappointing, no further development in an expensive prototype need occur.

Essentially, a WoO prototype can:

> Help you understand how potential users think about and react to new and unfamiliar advanced technology ideas.
> Allow you to explore usability requirements and issues at an early stage in the design process, particularly for concept systems that go beyond readily available technologies or for incomplete designs.
> Help the design team gain valuable insights from user participation.

STEP-BY-STEP GUIDE

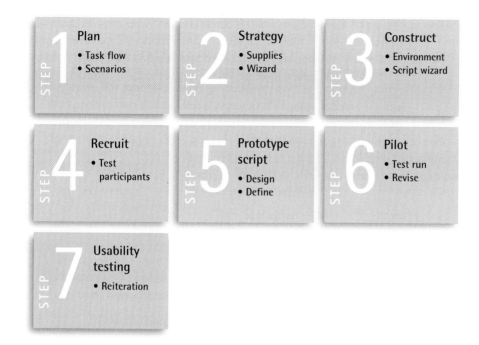

STEP 1 — Plan
- Task flow
- Scenarios

STEP 2 — Strategy
- Supplies
- Wizard

STEP 3 — Construct
- Environment
- Script wizard

STEP 4 — Recruit
- Test participants

STEP 5 — Prototype script
- Design
- Define

STEP 6 — Pilot
- Test run
- Revise

STEP 7 — Usability testing
- Reiteration

In this section, we cover adapting the steps for creating a WoO prototype to natural language or agent-based interactions, handhelds, and an unfinished design.

Procedure for a WoO Prototype for a Spoken Natural Language or Agent–Based Interaction

Step 1: Plan

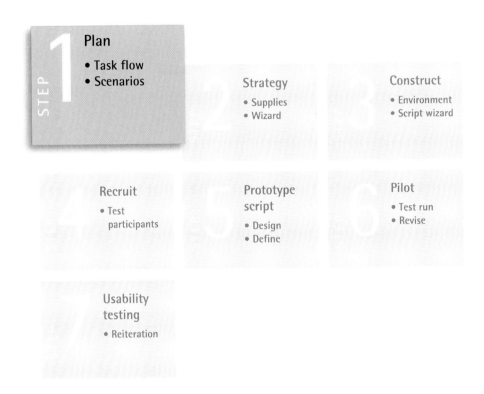

A WoO prototype involving user voice input and natural language responses or agent processes can be created using the following procedure:

Your plan should be based on a storyboard and interaction scenario for the desired task flow. For example, the task could be a hands-free user experience during the control of an automobile or airplane or a voice-based experience for getting information from a telephone service, such as the one offered by Amtrak, an American train company, to get train schedule updates.

Step 2: Strategy

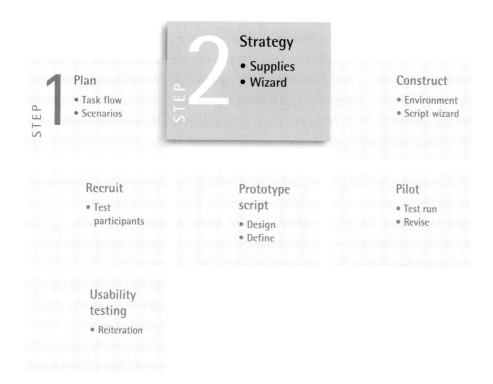

STEP 1

Plan
- Task flow
- Scenarios

STEP 2

Strategy
- **Supplies**
- **Wizard**

Construct
- Environment
- Script wizard

Recruit
- Test participants

Prototype script
- Design
- Define

Pilot
- Test run
- Revise

Usability testing
- Reiteration

Using the scenario and interaction script, determine the best artifacts, usage environment, and interaction method and environment for the system and its responses. The system could be scripted, involve a more complex system behind the scenes, or be done via "smoke and mirrors." An example of the latter would be having the natural language response simulated by someone providing scripted responses through an analog or digital audio system that represents the actual task environment, such as an automobile driver or airplane pilot cockpit working area.

Step 3: Construct

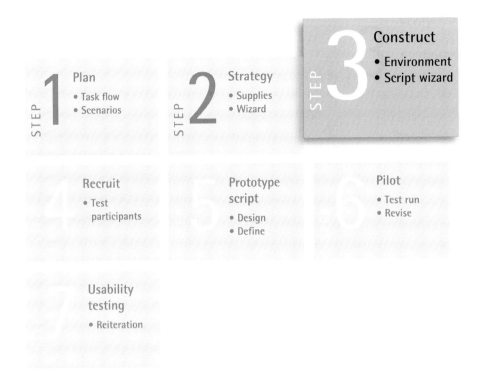

STEP **1** Plan
- Task flow
- Scenarios

STEP **2** Strategy
- Supplies
- Wizard

STEP **3** Construct
- Environment
- Script wizard

Recruit
- Test participants

Prototype script
- Design
- Define

Pilot
- Test run
- Revise

Usability testing
- Reiteration

The primary goal for building the WoO prototype is to create an environment that adequately suspends disbelief. This could involve something as elaborate as mocking up an airplane cockpit in an enclosed space such as a stage, jerry-rigging a prototype inside of an existing automobile, or building a tethered handheld device that provides natural language dialog with an assistive agent providing procedural instructions as needed to complete a task. The set up possibilities of WoO prototypes can go as far as your imagination and budget allow.

Step 4: Recruit

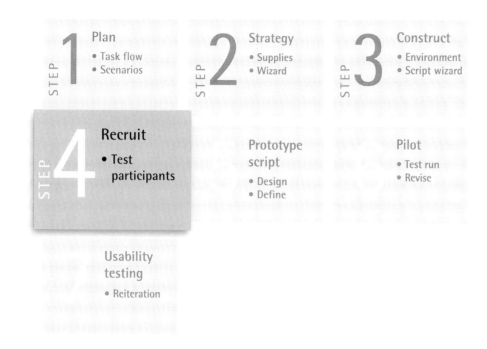

Recruiting participants is always the challenge. If you have access to your users directly, then it is easiest to contact them and involve them in the process. Users who will be directly affected are often eager participants. When you need to look for users, then it is often best to use recruiters who can find users for you based on a user profile and participant screener you provide. For more specialized or consumer oriented users, we have had very good luck with setting up booths at relevant tradeshows or conferences. General consumers can be found by setting up a stand at a shopping mall, preferably near a store that would attract users that would be interested in your software.

Step 5: Prototype Script

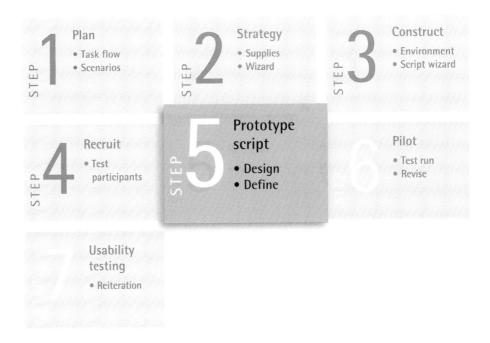

Script out the prototype based on your solution. This script will need to include what the video, audio, the different actors/players in the video will need to do. This should also include the design solution you want to prototype.

Designate the roles of wizard and facilitator then practice the interaction dialog using the storyboard scenario and interaction script. In terms of testing with participants (i.e., real users), the wizard may need to ad lib some responses to make them feel fluid and natural. Some teams may prefer to hire an actor to play the wizard role. This decision should be based on available budget and need for a steady, creative responder.

Step 6: Pilot

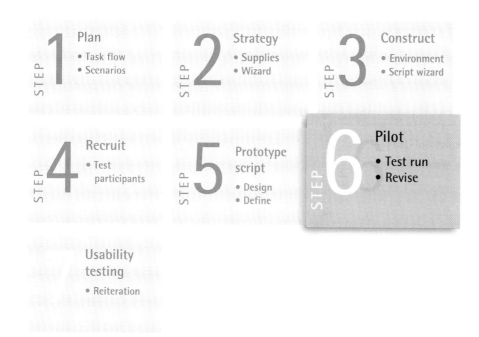

Once the prototype or prototype environment have been validated and the dialog script is well practiced, a pilot test should be conducted with a participant to detect any additional shortcomings or fixes that need addressing. If any modifications are needed, they should be made before continuing with usability testing.

Step 7: Usability Testing

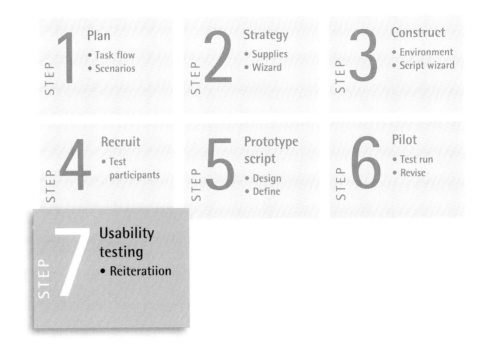

Test for usability. Be sure to videotape the sessions. Once the test sessions are completed and the results evaluated, the team can review and discuss any design implications and recommendations for improvements. The evaluation of WoO prototypes can yield a wealth of information regarding user expectations and requirements for novel technologies. The data gained from usability testing can be used by the team to informatively decide on next steps, such as continuing with more prototyping or transferring the ideas to a product development group.

Variation 1: WoO for Simulating Advanced Handheld or Portable Devices

The following variation on the step-by-step guide above represents a case study in which Michael used the WoO prototyping method to simulate an advanced hand-held device, a broadband wireless device used for field automation to access streaming video repair instructions. This prototype was implemented as a small device connected to a more powerful, large-scale system to simulate the interaction.

1. Similar to the prior procedure, start with a storyboard and interaction script of the task flow.
2. Based on the scenario and interaction script, determine the best technology artifacts, usage environment, and interaction method and environment for

the system and its responses. Our example could be tested in an actual field environment. A larger computer system would be hidden in a backpack carried by the field test moderator who would trail behind the test participant. The participant performs tasks with a hardware/software prototype of the device that is connected wirelessly, or tethered with a long cable, to the larger, more capable system in the backpack.

3. The prototype method and environment should be built to adequately suspend disbelief. As in the prior scenario, WoO prototypes dependent on more powerful systems are as capable as your imagination and budget allow.

4. To prepare a WoO prototype for usability testing, the participant recruiting process should begin when the prototype and any necessary environmental set up are near completion. To adequately detect user behavior patterns and interaction issues, five (minimum) to seven or more participants should be recruited.

5. Once the prototype method and environment set up are completed, a pilot test should be conducted to detect shortcomings and fixes that should be addressed before usability testing begins.

6. Test for usability. Once the test sessions are completed and the results (including videotapes) are evaluated, the team can review and discuss any design implications and recommendations for improvements.

Variation 2: WoO Method to Help Test an Unfinished Design

In an ideal world, you would only test a finished design, but the reality of time and resource constraints may require that you test long before then. Sometimes you need user input on the design before you finish, because the team has hit a roadblock or has two drastically diverging opinions on what the best design is. Worse yet, sometimes deadlines don't permit you to finish the design and testing must begin in parallel. An interactive prototype can incorporate characteristics of a WoO prototype to work around the empty spaces in the design.

1. Create an interactive prototype using whatever method will work best.
2. As usual, conduct an interactive session with the prototype.
3. For the designs that are not finished, either a computer operator mimics the resulting missing interaction behind the scenes or the test proceeds as if nothing out of the ordinary has happened.

Let's say you're testing a Web application. Instead of running the test in a Web browser, use a product that can mimic a browser's look and feel. For example, use Webex, a program in which the user can think he is using a computer but is actually being monitored by the hidden wizard who displays screens based on their input. Programs like Webex allow the wizard to assume control of the screen and simulate functionality by responding to user input. So when the participant finds a missing piece of interaction design, while the participant believes he is clicking a link that has the functionality to open a new Web page, the moderator changes the resulting screen based on the data; thus supplementing the missing functionality of the link.

Another method is to use an application that can be made to look like a Web browser. Most Microsoft Office products, for example, have a Web toolbar that makes the application look like a Web application if you hide everything except the Web toolbar. The Web links can be simple mockups in Excel, Word, or PowerPoint, and instead of functioning hyperlinks the wizard displays the appropriate system response screen. This strategy allows you to work with incomplete or not yet implemented functionality and applications, allowing stakeholder feedback on the design.

WHAT CONTENT ARE INCLUDED IN A WIZARD-OF-OZ PROTOTYPE?

WoO prototypes are driven by scenarios generally embodied in storyboards. The source of content for WoO prototypes that represent products comes from these storyboard scenarios derived from business and marketing requirements and user research, including site visits, task analyses, etc. The content source for WoO prototypes that represent an advanced technology exploration also come from storyboards, those arising from brainstorming and ideation sessions.

One of the unique aspects of WoO prototyping is its almost sole purpose for testing system behavior and performance. As such, WoO prototypes require fairly advanced interaction design concepts to be adequately used to test the designed system behavior. The prototype content includes the instructions and designed interactions that the system should respond to, if it really existed. Therefore, it is imperative that the wizard be thoroughly familiar with the design concept and the technical capabilities and limitations of the system.

NEXT ITERATION AFTER WIZARD-OF-OZ PROTOTYPING

The next iteration of a WoO prototype often depends on the various factors that impact design activity decision making, such as outcome of a first WoO prototype, project objectives, time, resources, etc. Considering these factors, the next iteration of a WoO prototype may be another WoO prototype, especially if it is a research project activity. Research project activities often don't have the same constraints, such as an aggressive timeline that a product effort has, allowing the luxury of multiple iterations.

Some lower fidelity WoO prototypes that require a larger, more powerful system behind the curtain, such as a hardware/software prototype of a mobile or portable device, can be prototyped within a week. If the original prototype is a quick, low-fidelity version, the likely next iteration is another WoO prototype of higher fidelity. Since WoO prototypes often portray advanced technologies that are not readily available, a time gap may occur between completion of WoO prototype testing and prototyping with the actual intended technology. This gap often occurs when advanced technologists identify a new emerging technology or scaling down of an existing technology; a WoO prototype allows trial and experimentation with a promising technology in advance of its availability.

REFERENCES

Nils Dahlback, Arne Jonsson, Lars Ahrenberg. Wizard of Oz studies: how and why. Proceedings of Intelligent User Interfaces Conference '93. New York: ACM, 1993, pp. 193–201.

James Lewis. Sample sizes for usability studies: additional considerations. Human Factors, 1994, vol. 36, pp. 368–378.

Wendy E. Mackay, et al. Video artifacts for design: bridging the gap between abstraction and detail. Proceedings of DIS '00. Brooklyn, NY: ACM, 2000.

David Maulsby, Saul Greenberg, Richard Mander. Prototyping an intelligent agent through Wizard of Oz. Proceedings of InterCHI '93. New York: ACM, 1993, pp. 277–285.

Jeffrey Rubin. Handbook of Usability Testing. New York: Wiley, 1994.

CHAPTER

22

DESCRIPTION

Coded prototypes come in many flavors ranging from those created in a comprehensive programming language such as C++ or Java to Visual Basic, from those
built in a markup language such as HTML to those built in a visual programming
environment such as Macromedia Director or Dreamweaver then scripted in
JavaScript or Macromedia Lingo. A coded prototype is usually concrete, high
fidelity, and fully interactive. Many coded prototypes are created in the target
development language and are meant to directly evolve into a final coded product. A coded prototype generally features a high-fidelity graphical user interface
and is best produced late in the design process after all large-scale design
changes have been completed. The intended audience is often internal upper
management, who generally require comprehensive, high-fidelity expressions of
products or services to help them visualize and understand full value and potential. The sales team also requires fully interactive simulations in advance of a finished product to be able to prime the marketplace. Lastly, a coded prototype is
especially good for capturing both qualitative and quantitative data via usability
validation testing.

What Is a Coded Prototype?

Coded prototypes can be created in several forms including a programming
language, a markup language, or in a visual programming environment in conjunction with a scripting language. All these forms are digital interactive expressions of
program code, each meant to portray a software product or one of its components
as similar to the finished coded result as possible. Figure 22.1, shows an interactive
TV prototype, created in Director with Lingo, that seamlessly simulates a full-
motion TV-based interactive shopping experience with full remote control
interactivity for broadband TV.

This prototype was based on a storyboard concept and used video, graphics
and animated special effects produced on video and special effects computer

FIGURE 22.1 *A product
category selection
menu from an
interactive TV shopping
environment.*

workstations. The preproduced content was imported and composited with other content in Director, and the interactivity was then coded using the Lingo scripting language.

Figure 22.2 is also a frame from an interactive TV prototype. This example used Java programming to schedule and trigger the display of preproduced graphics overlaid on a broadcast TV sports program. In addition, Java was used to fetch detailed information about sports players from a database and display it in a graphics composite.

CHARACTERISTICS

Audience–Coded prototypes are created for both internal and external audiences; however, given their high fidelity, they are the most appropriate form of prototype to show to the external world. For internal audiences, they are generally used for specification purposes. Marketing and sales use coded prototypes as demos to internal upper management in addition to prospective buyers and possible funding sources.
Stage–Late stage; all major requirements and design decisions should be finalized before investing in the effort needed to make this kind of prototype.
Speed–Coded prototypes require a generous amount of diligence to create because they both appear and behave as a final software product.
Longevity–Coded prototypes are generally created in the final stages of a software design effort. Because they are high fidelity and interactive, they can serve as a component of a software product or service specification used as a guide for the

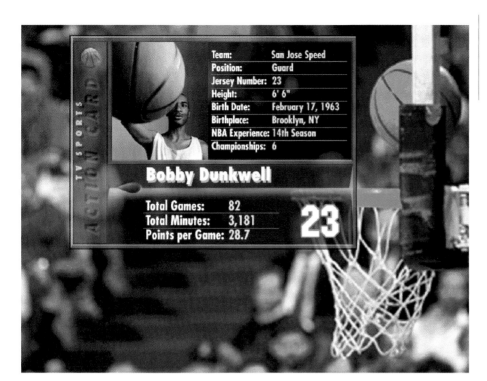

FIGURE 22.2 *A graphic information panel overlaid on TV sports content.*

programming team in implementing the user interface and user experience of a product. Thus, their longevity depends on the lifecycle of the specification, including whether it will be archived for future reference. Coded prototypes also have a natural durability, one that other prototype methods lack, due to their ability to run independently as self-contained executable programs. Furthermore, when a coded prototype is iterated and transformed into an actual coded product, its longevity is dependent on the life of the product, or at least the life of the initial version of the product. Since a coded prototype is also used as a marketing or sales demo, its longevity is contingent on its continued effectiveness and usefulness in the marketing and sales cycle. As mentioned above, since a refined prototype may require a sizeable investment of time and resources, its longevity may be considered as one component of justification for building it.

Expression–Coded prototypes are considered to be experiential because they attempt to portray a final software product and provide believable responses to user interactions.

Fidelity–Because they need to truly represent the final working product, coded prototypes generally tend to be high fidelity, especially if used for demonstrations.

Style–Coded prototypes are interactive; their main purpose is to mimic the actual product as closely as possible. Nevertheless, though they are capable of being interactive, they also can play a narrative role if someone drives the prototype in a presentation.

TABLE 22.1 Coded Prototype Content and Fidelity Matrix

Content	Very Low Fidelity	Low Fidelity	Medium Fidelity	High Fidelity	Highest Fidelity
Information design	−	−	+	+ +	+ +
Interaction design	NA	−	+	+ +	+ +
Visual design	+	+	+	+ +	+ +
Editorial content	NA	NA	+	+ +	+ +
Branding expression	− −	+	+	+ +	+ +
System performance	NA	− −	+ +	+ +	+ +

+ +, Most appropriate;

+, appropriate;

−, not appropriate;

− −, completely inappropriate;

NA, not applicable.

Medium–Because coded prototypes are developed in a programming, markup, or scripting language, they are purely digital.

Overview of What a Coded Prototype Looks Like

Figures 22.1 and 22.2 each show the most definitive visual aspects of a coded prototype in terms of the use of digital media:

> High-fidelity visual expression

> Ability to composite different media types into a single seamless display

> Ability to incorporate remotely stored informational content and data

As a paper medium, this book is incapable of effectively portraying the interactive, navigational, and audio aspects of coded prototypes, especially those that are meant to simulate rich multimedia expression, such as that required for interactive TV or interactive games prototyping. As such this book's website includes a video portrayal of an interactive TV prototype demonstrating the high-fidelity level of coded prototypes.

TYPES OF CODED PROTOTYPES

As mentioned, a coded prototype is any type of software that can be developed by software makers, including desktop software, websites, operating system software, software for handhelds, etc. We'll use the interactive TV example shown earlier to describe the creation of a coded prototype. The Director prototype shown in Figure 22.1 and the Java prototype shown in Figure 22.2 both represent examples of coded prototypes for interactive TV. Both prototypes involve seamlessly compositing video, graphics, text, and special effects into a user experience involving the use of remote control interaction.

The ambitious Director prototype involved:

- Hierarchical navigation through a menu of premium TV services to a merchant-based interactive shopping environment
- Interactive selection of product categories and products
- Interactive configuration of product ensembles, such as fashion items and suites of household furnishings
- Direct purchase business-to-consumer (B2C) electronic commerce (e-commerce) with credit cards

In comparison, the Java prototype focused on graphic and animated information provided as TV programming enhancements overlaid on broadcast content at the control of the user. In this case, the prototype focused on enhancing TV sports programming with information about a sporting event, including associated players, teams, organizational affiliations, etc. Below we will discuss each of these prototypes and their prototyping platforms in more detail.

Who Creates Coded Prototypes?

For the most part, coded prototypes are created by programmers, professional prototypers, and interaction designers. Coded prototypes created in a programming language, such as Java, C++, Visual Basic, etc. are generally built by experienced programmers. Prototypes created in a markup or scripting language are often done by a wider array of software makers in addition to programmers. User interface designers, interaction designers, product managers, and other non-programmer professionals have been known to create prototypes both in HTML with scripting and in visual programming environments. Visual programming environments open up the creation and production of fully interactive high-fidelity prototypes to a much larger base of creators than coding directly in a programming language allows.

What Are the Benefits of a Coded Prototype?

A coded prototype is usually developed in a programming or markup language and is most effective as an iteration of other forms of lower fidelity prototypes that have been validated with users. Otherwise, you risk developing a very expensive prototype that may be completely discarded or need major modifications. Depending on the programming language and amount of detailed coding, a coded prototype can have the advantage of allowing the software team to productively reuse the code for an actual finished product. A coded prototype can serve not only as a stimulus for usability testing but can equally well serve as an effective demonstration vehicle for sales and marketing. Coded prototypes meant to be used for design iteration and usability validation should not necessarily be driven by the needs and objectives of a sales or marketing demo. Likewise, the usability testing conducted on a more advanced coded prototype should return results that are a further refinement of the design rather than a redesign. Like the sales and marketing demo, this prototype should be the result of prior iterations of lower cost prototypes, usually providing feedback from potential users to drive small, incremental design refinements. If you end up with large-scale changes, your methodology needs reassessing—either you cut too many corners in the user-centered design process or the wrong people were making design decisions.[1]

What Is the Source for Coded Prototype Content?

Coded prototypes can be driven by a number of different methods that might precede them, such as storyboards, paper prototypes, wireframes, and others presented in this book. Content for a coded prototype can derive from the artifacts of these prior methods as well as the addition of high-fidelity content. This could include professionally produced video, graphics, and special effects in addition to refined editorial content and the application of a branding scheme. A very refined coded prototype can also connect to a database to supply content, including statistical, personal, address, news feed, image, telemetry, and other types of data. Any of this content can be accessed through the use of a programming language, markup language, or scripting.

What Is the Content of a Coded Prototype?

The content of a coded prototype can be anything and everything. It is indeed rare that a coded prototype just highlights one aspect of software content as discussed earlier in the content planning chapter because the effective prototyper first would have used cheaper prototyping methods to test certain critical aspects of the content. By the time the product team reaches the coded prototype stage, the team expects to know how all the content will be combined into a software product. Furthermore, since coded prototypes have the power of a programming, markup, or scripting language behind them, the content and interaction with it can be of high fidelity. The types of content and media can be almost anything that the software makers imagine, ranging from entertainment to business to communications to desktop applications to utility content. The biggest issue related to a coded prototype is not content but the potentially sizeable investment of time and resources needed to create both the content and the prototype. In the broadband shopping example above, a huge investment was made in the production of high-quality media, including expensive special effects. This investment and any associated risks must be considered for any highly refined and comprehensive prototype.

Step-by-Step Guide to Creating Sales Demos

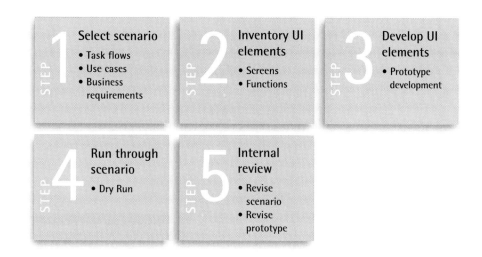

STEP 1 — Select scenario
- Task flows
- Use cases
- Business requirements

STEP 2 — Inventory UI elements
- Screens
- Functions

STEP 3 — Develop UI elements
- Prototype development

STEP 4 — Run through scenario
- Dry Run

STEP 5 — Internal review
- Revise scenario
- Revise prototype

Coded prototypes can be sales demos or the beginning of the development aspect of software making. Because it's used to tell a compelling story about an upcoming product, a sales demo is more narrative than interactive, while a late stage interactive prototype allows the design team to perform a last check on the design concept allowing for the refinements necessary to polish the software. Often, this late stage validation is characterized by small changes of a very light-weight nature. In our experience, that's wrong. Late stage coded prototypes often involve the most intensive design effort because making details work, solving concept problems in a way that conforms to predetermined goals and criteria, comprises the most challenging and time-consuming efforts. Also, reality usually strikes at this point, and software makers discover that those things that seemed so easy in concept are suddenly more difficult to code than expected. Workarounds will be needed as technical reality meets the original design concept. This process of working through design and technical issues is why we recommend short iterations for this phase; something akin to coaching sessions with the technical team should occur frequently to determine if the coded prototype development is running smoothly.

The steps involved in a coded sales demo prototype are outlined below.

In our experience, coded prototype creation for the average complex desktop application takes around 3 to 4 weeks. For websites and Web applications, which have much more limited interaction capabilities, the time can be trimmed to 1 to 2 weeks. Coded prototype iterations can usually be done in 1 to 2 days, depending on the complexity of the changes. If wholesale changes are needed, then usually half the time taken to create the original prototype is required.

Step 1: Select Scenario

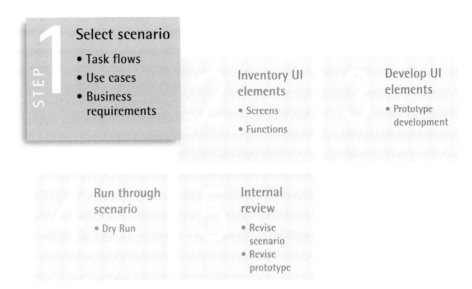

STEP 1

Select scenario
- Task flows
- Use cases
- Business requirements

Inventory UI elements
- Screens
- Functions

Develop UI elements
- Prototype development

Run through scenario
- Dry Run

Internal review
- Revise scenario
- Revise prototype

Create a new Scenario or select an existing scenario narrating the main business goals and tasks of the software to be used in the prototype (2–4 hours). All desired functionality for the demonstration (not all functionality in the software) should be included. This functionality should be known and should exist in documents or in the form of use cases, task flows, or stated business requirements. The scenario should follow a typical user on the routine usage of the product. Some common exceptions should be included, and user interface elements or functions that are not implemented should use a single under-construction screen or similar convention with the ability to return to the main or previous screen.

Step 2: Inventory UI Elements

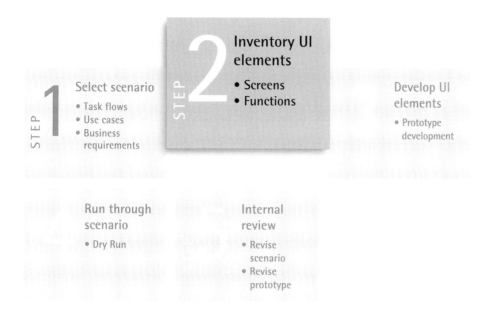

Create a checklist of all interface screens and functions needed to support the scenario. It is often most helpful if this is represented as a flow diagram. As items are developed, you can check them off on the flow diagram (1 hour, 5 hours maximum). Then, the scenarios are used to inventory the main screens, the information, and the secondary and other widgets and screens (e.g., modal dialogs, pull-down menus, messages, etc.) needed.

Step 3: Develop UI Elements

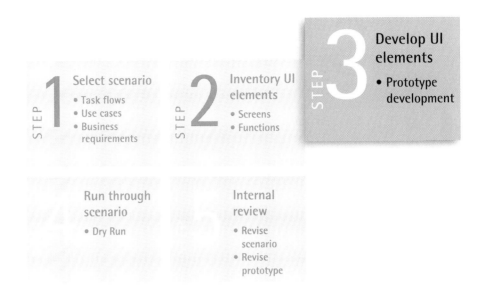

Every item on the checklist should be developed (average 1–3 weeks, 4 weeks maximum; complex systems, however, may require more time). It's useful to have the design specifications available, either in the form of previous prototypes or the specifications written from them.

Step 4: Run through Scenario

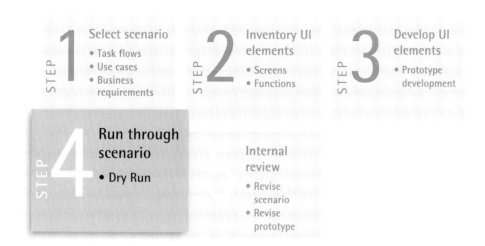

STEP 1 Select scenario
- Task flows
- Use cases
- Business requirements

STEP 2 Inventory UI elements
- Screens
- Functions

STEP 3 Develop UI elements
- Prototype development

STEP 4 **Run through scenario**
- **Dry Run**

Internal review
- Revise scenario
- Revise prototype

Perform your own dry run through the scenario with the prototype making sure to check for bugs and missing functions (4–8 hours, 1.5 days maximum). Step through the scenario by operating the prototype. You will probably catch many bugs this way. However, they really come out of the woodwork when you ask your cube mate or other colleague to actually use the prototype.

Step 5: Internal Review

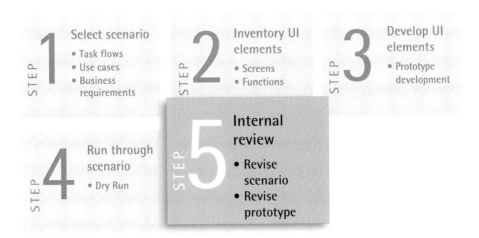

Show the prototype to requirements stakeholders (1 day, 1.5 days maximum). The internal review is most important for those who will give the demonstrations.

Step-by-Step Guide to Creating High-Fidelity Interactive Coded Prototypes

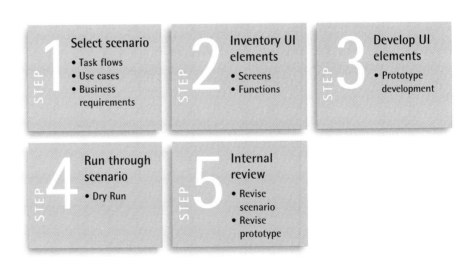

The steps involved in creating a late stage interactive coded prototype are outlined below and guide you to focus on getting the details of your coded prototype right for internal reviews and usability testing.

Step 1: Select Scenarios

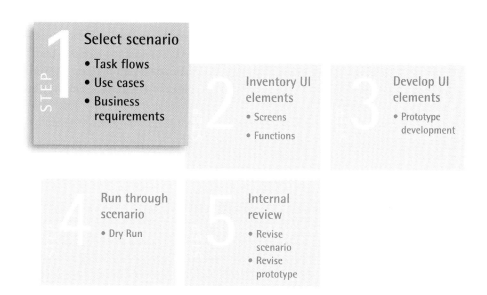

First, you need to determine which scenarios you want to implement. You can usually leverage scenarios you've already developed for storyboarding or prior low-fidelity prototyping (2–4 hours). These scenarios should cover distinct tasks that users can perform. They should not be single activities or functions that get strung together with a usability script, such as, logging in, entering data then looking for the print command. An example of a task is managing your bank account or transferring funds to an online bank account.

Step 2: Inventory UI Elements

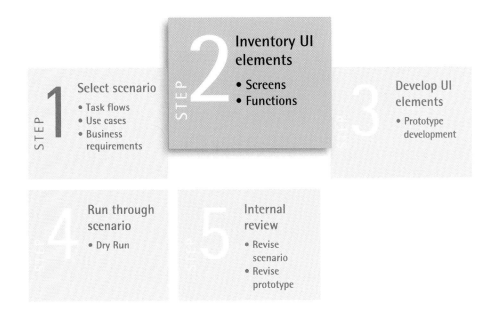

Creating the inventory of user interface elements to support the scenario is the same here as in the demonstration prototype (1–5 hours, depending on complexity). In addition to an inventory of screens, you also need to record the sample data required to perform the tasks. For example, if the task is to order a pizza, a menu needs to be presented offering all the options associated with specifying and ordering a pizza, including toppings, prices, available sizes, etc.

Step 3: Develop UI Elements

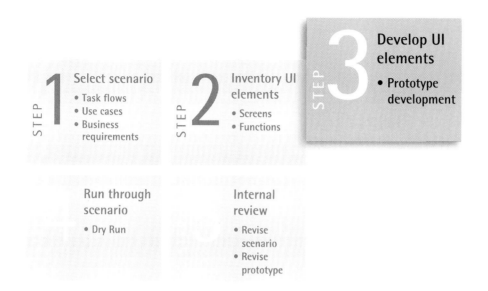

Develop every item on the checklist, including the test data. Earlier prototypes got away with greeking or other forms of finessing the design details, but a high-fidelity coded prototype needs to be as real looking as possible. It can easily become time consuming to complete the test data. Some teams even build latency into the prototype, especially when system performance is expected to be worse than in the prototype (1–3 weeks, 4 weeks maximum; complex systems may require more time). This step in the prototyping process assumes that little design work is necessary and that you're implementing an already existing design from a paper prototype, wireframe, or storyboard.

Step 4: Internal Review

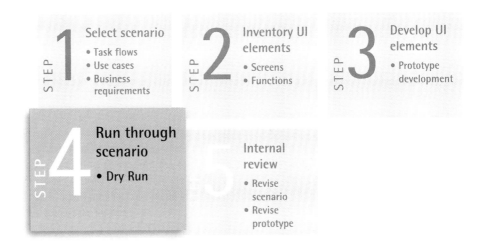

Similar to creating a sales demo, perform your own dry run through the scenario making sure to check for bugs and any other problems.

Step 5: Usability Testing

An internal review of the late stage prototype should be more thorough. You want to replicate the usability test in the review. You should ask both team members and colleagues unfamiliar with the work to test the prototype. Since you need to fix bugs before the test date, you may need some long hours and late night pizzas to get the prototype to its best quality (4–8 hours, 1.5 days maximum).

CASE STUDY: WORLD OF SHOPPING–CODED PROTOTYPE USING A VISUAL PROGRAMMING LANGUAGE

Director and its more recent cousin, Flash, are visual programming languages appropriate for representing interactive time-based multimedia and content, such as that of interactive TV and interactive games. The Director environment is based on a theater metaphor of a dynamically changing stage and cast of actors. The environment includes a script editor and a gallery of multimedia content in addition to features that support robust visual programming.

The World of Shopping interactive TV service represented in a single screen in Figure 22.1 required the dynamic combination of multimedia content with selection, navigation, product configuration, and e-commerce transaction interactivity. The World of Shopping was one component of a set of premium interactive subscription services that a regional telephone company envisioned offering to customers as enhancements to the array of standard telephone services. Once a strategic direction was defined in terms of service offerings, the design team was given the challenge to prototype an on-screen shopping experience including offerings from a variety of North American merchants, including a department store, a women's cosmetic company, a home furnishings company, a national florist, and others. The design team was composed of a manager, a design director, two interaction designers, a visual designer, a usability engineer, and a programmer/scripter. Prior to building the Director prototype, the team was engaged in a variety of design activities that led up to the interactive coded prototype. These activities included:

> Wireframes for ideation and discussion

> Paper prototyping

> Scenario and storyboard development

> Several iterations of rough (paper) to intermediate interactive prototypes (Director) of the following key components:

  • Hierarchical navigation scheme (service offerings to product offerings)

  • Product selection and configuration

  • E-commerce transaction procedure, including shopping cart and check out interaction

> Usability testing of prototype iterations

After these activities were completed and a refined interactive TV concept was validated by users, product management and the design team jointly decided to go forward with a complete, fully interactive, high-fidelity version of the prototype. A professional content producer needed to be hired to produce highly polished graphics, animation, video, and special effects in a TV production studio. Much of the video content were product marketing videos provided by the merchants themselves, but these videos needed to be edited and seamlessly woven into the overall shopping environment.

The final prototype also required the production of professional grade audio content for menu selection audio loops, background music audio tracks, and audio transitions. A professional audio producer was hired to create and produce the different audio expressions.

While the content was being produced, the design team:

> Prepared menu bar and other graphics components

> Set up the Director prototyping environment for remote control interactivity and navigation

> Prepared the content areas in which to import the produced content once it was ready

> Finalized the e-commerce transaction sequence, screens, and graphics

When the audio content was ready, the files were imported into Director. The video, animation content, and applied special effects were composited in Adobe Premiere, then imported into Director. The team then set about the diligent task of composing and sequencing all the media components within Director and tying them to the navigation and interaction components. This was a tedious iterative task which included refinement of the scripting and remote control functionality that allowed remote control interaction.

The final version of the World of Shopping prototype was then tested in usability sessions and, as a result, a few relatively minor refinements were made. The users, project management, and the design team were all pleased with the successful results of the user-centered design process. Unfortunately, due to many unplanned costs and the additional effort required to build and deploy a broadband infrastructure to effectively support the intended interactive TV services, the executive management decided not to deploy the World of Shopping.

CASE STUDY: INTERACTIVE TV–CODED PROTOTYPE USING A PROGRAMMING LANGUAGE

At another company, interactive TV was being explored as one of a number of new consumer services using the programming language, Java. Java on cable TV set-top boxes would allow major TV broadcasters and content providers to offer competitive enhancements to some of their standard broadcast programs. One area of opportunity was sports broadcasting. During a broadcast sports event, viewers wanted the ability to interactively receive more information about the teams and players overlaid on the broadcast. A number of application programmer interfaces were developed specifically for the purpose of allowing programmers to write code relatively easily to provide these content enhancements. The Java code allowed the following:

> Remote control interactivity with enhanced content

> Graphics overlaid on video

> Transparent graphics

> Fetching of informational graphics and text data from databases

> Synchronization of interaction commands, multimedia data, and content with a scheduled broadcast

During broadcasts that support interactive access to enhanced content, viewers could get real-time displays of this enhanced information with their remote controls, as shown in Figure 22.2. For sports-related content, these enhancements composited information available in the databases such as:

> Anecdotal, historical, and statistical information about leagues, divisions, teams, and stadiums

> Anecdotal, personal, and statistical information about past and current players

> Action, statistical, and scoring information about the viewed event

The Java prototype was built more along the lines of a traditional software application. Programmers did the actual prototype programming in close collaboration with designers. This type of collaboration underscores the labor and resource intensive nature of a coded prototype. But again, the result was an effective technological proof of concept ready for the next step.

Application Program Interface (API): A set of routines, protocols, and tools for building software applications. A good API makes it easier to develop a program by providing all the building blocks. A programmer puts the blocks together to create a working application.

NEXT ITERATION AFTER CODED PROTOTYPING

The next iteration of a coded prototype is often the actual software product that it represents. This is especially true for a prototype code base that is re-used and transformed into the final product. A coded prototype that is used for marketing or sales demonstrations may be iterated with new features to represent the next version of a product. A scripted prototype may have an iteration that refines the prototype based on feedback from usability testing or may, in fact, be used as a specification reference for programmers.

REFERENCES

Cay S. Horstmann. Java Concepts. Hoboken, NJ: Wiley, 2005.

Evangelos Petroutsos, Richard Mansfield. Visual Basic .NET Power Tools. San Francisco: Sybex, 2003.

Nicholas A. Solter, Scott J. Kleper. Professional C++ (Programmer to Programmer). Hoboken, NJ: Wrox, 2005.

CHAPTER

Prototyping Tools

23

PROTOTYPING WITH OFFICE SUITE APPLICATIONS

INTRODUCTION

Office suite applications are used around the world, in businesses of every size. These applications help us create formatted text documents, build and show presentations, and create spreadsheets. How have these kinds of applications, usually used by office workers, accountants, and managers, found their way into a book on prototyping? In this book, you would expect to find graphical and HTML-based programs such as Photoshop, Illustrator, Dreamweaver, and other traditional prototyping tools used by skilled interaction and visual designers. Surprising is that such mundane products as Microsoft Word, PowerPoint, and Excel, although not originally designed for prototyping and design, can be excellent prototyping tools. Each application has features that support varying fidelities and characteristics of prototyping. This chapter discusses the basics on how to use them.

For those who do not have the Microsoft Office Suite, most, if not all, of the tips and techniques discussed here are available in other office suites products from other vendors, like Apple Computer and Sun Microsystems. There is even a free suite of products called OpenOffice. These products have similar feature sets, but their command structures are slightly different. Consequently, you need to know not only where to find the similar commands but also what they are called in these different applications.

WHY COVER THREE OFFICE APPLICATIONS IN ONE CHAPTER?
Similarities and Differences

Since Word, PowerPoint, and Excel are all Microsoft products, they share many of the same features, such as menus and commands, which provide similar results. For example, entering text, adding graphics, or creating shapes each use the same menu commands across these three applications. Not all features and functions are the same across the Office suite applications, but those used for building prototypes are mostly similar. A list of common features among the three applications is shown below.

TABLE 23.1 **MS Office Features in Common**

Feature	Word	PowerPoint	Excel
Text	Yes	Yes	Yes
• Multiple styles	Yes	Yes	Yes
• Easy position control	No	No	Yes
• Find replace	Yes	Yes	Yes
Graphics	Yes	Yes	Yes
• Align graphics	Yes	Yes	Yes
• Imports graphics	Yes	Yes	Yes
• Graphic manipulation	Yes	Yes	Yes
• Creation	Yes	Yes	Yes
• Auto shapes	Yes	Yes	Yes
• Library	Yes	Yes	Yes
• Format painter	Yes	Yes	Yes
Animation	No	Yes	No[1]
Apply backgrounds	Yes	Yes	Yes
Apply comments	Yes	Yes	Yes
Presentation mode	Yes[2]	Yes	Yes[2]
Color	Yes	Yes	Yes
• Large palette	Yes	No	Yes
• Custom colors	Yes	Yes	Yes
• RGB/Web	Yes	Yes	Yes
Floating table cells	Yes	Yes	No
Grid cells	No	No	Yes
Save as HTML	Yes	Yes	Yes

1. Excel does not have the animation features of PowerPoint, however, by combining other features such as linking and multiple worksheets, the illusion of animations can be created in a useful and powerful manner.
2. These are not true presentation modes, however, they are Full Screen modes that can provide a presentation look and feel.

With all three applications having so many of the same features, you might think that there's no real difference in choosing one over another for prototyping. To a limited degree, this is true, because any one of these applications could be pushed to create a prototype that looks like one made by any of the other two. However, that effort may not be well spent as looks is not the same as behavior. You want to choose the application that best supports the style and method of prototype you need.

Choosing which application to use is decided by the differences between the applications rather than the similarities. The differences stem from each application's original purpose. Normally, you wouldn't use Excel for word processing nor would you choose PowerPoint to build your spreadsheets. But in redefining these as prototyping applications, you now need to compare their prototyping features. This doesn't imply that each application can only be used as described here. For example, many designers swear by PowerPoint as a great design tool, knowing all the tricks and shortcuts of a power user. This chapter is constrained to prototyping methods easily supported by each application's feature set without requiring you to be a power user.

Sophisticated Graphics: Something They're All Missing

Before going deeper into the differences among these applications, one additional similarity should be noted: a common deficiency. None of these applications have the ability to create sophisticated illustrations or graphics. If you want to create illustrations or graphic images, you'll need to use other programs, such as the basic paint application, Microsoft Paint, to the more feature-rich and sophisticated applications, Adobe Photoshop and Illustrator. However, you could also try an alternative to creating your own graphics. For example, if you are designing for an existing website you can copy the needed graphics from that site. If you're lucky, the design department in your company has all the graphics you need, so you can simply import these using the Insert Picture command on the Drawing toolbar or Insert menu. If your company cannot supply you with graphics, and artistic talent is not one of your strengths, then fear not—all three of the Office suite applications have the ability to create colored boxes and table cells, arrows, bars, and graphical text, all of which can be used to accurately represent many graphical aspects. All three applications also feature a clip art library, and you can find many license-free clip art sites on the Internet. To create sophisticated graphics though, you'll need to include a draw program or pixel editing application in your arsenal.

WHO WOULD USE OFFICE SUITE APPLICATIONS FOR PROTOTYPING?

One of the most compelling reasons to prototype with Office applications (Word, PowerPoint, and Excel) is their enormous installed base of users, resulting in very widespread availability and worldwide use. Since office applications of one sort or another are standard issue on most business computers, most people in the business world have proficiency in at least one of these applications. Taking your existing knowledge of Office applications and applying it to those applications for prototyping is a great opportunity for anyone lacking graphics applications or coding expertise. This gives everyone the opportunity to visualize ideas and readily share them with others. Using Office applications as prototyping tools expands the team participation to project managers, developers, analysts, product managers, and visual designers who can all collaborate in the same tool.

FIGURE 23.1 *Wireframe prototype built in Microsoft Word.*

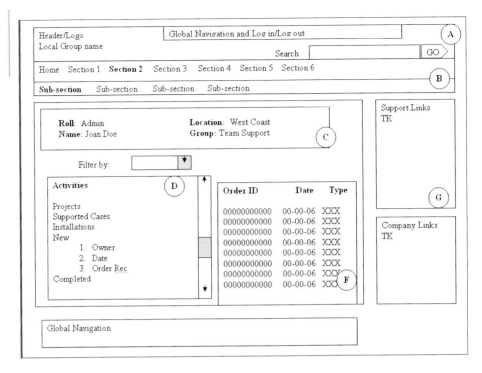

MICROSOFT WORD

MS Word is a word processing program that has become the industry standard for almost any kind of writing need.

Advantages

One great advantage of Word is its ease of use when applied to the appropriate method. Most everyone has experience using Word, making for a short learning curve. Because of its large user base, any prototype made in Word offers easy distribution to other team members. Word has good text handling capabilities and all the features that come with a word processing program, such as spell check, find and replace, and multiple text styles. Additionally, the drawing tools are simple and easy to use.

Disadvantages

As well as MS Word handles text, it has difficulty with graphics. Although graphics can be inserted, they cannot be placed with precision, such as with applications with real placement grids like Visio, Illustrator, In Design, etc. Building an interface that demands the exact positioning of graphics can become a frustrating experience using Word. Pagination is another limitation. For a word processing application, pages positioned one above another make sense as the text flows from one page to the next. However, building prototypes of many pages can become cumbersome and frustrating. Trying to control the depth of a page while making changes on others may shift the page up or down. Trying to keep pages in correct relationship to each other while maintaining their individual proportions can also be difficult.

Appropriate Method

MS Word best supports the wireframe method because its styles are conceptual, rapid, and require only low fidelity. As a conceptual prototype, correct proportions are not as important, so the graphics positioning issues become less important, making Word an effective conceptual prototyping tool. Conceptual prototypes are usually used in the early stages of the prototyping process. It is at this stage that fast-paced, iterative prototypes are needed most. The simplicity of Word's drawing tools makes it ideal for quick design iterations. Wireframes usually require only low-fidelity rendering, easily supported by the standard simple drawing tools offered in Word.

Example: Step-by-Step Guide to Building a Wireframe in MS Word

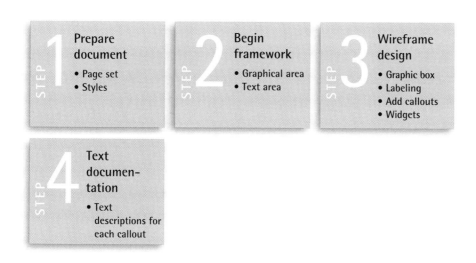

Franco is the product manager for a recently funded project. Since he will be meeting with the newly formed team for the first time tomorrow, he wants to visualize his initial thoughts for them. The design is for a section of a website where the navigation and branding are already established. Franco needs to focus on the structure of the new content areas of the site. There is no actual content yet, but he has an outline of what needs to be designed and wants to portray its structure. Due to the lack of concrete content at this point, a wireframe seems to be the best method to visualize his early concepts.In addition since it's early in the design process, Franco doesn't want to spend a lot of time building a prototype that will change as soon as his team begins working on it.

Step 1: Prepare Document

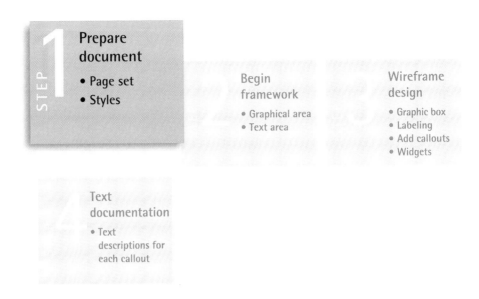

To build the first page of the wireframe, Franco begins by preparing a Word document for prototyping. He adjusts the default behavior of Word by choosing a horizontal orientation for the page so he can split each page into two and display both the wireframe and text documentation side by side. He decides that a horizontal layout is also a better match for the target screen resolution.

Franco then changes the text to the corporate standard for websites. He opens up the font format dialog (**Format**>**Font**) and changes the font settings to Arial Regular 12.

FIGURE 23.2 *MS Word page setup.*

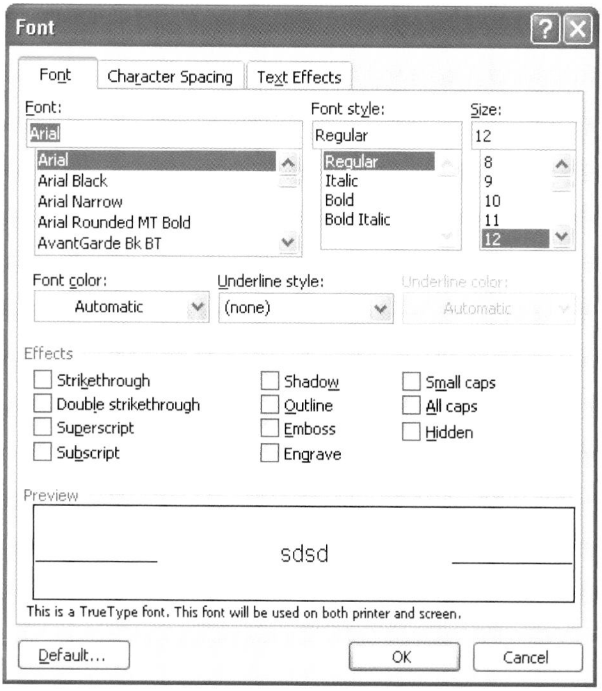

FIGURE 23.3 *Font dialog showing new settings to reflect the corporate standard.*

Step 2: Begin Framework

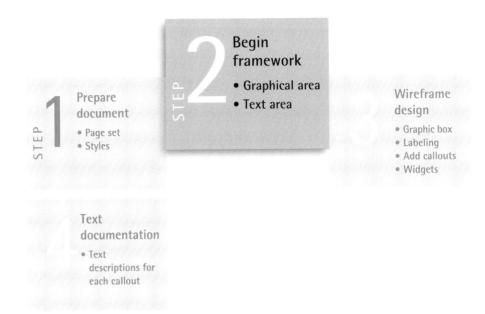

Franco now sets up his preliminary website layout by placing a graphic visualization on the left and annotations or descriptive text on the right. Having the description on the same page as the graphic provides an easy reference. It doesn't matter at this point that the graphic rendering portion will be small, because it lacks detail and the hierarchy and labeling are most important at this point—both of which are easily portrayed in this format. However, the text column could be made smaller to anticipate further development of the graphical area. For this example, we will keep the text area large. Franco goes through this procedure:

1. Opens the Drawing toolbar: **View**>**Toolbar**>**Drawing**.
2. Selects the rectangle tool.

FIGURE 23.4 *Selecting the rectangle tool.*

3. Creates a graphical rectangle (by clicking and dragging) half the width of the screen.

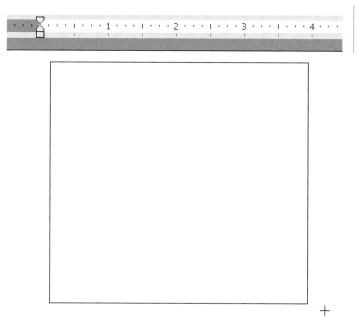

FIGURE 23.5 *Creating a graphic box.*

4. Selects the Text Box tool in the Drawing toolbar.

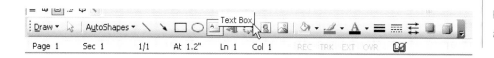

FIGURE 23.6 *Selecting the Text Box tool.*

5. Creates a Text Box rectangle to encompass the remaining available screen width.

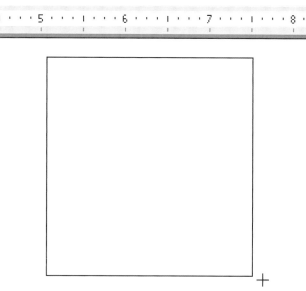

FIGURE 23.7 *Creating a text box.*

The end result: the graphic box and text box fill the entire screen (Figure 23.8).

FIGURE 23.8 *The graphic box on the left and text box on the right.*

Step 3: Wireframe Design

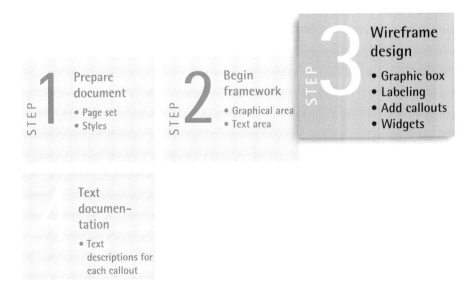

Franco now starts adding rectangles in the graphic box of the wireframe to create the screen areas that represent specific functional areas. He continues until he's added all the functional areas he thinks the screen needs. The functional areas are added by:

1. Clicking the rectangle toolbar button.
2. Dragging a rectangle area inside the larger graphical rectangle on the left.

In this abstract exercise, exact sizes and proportions are not important. The resulting page looks like Figure 23.9.

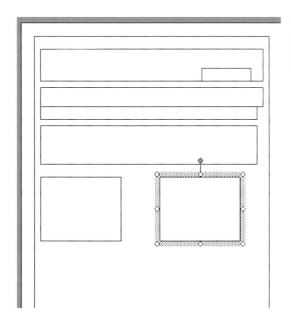

FIGURE 23.9 *The functional areas laid out in a Word wireframe.*

3. Adding reference letter codes to each rectangle by right-clicking on it and selecting Add Text from the context menu.
4. Entering a single letter or number within the rectangle to refer to each functional area.
5. In addition to the letter labels, using the Add Text feature from the context menu to add descriptive text to help the prototype audience. The prototype now looks like Figure 23.10.

FIGURE 23.10 *A Word wireframe prototype with text and labels.*

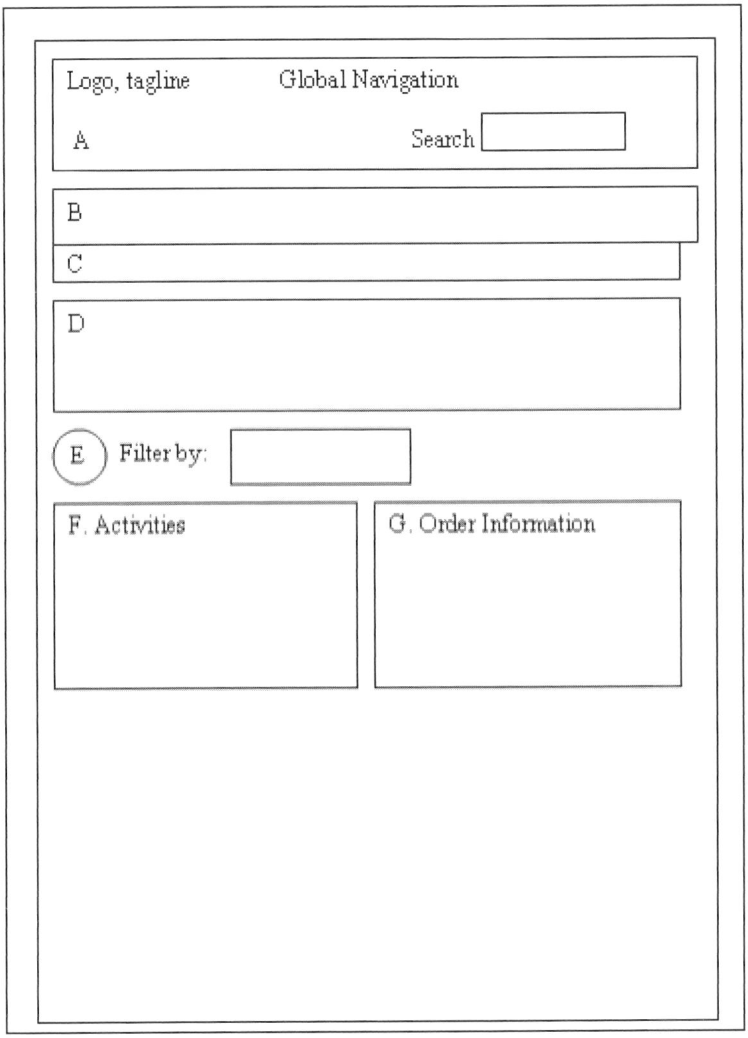

6. Adding widgets in areas where they may aid in communicating the functional idea. Widgets can be added from the Drawing toolbar, **Autoshapes**>**Block Arrows**. Other auto shapes, clip art, or any image from a file or screen capture can be used.

The Word wireframe is now visually complete. However, given the abstract nature of this prototype, annotations or descriptive text should be added to document the prototype.

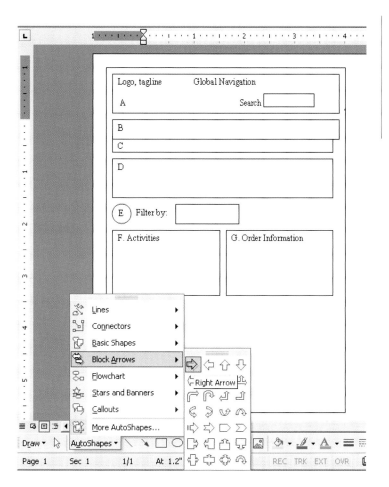

FIGURE 23.11 *A Word prototype with widgets and the AutoShapes menu active for inserting premade widgets and graphics.*

Step 4: Text Documentation

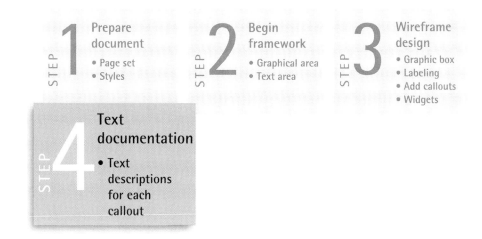

STEP 1 **Prepare document**
- Page set
- Styles

STEP 2 **Begin framework**
- Graphical area
- Text area

STEP 3 **Wireframe design**
- Graphic box
- Labeling
- Add callouts
- Widgets

STEP 4 **Text documentation**
- Text descriptions for each callout

Franco now documents his prototype by clicking inside the text box on the right side of the document page:

1. He starts by adding some descriptive text at the top, such as title, name of the product, release number, etc.
2. Then, he creates a numbered or lettered list (**Format**>**Bullets and Numbering**>**Outlined Numbered**) and enters a description for the first functional area label.
3. If further functional parts of the prototype need to be specified, he can use sub-bullet points in the outline to list them, as seen in Figure 23.12.
4. He then continues the list until every functional area created has been documented. The result looks like Figure 23.12.

FIGURE 23.12 *A Word wireframe prototype complete with documentation.*

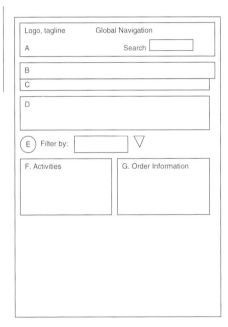

Some additional content that Franco considers adding are descriptions of each functional box, navigation description, website hierarchy description, including this screen's location in that hierarchy, project name and date, description of this screen. At this point Franco has quickly laid out the page with everything that is currently known about the design. He's now ready to begin conceptualizing the structure of the rest of the design.

By using **Rectangles** and **Text Boxes**, Franco can visualize how the page can be constructed. He adds descriptive text inside the boxes, where possible, using the text tool. When there is no space to add text, Franco enters a bold letter, referenced on the right side of the page, where he describes the content or functionality that goes there.

When this stage of the wireframe is finished, Franco has created a clear visualization of his ideas in a short time. He can show it to his team and distribute it, knowing that they will be able to open the design file and make any needed changes, comments, or iterations. With a minimal initial investment, team collaboration moves forward.

Usability Testing

Wireframes are not usually used for usability testing because they are often too conceptual for users to evaluate. However, the wireframe may be printed and used as a paper prototype, for evaluation in a focus group, if not actually usability tested.

MICROSOFT POWERPOINT

These days, almost any time you find yourself in a classroom or business meeting, a presentation program, such as PowerPoint, is being used. Business people, scientists, teachers, and students now use presentation programs to make pitches or communicate ideas. The popularity of PowerPoint is a testament to its ease of use as a presentation application, which also translates into its ease for prototyping.

Advantages

As a prototyping tool, PowerPoint has the same simple text boxes and graphical tools that MS Word has, making it easy for users to present ideas in both text and graphic formats. Also, the image import tool allows insertion of graphics, for use as

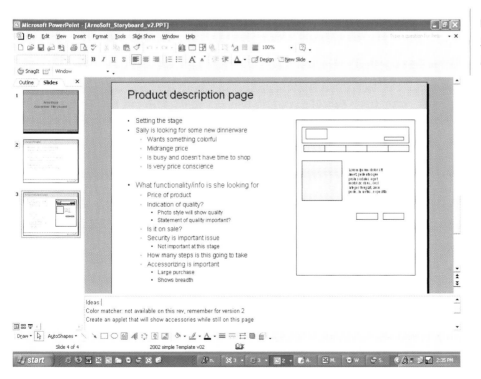

FIGURE 23.13

Storyboard in PowerPoint.

illustrations or complete designs, from any other application that saves images as GIF, JPEG, BMP, or any other common image formats. PowerPoint has the added feature of an underlying grid to help position objects. Another important distinction from Word is PowerPoint's ability to display screens in a slide presentation format. The presentations are free of any application controls and widgets, and are easy to navigate via single-click interactions. The ability to add animation allows PowerPoint to mimic application interaction with text or screens appearing with a mouse click.

PowerPoint offers strong text handling features for organizing ideas and presenting them as bulleted lists. When used with a projector, many people can collaborate during brainstorming sessions. The notes feature is a useful way to capture ideas that come up in a creative session but are not necessarily used; ideas can be stored on appropriate pages for later use or future design iterations.

For creating more accurate interface design, PowerPoint's underlying grid makes it easier to position objects more precisely on a screen, including graphics. By using backgrounds, combining shapes, coloring table cells, and adding text, PowerPoint can create complicated renderings of interfaces and designs. A note of caution though, you can end up creating designs with such complicated and accurate renderings that they become unmanageable and difficult to update.

PowerPoint's animations are not available in the other two MS applications covered here. These animation capabilities can simulate interface interaction to make a prototype more engaging and delivering possibly a more realistic user experience. Most of the animation features are geared for the purpose of enhancing your presentations with dissolves and screens sweeping into view. But by setting up screen actions to correspond to user clicks, screens can mimic application interaction.

Finally, PowerPoint presentation mode provides the most realistic environment of the three applications. After preparing all screens, you can transform the PowerPoint application interface with all its buttons and menus into a simple full screen presentation (without any menus or buttons) with fluid visual effects transitions from screen to screen.

Disadvantages

If you are looking to use PowerPoint as the creation tool for your screen designs, you should be aware of the one flaw that could be a showstopper–the screen of a slide show goes no further than what is displayed in the visible area of the window. The slide show presentation mode will not generate a scroll bar, so any content extending below the fold cannot be seen, or worse gets resized so maintaining a consistent screen size can be difficult. For some, this is not an issue. One of our colleagues says the design specification for her company demands that no content fall below the fold, making PowerPoint the perfect tool for her. However, for most designs, the need to show longer screens, ones that require scrolling, is a requirement, that makes PowerPoint inadequate. This doesn't imply that low-fidelity or more abstract prototypes don't demand precision or that higher fidelity prototypes can't be built in PowerPoint with success. However, if you're looking to build an accurate mid- to high-fidelity design with the ability to display a long screen, breadth and depth are definitely limiting factors.

Appropriate Method

The image, screen transition, and other features make PowerPoint ideal for narrative prototyping; narrative prototypes only need to show one screen at a time following a predetermined script. Presentation mode transforms PowerPoint into a mini-interactive mode allowing movement from one slide to another, creating a compelling narrative. In a narrative, the represented design doesn't necessarily need to be portrayed in a realistic manner, meaning the designs can be smaller than their true size or include only a portion of a complete design, making the single-page limitation less of an issue.

Creating a Storyboard in PowerPoint

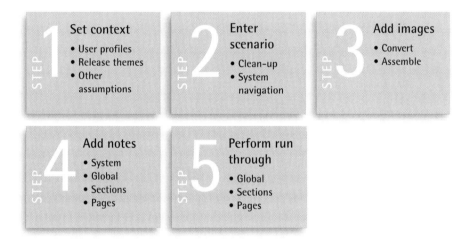

STEP 1 — **Set context**
- User profiles
- Release themes
- Other assumptions

STEP 2 — **Enter scenario**
- Clean-up
- System navigation

STEP 3 — **Add images**
- Convert
- Assemble

STEP 4 — **Add notes**
- System
- Global
- Sections
- Pages

STEP 5 — **Perform run through**
- Global
- Sections
- Pages

Scenario

An e-commerce company is adding a new section on bulk purchases to their website. Lisa, the company's new product manager, wants to be certain that the new site section is being designed with the appropriate customers in mind. She has developed some customer personas and wants to pull the team together in a series of brainstorming meetings to generate design ideas by reviewing the personas and other early work being done. Lisa plans to use one of the developed wireframes to discuss incorporating the personas into the proposed interface. She opens up a new PowerPoint file for the meeting.

Step 1: Set Context

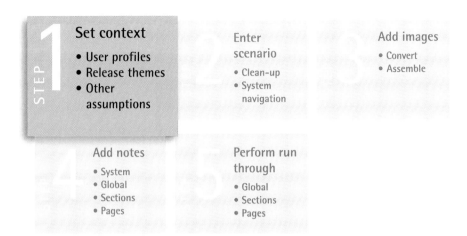

1. Lisa starts PowerPoint and creates a new file using her company's ArnoShop standard template. The file includes a title slide that Lisa uses for the product title

2. She then uses the first slides to set the context for the storyboard, listing her assumptions, product vision, and design principles at this phase of development on several slides.

3. Next, she adds the persona descriptions to another slide.

4. She adds the design principles to another slide.

5. Lisa then adds the scenario context of the storyboard.

Lisa's PowerPoint presentation looks like this:

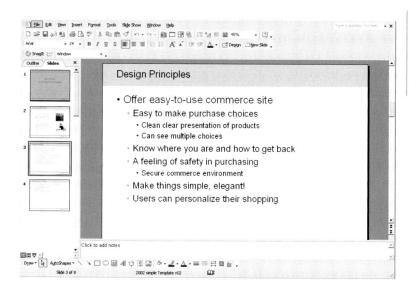

FIGURE 23.14

Storyboard brainstorming PowerPoint with context slides.

Step 2: Enter Scenario

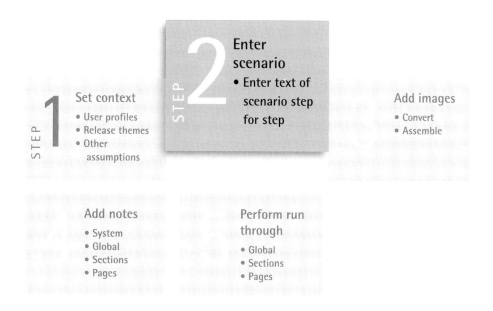

Next, Lisa enters the usage scenario that was created for the wireframe prototype. For every step in the scenario, Lisa creates a slide and enters short descriptive text for that step, like in Figure 23.15.

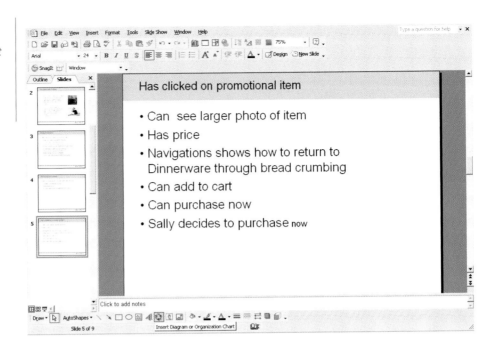

Step 3: Add Images

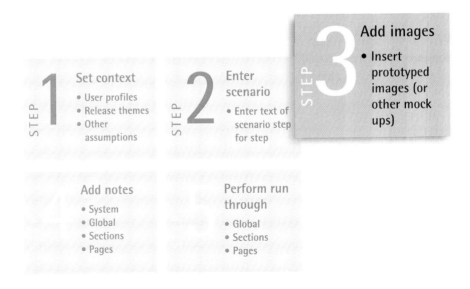

Lisa reviews the design team's wireframe work to ensure it aids in communicating the scenario and covers how the software will work in that scenario. She will use a combination of slides from the design team and may even decide to use scanned images or screen captures from competing products to provide an overview of the functionality needed.

1. Lisa adds the pictures to the text slides by using the command:
   Insert>Picture>From File.
2. She selects the picture.
3. Then, she resizes the picture and the text so they can both be seen on the slide.

The resulting screen looks like these:

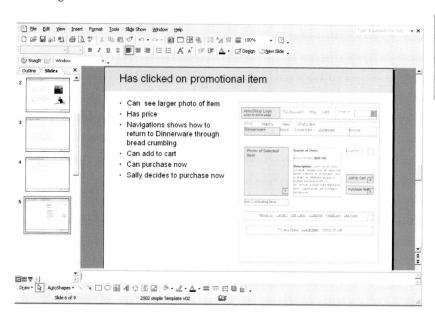

FIGURE 23.16

Storyboard PowerPoint slide including a Word wireframe graphic.

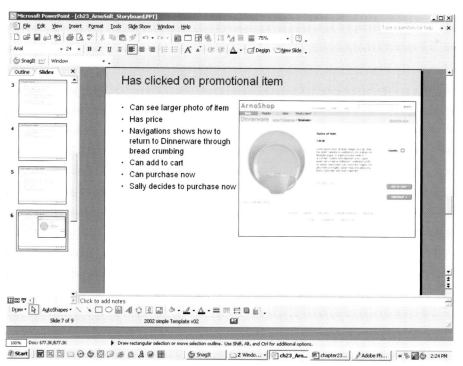

FIGURE 23.17

Storyboard PowerPoint slide including a higher fidelity Photoshop graphic.

Step 4: Add Notes

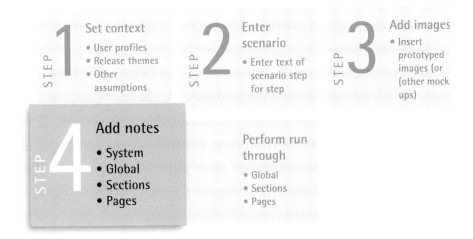

Lisa recognizes that the images need to be larger and she needs to be able to talk about several points on each slide, so she adds notes to the slides and deletes some of the text.

1. Lisa goes over each slide. If the scenario explanation is too long, she adds some of the text to the notes section of the slide and shortens the text included on the slide.
2. In the notes, she also includes future directions and functionality not displayed.
3. Finally, Lisa adds any content she wants to cover that hasn't been included on the slide.

FIGURE 23.18

Storyboard PowerPoint slide with notes added.

Idea: Can we make the photo of the item interactive so on rollover options to see other styles appears? Would like link to accessories.

Step 5: Perform Run Through

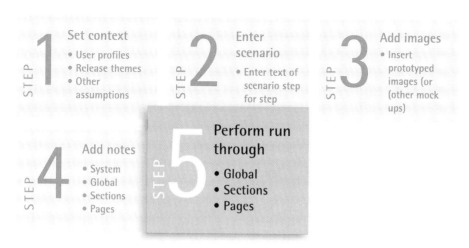

Prior to the brainstorming meeting, Lisa wants to determine if the storyboard is complete, so she runs through the presentation from the beginning and takes notes on steps that need to be added, deleted, or edited. For any project, the first run-through almost always results in many storyboard changes.

MICROSOFT EXCEL

Using Excel as a prototyping application is a foreign idea to most people. Looking at the example in Figure 23.19, it's hard to imagine that it was built in Excel and not just a flat piece of art inserted on a worksheet. When explaining to seasoned designers and prototypers how Excel can be a professional prototyping tool, the claim is usually greeted with a look of incredulity or a smile of someone waiting for the punchline. Once they get it, though they wonder how they ever did without it. Using Excel to create prototypes is a new process that has had little exposure in the software design world, but will be embraced by the larger community once it is understood.

Advantages

One of the features that make Excel a powerful prototyping tool is the inherent table cell grid. As a spreadsheet application, the grid is the dominating visual feature that contains all the numbers and text. As a prototype application, the grid still plays a primary role as a structural backdrop to design by providing form and precision. Once the grid is transformed into a canvas (see scenario below), the cells become more than just empty boxes for numbers and calculations The cells are the design tool, the alignment, and the canvas. The table cells are comprised of the screen elements because they can be filled with colors to represent backgrounds or functionality such as buttons and fields. Text in Excel also uses all the font attributes of an Office application.

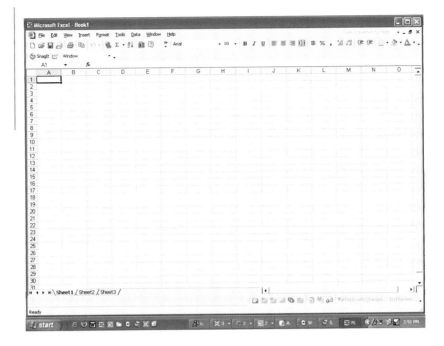

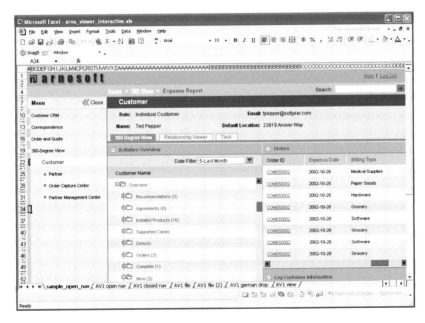

Another feature of the grid cells is their copy and paste ability. This doesn't seem like much of a feature and is definitely not exclusive to Excel, but the copy/paste features in Excel make screen creations quick and easy by taking design elements from one mockup and accurately placing them on another mockup with the same grid proportions. Excel has some special copy/paste features that other applications lack, such as pasting a large area by selecting just one cell in the target location.

All Office applications have the ability to import graphics and use them in conjunction with the many shape tools. What makes this feature so successful in Excel, more so than in PowerPoint, is that the graphics can be combined with table cell attributes to create effective and high-fidelity designs by combining cell attributes with graphic widgets.

Excel doesn't include the animation features that PowerPoint has. However, Excel competes with PowerPoint's animation features through the use of hyperlinks. As with all the Office applications, both text and graphics can become hyperlinks that connect to worksheets or workbooks or even websites. This linking feature allows many types of interface interactions to be simulated, even to the degree of enabling interactive usability testing with an Excel prototype.

Excel has the ability to expand to meet the design needs of any designer. Unlike PowerPoint, which only shows one page length at a time, Excel generates a scroll bar, extending the length or width to whatever is needed.

Different screens are created as worksheets, which act independently from each other but are all included in the same file. Each worksheet is represented as a tab at the bottom of the Excel application, a helpful feature when designing multiple pages. The worksheet tabs can be renamed, moved, linked, deleted, or hidden, making it easy to save, present, and share multiple-screen designs.

Disadvantages

The main disadvantage with using Excel is its newness as a prototyping tool. Even though most people have Excel on their computers, have some experience with it as spreadsheet application, and would be able to view a prototype in Excel, they usually don't know what to do with it without some introduction. In comparing Excel to PowerPoint, Excel's main disadvantages are its lack of any presentation mode or hide and show elements like PowerPoint's animations.

Appropriate Method

Excel's flexibility allows it to be used for many methods. For example, you can easily create low-fidelity wireframes and create a Wizard-of-Oz prototype with imaginative use of navigating to worksheet tabs and other internal hyperlinking to mimic a website. Excel's strong design abilities and accurate grid features make it best when used for mid- to high-fidelity interactive design renderings.

Creating a Prototype in Excel

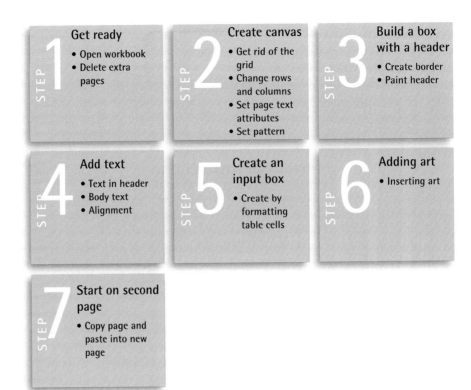

STEP 1 — **Get ready**
- Open workbook
- Delete extra pages

STEP 2 — **Create canvas**
- Get rid of the grid
- Change rows and columns
- Set page text attributes
- Set pattern

STEP 3 — **Build a box with a header**
- Create border
- Paint header

STEP 4 — **Add text**
- Text in header
- Body text
- Alignment

STEP 5 — **Create an input box**
- Create by formatting table cells

STEP 6 — **Adding art**
- Inserting art

STEP 7 — **Start on second page**
- Copy page and paste into new page

Step 1: Get Ready

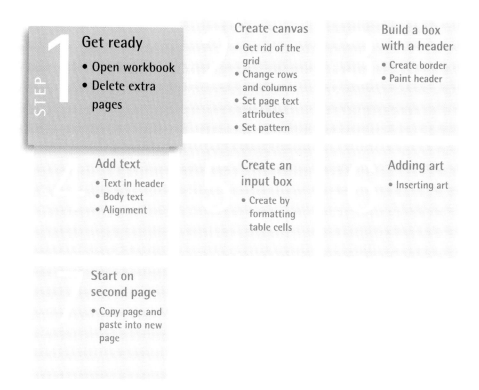

STEP 1

Get ready
- **Open workbook**
- **Delete extra pages**

Create canvas
- Get rid of the grid
- Change rows and columns
- Set page text attributes
- Set pattern

Build a box with a header
- Create border
- Paint header

Add text
- Text in header
- Body text
- Alignment

Create an input box
- Create by formatting table cells

Adding art
- Inserting art

Start on second page
- Copy page and paste into new page

From the time when we first began figuring out how to use Excel for prototyping we realized that the way to maximize the process of creating multiple prototypes was to create a template to be the starting point for every design. The template is a workbook comprised of a few worksheets that include all the pieces and styles that a designer needs to begin a project. In this example, I start from the beginning with a standard Excel worksheet and want to convert it to what I call a "canvas" for my project.

1. Open an Excel workbook.
2. Delete the third worksheet by right-clicking on the tab and choosing Delete, or choosing Delete Sheet from the Edit menu.
3. Do the same for the second worksheet.

Step 2: Create Canvas

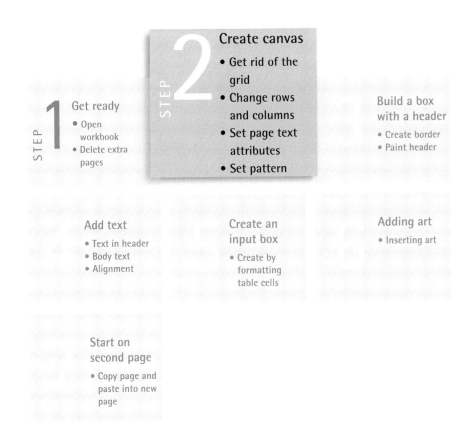

Because we're no longer working with spreadsheets, the Excel interface needs to be converted to a prototyping "canvas." Now, we will remove the grid. Actually, the grid will still be there, but will be invisible.

1. Select **Tools**>**Options**.
2. In the View tab, uncheck the box for Gridlines and click OK.

The gridlines are now invisible.

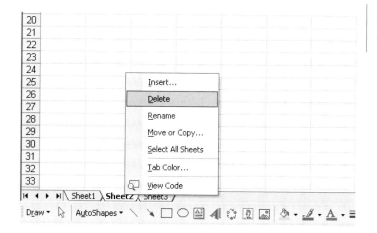

FIGURE 23.20 *Delete extra workbook pages.*

The rows and columns need to be set to new increments that best support interface design and give greater flexibility to placement.

1. Click on the rectangle where the columns and rows meet to highlight the entire worksheet.

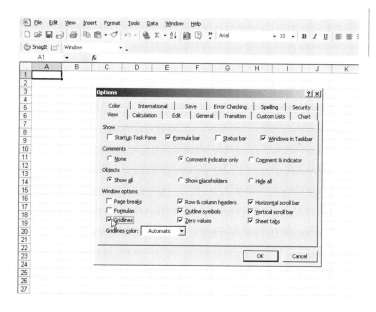

FIGURE 23.21

Removing the gridlines.

2. While the worksheet is highlighted, select **Format**>**Row**>**Height** and enter 13 as the row height.

FIGURE 23.22
Highlighted worksheet.

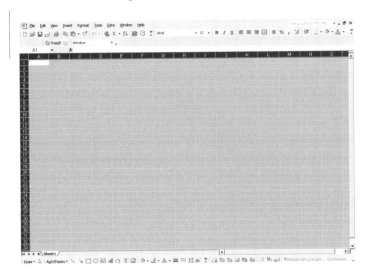

FIGURE 23.23 *Select row height.*

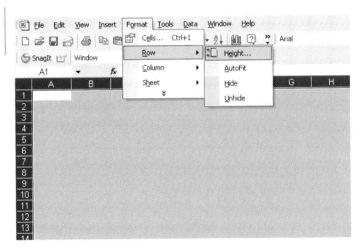

3. Follow the same process with **Format**>**Column**>**Width**, and select a width of 1.

FIGURE 23.24 *Input new row height.*

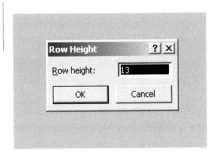

4. While the page is still highlighted, right click any cell and go to Format Cells.

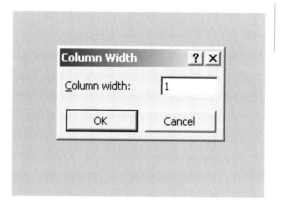

FIGURE 23.25 *Change column width to 1.*

5. The dialog box opens with the Number tab displayed.
6. Select "Text" as the Category. This interprets any numbers entered into cells as text, which informs Excel to avoid conversion of any numbers used in your design to Excel's number storage format, a problem particularly with dates.

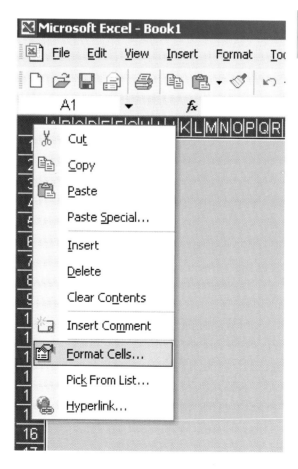

FIGURE 23.26 *Format all the table cells.*

7. With the dialog box still open, go to the Font tab to set the type style.

FIGURE 23.27 *Change cells to display text only.*

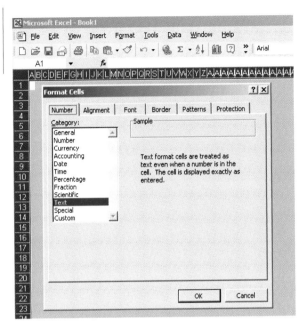

8. Finally, go to the Patterns tab, which allows you to choose a color for all the table cells if your design style calls for something other than white.
9. Click OK. The canvas is complete—a clean page with text, background and color styles to match your specifications.

FIGURE 23.28 *Set font style.*

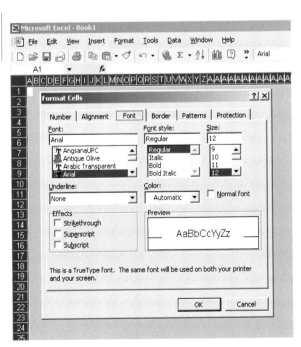

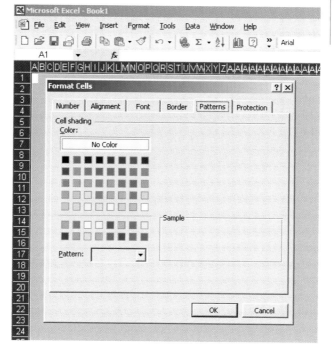

FIGURE 23.29 *Set cell background color.*

Step 3: Building a Box with a Header

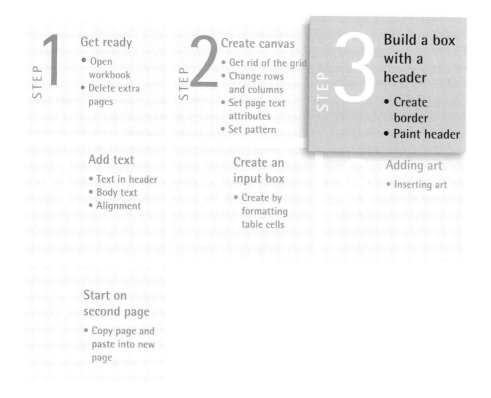

STEP 1 Get ready
- Open workbook
- Delete extra pages

STEP 2 Create canvas
- Get rid of the grid
- Change rows and columns
- Set page text attributes
- Set pattern

STEP 3 Build a box with a header
- Create border
- Paint header

Add text
- Text in header
- Body text
- Alignment

Create an input box
- Create by formatting table cells

Adding art
- Inserting art

Start on second page
- Copy page and paste into new page

Now that I have an empty canvas, I can begin working on the prototype. This first page calls for a box with a header bar and three labeled entry fields. First, build the box and header bar.

1. Highlight an area the size of the box you want to create.

FIGURE 23.30 *Finished Excel prototyping canvas.*

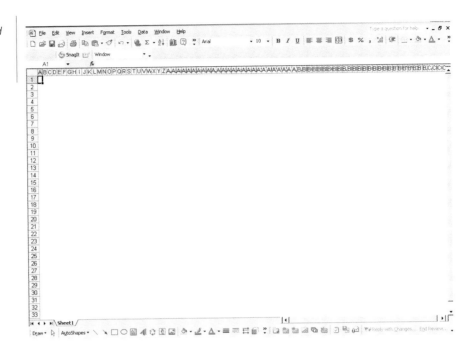

2. Right click in the area and choose Format Cells.

FIGURE 23.31 *Highlight box area.*

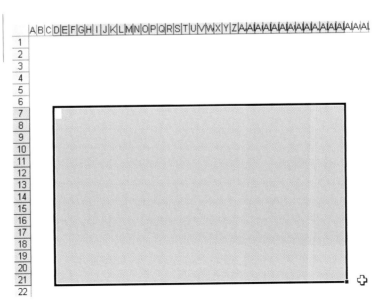

3. Go to the Border tab. To choose a border color, click on the pull-down menu under Color. You can create a customized palette if you have specific color requirements, but we won't cover that here as that is a more power user feature.

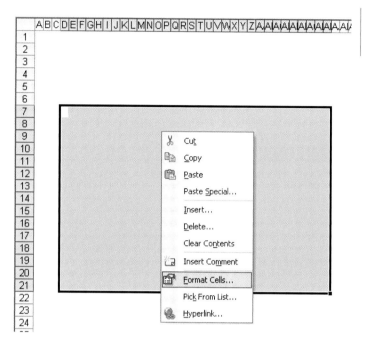

FIGURE 23.32 *Select Format Cells.*

4. Then choose the correct line width in the **Line>Style** menu.
5. To create the box outline, click on the Outline icon. You will see a border preview in the dialog box.

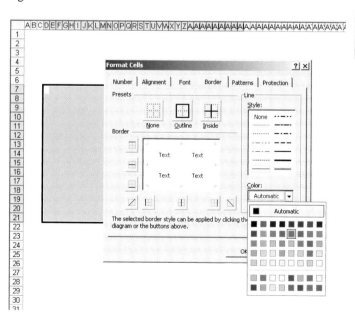

FIGURE 23.33 *Choose border color.*

6. Click OK to see the box created.

FIGURE 23.34 *Create border.*

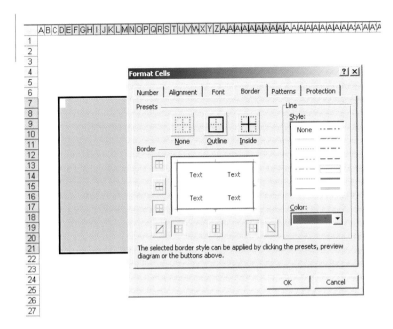

7. To create the header, highlight the top row, right-click on highlighted cells, and select Format Cells.

FIGURE 23.35 *Defined box.*

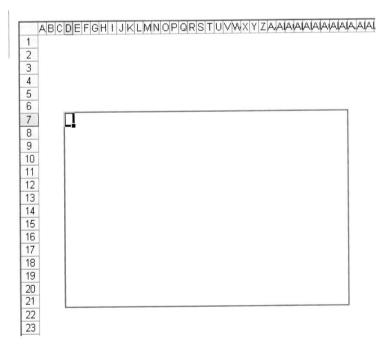

8. Go to the Patterns tab, select the desired color, and click OK.

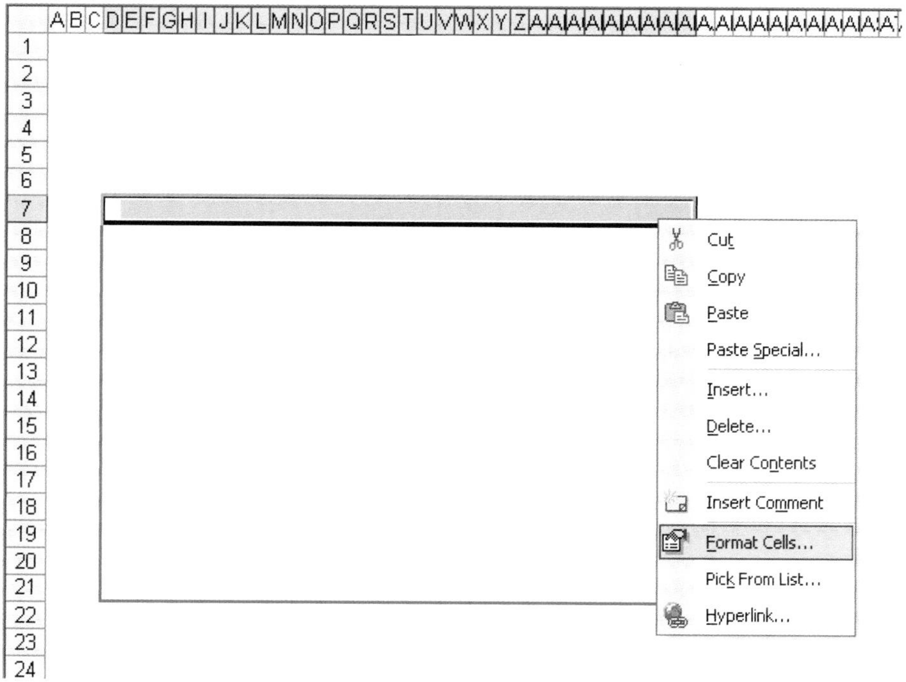

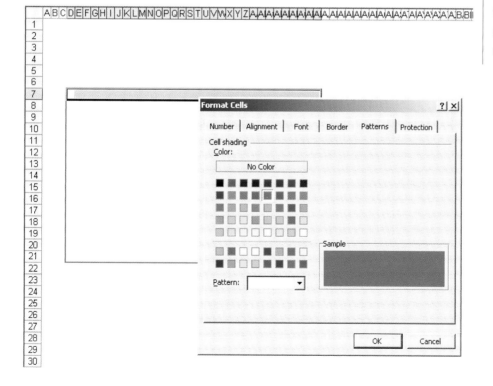

FIGURE 23.36 *Header area defined.*

The box and the header are finished.

FIGURE 23.37 *Choose Pattern and background color for the header.*

Step 4: Add Text

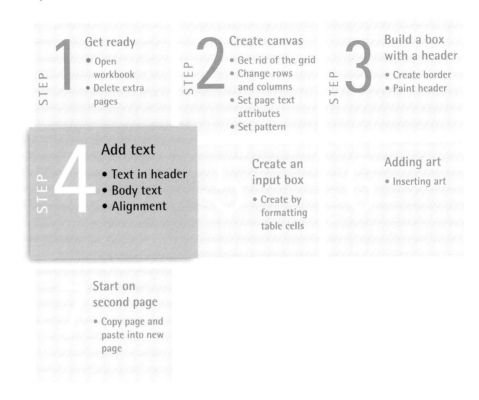

STEP 1 — Get ready
- Open workbook
- Delete extra pages

STEP 2 — Create canvas
- Get rid of the grid
- Change rows and columns
- Set page text attributes
- Set pattern

STEP 3 — Build a box with a header
- Create border
- Paint header

STEP 4 — Add text
- Text in header
- Body text
- Alignment

Create an input box
- Create by formatting table cells

Adding art
- Inserting art

Start on second page
- Copy page and paste into new page

Now we want to add a name to the box and create the labels for the input fields.

1. Position the cursor in the far left cell of the header bar and enter text. The text appears both in the cell and formula bar. By highlighting the text in the formula bar, you can choose text styles in the Formatting toolbar. Arial, 12 point, Bold, and white text color will work for the header text.

FIGURE 23.38 *Finished box and header.*

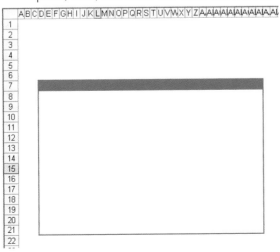

2. Next, we enter the text for the field labels. We want to right-align the text within the body of the box, so we select table cells that are well within the left border of the box to leave space for labels and enter the text on different rows.

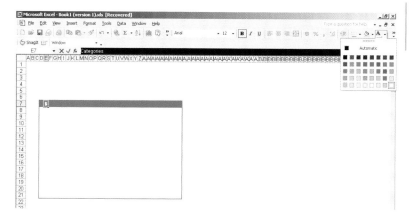

FIGURE 23.39 *Add text and define text style.*

3. Then, the text is aligned by highlighting all the cells that contain the text and choose the correct alignment icon in the Formatting toolbar, the right-align icon, reorienting the text to the proper position.

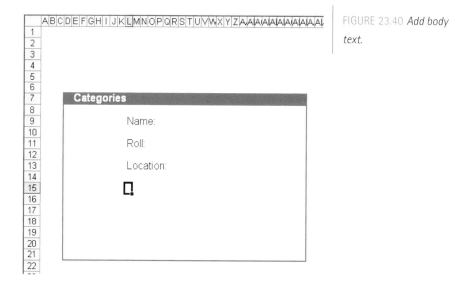

FIGURE 23.40 *Add body text.*

Step 5: Create an Input Field

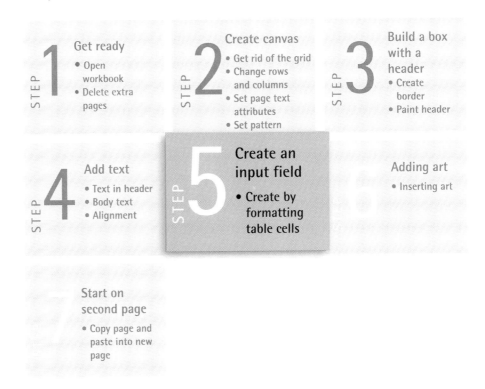

The next step is to create the input fields for each label. With a template, we would only need to go to a screen with preconstructed input fields, find the appropriate size, copy, and then paste it in the box, which would take only a moment. Since we don't have a template, we'll build it now.

1. Highlight the table cells to the right of the label that should represent the width of the input field. While highlighted, right-click and select Format Cells.

2. Go to the Border tab. Similar to the way the large box was created, choose a gray as the border color and choose a wide border for the left and top sides of the field. This border can be applied by either clicking on the appropriate icon or on the desired position in the dialog box.

3. For the right and lower sides of the field, choose a thinner line.

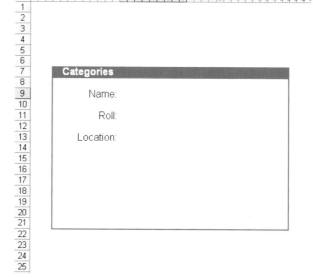

FIGURE 23.41 *Box with header and field labels.*

4. Rather than going through this process of defining the field border two more times, you can simply copy and paste the box twice. Highlight the box, right click, and select Copy, then click on the **one** table cell where you want the box to begin and paste the copied cells. It's best to select only one box when pasting, because if you don't select the same number of cells as you included in the copy, Excel won't be able to paste it.

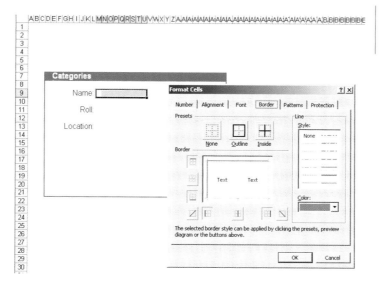

FIGURE 23.42 *Define input box border.*

Step 6: Adding Art

Adding images to the prototype is best used for design elements that don't need editing. In this case, we'll add the screen header, which includes the logo and some links that are present on all the screens but do not need to be editable. Graphics, such as icons, buttons and widgets, can also be used throughout the prototype to lend a realistic look and feel.

1. Highlight the upper left table cell and go to **Insert**>**Picture**>**From File**.

FIGURE 23.43 *Copy input box.*

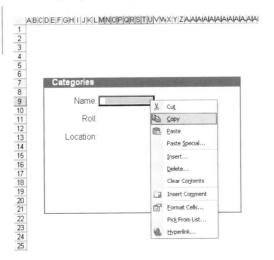

2. Find the premade graphic using the Browse feature. The logo image appears perfectly positioned in the initially selected cell.

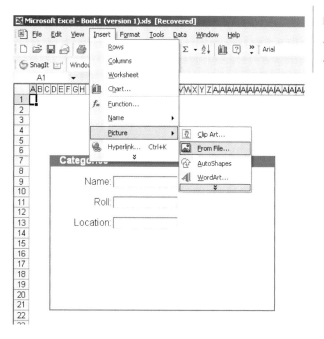

FIGURE 23.44

Positioning and inserting an image.

Step 7: Start on Second Page

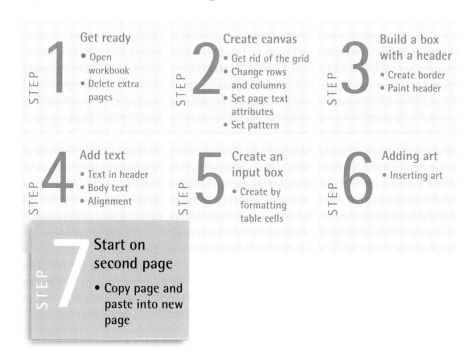

STEP 1 — **Get ready**
- Open workbook
- Delete extra pages

STEP 2 — **Create canvas**
- Get rid of the grid
- Change rows and columns
- Set page text attributes
- Set pattern

STEP 3 — **Build a box with a header**
- Create border
- Paint header

STEP 4 — **Add text**
- Text in header
- Body text
- Alignment

STEP 5 — **Create an input box**
- Create by formatting table cells

STEP 6 — **Adding art**
- Inserting art

STEP 7 — **Start on second page**
- Copy page and paste into new page

Rather than start over from the beginning for the next prototype screen, simply copy this worksheet and make the necessary changes.

1. Right-clicking on the worksheet tab and select Rename to provide an understandable name for this worksheet.

FIGURE 23.45 *An image placed in the worksheet.*

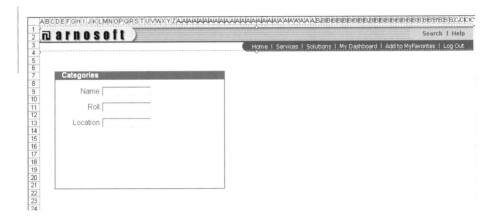

2. Then, right-click on the tab again and select Move or Copy.
3. In the dialog box, check the Create a Copy box at the bottom and select the (move to end) option. Click OK to create a copy of the worksheet.

FIGURE 23.46 *Rename worksheet.*

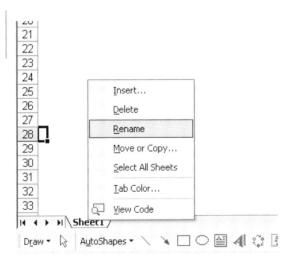

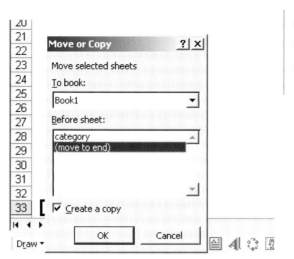

This exercise is a very simple example of what can be done in Excel. More sophisticated prototypes can also be created, as seen in Figure 23.19. In that example, a template was created, which enabled that mockup to be built in less than 20 minutes.

Testing

Designs built in Excel can be used in various validation testing methods. The screens can be printed and used in paper prototyping, or if the prototype has been built using links to tie the screens together, then a certain amount of interactive usability testing can be undertaken.

MS OFFICE APPLICATIONS

The MS Office Suite offers a wide range of opportunities for prototypers. Word, when used for wireframes, is fast, easy, and accessible to most anyone. PowerPoint can be used solely to create designs as well as an effective tool when used to create narrative prototypes shown in the powerful presentation mode. Excel, the unexpected newcomer to the prototyping world, offers strong design and interaction capabilities for medium- to high-fidelity prototypes.

REFERENCES

Nevin Berger. "The Excel Story," from Interactions Magazine, Volume 13 , Issue 1, pages 14–17 (January + February 2006). New York, ACM, 2006.

Microsoft Office Suite at http://office.microsoft.com/en-us/default.aspx. (accessed 4 May 2006).

OpenOffice at http://www.openoffice.org/ (accessed 4 May 2006).

Prototyping Tools

24

PROTOTYPING WITH VISIO

Ji Kim

INTRODUCTION TO VISIO AS A PROTOTYPING TOOL

Microsoft Visio is diagramming software used to create business and technical diagrams that document and organize complex ideas, processes, and systems. Visio diagrams allow communication of ideas in a way that text and numbers cannot. As a prototyping tool, Visio is as easy as dragging and dropping shapes to represent anything from desktop software to websites.

Some benefits of Visio are its fairly low learning curve, the powerful template-making capabilities that allow easy reuse with a library of user interface objects, the grid to support drawing and layout control, and the incorporation of high-fidelity graphics.

OVERVIEW OF EFFECTIVE PROTOTYPING WITH VISIO
Ideal Methods for Using Visio

Storyboard prototypes–Visio is an ideal tool for translating business and marketing requirements into usage scenarios. For example, Visio comes with out-of-the-box business process, brainstorming, flow chart, and UML templates and stencils that can be used to create storyboards.

Wireframe prototypes–The most popular application for the use of Visio as a prototyping tool. Out-of-the-box shapes with its low learning curve ensure that virtually anyone can create prototypes.

Paper prototyping–Visio drawings can be printed for use as paper prototypes. Even if the paper prototype is damaged or lost, it's easy to recreate.

CHARACTERISTICS

Visio is useful for testing the following design facets:

Information design–Low-fidelity prototypes such as wireframes for representing information design are a common application of Visio. Free third-party stencils are also available to help you quickly build the wireframe.

TABLE 24.1 Visio Prototyping Characteristics Matrix

Characteristics		Visio
Audience	Internal	−
	External	+
Stage	Early	+ +
	Midterm	+
	Late	− −
Speed	Rapid	+ +
	Diligent	−
Longevity	Short	+ +
	Medium	+
	Long	−
Expression	Conceptual	+
	Experiential	−
Style	Narrative	+
	Interactive	−
Medium	Physical	−
	Digital	+ +

Content Fidelity		Visio
High fidelity	Information	+ +
	Interaction	− −
	Visual design	+
	Branding	−
	System	NA
Low fidelity	Information	+
	Interaction	+ +
	Visual design	+
	Branding	+
	System	+ +

+ +, Most appropriate;

+, appropriate;

−, acceptable;

− −, not appropriate;

NA, not applicable.

Interaction design and navigation model–Form control states or dialog windows can be created, and simple interaction can be added by inserting hyperlinks into the Visio shapes.

Visual design–High-fidelity software representations are possible with Visio, but tools such as Adobe Photoshop and Illustrator are recommended as the means for creating visual design elements, especially medium- to high-fidelity elements.

Branding–Visio can be an effective tool for creating designs that incorporate branding expression as embodied in the visual, information, and interaction design.

Target Audience for Visio

Although Visio can be used by people with a variety of skills, it's especially useful for those with little or no drawing skills. For example, product managers or engineers with no previous background in user interface design can quickly start prototyping with Visio with little or no training. Visio may be a good prototyping tool for your next project if:

> - You are familiar with using Microsoft Office products like Word, PowerPoint, or Excel.
> - You don't have lot of time to learn how to use professional design software like Photoshop or Illustrator, but you want to have access to basic drawing and picture customization features.
> - You don't want to start your designs without a template but rather design from libraries of useful shapes and templates.
> - In addition to creating a prototype, you would like to use a single software product to create task flows and use cases.
> - The prototype you want to create doesn't need to look exactly like the final product.
> - The prototype you want to create doesn't need to be fully interactive.

USEFUL PROTOTYPING FEATURES IN VISIO

Visio provides useful features for quick and effective prototyping, including a collection of useful shapes and templates, powerful drawing tools, snap and group shapes, show-and-hide drawings using layers, adding interaction using hyperlinks, importing various image formats, powerful print and export features, and setting the background image.

Reuse

Visio allows importing a variety of files, including clip art and popular picture formats such as GIF, JPG, PNG, BMP, etc. You can also import templates and stencils—templates in the form of environments created for a particular kind of drawing, such as the Windows user interface platform or Charts and Graphs. Stencils are useful collections of shapes for use in a drawing.

Visio drawings can be exported in a variety of file formats for integration with other applications or media. They can specifically be exported in the following formats:

> - Popular picture formats such as GIF, JPG, etc. for use in other prototyping tools such as Visual Studio, Dreamweaver, Illustrator, Acrobat, PowerPoint, etc.
> - Web pages (.html) or PDFs (if you have Acrobat Professional installed), useful for sharing files with team members who don't have Visio

> › Visio templates or Visio stencils for later use

Visio files can be also printed to be used for paper prototyping purposes

ADVANTAGES AND DISADVANTAGES OF USING VISIO FOR PROTOTYPING
Advantages

Visio is an object-based diagramming tool, meaning that one or more shapes can be selected to make quick changes. If you use form control shapes from Windows User Interface stencils, all the form control shapes can quickly be made to look enabled or disabled by selecting them all and applying the appropriate setting. You can apply changes to multiple shapes as long as the selected shapes share common attributes. Prototypers can use drag-and-drop stencil shapes for quick prototype creation. You can easily customize these shapes, such as changing the border width or adjusting the shape's transparency. Some shapes (for example, the Windows User Interface stencils) allow quick modifications such as making a radio button shape look selected or deselected. The only caveat is that you have to be careful using transparency settings because Visio doesn't print shapes with transparency well.

Meanwhile, if you can't find the stencils you want, third-party stencils can be downloaded or new custom shapes created. Visio also supports integration of other Microsoft Office document objects into a drawing, like inserting and editing Excel worksheet objects. You can insert an Excel prototype as simply another shape inside Visio.

Lastly, global search and replace is a handy Visio tool to quickly change things like text labels in a prototype.

Disadvantages

When prototyping, there is an important difference between Visio Standard and Visio Professional. Only Visio Professional has the useful stencils that will help with prototyping, making it worth the extra expense. That said, Visio is not a professional illustration or image editing tool. Although Visio supports some basic drawing and image editing features such as layers and image resizing, you will not be able to perform more advanced operations such as image filters that are available in tools like Photoshop. When more advanced image customization is needed, it's best to use tools like Photoshop or Illustrator, then import those images into Visio.

In Visio certain shapes don't support advanced customization. For example, there is a limit to the number of rows that can be set in a grid shape provided by the Windows User Interface stencil. Also, you'll need to take care in selecting multiple shapes because the mouse pointer may not select all the shapes, leading to unexpected results. Try using the Select All command or manually select each individual shapes using the Shift key. You also need to remember the order of shapes placed in the drawing. Shapes can be obscured by others placed more recently in the drawing or moved on top of them. The Send to Front and Send to Back commands are easy solutions to this problem. Also, if you change the dimension of the drawing area, the drawing may not print correctly without additional adjustments in Print Setup. In most cases, setting Visio's print zoom to "fit to 1 sheet across and 1 sheet down" takes care of this problem.

It's difficult to see and use several Visio documents simultaneously. For example, copying and pasting multiple shapes between two Visio documents is tedious. One workaround consists of launching separate Visio processes, with each having a different Visio file. You have the ability to reorder pages in a Visio document, but you have no control over the order in which a new page is inserted. Unfortunately, there is no easy solution. When possible, try using layers or separating the drawings into separate Visio documents.

Other than the hyperlink and macro features, Visio doesn't support interaction very well. Therefore, Visio is best used as a low- to medium-fidelity static prototype. Visio drawings can be imported into Visual Studio or Dreamweaver to create more interactive prototypes.

DOCUMENTING A DESIGN IN VISIO

It's easy to specify designs in Visio. For example, if you want to display design notes or comments on every page of the Visio file, you can create a shape to represent this area as part of the page background. This is a useful method for providing developers with additional specifications or for sharing the prototype with others who don't have Visio installed on their computers.

Another method for adding comments and annotations is to use Visio's Comment and ScreenTips features. With the Comment feature, you can place the notes anywhere in the Visio drawing, similar to using a sticky note. (As an alternative to using the Comment feature, you can convert the Visio drawings into a PDF and make your comments in Acrobat.) The ScreenTips feature provides extra information for a shape, appearing when the mouse is positioned over the shape.

In addition, you can use the Track Markup feature in Visio to easily make and view drawing changes. Proposed changes and markups are tracked on a separate colored and tabbed overlay for each person who opens the drawing.

BUSINESS SCENARIO

As a product manager at a software company, you're responsible for delivering the new Acme FTP Tool. This new product will transfer files between a user's computer and a remote FTP (File Transfer Protocol) server.

Users of this new software will have the ability to transfer files of any size or type, including Web pages and multimedia files to and from a server via FTP, the standard for moving files across the Internet. Basic features will include the ability to make new FTP connections, upload and download files, manage folders on both the user's computer and a remote FTP server, and view information about files and folders.

This new software will be based on a thick client (compiled desktop application) for the Windows XP operating system. The software creation team has already defined an interface and an initial set of desired functionality. To start the project, you will create a low-fidelity prototype that can be tested with the use case below.

Use Case Description

The user successfully uploads files to the FTP server. As a precondition, the user has already provided the necessary information to connect to the FTP server.

TABLE 24.2 **Sample Use Case: Upload Files to Remote Server**

User Intention	System Responsibility
1. The user wants to upload files to his or her remote FTP server.	2. Show that the user's computer is connected to the FTP server.
3. The user browses for the files to upload to the FTP server.	4. Show file structure of the user's computer.
5. User selects the files.	
6. The user browses for the folder on the FTP server where the files need to reside.	7. Show a list of folders on the FTP server where the files can be uploaded.
8. Select action to upload the files.	9. Show progress of the files being uploaded.

Step-by-Step Example

Step 1: Getting Started (Set Up Your Environment and Stencils)

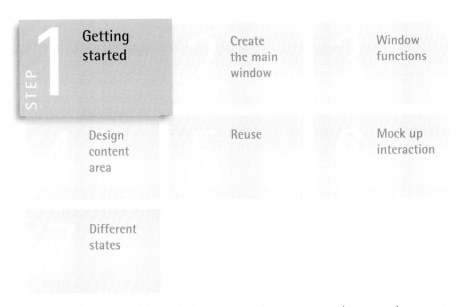

1. Set up the Visio grid to suit the prototype's purpose, and turn on the snap to grid functionality to ease object alignment.
2. Select the stencils to use for the interface. For example, Visio comes with Windows XP User Interface widgets available as stencils.

COM and OLE (Metric)

COM and OLE (US units)

Data Flow Model Diagram (Metric)

Data Flow Model Diagram (US units)

Enterprise Application (Metric)

Enterprise Application (US units)

Jackson (Metric)

Jackson (US units)

Program Structure (Metric)

Program Structure (US units)

ROOM (Metric)

ROOM (US units)

UML Model Diagram (Metric)

UML Model Diagram (US units)

Windows XP User Interface (Metric)

Windows XP User Interface (US units)

3. Choose the appropriate stencil by going to File>New>Software> Windows XP User Interface (US units).

Step 2: Create the Main Window

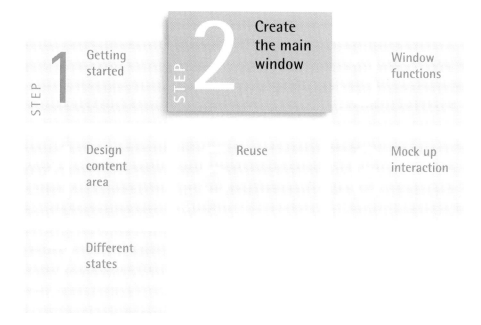

STEP **1** Getting started	STEP **2** Create the main window	Window functions
Design content area	Reuse	Mock up interaction
Different states		

To create the prototype, a main window is needed to contain the user interface elements:

1. From the Windows and Dialogs stencil, drag and drop a Blank form shape to the drawing page.

FIGURE 24.2 *The Windows and Dialogs stencils Blank window selection.*

2. Next, the Windows OS buttons needed to be added for the main window. From the Windows and Dialogs stencil, drag and drop the Windows button shape to the top right corner of the main window drawing.

FIGURE 24.3 *Windows buttons stencil shape.*

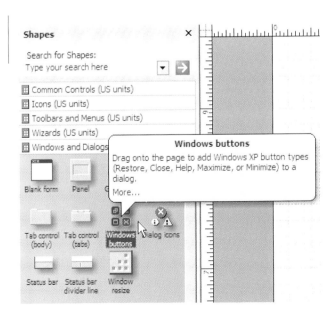

Note: When you drag and drop the Windows button shape, you will need to select a type of button to create. For the use case outlined above, we will create three Windows buttons: **minimize**, **maximize**, and **close**.

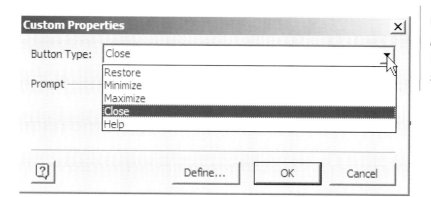

FIGURE 24.4 *Custom properties dialog for the Windows buttons stencil shape.*

3. For this use case, the main window should be gray. Select the main window drawing, right-click, and choose the Gray Background option from the context menu.

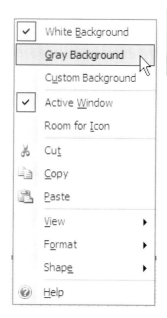

FIGURE 24.5 *Visio context menu for a window.*

Tip: You can also change the background color of the Blank form shape by selecting the shape and choosing: Shape>Actions>Gray Background.

4. Now, the main window needs to be made larger. It can be proportionally resized by selecting the main window drawing and dragging the bottom right corner handle to the desired size.

FIGURE 24.6 *Element resize handle.*

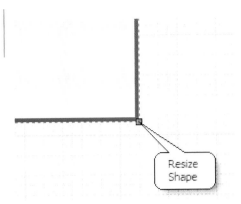

5. According to our use case, we need to show a connection status between the user's computer and the remote FTP server. We can show this in the main window status bar. To create the status bar in the main window, drag and drop the Status bar shape from the Window and Dialogs stencil to the bottom of the main window drawing.

FIGURE 24.7 *Status bar shape.*

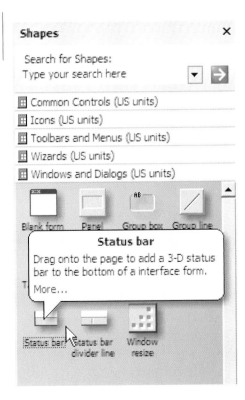

6. Double-click on the Status bar shape and change the text to "Connected to: ftp.acme.com." Then resize the width of the Status bar shape by dragging the endpoint to be the same length as the main window.

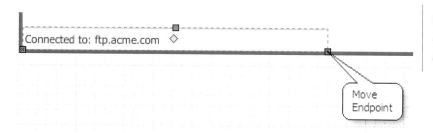

FIGURE 24.8 *Status bar endpoint can be dragged for resizing.*

7. Finally, we need to provide a title for the main window by double-clicking the Blank form shape in the main window drawing. Change the title to "Acme FTP Tool."

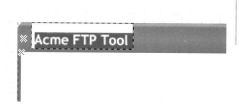

FIGURE 24.9 *Changing the window title.*

Progress Check:

Note: After setting up the application, the main window appears as shown in Figure 24.10.

FIGURE 24.10 *New window created using standard shapes and stencils in Visio.*

Step 3: Window Functions (Design Top-Level Menu and Toolbar)

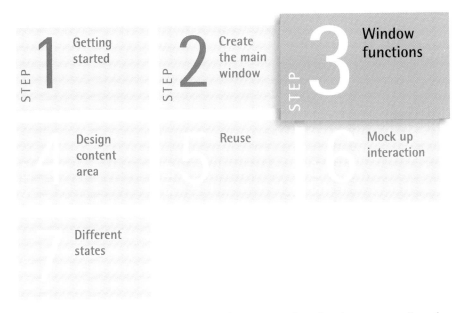

The application design calls for top-level menus and toolbar buttons to allow the user to transfer files between the user's computer and the remote FTP server.

1. First, we'll create a top-level menu bar. From the Toolbars and Menu stencil, drag-and-drop Menu bar shape to the top left corner of the gray background area of the main window drawing.

   Tip: The Menu bar shape should snap to the top corners of the Blank form shape.

FIGURE 24.11 *Menu bar shape.*

2. Resize the width of the Menu bar shape by dragging the endpoint to be same length as the main window.

FIGURE 24.12 *Dragging the menu bar shape to create a menu bar.*

3. Now, we need to create top level menus. We can always add or remove menus later. From the Toolbars and Menus stencil, drag and drop the Top-level menu item shape to the Menu bar shape in the drawing. Repeat this process until five Top-level menu item shapes are aligned horizontally across the Menu bar shape.

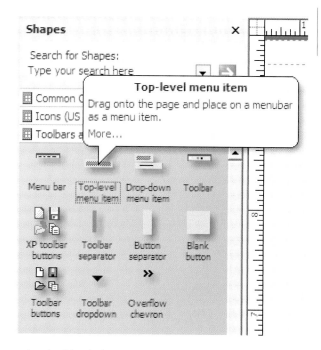

FIGURE 24.13 *Top-level menu item shape.*

4. Change the menu names by double-clicking each Top-level menu item shape and editing the text. For this use case, the menus are **File**, **Edit**, **View**, **Actions**, and **Help**.

FIGURE 24.14 *Menu bar items created.*

5. Next, we need to create a toolbar for placement of the toolbar buttons. From the Toolbars and Menus stencil, drag and drop the Toolbar shape below the Menu bar shape in the drawing. Resize the width of the Toolbar shape by dragging the endpoint to be the same length as the Menu bar shape.

FIGURE 24.15 *Toolbar shape.*

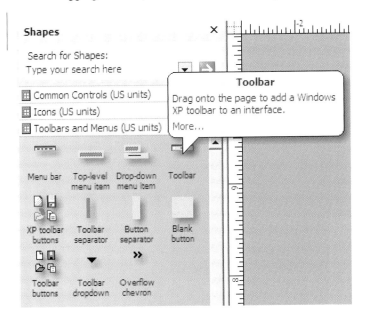

6. Now, we need to create the toolbar buttons with labels. We can always add or remove toolbar buttons later. From the Toolbars and Menus stencil, drag and drop the Blank button shape to the Toolbar shape in the drawing.

FIGURE 24.16 *Blank button shape.*

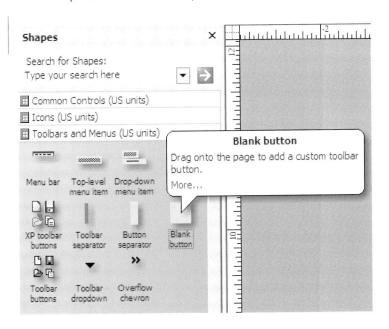

7. To make the new toolbar button more visible, select the Blank button in the drawing, right-click the shape, and choose the Show Button option from the context menu.

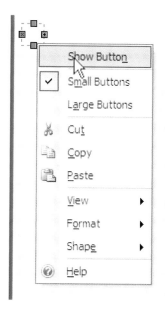

FIGURE 24.17 *Blank button context menu.*

8. Also, create a button label using the Text Tool in Visio's toolbar.

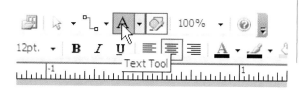

FIGURE 24.18 *Visio's text tool toolbar command.*

9. Create a text shape next to the Blank button shape in the drawing and enter "New Connection."
10. Be sure that the text shape has font settings of Tahoma 8 point.

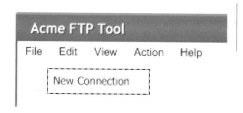

FIGURE 24.19 *Button text label.*

11. Using the same process that was used to create the "New Connection" toolbar button and label, create buttons and labels for **Stop**, **Upload**, **Download**, **New Folder**, **Edit**, and **Delete**.

Note: The toolbar buttons should be left aligned on top of the Toolbar shape in the drawing.

FIGURE 24.20 *Button bar creation.*

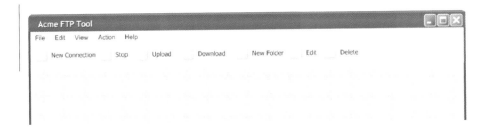

Progress Check:
Note: The main menu and toolbar area should look similar to the one shown in Figure 24.21.

FIGURE 24.21 *New window with Menus and Toolbar.*

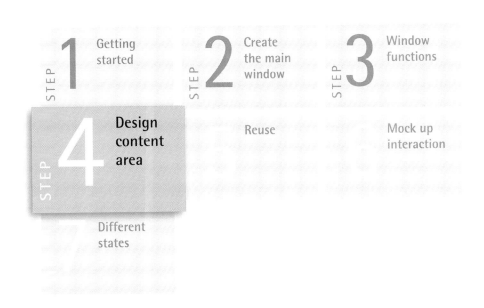

Step 4: Design Content Area (Mockup Areas to Display Files on the User's Computer and Remote FTP Server)

According to the use case, the application needs to be able to allow the user to browse and select files on both the user's computer and the remote FTP server. First, we're going to design the user interface that allows the user to select a directory on his computer and view the relevant sub-directories and files. A combo box is probably the best mechanism to allow the user to select a directory and view the file structure.

1. To begin, the combo box label, "Local Site" can be created with the Text Tool and located below the Toolbar.

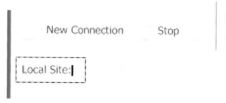

FIGURE 24.22 *Creating a Combo box label.*

2. Next, the combo box is created from the Combo box shape in the Common Controls stencil.

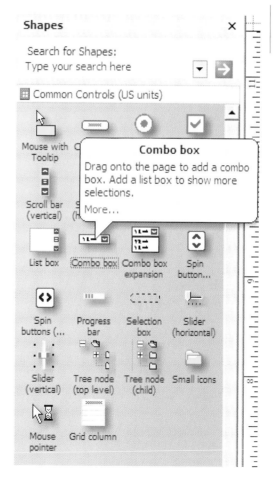

FIGURE 24.23 *Combo box shape.*

3. Double-click on the Combo box shape just added to the drawing and change the text to "C:\my files."

FIGURE 24.24 *Combo box with prefilled text.*

4. Next, we need to show the files and directories on the user's computer. A List box can be used to display the file name and file type. From the Common Control stencil, drag and drop the List box shape below the Combo box shape in the drawing.

FIGURE 24.25 *List box shape.*

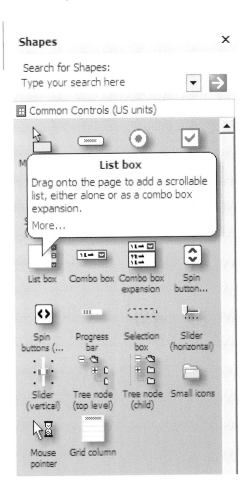

5. Drag the bottom right corner handle to resize the List box shape to accommodate multiple files and column headers.
6. Double-click the List box shape and delete the default text, "Enter Text."

FIGURE 24.26 *An expanded List box.*

7. Now, we're going to add column headers to the List box by dragging the Grid column shape from the "Common Controls" stencil to the top of the "List box" shape in the drawing.

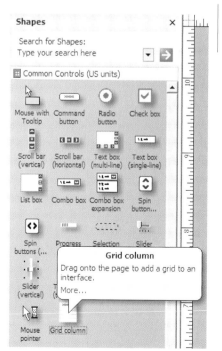

FIGURE 24.27 *Grid column shape.*

8. Select the Grid column shape and make the first row a header cell using the right-click menu.

FIGURE 24.28 *Column grid shape context menu.*

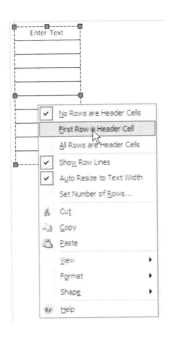

9. Then left align the shape's text by clicking on the Align left toolbar button in Visio.

FIGURE 24.29 *Visio's text alignment Toolbar commands.*

10. The Grid column shape should look similar to Figure 24.30.

FIGURE 24.30 *One grid column.*

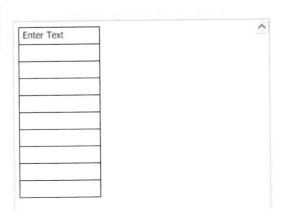

11. Select the Grid column shape and make a duplicate using **Edit** > **Duplicate**.

12. Now, there are two Grid column shapes in the drawing. Place them next to each other within the List box shape and resize the width of the Grid column shapes so that the first shape takes 70% and the second shape takes 30% of the space in the List box.

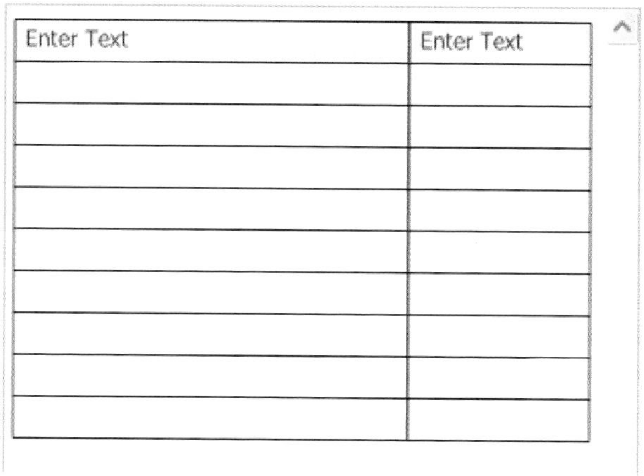

Enter Text	Enter Text

FIGURE 24.31 *Building a table with two grid columns.*

13. Next, we add mock data to make the prototype more realistic. The left column should display "Name" in the header row, which can be done by selecting the first row in the Column grid shape, and entering the text. The following rows should include the text "Web Pages," "Music." "Report1.txt," and "Report2.txt" as shown in Figure 24.32.

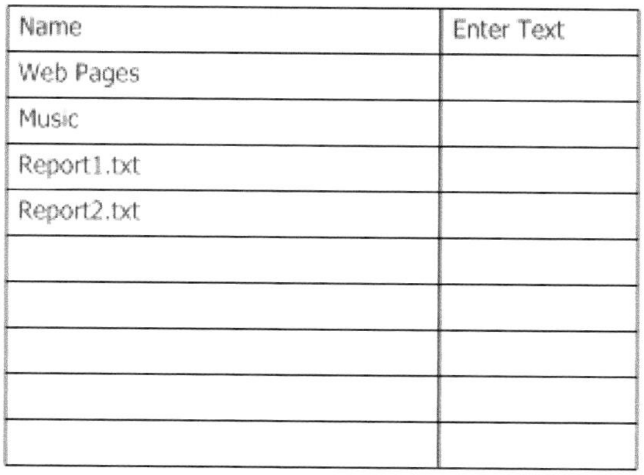

Name	Enter Text
Web Pages	
Music	
Report1.txt	
Report2.txt	

FIGURE 24.32 *Column grid with entered text.*

14. The right column should display the **file type**. Select the first row in the right Column grid shape and enter "Type." The following rows should read "File Folder," "File Folder," "Text Document," and "Text Document" as shown in Figure 24.33.

FIGURE 24.33 *Text entered in both column grids.*

Name	Type
Web Pages	File Folder
Music	File Folder
Report1.txt	Text Document
Report2.txt	Text Document

15. For the final step, we'll hide the grid column lines by selecting each column, right-clicking, and deselecting the Show Row Lines option.

FIGURE 24.34 *Grid context menu.*

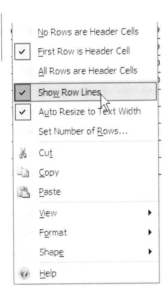

Progress Check:
Note: The file list columns should appear similar to Figure 24.35.

FIGURE 24.35 *Final grid design.*

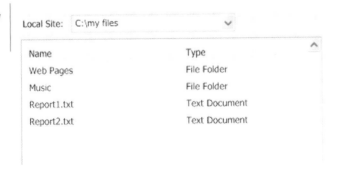

Step 5: Reuse

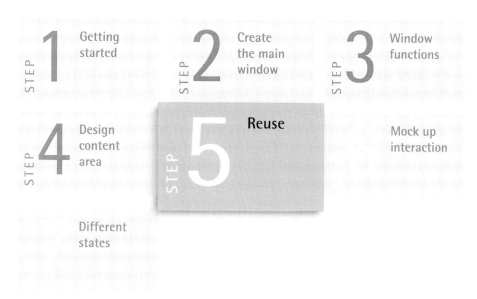

STEP **1** Getting started

STEP **2** Create the main window

STEP **3** Window functions

STEP **4** Design content area

Reuse

STEP **5**

Mock up interaction

Different states

Next, we need to design the display of files and directories on the remote FTP server. For this, we will reuse the shapes created in Step 4.

1. Select the shapes created in Step 4 and duplicate them using **Edit** > **Duplicate**. Then align the duplicated shapes next to the initial file list.

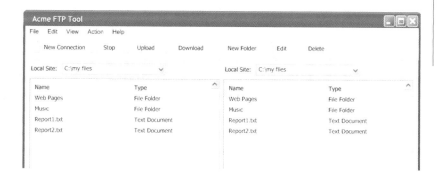

FIGURE 24.36

Prototype design with duplicate column grid.

2. Make the following text changes for the duplicated shapes:
   ‣ Change "Local Site:" to "Remote Site:"
   ‣ Change "C:\my files" to "\pub\ftp_files"

Note: We won't change the text in the column grid.

Remote Site: /pub/ftp_files   ⌄

FIGURE 24.37 *Remote Site pull-down.*

Step 6: Mockup Interaction

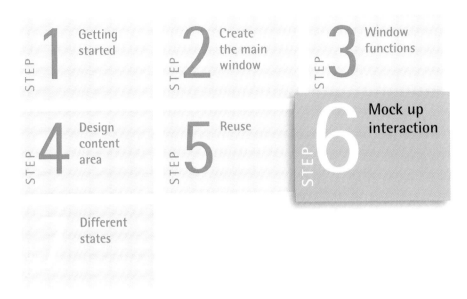

Finally, we are going to hide the duplicate column grids to illustrate how the remote FTP server directory might look before files are uploaded from the user's computer. Visio's layer feature will be useful for this task.

1. Select the Remote Site column grid, right-click, and assign a new layer to the columns by choosing Format>Layer from the context menu. Enter "after_upload" as the new layer name close the dialogs.

2. To hide the newly created layer, go to **View**>**Layer Properties** . . . to launch the Layer Properties dialog. Deselect the checkmark in the Visible column of the "after_upload" layer.

FIGURE 24.38 *New layer dialog.*

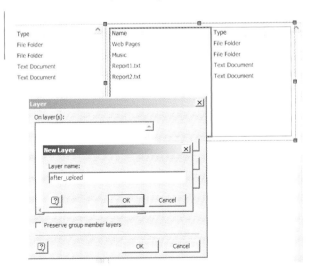

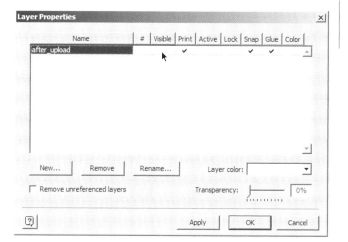

FIGURE 24.39 *Layer Properties dialog.*

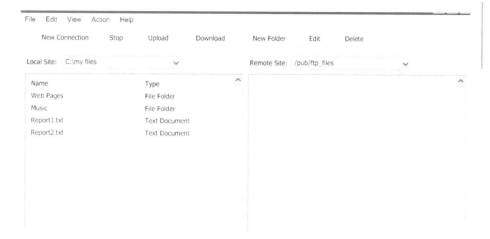

FIGURE 24.40

Prototype with hidden layer properties applied.

Note: At this point, the "after_upload" layer is hidden, as shown in Figure 24.40.

3. As the last part of the prototype creation, we're going to create a progress dialog to show files being transferred between the user's computer and FTP server. From the Windows and Dialogs stencil, drag and drop a new Blank form shape to the center of the main window drawing. This is going to be the new Progress dialog. The Progress dialog drawing will have the title of "FTP Progress," a gray background color, and resized to approximate the size of a dialog. This size can be later modified if it's too large or too small.

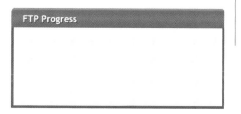

FIGURE 24.41 *FTP Progress dialog.*

4. Now add a progress indicator to the dialog by dragging a Progress bar shape from the "Common Controls" stencil to the Progress dialog in the drawing.

FIGURE 24.42 *Progress bar shape.*

5. Then, using Visio's Text Tool, we add the following text to the dialog: "Uploading files . . . please wait."

FIGURE 24.43 *Adding text to the Progress dialog.*

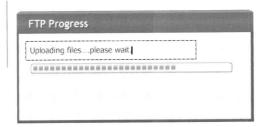

6. We also need to create a Cancel button for the Progress dialog. From the Common Controls stencil, drag and drop the Command button shape below the Progress bar shape. Then, double-click the Command button and change the text to "Cancel." Also, make the button the default action by selecting the Command button shape, right-click, and choose Enabled/default from the context menu.

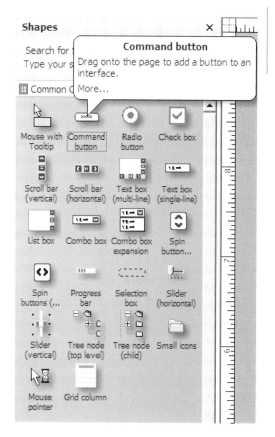

FIGURE 24.44

Command button stencil.

Progress Check:

Note: The FTP Progress dialog should look similar to the one shown in Figure 24.45.

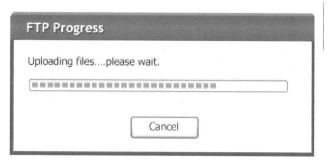

FIGURE 24.45 *Finished FTP Progress dialog.*

7. Finally, hide the Progress dialog drawing until it is needed by using the Layer feature. Assign a new layer to the Progress dialog. Select the dialog, right-click, and choose Format>Layer from the context menu. In the Layer dialog, click the "New . . ." button and enter "Upload Progress" for the new Layer name. Save the changes.

FIGURE 24.46 *New Layer dialog.*

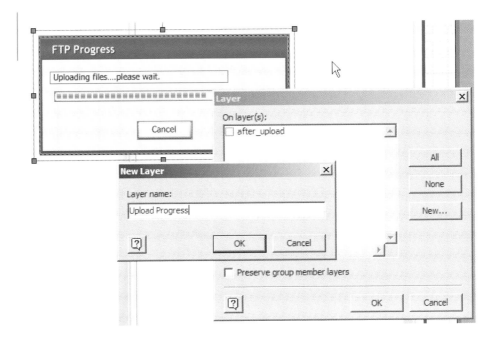

8. Hide the layer by going to **View**>**Layer Properties** . . . to launch the Layer Properties dialog.

9. For the Upload Progress layer, deselect the Visible checkmark.

FIGURE 24.47 *Layer Properties dialog.*

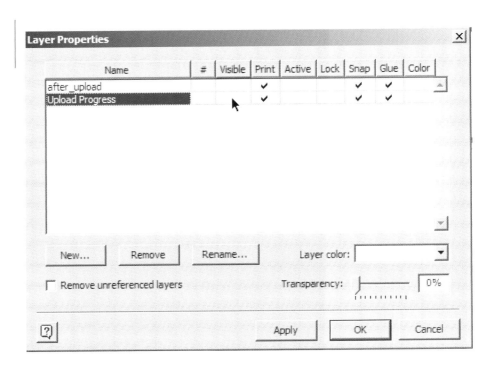

Step 7: Different States

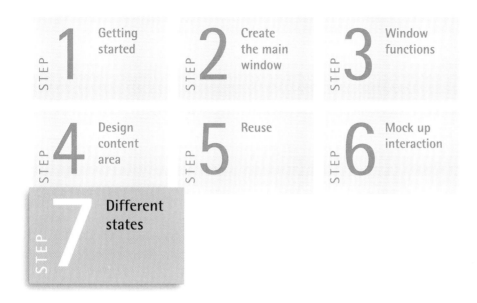

STEP **1** Getting started

STEP **2** Create the main window

STEP **3** Window functions

STEP **4** Design content area

STEP **5** Reuse

STEP **6** Mock up interaction

STEP **7** **Different states**

State 1: Before Files Are Uploaded

To show the Acme FTP Tool *before* files are uploaded from the user's computer to the FTP server, make sure that the after_upload and Upload Progress layers are hidden.

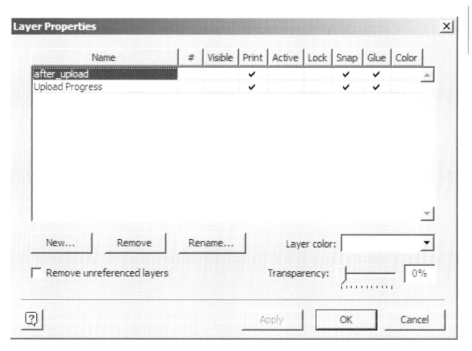

FIGURE 24.48 *Layer Properties settings.*

FIGURE 24.49 *Acme FTP Tool before files are uploaded.*

State 2: Files Are Currently Being Uploaded

To show the Acme FTP Tool *while* files are being uploaded from the user's computer, the after_upload layer should be hidden but the Upload Progress layer should be visible.

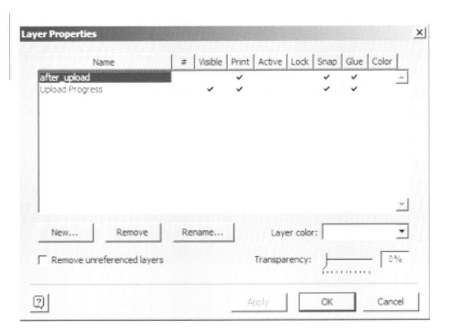

FIGURE 24.50 *Layer properties for the main screen.*

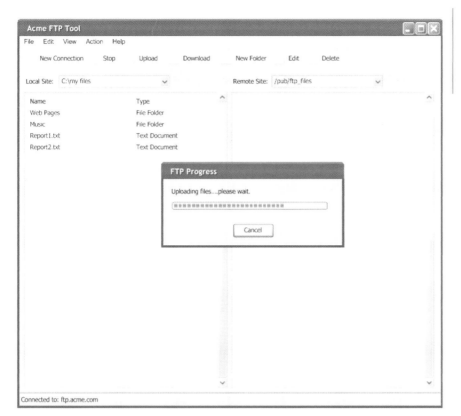

State 3: After Files Are Uploaded

The Acme FTP Tool, after files are uploaded from the user's computer to the FTP server, will have the after_upload layer visible and the Upload Progress layer hidden.

PRESENTING AND DISTRIBUTING A VISIO PROTOTYPE

Once you have finished creating a low-fidelity prototype in Visio, you'll probably want to distribute and present the prototype to members of your team or target users of the product. Fortunately, this task is fairly easy to accomplish using Visio.

When project team members or stakeholders are co-located, experience shows that receiving feedback and making prototype changes is much faster and more informative with paper, thus printing Visio drawings works best.

However, there will be times when you'll need to show your prototype with the team members located in other geographic locations. For this type of situation, you can distribute the Visio drawings digitally using e-mail or making the Visio document available in a shared network folder, external or internal website, or FTP site.

To allow others to view your digital Visio drawings, team members either need to have Visio or Visio Viewer (free) installed on their computers. Alternatively, you can save the Visio file as a PDF and distribute the PDF.

CHAPTER

Prototyping Tools

25

PROTOTYPING WITH ACROBAT

Dave Rogers

INTRODUCING ACROBAT

Adobe Acrobat is *not* a design or prototyping application. It is a document-sharing platform *par excellence*, one that not only preserves the exact formatting of documents but that also includes powerful reviewing and security features.

OVERVIEW OF EFFECTIVE PROTOTYPING WITH ACROBAT

Due to its accurate screen rendering and linking abilities, Acrobat is an ideal tool to use for digital interactive prototypes. Acrobat is a ubiquitous tool with read-only protection that allows for secure documents. It's a scalable tool; you can start simply and grow with the tool as your needs or proficiency expands.

Characteristics
PDF = Portable Document Format

The heart of Acrobat is the Portable Document Format (PDF). Adobe bills it as "a widely-accepted specification used by standards bodies around the world for more secure, reliable electronic document distribution and exchange." You'll find that these claims are not only true but critically essential when prototyping with Acrobat. PDFs can be created from nearly any application, from e-mail to AutoCAD, from paper to websites, preserving the look, design, and integrity of documents. Fonts, formatting, illustrations, media, and forms appear exactly as designed. Also, PDFs are easily repurposed for delivery as printed material, Web pages, e-books, CD-ROMs, and even prototypes.

The Flavors of Acrobat

Acrobat applications come in several varieties, each with their own purpose and audience. First, the omnipresent **Acrobat Reader** is freely distributed by Adobe; you probably already have it installed on your computer. Reader permits users to

TABLE 25.1 Acrobat Prototyping Characteristics Matrix

Characteristics		Acrobat
Audience	Internal	+
	External	++
Stage	Early	−
	Midterm	++
	Late	−
Speed	Rapid	+
	Diligent	+
Longevity	Short	+
	Medium	++
	Long	−
Expression	Conceptual	−
	Experiential	++
Style	Narrative	−
	Interactive	++
Medium	Physical	− −
	Digital	++

Content Fidelity		Acrobat
High fidelity	Information	++
	Interaction	++
	Visual design	++
	Branding	++
	System	NA
Low fidelity	Information	−
	Interaction	− −
	Visual design	+
	Branding	+
	System	++

++, Most appropriate;
+, appropriate;
−, acceptable;
− −, not appropriate;
NA, not applicable.

effortlessly view, print, and search PDF files and works seamlessly with most Web browsers. As nifty as it is, Reader is *only* a viewer and cannot create prototypes. However, it permits viewing and interaction with digital prototypes created by any PDF generator. Therefore, Reader is ideal as a prototype delivery mechanism.

The flagship of the Acrobat line is **Adobe Acrobat Professional**, an application that gives users the power to create, control, and deliver PDF documents to anyone with Reader or comparable software. Acrobat Pro isn't for everyone. Its primary users are those who need to securely share documents for review, distribute documents for websites or e-books, and produce print materials.

Besides Acrobat Pro, a number of other applications permit the creation and manipulation of PDF documents:

> **Adobe Acrobat Standard** is a subset of Pro, lacking the latter's robust form tools, multimedia capabilities, and more.
> **Adobe Acrobat Elements** is an enterprise-wide application intended only for the creation of simple PDF files for document sharing.
> Other Adobe products (such as Photoshop) can natively create and read Acrobat files.
> A number of independent PDF-related applications are also available.

ACROBAT AND PROTOTYPING

Although Acrobat is not a design application, it includes a suite of utilities that make the creation of digital prototypes possible. Using these tools, you can easily:

> Add and edit hyperlinks to content within and beyond the PDF document. Links can spawn a number of different actions, including media playback and menu item execution.
> Add and edit forms (buttons, text fields, check boxes, radio buttons, etc.) that simulate full functionality without coding.
> Include multimedia content such as sound, animation, and video.
> Insert, remove, replace, and rearrange pages; and combine documents created in different source applications into a single PDF.
> Edit text and other objects.
> Write custom JavaScript for advanced functionality and extensibility.

These features make it possible to build digital prototypes with the approximate effort of paper prototypes. Application-agnostic Acrobat handles high- and low-fidelity prototypes with equal aplomb. Designs do not need to be recreated within a programming environment, which is a real time saver. And perhaps most important of all, Acrobat forces you to separate the design process from prototype creation. You create, modify, and polish your design *first*; only when it is completed does Acrobat come into play.

That said, Acrobat is not an ideal prototyping environment for everyone and every situation. Prototyping in Acrobat requires some sleight of hand and pushing beyond the product's intended use—efficient link and form handling requires a plugin (more on this below); PDFs do not respond to Web browser navigation tools (Back, Forward and scrolling); and forms are not "real" forms, only simulations.

Some may think that using Acrobat for prototype creation is wasted effort, that the same features are available in diagramming or other applications. Yet whether you add links in Visio or Acrobat is immaterial; both require equal amounts of effort. And building working form simulations in Visio and other applications requires the use of Visual Basic; whereas in Acrobat, it's simply a matter of dialog boxes. Once you're past the initial learning curve, you'll be surprised at how easy it is to create PDF prototypes.

Prototype Characteristics

As with other prototyping tools in this book, Acrobat is not suited for creating every kind of prototype. It is most ideal for creating digital interactive prototypes. For rapid prototyping, only paper prototypes exceed Acrobat's speed and ease. Acrobat's ability to quickly convert static wireframes to working mockups that replicate functionality and interaction is a diligent trait.

Similarly, by offering models that approximate the user experience of the final product, PDF prototypes are strongly experiential in nature. Even so, they can also test rough concepts. For example, you can use PDF prototypes to assess interaction design apart from visual design, which is ideal for ideation early in the design process. Later, PDF prototypes are ideal for validating designs.

Easily created from paper and digital design documents, PDF prototypes are excellent low-fidelity prototypes. It's possible to scan quick sketches into Acrobat, add interactivity, and submit a prototype for usability testing in the course of a business day. More detailed designs, such as wireframes, take a bit more time, but rarely more than a day or two. You can also build PDFs from visual comps and screen captures for high-fidelity prototypes. These capabilities make Acrobat best for midterm and late prototypes.

PDF prototypes are most effective for usability testing with external audiences, especially end-users. While members of the internal team are certainly welcome to explore Acrobat prototypes, they should have already commented on the designs *before* they went to PDF. Remember, PDF prototypes are best created *after* the team has signed off on the design iteration. That said, PDF prototypes shine as a demonstration tool for upper management.

Prototype Content and Methods

Because they can include links and a variety of forms, even at low-fidelity, Acrobat prototypes are ideal for testing interaction design and navigation. At higher fidelities, especially when actual content can be included, PDFs can be used to assess information design. And while high-fidelity prototypes can be used to validate nearly completed visual designs, HTML prototypes are a better solution.

As we've seen, a primary strength of PDF prototypes is their ability to transform *narrative* documents to *interactive* simulations of a website or software product. Wireframes, whether paper or digital, demonstrate this most powerfully. PDF prototypes can test early pencil sketches through to the almost-ready-for-production wireframe iteration from a digital source. Created and revised quickly, PDFs scanned from paper retain some of the flexibility of paper prototypes with the addition of digital functionality. It's even possible to modify such a prototype *between test sessions* by redrawing a page, scanning it to PDF, inserting it into the prototype, and adding interactivity.

Thus far, we've painted a compelling and rosy picture of Acrobat's capabilities as a prototyping tool, but how does it measure up in the real world? The following case study demonstrates Acrobat's versatility and rapid prototyping capabilities in a time-critical situation.

CASE STUDY

Jack, an information architect, was hired at the last minute for a major expansion and redesign of a website promoting a prominent convention location. The site was targeted to professional meeting planners and, although the project had been underway for several months, there was no progress on the information structure or interaction design of the site. Site maps were due six days after an emergency kickoff meeting with *final* wireframes for the 300-plus page site required 6 weeks later.

While the team had basic demographic and psychographic profiles of end users–and outstanding domain experts–time precluded any user analysis such as usability testing of the current and competitive sites, user surveys, and card sorting exercises. Jack's challenge was to devise a way to bring user input into the design process before it progressed so far into development that changes would be impossible.

A major convention for meeting planners occurring 3 weeks after the kickoff provided an ideal venue for usability testing. But could a prototype be ready in time? Having worked with Acrobat before, Jack proposed PDF prototypes as a solution, emphasizing their ability to create just-in-time prototypes from whatever wireframes were available. The team immediately approved the idea.

Driven by the tight timeline, Jack completed a second iteration of wireframes 5 days before the convention began. He converted each of the 20 wireframe Visio files to PDF and assembled them into a single 215-page file.

Because the design featured a highly persistent global navigation scheme, Jack had created the wireframes on templated background pages, ensuring that all critical global links were in the same position throughout the PDF. He quickly created links for all the persistent global elements on the wireframe home page. Then, using an Acrobat plugin, Jack duplicated the links across the document in one step. He used a similar process on a smaller scale for persistent section navigation. Finally, Jack added the remaining links to each page in the document, taking every opportunity to use the plugin's link copying ability.

The site included an especially thorough user registration process and the ability to submit digital RFPs (requests for proposals), making the addition of interactive forms a particular challenge. Jack again began at the global level, working his way down to individual pages, copying and pasting duplicate fields whenever possible.

The morning before the convention, Jack completed the 2.5-megabyte prototype. Using the five tasks identified for usability testing, he repeatedly tested the prototype to ensure its readiness. After some tweaks and corrections, he used Acrobat's tools to secure the prototype against inadvertent changes. The last step was e-mailing the prototype to the project producer at the convention site along with instructions and usability test documentation. Ultimately, building the prototype took 4 (admittedly long) days.

Over the next 2 days, the producer used the prototype to test the design with 10 meeting planners. Beyond expectations, the test participants successfully completed all five test tasks. More important, their comments and ideas suggested significant improvements to the site's navigational scheme, priority of content elements, and terminology.

Jack immediately incorporated the test findings into a new iteration of the wireframes. The site launched on schedule and immediately saw a significant increase in traffic. Subsequent user surveys indicated that meeting planners were delighted with the site. A redesign several years later retained the information structure and interaction design that had been validated by the PDF prototype.

BUILDING PDF PROTOTYPES

Hopefully we've convinced you that Acrobat is a viable platform for creating digital prototypes. But now it comes to the nitty-gritty: How easy *is* it to build a PDF prototype? In this section, we'll convert Visio wireframes into an interactive, rapid, low-fidelity Acrobat prototype ready for usability testing.[1] A few caveats:

> This tutorial assumes the use of Adobe Acrobat Professional 7.0. If you use another version, you may need to make minor adjustments to the process.

> Although this tutorial demonstrates prototype creation for a website, the process is very similar for a software application.

> While some steps may differ depending on the source format and prototype purpose, you should be able to extrapolate procedures as needed.

> While not required, ARTS PDF Aerialist™ (an Acrobat plugin[2]) eases the chore of link and form creation. If you routinely create PDF prototypes, it is a significant time saver.

> Because Acrobat was not designed as a prototyping tool, you'll be pushing its envelope. Some of the procedures are clumsy, others are kludges. In other cases, Acrobat's limits will force you to scale down expectations. Despite the challenges, you'll be surprised at what you can do and how quickly you adapt.

> Finally, in the spirit of our purpose to demonstrate prototype creation using tools you already know, we assume that you have at least a working knowledge of Acrobat.

The wireframes in this example represent a generic e-commerce website. You can download copies of the prototype (with and without interactivity) and other extras at www.effectiveprototyping.com.

---

1. *A much shorter version of this chapter originally appeared in the newsletter of gotomedia in May 2005 (http://www.gotomedia.com/gotoreport/may2005/news_0505_usable1.html).*
2. *Available at http://www.artspdf.com/arts_pdf_aerialist.asp.*

The procedure for creating PDF prototypes consists of seven steps:

While the exact process you follow will vary based on the prototype's requirements and your personal preference, you will usually perform each step in one way or another.

Step 1: Get Ready

We have noted that one of the benefits of using Acrobat for prototypes is that it permits you to focus exclusively on design without distraction. Create the best wireframes possible, get the project team's approval to create interactive prototypes, *then* move to Acrobat for prototyping.

That said, here are a few things to keep in mind while wireframing:

Depict all interactive elements on your wireframes or application mockup–links, forms, media controls, etc. It's much easier to create and align these in your diagramming application than in Acrobat. Use Acrobat only to overlay interactivity.

Leverage Visio's features to make wireframing *and* prototyping easier. A previous chapter discusses Visio prototyping in greater detail. The following are some Visio features that are especially useful in combination with Acrobat:

> ➤ Make liberal use of nested background pages. This provides flexibility during wireframing and ensures that persistent elements are in static locations on every screen, which greatly speeds the linking process.

> ➤ Place callouts and notes on separate layers to ease their removal before converting to PDF.

> ➤ Hyperlinks created in Visio (especially on background pages) do not always convert smoothly to PDF, so use Acrobat to add links.

> ➤ Similarly, while it is possible to add interactive forms within Visio, it requires the use of Visual Basic, so stick with nonfunctional shapes and add the interactivity in Acrobat.

Step 2: Prepare for Conversion

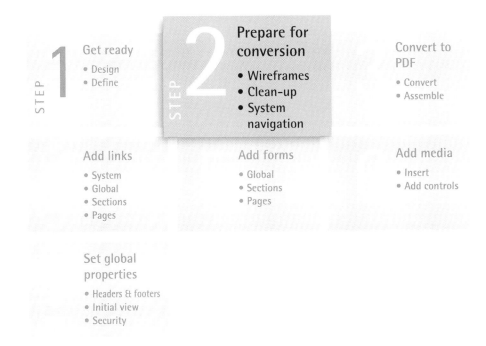

Although you can convert your wireframes to PDF with a single click in Office applications, you must first optimize them for prototyping. For our purposes here, we assume Visio wireframes but these steps can easily be adapted to Photoshop or other tools.

1. Save the document under a new name to create a backup copy of the original in case you have any problems.
2. Strip out any callouts and notes. If you assigned them to specific layers, use "Layer Properties" to remove them from each page.
3. On your primary background page, remove any administrative details so only the page schematics remain.
4. Because PDFs do not respond to browser commands, you must add substitute system icons to your wireframes.

   ‣ On the primary background page, create and add *Back* and *Forward* icons to the upper left corner (Figure 25.1). You will later add interactivity to these in Acrobat.

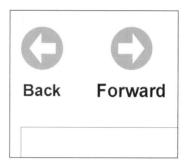

FIGURE 25.1 *Substitute Back and Forward browser icons.*

   ‣ If you use multiple wireframes for pages that extend below the fold, create *Scroll Down* and *Scroll Up* icons (Figures 25.2 and 25.3) at the bottom and top of applicable pages.

FIGURE 25.2 *Scroll Down icon.*

FIGURE 25.3 *Scroll Up icon.*

5. Create an *Under Construction* page (Figure 25.4) to display when usability test participants click an inactive link.

FIGURE 25.4 *Under Construction page.*

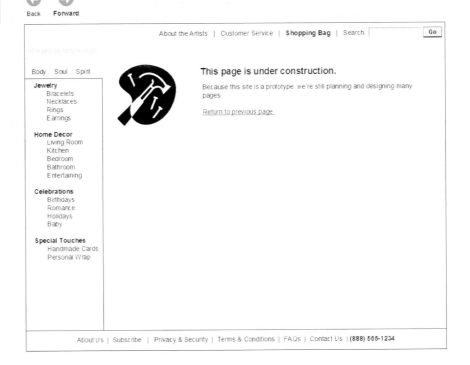

Step 3: Convert to PDF

You're ready to convert the wireframes to PDF. If you created the wireframes in an MS Office application, Adobe's PDFMaker toolbar (Figure 25.5) makes this a snap. Be sure the conversion settings (Adobe PDF>Change Conversion Settings . . .) are set to Standard (Figure 25.6); then click the Convert to Adobe PDF button.

FIGURE 25.5 *PDFMaker toolbar.*

FIGURE 25.6 *PDFMaker Change Conversion Settings dialog.*

1. In a few moments, the PDF file will open in Acrobat. If the wireframes consist of more than one file, repeat this step until all are converted.
2. Now assemble the prototype based upon the requirements and goals.

    ➤ If a *single* prototype will meet your needs, use Acrobat to piece together all the wireframe PDFs into one file (Document>Insert Pages). If you own the Aerialist plugin, its Merge Files command streamlines this process.

    ➤ If you need *multiple* prototypes, for example, one prototype for each usability test task, list the pages each task requires. Then, assemble the prototype page by page from the wireframe PDFs using Acrobat's Document>Pages Insert, Delete, Replace and Extract commands. With Aerialist, you can also split PDFs by several variables.

3. Open the prototype in Acrobat. To facilitate navigation while setting links, select the Pages tab at the left to open the corresponding pane (Figure 25.7).

FIGURE 25.7 *Acrobat Pages tab.*

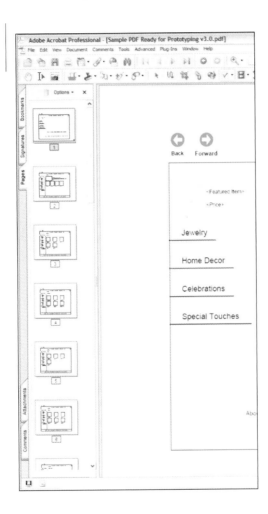

4. You will also need Acrobat's Basic and Advanced Editing toolbars. Aerialist offers its own as well as the ability to create custom toolbars (Figure 25.8).

FIGURE 25.8 *Acrobat and Aerialist toolbars used for prototyping.*

You're ready to bring the prototype to life.

Step 4: Add Links

If you are building a website prototype (as we are in this example), links are the easiest interactive elements to add, because setting their actions is simply a matter of selecting options in a dialog.

Adding Links to System Icons

Begin by adding links to the system icons you created, starting with the persistent *Back* and *Forward* icons. While creating these links, you'll also set the appearance defaults for other document links. We'll start with the Back symbol.

1. Select Acrobat's **Link Tool** on the Advanced Editing toolbar. On the first page of the prototype draw a rectangular outline over the Back icon (Figure 25.9).

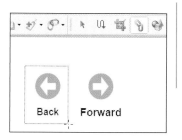

FIGURE 25.9 *Drawing a rectangular outline with Acrobat's Link Tool.*

2. The Create Link dialog opens. The Back icon is already a visible element in the PDF, so set the Link Type to **Invisible Rectangle**. Set the Highlight Style to **Invert**. For the Link Action, select **Custom Link** and click Next (see Figure 25.10).

FIGURE 25.10 *Create
Link dialog with
Custom Link selected.*

3. When the Link Properties dialog opens, go to the Actions tab. Select **Execute a Menu Item** from the Add an Action pull-down and click the Add . . . button. Use the resulting Menu Item Selection dialog to select **Previous View** (View>Go to>Previous View) as shown in Figure 25.11. Confirm the dialog changes to finalize the link.

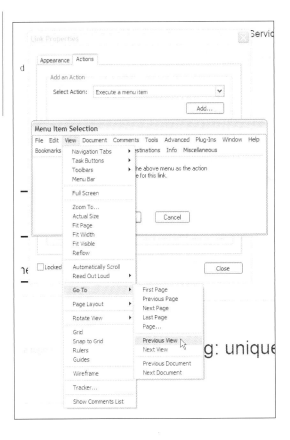

4. Finally, right-click on the new link and select **Use Current Appearance as New Default** (Figure 25.12). This ensures that all subsequent links will also be invisible.

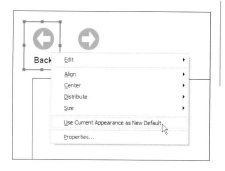

FIGURE 25.12 *Right click menu with use Current Appearance as New Default.*

5. Repeat steps 1 through 3 to create the link for the *Forward* icon–this time setting its menu action to **Next View** (View>Go to>Next View).

6. To test the links, use Acrobat's Hand Tool in the Basics toolbar. In the Pages pane, go to page 2. Click on the Back icon on page 2; it should take you to page 1. Click the Forward icon, and it should take you to page 2. If not, double-click the links and check to be sure you have them set as described above.

7. Now, because they appear throughout the prototype, copy the Back and Forward links to every page. There are two ways to do this:

   › If you do not have the Aerialist plugin, use Acrobat's Link or Select Object Tool to select both links and copy them to the clipboard. Then, manually paste and position them over the Back and Forward icons on every page.
   › The Aerialist plugin automates the process. Click the Link Select tool in the Aerialist toolbar. Select both links and *copy them to the clipboard*. Click the down arrow beside the Link Select Tool in the ARTS PDF Aerialist toolbar and select **Paste links across multiple pages** . . . (Figure 25.13).

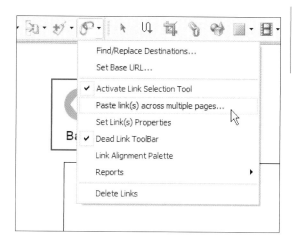

FIGURE 25.13 *Link Select tool options in the Aerialist toolbar.*

8. In the resulting dialog, go to the Pages radio button and select **All Pages** in the corresponding pull-down (Figure 25.14). Confirm to copy the links to all pages in their assigned positions instantly.

FIGURE 25.14 *Aerialist Paste Links dialog.*

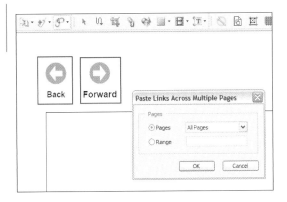

9. Test the links again to be certain they function as expected.
10. Next, page by page, add links to any *Scroll Down* icons. Following steps 1 through 3 above, create the first Scroll Down link, setting its Action to **Next Page** (Figure 25.15). Test the link to be certain it moves to the next page. Then, copy the link to the clipboard and paste it over every Scroll Down icon in the document.

FIGURE 25.15 *Link Properties>Actions> Menu Item Selection dialog with Next Page selected.*

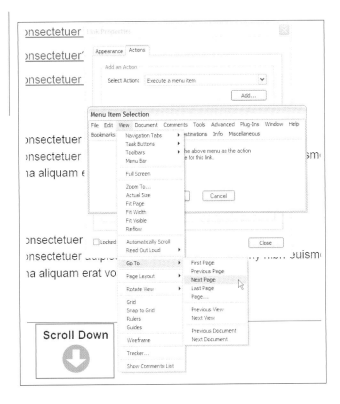

11. Repeat the process for the *Scroll Up* links, this time setting its Action to **Previous Page** (Figure 25.16).

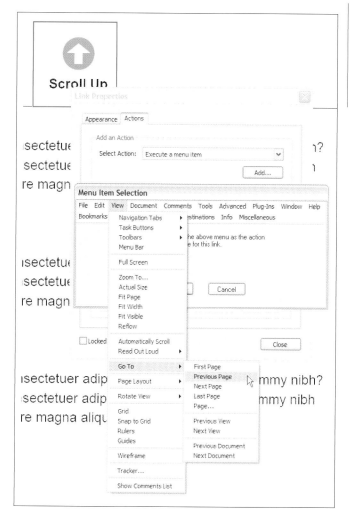

FIGURE 25.16 *Link Properties>Actions> Menu Item Selection dialog with Previous Page selected.*

Adding Links to Persistent Elements

With the system icon links in place, add links to persistent elements. These typically include global navigation, site-wide utilities and section navigation. It's most efficient to begin on the global scale and drill down to sections and subsections, creating and copying links in stages.

Regardless of their place in the site hierarchy, linking persistent elements follows the same procedure:

1. Navigate to the page where the particular persistent links (whether global, section or subsection) first appear.
2. Using the Link Tool, overlay links on each persistent element. Select **Go to a page view** as the Link Action and click Next (Figure 25.17).

FIGURE 25.17 *Create Link dialog with Go to a page view selected.*

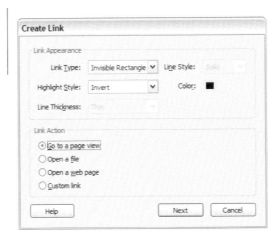

3. Following the directions in the Create Go to View dialog (Figure 25.18), navigate to the desired page within the prototype and click **Set Link**. (Tip: Use the Page pane for speedy navigation.)

FIGURE 25.18 *Create Go to View dialog.*

4. Right-click the new link and select Properties. On the Actions tab (Figure 25.19), verify that the Zoom level is set to Inherit Zoom. If not, click the Edit button and select **Inherit Zoom** from the Zoom pull-down (Figure 25.20) in the resulting dialog. Confirm and close the Link Properties dialog. This important step ensures that all linked pages display at the same magnification.

FIGURE 25.19 *Link Properties>Action tab dialog.*

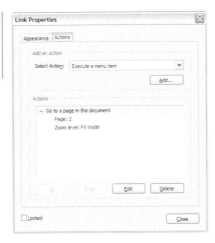

FIGURE 25.20 *Link Properties>Action tab dialog with Inherit Zoom selected.*

5. Switch to Acrobat's Hand Tool and verify that the link connects to the appropriate page.

6. When the links for each level are completed, select them as a group and paste into the appropriate pages using Acrobat or Aerialist (which can batch-paste to a specified range of pages). For example, after setting links for global navigation on one page, copy them across the prototype. Copy section links, of course, only within the applicable section.

Adding Links to Individual Pages

Finally, add links to individual pages using a similar process. While they are likely to link to a myriad of locations within the prototype, keep alert for opportunities to copy and paste whenever possible.

Tips for Adding Links

While the linking process may appear onerous in print, you will find that with just a little practice it proceeds rapidly, especially when using Aerialist. In addition, consider the following suggestions:

> Test every link *before* copying them to other pages.

> To edit a link, select Acrobat's Link or Select Object Tool. Double-click the link to open the Link Properties dialog.

- Since usability test participants may click anywhere on a page, add links to *all* link-like elements, even if they're inactive or unnecessary. Inactive links can link to the prototype's "Under Construction" page.
- When buttons in the prototype link to a destination, *overlay them with links* instead of using Acrobat's dedicated button tool. Use the Go to a Page View option to link to the appropriate location, whether it's a search result, login page or other destination.
- Links can do much more than navigate to other pages. You can use them to open other PDFs (meaning that you can create a mini-Web of PDF proto-types). They can open URLs or control sound and video. They can also exe-cute any Acrobat menu function. Acrobat includes JavaScript capabilities that give links almost unlimited power. Of course, you'll need some coding experi-ence or a friendly engineer's assistance. John Deubert's *Extending Acrobat Forms with JavaScript* is an excellent resource for more information.

Step 5: Add Forms

While you can certainly add linking functionality to prototypes in other programs, Acrobat permits you to add text fields, buttons, check boxes, radio buttons, list boxes, and combo boxes that simulate working forms and more—*all without coding*.

A brief primer: In addition to its document sharing features, Acrobat Professional includes the tools to create digital documents that gather data from users and transmit it by e-mail or the Web. Form fields can hold data, initiate actions, and call scripts. They can even be dynamic, drawing information from databases and populating other fields on the fly. They're immensely powerful. A helpful, though dated, resource is John Deubert's *Creating Adobe Acrobat Forms*, or you can check any of the numerous Acrobat reference works.

Although you could delve into JavaScript and CGI to build genuine working forms in PDF prototypes, it's wholly unnecessary. First, it's antithetical to producing prototypes quickly in numerous iterations without busting the budget or deadline. More to the point, prototypes don't *need* fully functional forms; instead, the *appearance* of working forms is sufficient, especially for early and midterm rapid prototypes intended for usability testing. Acrobat's power for digital prototyping lies in its basic tools for creating *simulated* forms that act like real ones.

As with links, adding form interactivity to PDF prototypes means drawing a shape and setting a series of options in dialog boxes, but there are important differences. When you added links to your prototype, you overlaid *invisible* links on link elements in the PDF. In contrast, forms are *visible* elements that obscure the underlying image. While links may span a number of pages, most forms are page specific, so you create them on a page-by-page basis. Finally, links are the most common features of website prototypes while forms dominate software prototypes.

Acrobat's form tools appear on the Advanced Editing Toolbar. To speed your work, display the palette of form types by selecting **Show Forms Toolbar** (Figure 25.21) from the Forms button menu.

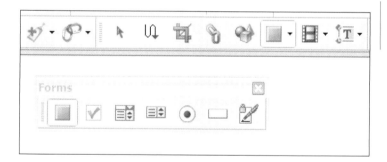

FIGURE 25.21 *Acrobat Forms Toolbar.*

Adding Text Fields

Text fields (Figure 25.22) are simple boxes for entry of text or numbers and are a great way to become familiar with Acrobat's form capabilities.

> enter email for newsletter signup

FIGURE 25.22 *Text field in Acrobat.*

1. Select the Text Field Tool from the Forms toolbar.
2. Draw the field *over* the wireframed field on the page, making it small enough to fit just within the borders of the original.

3. On the General tab of the Text Field Properties dialog (Figure 25.23), type a name for the field. It can be anything you like, but choose a title that clearly describes the contents, something like "FirstName." For later reference, note the field's title and location in a text document. If your design specifies, add a Tooltip such as "Type your first name." Under Common Properties, *be certain to set the field as* **Visible**; otherwise, test participants will not be able to see or use it.

FIGURE 25.23 *Text Fields Properties> General dialog.*

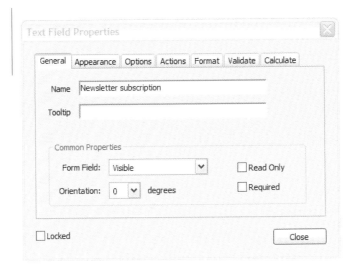

4. On the Appearance tab (Figure 25.24), set the Border Color to **No Color**, but make the Fill Color white. Set the Font Size to 9 or 10 and stick with a common font, such as Arial or Helvetica.

FIGURE 25.24 *Text Field Properties>Appearance dialog.*

5. In the same dialog's Options tab (Figure 25.25), type the text that you'd like to appear in the field by default. Set the Alignment and other options as needed.

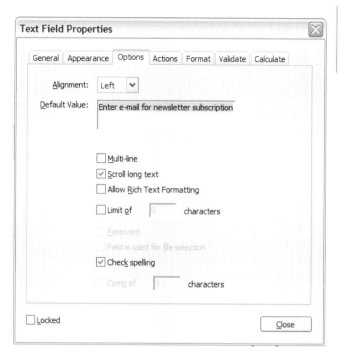

FIGURE 25.25 *Text Field Properties>Options* dialog.

6. For simple text fields, you're finished. But for numeric and other data, you can select a number of settings on the Format tab (Figure 25.26).

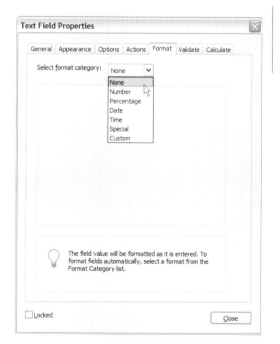

FIGURE 25.26 *Text Field Properties>Format* dialog.

7. Close the dialog. To test the field, select Acrobat's Hand Tool, click the field and type. Delete your test text so Acrobat doesn't save it as part of the document.

8. If you need to edit the field, switch back to the Text Field Tool and double-click the field to open the Text Field Properties dialog. You may also need to fine-tune the field's size and placement to ensure it fits within the underlying image.

How would you like your prototype to refer to users by their names? If your prototype includes a field where users enter their names, you can use the data to display their names elsewhere. You do this by creating another field *with the same title*. For example, if the "FirstName" field is on a registration page and you'd like to thank users for registering on a subsequent confirmation page, either (1) create a text field on the confirmation page and name it "FirstName" or (2) simply copy your original field to the confirmation page. The user's first name will appear where you place the field.

Adding Check Boxes

Check boxes (Figure 25.27) usually appear in groups where users can select one or more options. They are quick to add to the prototype.

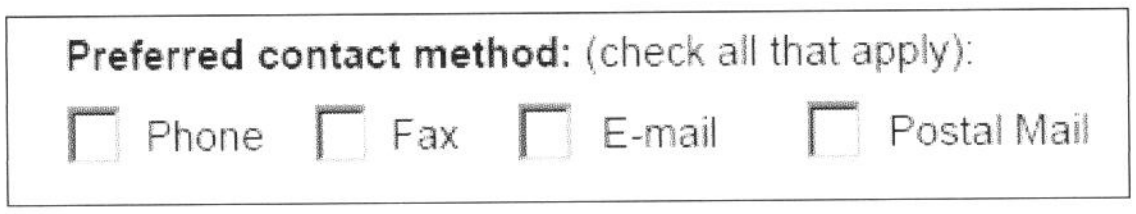

FIGURE 25.27 *Check boxes in Acrobat.*

Preferred contact method: (check all that apply):

☐ Phone ☐ Fax ☐ E-mail ☐ Postal Mail

1. Select the Check Box Tool from the Forms Toolbar.
2. Draw the field over the check box depicted on the wireframe page, making it slightly larger.
3. On the General tab of the Check Box Properties dialog (Figure 25.28), assign a descriptive name. Add a Tooltip if you wish and set the Form Field to **Visible**.

FIGURE 25.28 *Check Box Properties>General dialog.*

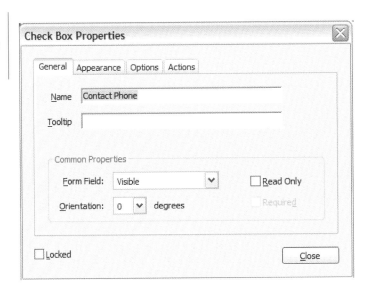

4. On the same dialog's Appearance tab (Figure 25.29), set the Border Color to black and the Line Thickness to **Thin**. Make the Fill Color white and the Line Style **Solid**. Set the Font Size to **Auto**.

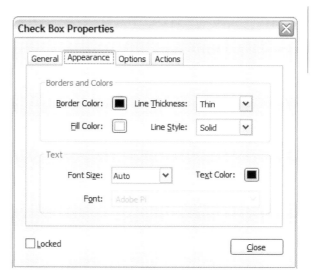

FIGURE 25.29 *Check Box Properties> Appearance dialog.*

5. On the Options tab (Figure 25.30), select a Check Box Style from the pull-down. Leave the Export Value at **Yes**. Set the box as **checked by default**, if desired.

FIGURE 25.30 *Check Box Properties> Options dialog.*

6. Close the dialog. Switch to the Hand Tool and toggle the check box on and off several times. If you need to adjust its properties, double-click it with the Check Box Tool to open the Properties dialog.

If you have any reason to display the check box at another location while retaining its user setting, you can copy and paste the original or draw a new one and assign it the same title.

Adding Radio Buttons

Radio buttons (Figure 25.31) are employed when users can select only one of two or more options. With a little trick, you can create radio buttons in the prototype that ensure only one selection. In this example, we'll create two radio buttons for subscribing or unsubscribing to a newsletter.

FIGURE 25.31 *Radio Buttons in Acrobat.*

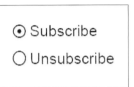

1. Select the Radio Button Tool from the Forms Toolbar.
2. We'll start with the Subscribe button. Draw a button over the corresponding image on the prototype's page, making it slightly larger than the original.
3. On the General tab of the Radio Button Properties dialog (Figure 25.32), assign a title (and Tooltip, if desired). Set the Form Field to **Visible**.

FIGURE 25.32 *Radio Button Properties> General dialog.*

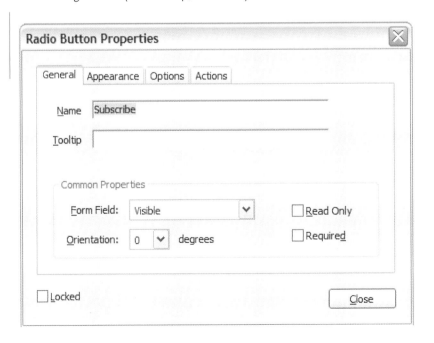

4. On the Appearance tab (Figure 25.33) of the same dialog, set the Border Color to black and its Line Thickness to **Thin**. Set the Fill Color to white and the Line Style to **Inset**. Set the Font Size to **Auto**.

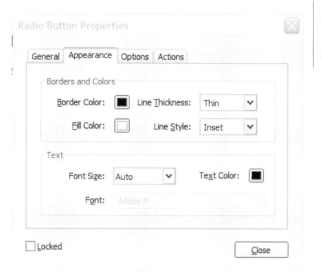

FIGURE 25.33 *Radio Button Properties> Appearance dialog.*

5. On the Options tab (Figure 25.34), set the Button Style to **Circle** (the most common). Set the Export Value to **Yes** (this is very important). Finally, set the button to be **checked by default**. Close the dialog.

FIGURE 25.34 *Radio Button Properties> Options dialog.*

6. Now comes the trick. *Copy* the Subscribe radio button to the clipboard and paste it over the Unsubscribe button in the prototype.

7. Double-click the new button to open its Properties dialog. On the Options tab, *change the Export Value to* **No** (Figure 25.35) and be certain this button is *not* checked by default. Don't make any other changes to the new radio button's properties.

FIGURE 25.35 *Radio Button Properties> Option dialog with Export Value set to No.*

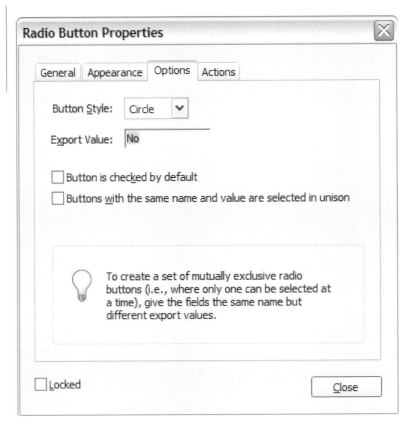

8. Close the dialog. You will see that the Subscribe radio button is filled. Select the Unsubscribe radio button with the Hand Tool; the Subscribe radio button should clear and the Unsubscribe button fill. Select the Subscribe radio button, and it should fill while Unsubscribe clears.

Adding Buttons

Buttons typically initiate some kind of action. In Acrobat, button forms are extremely versatile. They can change appearance when moused over, activate a number of actions with just one click, or initiate several series of actions. You rarely need such power for prototyping, however. As mentioned earlier, simply overlaying a prototype's buttons with links handles most button-related chores.

Here we'll demonstrate a behind-the-scenes administrative use for buttons. When users complete forms within the prototype (for example, during usability testing) their entries and settings are stored in the document. To clear the fields, you must close the document (without saving if using Acrobat Professional) and reopen it. Alternatively, you can create a subtle just-for-the-moderator button that resets all fields with a single click. It's a real time saver.

1. Select the Button Tool from the Forms Toolbar. On a little-used page such as the Under Construction page, draw a button outside the boundaries of the wireframe near the bottom right corner (Figure 25.36).

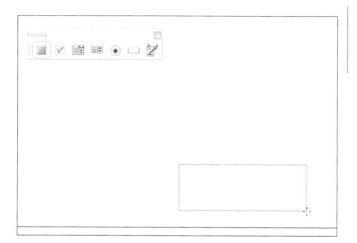

FIGURE 25.36 *Drawing a button outside the wireframe boundaries.*

2. In the General tab of the Button Properties dialog (Figure 25.37), assign a name and set the Form Field to **Visible**.

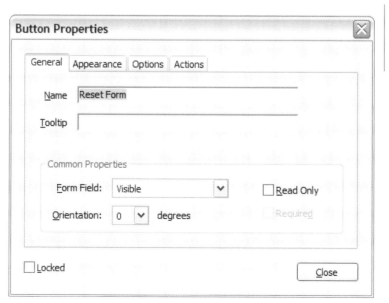

FIGURE 25.37 *Button Properties>General dialog.*

3. On the Appearance tab (Figure 25.38), set the Border Color to a light gray, the Line Thickness to **Thin**, and the Line Style to **Solid**. Set the Fill Color to **No Color**. Because you will leave the button unlabeled, leave the Text settings at the defaults.

FIGURE 25.38 *Button Properties>Appearance dialog.*

4. On the Options tab (Figure 25.39), set the Layout to **Label only**, the Behavior to **Invert**. Leave the Label field blank.
5. On the Actions tab (Figure 25.40), set the Trigger to **Mouse Up** and the Action to **Reset a form**. Click the Add . . . button.

FIGURE 25.39 *Button Properties>Options dialog.*

FIGURE 25.40 *Button Properties>Actions dialog.*

6. Select all forms listed on the resulting Reset a Form dialog (Figure 25.41). Close the Button Properties dialog.
7. Use the Hand Tool to test resetting all form fields in the prototype with a single click.

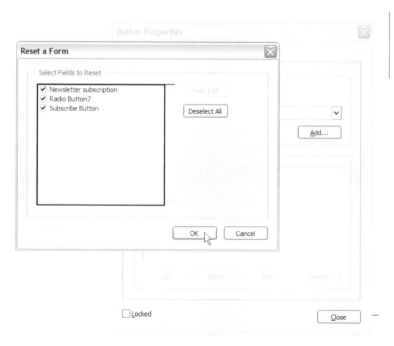

FIGURE 25.41 *Button Properties>Actions> Reset a Form dialog.*

Adding List and Combo Boxes

List boxes and Combo boxes (Figure 25.42) are similar in function. Both present the user with a number of options and both can permit the selection of multiple options. Combo boxes can also allow users to enter their own values.

FIGURE 25.42 *List Boxes and Combo Boxes in Acrobat.*

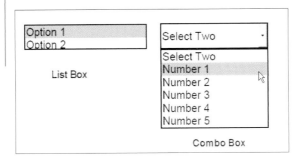

Unfortunately, Acrobat's List and Combo boxes don't work "out of the box" as we might wish. They're fine for *simulating* the selection of options such as a clothing size, but they require JavaScript to *take action* based on a selection, at least through Acrobat 7.0 Professional. This is a situation where we have to compromise for prototyping.

In this example, we'll approximate the ideal by using a combo box with a button and a little JavaScript.

1. Select the Combo Box Tool from the Forms Toolbar.
2. Draw a box over the combo box on the prototype's page, making it small enough to fit just within the original's borders.
3. On the General tab of the Combo Box Properties dialog (Figure 25.43), name it "Nav Box" (add a Tooltip if you wish) and set the Form Field to **Visible**.

FIGURE 25.43 *Combo Box Properties> General dialog.*

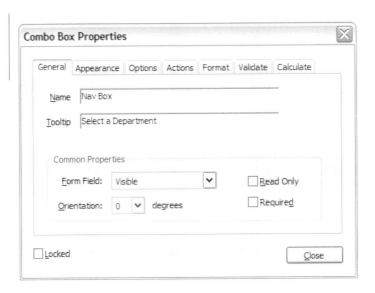

4. On the Appearance tab of the same dialog (Figure 25.44), set the Border Color to **No Color**. Set the Fill Color to white. Set the font size to your desired preference and use a common font like Arial or Helvetica.

FIGURE 25.44 *Combo Box Properties> Appearance dialog.*

5. On the Options tab (Figure 25.45) things get interesting because you want to take users to the page of a store department selected in the combo box. For each option, you must enter an Item, its Export Value, and press the Add key. In this case, the Export Values will be the page number of the corresponding department according to the following:

FIGURE 25.45 *Combo Box Properties> Options dialog.*

TABLE 25.2 **Sample Prototype Export Values**

Item	Export Value
Select a department	Leave blank
Jewelry	4
Style	6
Celebrations	8
Special Touches	10

Note that Acrobat considers page 1 as *page 0*, so numbers are actually one less than their actual position. These Export Values are very important to the simulation, so check them carefully.

6. Still on the Options tab, choose **Select a Department** in the Item List to set it as the default. Because we entered the Items in the desired order, clear the Sort Items check box. Be sure that Allow User to Enter Custom Text and Commit Selected Value Immediately are unchecked (Figure 25.46).

FIGURE 25.46

Completed Combo Box Properties>Options dialog.

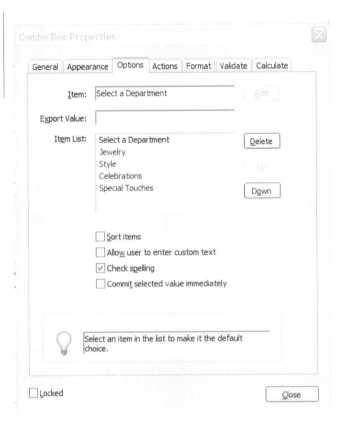

7. Close the Combo Box Properties dialog. Use Acrobat's Hand Tool and experiment with the combo box. You'll see that you can select an option but nothing happens as a result.

Now we begin the workaround.[3] We're going to add a *button* that, with a single line of JavaScript, will read the selected option's export value and display the corresponding page. Use the Button Tool on the Form Toolbar to draw a small button immediately to the right of the combo box (Figure 25.47).

FIGURE 25.47 *Drawing a button next to a combo box.*

8. On the General tab of the Button Properties dialog (Figure 25.48), name the button "Go Button" and set the Form Field to **Visible**.

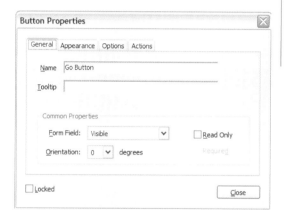

FIGURE 25.48 *Button Properties>General dialog with button name.*

9. On the Appearance tab (Figure 25.49), set the Border Color to black, the Line Thickness to **Thin** and the Line Style to **Solid**. Set the Fill Color to light gray. Set the Font Size to **Auto** and use a common font like Arial or Helvetica.

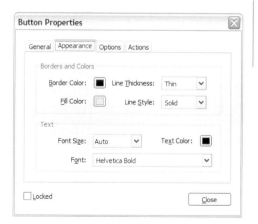

FIGURE 25.49 *Button Properties>Appearance dialog.*

---

3. *Thanks to George Johnson for his contribution of this elegant trick on Usenet's comp.text.pdf newsgroup (June 15, 1999).*

10. On the Options tab (Figure 25.50), set the Layout to **Label Only** and the Behavior to **Invert**. Label the button "Go."

FIGURE 25.50 *Button Properties>Options dialog.*

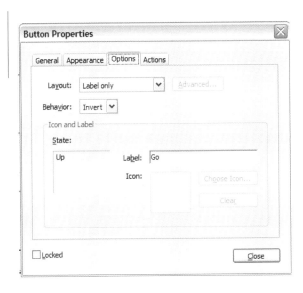

11. Now for some JavaScript. On the Actions tab (Figure 25.51), set the Trigger to **Mouse Up**. In the Select Action pull-down, select **Run a JavaScript**. Click Add.

FIGURE 25.51 *Button Properties>Actions dialog.*

12. In the resulting JavaScript Editor (Figure 25.52) dialog, type in this line of code: this.pageNum = this.getField("Nav Box").value

This tells Acrobat to look up the export value of the option selected in the combo box and display the equivalent page. Click OK to close the JavaScript Editor, then close the Button Properties dialog.

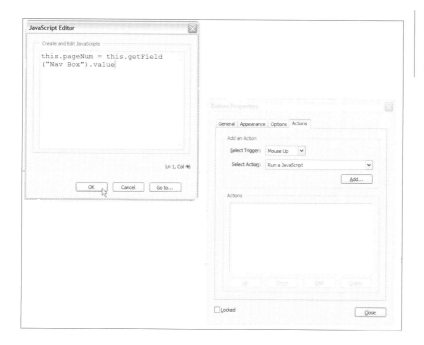

FIGURE 25.52 *Button Properties>Actions> JavaScript Editor.*

13. Use the Hand Tool to select any of the departments listed in the combo box and click the Go button. Acrobat will take you to the corresponding page.

Tips for Adding Forms

As with links, adding forms to prototypes will become second nature with a little practice. The following suggestions will add even more efficiency to your efforts:

› Before adding forms, go to Edit>Preferences and select the Forms option in the left pane of the dialog (Figure 25.53). The settings shown here should work well for almost everyone. Take special care to hide the forms document message bar and to disable the Auto-Complete function to avoid unnecessarily distracting the prototype's users.

› You can quickly locate and navigate to any form using the Fields navigation tab (Figure 25.54). Go to View>Navigation Tabs and choose the Fields tab. The tab lists all of the prototype's form fields, indicating their types. To go to a form, click on it. To rename, edit, or delete a form, right-click it. Additional procedures are available using the tab's Options pull-down menu.

FIGURE 25.53 *Acrobat
Preferences>Forms
dialog with recom-
mended settings.*

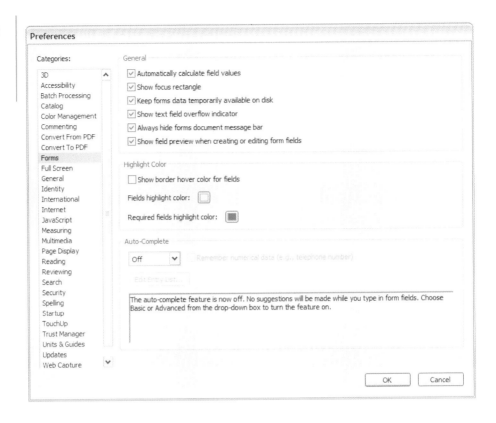

FIGURE 25.54 *Fields
Navigation Tab.*

> ▸ To open a form's Properties dialog quickly, double-click it while using
>   Acrobat's Select Object tool or the appropriate tool from the Forms toolbar.
> ▸ If a form appears on a number of pages in the same position, you can copy it
>   in one action. Right-click the form and select Duplicate . . . In the Duplicate
>   Field dialog (Figure 25.55), copy the form to all or a designated range of pages.
>   Keep in mind that these are all copies of the *same* field, not new ones. If you
>   want to use these fields for different data, be certain to change their names.

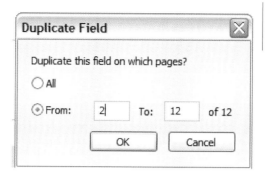

FIGURE 25.55
Duplicate Field dialog.

> If a page features a number of similar fields (for example, a series of text boxes), Acrobat includes an interactive tool that speeds the process of creating them. Right-click on the form you want to copy and select Create Multiple Copies . . . The dialog (Figure 25.56) permits you to dynamically specify the field size, placement, and number to create. When you click OK, Acrobat automatically titles and numbers new fields based on the original. You can now edit them to your specifications.

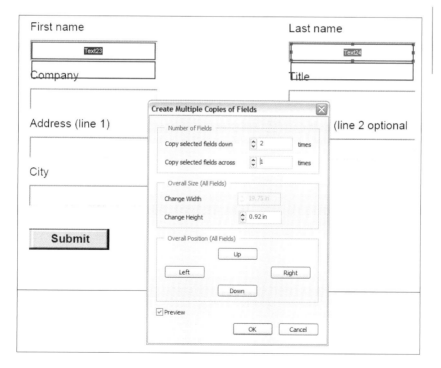

FIGURE 25.56 *Create Multiple Copies of Fields dialog.*

> As you create fields, Acrobat automatically sets their tab order. If you want to rearrange the order, Acrobat provides a tool, but it's a bit tricky.

1. In Acrobat's Pages pane, right-click the page and select Page Properties . . . On the Tab Order tab (Figure 25.57), select **Unspecified** and close the dialog.

FIGURE 25.57 *Page Properties>Tab Order dialog.*

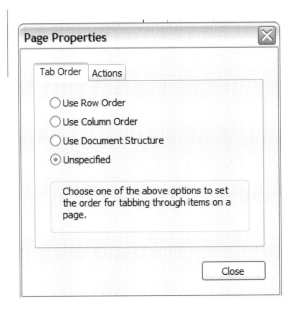

2. Choose the Select Object Tool on Acrobat's Advanced Editing toolbar. Right-click any form on the page and select Set Tab Order. This adds a small number at the upper left corner of each field (Figure 25.58), showing its place in the tabbing sequence.

FIGURE 25.58 *Tab Order display.*

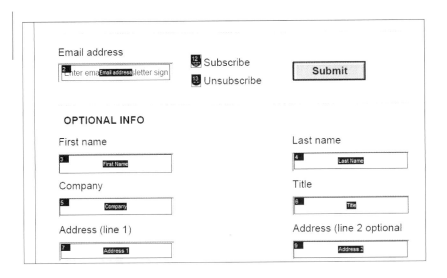

3. To change the tab order, click through the field numbers in the desired sequence. If the numbering initially seems incorrect, just keep clicking through all the fields. If you make a mistake, or the final tab order is incorrect, click anywhere on the page, right-click on any form, reselect Set Tab Order and try again.

> ▸ As noted above, JavaScript can add amazing abilities to the prototype's forms if you have the requisite abilities or a friendly programmer nearby. To enable JavaScript in Acrobat, go to Edit>Preferences, choose the JavaScript option, and verify that the Enable Acrobat JavaScript check box is filled.

Step 6: Add Media

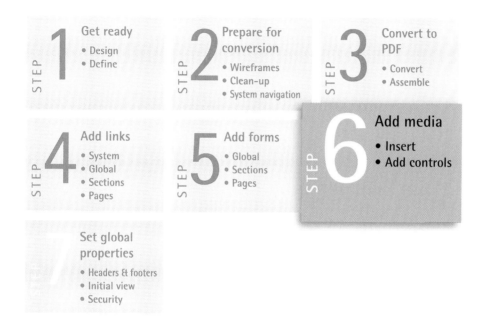

You can include a wide variety of sound, video and animation files in a PDF prototype. Acrobat 7.0 plays all media elements compatible with Flash, QuickTime, Windows Media Player, RealOne, and Windows' built-in player. Clips can either be embedded in the prototype, increasing the file size, or links to clips in an external location can be added. Playback may be controlled using links and forms. In this example, we will add a movie and control playback with links.

1. When designing wireframes in your diagramming tool, include an image of a media player with a playback area and desired basic controls.

2. After converting the wireframes to PDF, select the Movie Tool on the Advanced Toolbar. If the Movie Tool is not visible, find it using the pull-down next to the Sound Tool.

3. Using the Movie Tool, draw a square within the wireframe media player's playback area (Figure 25.59).

4. In the Add Movie dialog (Figure 25.60), select **Acrobat 6 (and Later) Compatible Media** to apply the most robust media tools. If you are uncertain whether prototype users will use version 6.0 or later of Acrobat or Acrobat

Reader, select Acrobat 5.0 instead. Insert the appropriate movie using the
Location Browse button.

<project video>

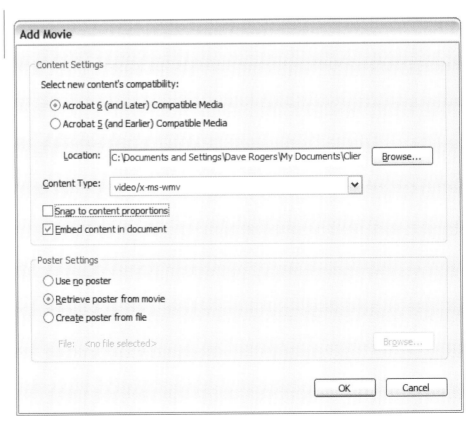

5. Clear the **Snap to content proportions** check box to ensure that the movie plays within the defined boundaries. It's usually best to mark the **Embed content in document** option.

6. You can choose to show a movie "poster" in the playback area when the clip is not playing. To automatically create a poster from the first frame of the clip, choose **Retrieve poster from movie**. A few moments after closing the dialog, the poster appears within the playback area.

7. Now we'll set links to control the movie's playback. Use the Link Tool in the Advanced Editing toolbar to draw a link over the Play button image in the prototype (Figure 25.61).

FIGURE 25.61 *Drawing a link for the Play button.*

8. In the Create Link dialog (Figure 25.62), set the Link Type to **Invisible Rectangle** and Highlight Style to **None**, select the **Custom link** radio button, and click Next.

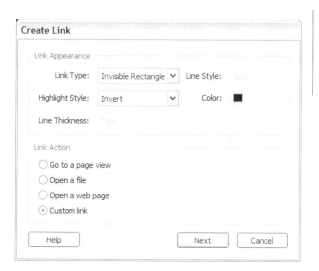

FIGURE 25.62 *Create Link dialog with custom link selected for media controls.*

9. On the Actions tab of the Link Properties dialog (Figure 25.63), select **Play Media** (Acrobat 6.0 and Later Compatible) from the pull-down menu. Click Add. (Select the Acrobat 5.0 Compatible option if you chose that while adding the media clip.)

FIGURE 25.63 *Link Properties > Action dialog with Play Media selected.*

10. In the Play Media dialog (Figure 25.64), select **Play** in the Operation to Perform pull-down. The Associated Annotation section lists all compatible media in the prototype. Select the desired clip and close the Link Properties dialog.
11. To play the movie, switch to Acrobat's Hand Tool and click the Play button.
12. Repeat this process to add links for the player's other controls.

We have only scratched the surface of Acrobat's media abilities. For more information, refer to Acrobat's documentation.

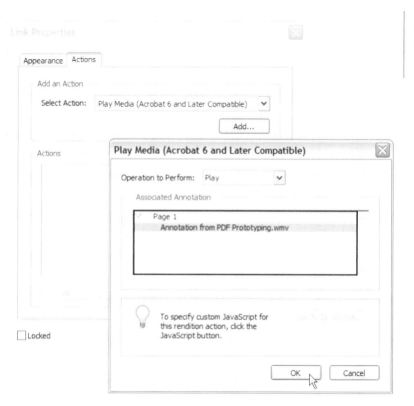

FIGURE 25.64 *Play Media dialog with media file selected.*

Step 7: Set global properties

STEP **1** Get ready
- Design
- Define

STEP **2** Prepare for conversion
- Wireframes
- Clean-up
- System navigation

STEP **3** Convert to PDF
- Convert
- Assemble

STEP **4** Add links
- System
- Global
- Sections
- Pages

STEP **5** Add forms
- Global
- Sections
- Pages

STEP **6** Add media
- Insert
- Add controls

STEP **7** Set global properties
- Headers & footers
- Initial view
- Security

After adding all links, forms, and media clips, test the entire prototype thoroughly and repeatedly. Assess the prototype against its expressed purpose. Can you successfully complete every task for the usability test? Does it operate smoothly as a proof of concept? Would you feel comfortable showing it to upper management?

Once you're satisfied, use Acrobat to add headers and footers to the prototype's pages (Document>Add Headers & Footers . . .). These should be small, serving as subtle reference points for usability test moderators and observers. See Acrobat's documentation for instructions.

Next, prepare the prototype for display in a Web browser. This essential step eliminates the possibility of inadvertent or unexpected events due to Acrobat's interface.

1. Transfer the prototype to a testing or demonstration computer with Acrobat Pro or Reader installed. Open the Web browser you will use for testing or demonstration and maximize its window. Remove all unnecessary toolbars from the browser interface, making the document window as large as possible.

2. Open the prototype in the browser. Use the Dynamic Zoom on the browser's Acrobat toolbar (Figure 25.65) to set an optimal magnification, one in which the *entire page* (from top to bottom and side to side) is visible *without horizontal or vertical scrolling required*. The Back, Forward, and any Scroll Up and Down buttons should be clearly visible. When satisfied, note the magnification percentage in the toolbar for later reference and close the prototype.

FIGURE 25.65 *Acrobat Reader's Zoom pull-down menu in a browser.*

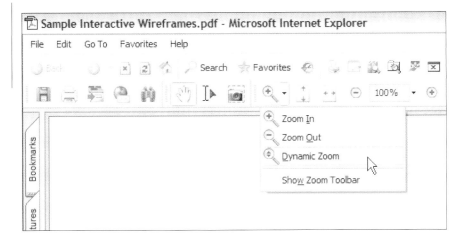

3. In Acrobat Professional, open the prototype again. Go to File>Document Properties and select the Initial View tab (Figure 25.66). In Document Options, set Show as **Page Only** and Page Layout as **Single Page**. In the Magnification field, select the option closest to the percentage you established earlier in the browser view. The document should open to page **1**.

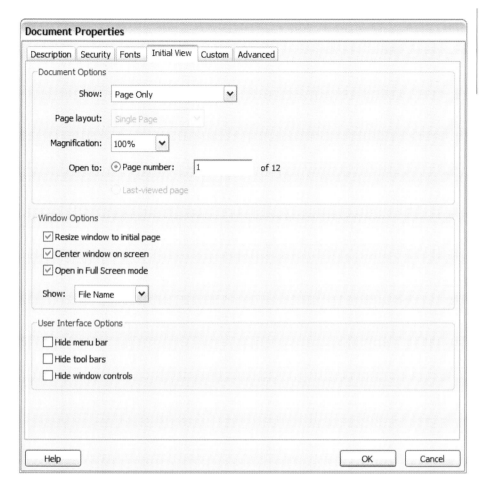

FIGURE 25.66

*Document Properties >
Initial View dialog with
recommended settings.*

4. In Window Options, check all three boxes. **Open in Full Screen Mode** is the most important, maximizing the document window and eliminating all Acrobat controls. This is why you created the system icons for navigation.

5. Save the prototype and transfer it to the testing or demonstration computer. Open the file in the maximized Web browser to confirm that the magnification setting is acceptable. (If you need to restore the Acrobat interface in the browser, press the ESC key.) Run through one more test of the prototype.

6. If a page size changes after clicking a link, it is likely that the target's Zoom Level is incorrectly set. Open the prototype on the development computer and use the Action Tab in the Link Properties dialog to set it to **Inherit Zoom**. If you have the Aerialist plugin, you can set *all* links to Inherit Zoom in one action. Click the Link Select Tool in the Aerialist toolbar, right-click any link and select Set Link(s) Properties. In the Link Magnification section of the Set Link Properties dialog (Figure 25.67), set From as **All Magnifications** and To as **Inherit Zoom**. Confirm the changes.

FIGURE 25.67

Aerialist's Set Link
Properties dialog.

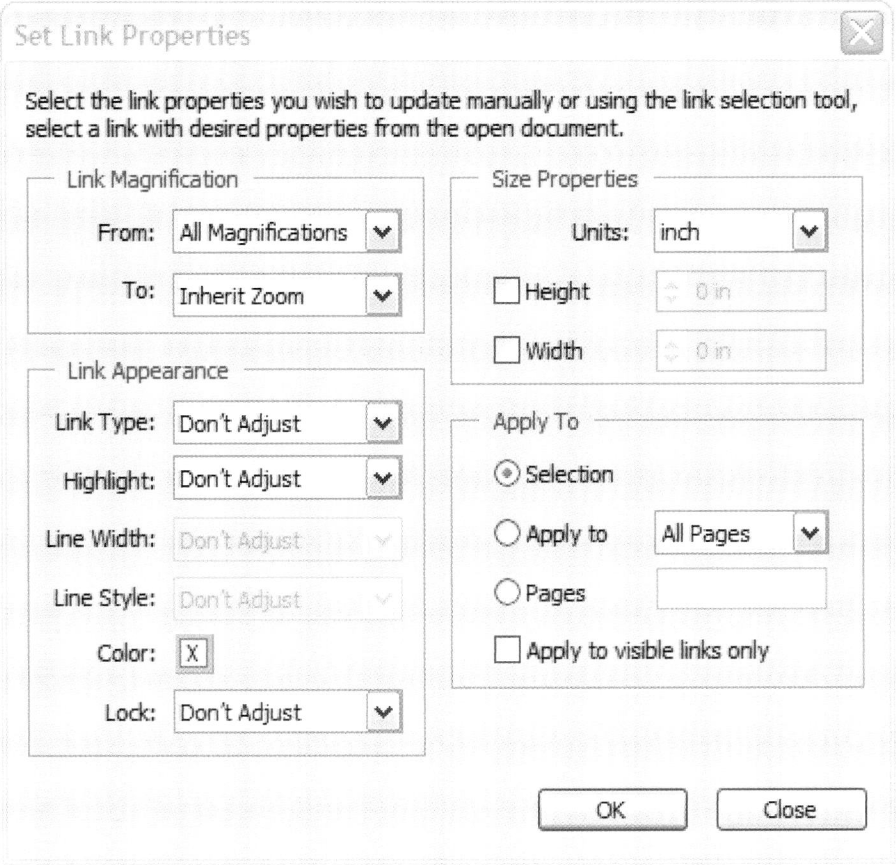

When you're *certain* that the interactive prototype is finished, you may wish to use Acrobat's security functions to protect the prototype from changes. Go to File>Document Properties and select the Security tab. Using Password Security to prevent changes to the document is usually sufficient. Refer to Acrobat documentation for further details.

Sample Files

For demonstration and experimentation, we have provided sample files at www.effectiveprototyping.com:

> A Visio wireframe set up and ready for conversion to PDF
> A PDF prototype *without* interactivity
> A completed PDF prototype

PUTTING THE PROTOTYPE TO WORK

Congratulations—your PDF prototype is ready for its debut!

Team Review

Your first audience is likely the project team. Distribute the prototype to your work-group for review via e-mail or access to a server location. Include a list of the usability or demonstration tasks along with brief instructions asking the team to test its readiness. Because Acrobat Reader is so widely distributed, it's likely every member can run the prototype. If they have Acrobat Pro or Standard installed, your coworkers can use its powerful reviewing and commenting features to respond with feedback.

When you've gathered the team's responses and made any necessary corrections and changes, it's time to introduce the prototype to end users.

PDF Prototypes in Usability Testing

Running a usability test with an Acrobat prototype requires only a few adjustments. Before the participant arrives, open the prototype within the browser. Run through the test tasks for a last-minute check.

During the introduction, set the participant's expectations by explaining that a prototype will be used, not a final product. One way to do this is to say: "We'll be working with an early version of a new website. It definitely has some rough edges–there are no graphics, the text may be gibberish and things may not work the way you expect. In fact, it's pretty ugly! But that's OK–because we need the opinions of people like you to help us finish it in the best possible way."

Next, explain, and even demonstrate, how to navigate through the prototype: "Because this is a prototype, there are some differences in how you'll navigate. Instead of using the browser's Back and Forward buttons, we've made some special ones for you to use. They're right here at the top left corner of every page.

"Some pages of the prototype may extend beyond the bottom of the screen. Because the usual scroll bar at the right of the screen is absent, you'll use this special Scroll Down button to see the rest of the page. Then you'll see the Scroll Up button that moves to the top of the page. You can also use the Page Down and Page Up buttons on the keyboard."

To enhance the introduction, you may wish to create a lighthearted little PDF prototype with three or four pages so participants can practice before beginning the usability test. If you make the subject of this demonstration prototype humorous, it's a great way to break the ice with participants. Test participants are usually nonplussed about using prototypes. They understand the limitations and are usually delighted to be a part of the design process. Even so, ask if there are any questions before beginning the test.

You can conduct the usability test in your typical manner. If you're using separate PDFs for each test task, you'll have to open them as each task is completed. Otherwise, you'll find that using a PDF prototype requires no special procedures.

NEXT STEPS

After testing or demonstration, it's back to the virtual drawing board. Return to your wireframing application to incorporate revisions and corrections to the design.

If the changes are relatively minor, affecting only a small number of pages, you may be able to reuse the prototype, replacing only the pages where the design was changed. If the changes are very minor, you may be able to make them overnight, or even between usability test sessions:

1. Make the necessary corrections and changes in your diagramming tool.
2. Convert *only* the changed pages to PDF. The Acrobat PDFMaker macro for Visio includes a handy option for converting single pages. Click Adobe PDF in the application menu and uncheck Convert All Pages in Document.
3. Open the prototype. Using Acrobat's Document>Pages commands and, working page by page, replace the original pages with those you revised. Some suggestions for a smooth makeover:

> Simple page-for-page replacements are the easiest because Acrobat retains the original links and forms. If you moved, added, or removed any such elements on your revised wireframe, do the same on the new page in the prototype.

> While replacing single pages is a breeze, *adding* or *deleting pages* can be problematic as they may confound Acrobat. Links automatically adjust, but if you use forms for navigation, you may need to reset the destinations. Aerialist includes search and replace abilities that can speed the process. Right-click the Link Select tool in the Aerialist toolbar and select Find > Replace Destinations . . . In the resulting dialog, set Search For as **Page Number**, then enter the appropriate information in Find What and Replace With (Figure 25.68), being sure to check the **Search in form fields** box.

FIGURE 25.68 *Aerialist Find and Replace Destinations dialog.*

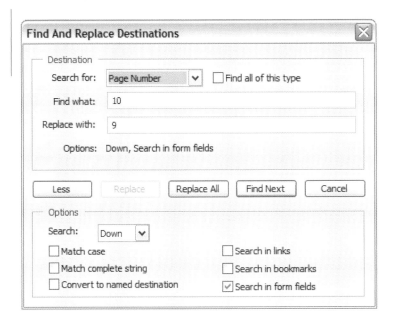

> ➤ If you revised global, section or other persistent elements (such as global navigation links), it's most efficient to delete *all* the original links page by page, then recreate and copy them as described earlier. If you own Aerialist, you can use its Dead Link Toolbar to quickly search for broken links.

SOME CLOSING THOUGHTS

In this chapter, we've seen how Acrobat can transform static wireframes into functional simulations of an application or website. Because its tools require no coding, practitioners can quickly create interactive prototypes directly from digital or paper designs. Acrobat's robust form tools are especially user-friendly while other applications require programming experience. And should the need arise, the sky's the limit for PDF prototypes due to Acrobat's integrated JavaScript.

Best of all, Acrobat prototyping is versatile, ready to handle prototypes of low or high-fidelity, rapid or diligent, concrete or abstract, midterm or late, and intended for a variety of purposes and audiences. While PDF prototypes take some initial work and a few workarounds, creating them demands no more effort than creating paper prototypes but PDF prototypes are definitely a step closer toward reality.

REFERENCES

John Deubert. Creating Adobe Acrobat Forms. Berkeley, CA: Adobe Press, 2002.

John Deubert. Extending Acrobat Forms with JavaScript. Berkeley, CA: Adobe Press, 2003.

EFFECTIVE PROTOTYPING

Term	Definition
arrangement and sequencing	To allow focus on these aspects for design and usability testing, wireframes and other types of prototypes can depict arrangement and sequence flows, how elements are arranged on a screen, and navigation sequencing possibilities.
assumption	An unvalidated requirement.
audience	Prototyping characteristic: Who prototypes are designed for. Audiences fall roughly into two categories – internal and external to the software creation and development team.
balance	Design Guideline: The harmony of design and proportion of content and user interface elements that expresses an even distribution of weight and a feeling of stability.
characteristics	Traits that define or characterize a prototype. Until recently, high and low fidelity in addition to rapid have been the primary focus on traits, and even those terms are often misunderstood. Eight high level prototyping characteristics have been defined in Chapter 3.
conceptual model	The model a software maker designs to enable an end user to form their mental model of how to use the software.
content	The elements that make up a prototype, such as blocks of text, branding, icons, graphics, etc.
critical incidents or critical task situations	Key defining moments or incidents where extraordinary usage, as opposed to everyday usage, proves the real value of a software product.

design criteria	A collection of design guidelines used as guiding principles of a design that support the design rationale and by which design decisions are made.
design guidelines	A set of design rules that inform the design and layout of screens. They do not guarantee a good design but rather provide guidance in the analysis of good design ideas for a prototype.
design rationale	The reasons and justification for creating a specific design.
editorial content	Prototyping content: Information in the form of text and image content of the viewed screen that is communicated to the user.
effective prototype	An effective prototype has the right mix of concrete and abstract aspects to accurately express the current state of under-standing for the software product or to represent the current salient issues of the design team. Effective prototypes reflect stakeholder knowledge and concerns and also venture to foster discussion by addressing next steps or possible directions.
effective prototyper	A person who effectively analyzes the current state of software requirements with the needs of the organization in mind and translates that knowledge into a prototype with the right levels of fidelity at appropriate stages of the software creation process.
effective prototyping	A learnable, repeatable process where the prototype lives or dies by how effectively the prototyper analyzes the current state of the requirements in relation to business/marketing, functional, technical and usability needs.
efficiency	Design Guideline: A screen layout/organization and task flow attribute that allows users to easily and effectively navigate through the interface to accomplish tasks.
end user	The people who ultimately use your software to perform tasks or activities.
expression	Prototyping characteristic: The degree of abstraction as por-trayed by the visual and interaction aspects of the user interface, ranging from rough and very abstract (conceptual), such as a napkin sketch versus actual and concrete (experiential), such as an accurate portrayal of finished software.
fidelity	Prototyping characteristic: The degree of detail and finish to which the prototype represents real system design – graphics, content, interactivity, functionality, and performance. Fidelity ranges from very low to very high.

Fitts' Law	A mathematical function that predicts the time required to rapidly move a cursor from a starting position to a final target area, as a function of the distance to the target and the size of the target. Frequently used as a screen design metric, the law is interpreted as the smaller and farther away a screen target is located, the more difficult it is for users to reach the target and interact with it.
Greeked text	Using Latin text to mock up editorial content.
grid-based organization	Design Guideline: A matrix-base organization and alignment structure used as a framework for the layout of typographic information and graphic elements on a screen and across related screens, and its translation into a final cohesive design. [Hurlburt, p 86] Grid-based organization is the process of laying out a sequence of related screens so they are consistent and the user can find information quickly.
hardware prototype	A prototype as physical artifact or stimulus.
information design	Prototyping content: Information structure of the software content, characterized by the hierarchical and priority relationships between and among the various elements of content.
information flow	Design Guideline: The path on which the human eye is meant to travel while viewing information on a display screen. The path and general layout of information should map to what users expect to see and where they expect to see it.
interaction design	Prototyping content: The layout of the interaction controls (such as buttons and links), definition of navigation paths (including origin and destination points), and sequencing of the interaction flow.
learnability	Design Guideline: Ability of users to understand and easily learn a user interface. This is based on users' ability to reuse current knowledge or knowledge gained from using one aspect of the application to learn other aspects.
logical grouping	Design Guideline: The contextual and relational grouping of screen information and user interface elements that enables users to find and comprehend information more quickly and easily in ways that users expect and comprehend. Groupings facilitate users' ability to form a mental model about associations between and among items and information sets.
longevity	Prototyping characteristic: The life expectancy of a prototype, characterized as short, medium, or long.

medium	Prototyping characteristic: The physical or digital state in which a prototype will be rendered, not the state in which it is created.
methods	Various systematic techniques used to create a prototype, including storyboards, wireframes, and paper prototypes.
mental model	A mental image that the user forms to understand how software works and how to operate it.
mock up	A general term for any prototype.
over-achieving prototype	A high fidelity prototype that is meant to wow an audience but is generally introduced too early in the software design process. Often causes design decisions to be made prematurely allowing little or no room for adapting or extending a concept.
product branding	Prototyping content: Product characteristics and how they are expressed to the outside world, including product users.
progressive disclosure	Design Guideline: A method for reducing user memory and cognitive overload by preventing the display of overly complex and overwhelming amount of information to users. Progressive disclosure occurs within a screen or across multiple screens by breaking information into task-relevant sequential chunks that are easy to comprehend, consume and interact with and appear as necessary for the user to complete tasks.
prototype	A model used to represent a software and/or hardware idea for the purpose of trying new design concepts and determining their efficacy. Relative to design objectives prototypes can be rendered with varying degrees of completeness.
prototyping	Act of conceptualizing, creating, and building prototypes.
rapid prototyping	A type of prototype conceived and built in a very short time frame.
requirement	What the software needs to fulfill to be successful.
rhythm and pattern	Design Guideline: Regular and intelligible form or sequence discernible in certain visual arrangements or interaction situations. Rhythm and pattern allow the design of different information and navigation flows appropriate to design objectives, including the top left to bottom right and top right to bottom left patterns.
scenario	The description of a user activity or task in the form of a narrative presentation.
software makers	People who create and produce software, such as developers, user interface designers, business analysts, product

	managers, etc. Software maker acknowledges the multi-disciplinary, collaborative and collective characteristics of software creation better than the more exclusive terms such as developer and designer.
software making	Act of creating software, in its many stages, undertaken by software makers.
speed	Prototyping characteristic: The amount of time it takes to create a prototype. In this book speed is characterized in terms of rapid and diligent.
stage	Prototyping characteristic: Phase in the software making process in which a prototype is developed, the phases discussed in the book are high level stages: early, midterm and late.
style	Prototyping characteristic: The presentation of a software design concept ranging from a story presentation (narrative) to a fully interactive representation (interactive).
swim lane diagram	Task flow representation as broken down into subtasks and aligned with user roles.
system performance	Prototyping content: Speed and accuracy with which the computer system responds to user commands and interactions.
task analysis	Mapping what users do in the context they perform activities in. This information informs design.
task flow	Required user actions and cognitive processes to achieve completion of a task or series of tasks.
task layer map	Dependency diagram representing a series of tasks or task steps required to complete an action or work process.
tool	A software application or other media used to create prototypes.
tools	Software and physical tools used to create a prototype. Software tools can include almost any software application such as word processors and spreadsheets along with the more traditional prototyping applications of Dreamweaver, Flash, Authorware and Visual Basic. Physical tools include paper, clay, foam, pencils, pens, arts and crafts materials, etc.
typographic structure	Design Guideline: The layout and organization of the typographic elements in a user interface, such as content text, help and error messages, field labels, titles, etc.
under-achieving prototype	An under-achieving prototype underwhelms an audience by omitting detailed design. As a poorly defined prototype, it is too vague to be of much use later in the software creation process.

Under-achieving prototypes fail to account for known require-ments and stakeholder needs and provide few ideas to inspire next steps.

unity
Design Guideline: In terms of design, a state of forming a complete and pleasing whole.

variety
Design Guideline: Design presented in new but still recognizable forms for the purpose of emphasis or controlled visual impact.

visual design
Prototyping content: Software look and visual language, including visual arrangement of content and user interface elements in addition to typographic design, icons, graphic elements, color, etc.

waterfall method
A traditional software development process broken down into discreet, isolated sequential phases – strategy, analysis, design, build, test, then transition.

Longevity (*Continued*)
digital interactive prototyping and, 345
long, 121
medium, 121
overview, 110
paper prototyping and, 318–319
short, 120–121
storyboard and, 297
video prototyping and, 390
wireframes and, 275
Wizard-of-Oz prototyping, 405–406

M

Macromedia Director, 421
Management, upper, 112
Managers
marketing, 112
product, 112
sales, 112
Marketing
manager, 112
requirements, 32
Media, using Adobe Acrobat, 559–563
Medium, 126–128
blank model prototyping and, 364
for card sorting, 252
coded prototyping and, 424
definition, 574
digital, 128
digital interactive prototyping and, 345
fidelity, 133
overview, 110
physical, 127–128
storyboard and, 298
video prototyping and, 391
wireframes and, 276
Wizard-of-Oz prototyping, 406
Memory load, 197–198
Mental model, 256
definition, 574
mapping for paper prototyping, 322–323
Menu structure, 255
Methods, 137–154
blank model prototyping, 143–144
card sorting, 137–138

choosing the right prototyping
method, 147–150
coded prototyping, 146
definition, 574
digital prototyping, 141–142
paper prototyping, 140–141
presentation agenda, 228–238
prototyping, 137
selection, 226
storyboard prototyping, 139–140
video prototyping, 144–145
wireframe prototyping, 138–139
Wizard-of-Oz prototyping, 145–146
Microsoft Excel, 463–485
advantages, 463–465
creation, 466–485
disadvantages, 465
method, 465
testing, 485
Microsoft Office, 442
Microsoft PowerPoint, 164, 169, 455–463
advantages, 455–456
disadvantages, 456
learning new tricks from team members, 166
method, 457
storyboard, 455, 457–463
worksheet, 169
Microsoft Visio, 487–517
Adobe Acrobat and, 526
advantages, 490
audience, 489
business scenario, 491
characteristics, 487–488
combo box, 503–504
context menu, 495
design content area, 502–508
different states, 515–517
disadvantages, 490–491
documenting a design, 491
features, 489–490
main window creation, 493–497
methods, 487
mockup interaction, 510–514
overview, 487
for paper prototypes, 487

presentation and distribution of
prototype, 517
reuse, 489–490, 509
for storyboard prototypes, 487
use case description, 492–493
window functions, 498–502
for wireframe prototypes, 487
Microsoft Word, 164, 169, 444–455
advantages, 444
building a wireframe, 445–455
disadvantages, 444–445
method, 445
prototype, 444
text documentation, 453–455
usability testing, 455
Mock up, definition, 574

N

Natural language interface, 404, 406
Navigation model, 255

O

Office suite prototyping, 441–485
applications, 485
graphics, 443
Microsoft Excel, 463–485
Microsoft Office features
in common, 442
Microsoft PowerPoint, 455–463
Microsoft Word, 444–455
overview, 441
similarities and differences, 441–443
users, 443
Organization, grid-based, definition, 573
Over-achieving prototype, definition, 574

P

Palm Pilot, 13
Paper prototyping, 140–141, 153, 164, 169, 317–341
benefits, 319–323
characteristics, 318–319
content and fidelity matrix, 319
description, 317–318
digital advantages over, 348–349

versus digital interactive prototyping, 349–350
feedback session, 331
guidelines, 324–331
iteration, 340
making a prototype from paper, 329–330
with Microsoft Visio, 487
operating, 330–331
overview, 323–324
points in common with digital interactive prototyping, 347–348
reiteration, 339–340
session, 338
testing, 331–340
Participatory design, 14
Pattern, 182–183
definition, 574
PDF. *See* Adobe Acrobat, prototyping
Peer reviews, 238
Photoshop, 164, 169
Pince, Art, 17
Plan, 29–105
Plot, 75–78
Portable document format (PDF). *See* Adobe Acrobat, prototyping
PowerPoint. *See* Microsoft PowerPoint
Process tips, 36
Product branding
brand expression, 97–99
decreasing, 98–99
definition, 574
increasing, 98
Product Design, 15
Product Design Guide, 248–249
Product managers, 112
Progressive disclosure, 191–193
definition, 574
Protagonist. *See* Users
Prototype. *See also* Fidelity; Ideas; Prototyping
background, 226
characteristics, 226
components and content, 207
definition, 3–4, 574

design, 208–215, 509
approach from concept to product, 14–15
deployment, 243–249
economics, 11–12
evaluating, 237–239
function, 10–11
guide, 248–249
review, internal, 221–232
schedule and budget planning, 15–16
specification, 15
user response, 12–14
distribution strategies, 244–248
effective, xxx
definition, 572
handoff, 244
closed versus open, 245–246
narrative versus interactive, 246
hardware, definition, 573
iteration, 235–241
midterm, 117
narrative, 124, 125
outcome expectation, 226–227
over-achieving, xxix
definition, 574
from paper to coded, 44–45
presentation, 227–228, 229
agenda, 228–230
presenting wrong content, 99
under-achieving, xxix
definition, 575–576
usability, 235–241
testing, 236–237
validation, 207–208, 235–241
strategy, 235–236
Prototyping.
with Adobe Acrobat, 519–569
blank model, 143–144, 363–385
characteristics, xxi, 22–23, 109–134
coded, 146, 154, 421–439
content and fidelity, xxxi, 22, 85–105
definition, 85–86
creation, 24
definition, 574
design
criteria, 24, 177–202

implementation, 25
validation, 24
digital, 141–142
digital interactive, 343–361
documenting results, 248
effective, definition, 572
historical perspective, 4–9
methods, xxxii, 23, 137–154. *See also* individual methods
choosing the right method, 147–150
with Microsoft Visio, 487–517
with office suite applications, 441–485
paper, 140–141, 153, 164, 169, 317–341
predecessors, 10
prioritizing, xxxi
process, 21–29
design, 23–24
planning, 21–22
results, 24–25
specifications, 22–23
rapid, definition, 574
requirements, 22, 30–48
from coded prototype to software requirements, 45–46
from idea to visualization, 38–40
from paper prototype to coded prototype, 44–45
from quick wireframe to wireframe, 41–42
versus software requirements, 32
from storyboard to paper prototype, 43–44
transformation of assumptions, 33–38
from wireframe to storyboard, 42–43
reviewing the prototype, 24
storyboard, 139–140, 152, 295–315
task/screen flow, 22, 50–82
tools, xxxii, 23, 157–173
choice of, 159–163
complementary, 158
overachieving, 158
selection, 168–169

T

Task analysis, definition, 575
Task flow
    after handing off the prototype, 247
    definition, 575
    paper prototyping and, 331
Task layer map, definition, 575
Task/screen flow, 22, 50–82
    creation of list of tasks, 53–54
    dependencies
        diagram, 59–60
        of each item, 54–56
        removal, 58
    development, 206
    flow step diagrams, 63, 64, 80
    highlighting key tasks, 60–62
    identification of needs, 62–64
    layering listed items, 57
    prioritization of requirements, 60
    sketching, 51
    swim lane diagrams, 65–72
    task layer maps, 52, 54, 55, 56, 59, 61
    usage scenarios, 72–78
Teams, design, 112
Technical requirements, 33
    after handing off the prototype, 247
Technical writers, 113
Terminology, validation, 255
Testing
    focus group, 238
    usability, 236–237, 238
Tools
    definition, 575
    prototyping, 157–173
Travel and expense software, 39–40
Typographic structure, 184–185
    definition, 575

U

UCD. *See* User-centered design
Under-achieving prototype,
        definition, 575–576
Unity, 183–184
    definition, 576
Usability
    after handing off the prototype, 247
    requirements, 33
    validation, 33

User-centered design (UCD), 9
User experience design, 8
User interface guidelines, 190–198
Users
    control, 197
    memory load, 197–198
    response to design, 12–14
    roles, 68–70
    scenarios, 72–78
    storyboard and, 300

V

Variety, 183–184
    definition, 576
Verplank, Bill, 4
Video prototyping, 144–145, 153–154
    animatic, 400
    benefits, 389
    brainstorming, 391, 396–397
    characteristics, 390–392
    creation process, 393
    description, 388–389
    guidelines, 394–399
    holistic, 387–388, 389–390
    iteration, 401
    observation of users, 395–396
    overview, 387
    storyboarding, 392
    users, 389
    visionary prototypes, 387,
        399–401
Virtual design, definition, 576
Visio. *See* Microsoft Visio
Vista, Valmar, 17–18
VisualBasic, 171, 421
Visual design, 94–96
    for digital interactive prototyping,
        354
    guidelines, 179–190
    Microsoft Visio and, 488
    techniques to adjust fidelity,
        95–96
VisualStudio, 171

W

Walkthroughs, cognitive, 238
Waterfall method, xxxiii–xxxiv
    definition, 576

Website
    navigation model, 255
    site map diagram, 263
Wireframe, 79
    arrangement and sequencing, 274
    characteristics, 274–276
    conceptual prototype, 122
    content and fidelity matrix, 276
    content source, 283–285
    creation process, 281–282
    description, 273–274
    design, 450–453
    digital skeletal, 277
    evolution, 291–292
    goals, 279–281
    hand-drawn image, 277
    high-level structure, 274
    iteration, 292
    medium, 281
    with Microsoft Visio, 487
    in Microsoft Word, 445–455
    perspectives, 273–274
    prototype in Microsoft Word, 444
    prototyping, 138–139, 152, 273–292
        guidelines, 282–292
        iteration, 292
        methods, 281
        overview, 276–279
    requirements, 41–42, 280
    single-path, 274
    stakeholders, 285–286
    to storyboard, 42–43
    tool selection, 286–288
    visualization, 280, 281
    web page, 278, 279
Wizard-of-Oz prototyping (WoO),
        145–146, 154
    benefits, 408
    characteristics, 405–406
    construct, 412
    content, 418
    description, 403–404
    digital interactive prototyping and,
        345
    disclaimer statement, 405
    ethical consideration, 404–405
    guidelines, 409–418
    iteration, 418–419

Wizard-of-Oz prototyping (WoO) *(Continued)*
with Microsoft Excel, 465
overview, 406–407
participants, 407–408
pilot, 415
planning, 410
prototype script, 414
recruiting participants, 413
session, 407
strategy, 411
usability testing, 416–418

WoO. *See* Wizard-of-Oz prototyping
Word. *See* Microsoft Word
Worksheets, 23
Acrobat, 169
choosing a prototyping tool, 161–163
determination of prototype characteristics, 132
evaluation method choice, 239
inventory requirements, 36

PowerPoint versus Acrobat, 169
prioritizing design guidelines, 200
requirements for time management software, 35
selection of a prototype method, 148–150
storyboard, 165
task flow step to requirements mapping, 64
time requirements, 38
Writers, technical, 113

Jonathan Arnowitz is the User Experience Architect at SAP Labs and is the co-editors-in-chief of *Interactions Magazine*. Most recently Jonathan was a senior user experience designer at Peoplesoft and a leading HCI consultant in the Netherlands. He is a member of the SIGCHI extended executive committee, and was a founder of DUX, the first ever joint conference of ACM SIGCHI, ACM SIGGRAPH, AIGA Experience Design Group, and STC.

Michael Arent is the director of user interface standards at SAP, and has previously held positions at Peoplesoft, Inc, Adobe Systems, Inc, MetaDesign, Sun Microsystems, and Apple Computer, Inc. He holds a number of U.S. and international patents.

Nevin Berger is design director at Ziff Davis Media. Previously he was a senior interaction designer at Oracle Corporation and Peoplesoft, Inc., and has held creative director positions at World Savings and OFOTO, Inc.

CONTRIBUTORS

Ji Kim is a Senior UI designer at Moody's KMV with over 10 years of experience in interaction design and user research. In the past, he has designed for both Web Applications and desktop products in the areas of network security, business intelligence, personalization, video search, and developer tools.

Dave Rogers is an independent user experience specialist and information architect practicing in Los Angeles, California. A multiple award-winner, he has an extensive background in interactive multimedia, instructional design and marketing.